UNLOCKING

ACTIVE
SERVER PAGES

CHRISTOPH WILLE

WITH
PAUL THURROTT

D1592341

New
Riders

New Riders Publishing, Indianapolis, Indiana

Unlocking Active Server Pages

By Christoph Wille with Paul Thurrott

Published by:
New Riders Publishing
201 West 103rd Street
Indianapolis, IN 46290 USA

Printed in the United States of America 1 2 3 4 5 6 7 8 9 0

Library of Congress Cataloging-in-Publication Data

97-067684

ISBN: 1-56205-752-9

Warning and Disclaimer

Publisher	*Don Fowley*
Associate Publisher	*David Dwyer*
Marketing Manager	*Mary Foote*
Managing Editor	*Carla Hall*
Director of Development	*Kezia Endsley*

Product Development Specialist
Brad Jones

Acquisitions Editor
Danielle Bird

Senior Editors
Sarah Kearns
Suzanne Snyder

Development Editor
Danielle Bird

Project Editor
Howard A. Jones

Technical Editor
Marc Gusmano

Software Specialist
Steve Flatt

Assistant Marketing Manager
Gretchen Schlesinger

Acquisitions Coordinator
Stacey Beheler

Administrative Coordinator
Karen Opal

Manufacturing Coordinator
Brook Farling

Cover Designer
Anne Jones

Cover Production
Aren Howell

Book Designer
Glenn Larsen

Director of Production
Larry Klein

Production Team Supervisors
Laurie Casey
Joe Millay

Graphics Image Specialists
Steve Adams, Oliver Jackson

Production Analyst
Erich J. Richter

Production Team
Tricia Flodder, Mary Hunt,
Daniela Raderstorf, Maureen
West

Indexer
Sandy Henselmeier

About the Authors

Christoph Wille, an MCSE and MCSD, has an extensive background working with OLE, MFC, Microsoft SQL Server, Microsoft operating systems, and Access. He is currently developing web sites with integrated e-commerce as well as working as a consultant for companies that want to connect their private networks to the Internet and who need someone to design their Internet presence.

Paul Thurrott is the Webmaster at Big Tent Media Labs, a publishing company in San Francisco, where he creates dynamic, data-driven web sites with Microsoft Visual InterDev and SQL Server. Paul is the author of several books, including the Delphi 3 SuperBible, and titles about Visual Basic, Visual Basic Script, Windows NT 4.0 and 95, Excel and Office 95, and other Windows-related technologies. Paul lives in Phoenix with his wife Stephanie and their two bilingual cats, Fred and Barney.

Acknowledgments

I'd like to thank the editors at New Riders for helping me in getting this book done. Doing a 500+ pages book—compounded by the fact of not doing it in my native tongue—is what you surely do not learn in English classes at your local high school. Thanks to Danielle Bird, Howard Jones, Christopher Cleveland and Kezia Endsley, the text I have supplied is now standard English and I have learned a great deal! Marc Gusmano, the tech editor on this project, always pointed me to—of course—my errors and helped in fixing these.

Further thanks go to Brad Jones at New Riders, who came up with the preliminary outline and commented on it at the beginning of the project; he also presented the book idea to the sales force and the rest of the editorial board. I want to thank the many dedicated people in Proofreading, Layout, and Illustration whose work you can see on every page of this book.

I'd also like to thank my roommate, who accepted a television ban for the time I was writing on this book, because the TV set and my computer are in the same room. I have to admit that two months are a long time. Thanks for pulling me away from the computer for a beer or two.

Finally, I'd like to thank my parents and my brother Claus for their continual support—not only during the process of writing this book, but every day.

Trademark Acknowledgments

All terms mentioned in this book that are known to be trademarks or service marks have been appropriately capitalized. New Riders Publishing cannot attest to the accuracy of this information. Use of a term in this book should not be regarded as affecting the validity of any trademark or service mark.

Contents at a Glance

Table of Contents

Introduction

The Internet world is spinning quickly and development cycles on products are very short. Microsoft's Internet Information Server hit the streets in its first version in early 1996. Now, in early 1997, version 3.0 has arrived and with it a new technology— Active Server Pages (ASP).

To program web applications only about 2 years ago you either needed a C expert or someone familiar with PERL. The development took an extremely long time and the approach was error-prone. The motto was "Don't change anything about the application after you've finished it."

Prior to Active Server Pages, Internet Information Server 1.0 already offered powerful database access via the Internet Database Connector (IDC). However, with the new Active Server Pages technology, following that method is like living in the days of the dinosaur. Now pages are easy to create and maintain. One of the best features is that you can mix programming code and HTML code. You also can choose any programming language you like—as long as it supports the ActiveX Scripting Interface. These languages include VBScript, JScript, and PerlScript, and more will be added in the future.

The power you receive with Active Server Pages is amazing; taking full advantage of this power is what this book is aimed at helping you to achieve.

Is This the Book for You?

A question I'm always asking myself when looking at books on a shelf in the bookstore is "Is this the book for me?" Now I can ask "Is this the book for you, reader?" Who is the audience of this book?

- The IS manager responsible for making technology and implementation decisions for the corporate web site.

- The web development professional who is responsible for creating high-performance—and, of course, high-quality web applications—who wants to make the move to ASP.

- The web development professional already familiar with ASP, who wants to learn more about components, personalization, sophisticated database access, and tools for ASP.

- The web page programmer new to server-side programming who wants to get up-to-speed with this new technology as quickly as possible.

This book requires that you be familiar with HTML and know how to deal with databases, which are at the heart of every dynamic web site. It would be advantageous if you are most familiar with Microsoft SQL Server. Basic knowledge of Windows NT is an advantage, but is not a requirement.

What's in This Book?

Each of the following paragraphs presents an overview of a single chapter in this book. Of course, these are only appetizers for the actual chapter.

The client-server model of the Web was limited for a long time to using the server as data sender only and providing all the functionality of the Web on the client. Chapter 1, "An Overview of Active Server Pages," shows the new concept of preparing the content for the client on the server and where Active Server Pages fits into this scenario.

Before jumping into page creation, topics like site planning, look and feel, and navigation should be considered. In "Designing Active Server Pages," Chapter 2 presents the dos and don'ts of the trade.

Chapter 3, "Foundations for Creating Active Server Pages," provides you with the first steps in creating pages with Active Server Pages. The coding structure is explained, along with the basic directives needed to get up and running.

In "Working with Visual InterDev," Chapter 4 presents an overview of Microsoft's new Active Server Pages programming tool. All the features that make an ASP programmer's life easier are covered here, but this chapter is only a quick overview of this hot topic.

Now that you have already seen what is possible with ASP, Chapter 5, "Programming Active Server Pages," takes you on a step-by-step tour of the basic objects of ASP. You will learn how to handle user input, write sophisticated HTML back to the user, create web applications, and manage state information for the users.

Perhaps the biggest advantage to ASP is its extensibility with ActiveX components. In Chapter 6, "Using ActiveX Components," you examine the core components that come with ASP.

If you're creating dynamic web sites, databases are a must-have for storing and retrieving data. Chapter 7, "Database Access with ActiveX Data Objects," is dedicated to showing you all the tricks of the trade to get the most out of your database for your web application.

When you're in business with Internet Information Server for a longer time period, Chapter 8, "Converting IDC Applications to Active Server Pages," saves you time in making the move from IDC to modern ASP applications.

Being a new kid on the block and part of Microsoft's new Commercial Internet System, "The Microsoft Personalization System" presented in Chapter 9 brings you up to speed in enabling personalization of your site for visiting users.

"Security," discussed in Chapter 10, deals with all the issues of securing a web server against intruders, protecting your data, and setting up member-only areas on your server.

Developing extensively with ASP guarantees that you will run into errors others have figured out before. Learning from others, Chapter 11, "Troubleshooting Active Server Pages," is your chance to avoid these errors without being stuck for hours.

If the components delivered with ASP aren't powerful enough for you, Chapter 12, "Extending Active Server Pages with Components," is your best bet. In this chapter, component creation with Java, Visual Basic, Microsoft Foundation Classes, and the ActiveX Template Library is presented.

As the first chapter of the examples part of this book, Chapter 13, "Creating a Guest Book," walks you through all the steps of creating a totally cool guest book that you can immediately incorporate into your web site.

Setting up shops online is not uncommon nowadays, so you're facing problems of an online shop that need a solution. Chapter 14, "Creating a Shopping Bag," shows two different approaches to creating a shopping bag for your customers.

With the number of search engines on the Internet growing constantly, you have to remember many different URLs when trying to find something on the Internet. Chapter 15, "Implementing a Search Wizard," shows you how to create a one-stop solution for querying different search engines.

Databases are at the heart of every dynamic web site. Management of Microsoft SQL Server over the Internet is the topic of Chapter 16, "Creating a Web Front-End for SQL Server." It shows how to leverage the component architecture of the SQL Distributed Management Objects in a web application.

Personalization was already the topic of Chapter 9. In "Adding Personalization to Your Site," Chapter 17 presents a full-featured solution you can incorporate into your site.

The back matter of this book starts with Appendix A, "Installing Visual InterDev," in which you are presented with coverage of installing Visual InterDev in a development environment.

Intended as a point of reference for you, Appendix B, "Server-Side Directives," provides a recap of these in a single place.

Tuning is not only for cars—you also can tune your web server. Appendix C, "Configuration Tips for Active Servers," shows you how to do this with the almighty registry.

About the CD-ROM

On the CD

The examples described and referenced in this book can all be found on the accompanying CD. They are organized in folders with the chapter's name, and unless otherwise noted in the heading for the listing, named

```
chaptername\chapternumber\listingnumber.fileextension
```

For example, an ASP page presented in Listing 7 of Chapter 7 will be named listing77.asp.

In addition to the examples in the book, there are more components, tools, and programs on this CD. The next paragraphs describe these to assist you in finding the components or tools you need.

To help you set up your web server, all the software needed is included: **Peer Web Services** for Windows 95 (**Internet Information Server** is part of the Windows NT Distribution), the installation for **Active Server Pages** and for indexing your web site, **Index Server**. Additionally, the latest **Service Packs** for Microsoft Windows NT 4.0 (SP2) and Microsoft SQL Server 6.5 (SP2) are contained on the CD as well.

HTTPSpy was created because web developers occasionally need to view the raw HTTP transactions during web development. HttpSpy logs each ISAPI event to a text file as they occur. This tool is intended for testing purposes only.

IISCfg was developed to help IIS users configure a number of IIS parameters that are not (and some that are) available from the IIS Service Manager program. IISCfg helps you to adjust these parameters without the use of RegEdit.

WebHammer 2.0 is a new version of the utility designed to test web applications and servers. It features GET, POST, and HEAD request methods, authentication, cookies, user-agent headers, redirects, and more. It is capable of calculating Seconds Per Request/Requests Per Second and Maximum Request Time.

To assist you in converting IDC applications to ASP, the tool **IDC2ASP** from IntraActive Software is included on the CD. To see how to use this tool, refer to Chapter 8, "Converting IDC Applications to Active Server Pages."

For all of you that prefer writing scripts with PERL, the **PerlScript** implementation for Active Server Pages is included on the CD. It provides powerful access to the operating system you won't gain without components in JScript or VBScript.

A selection of industry-strength **components** from Stephen Genusa's premier "unauthorized" ASP Developer's Site is on the CD too. These include components for executing applications, ftp transfers, process lists, and more.

New Riders Publishing

The staff of New Riders Publishing is committed to bringing you the very best in computer reference material. Each New Riders book is the result of months of work by authors and staff who research and refine the information contained within its covers.

As part of this commitment to you, New Riders invites your input. Please let us know if you enjoy this book, if you have trouble with the information and examples presented, or if you have a suggestion for the next edition.

Please note, however, that New Riders staff cannot serve as a technical resource for information about Active Server Pages or for questions about software- or hardware-related problems. Please refer to the documentation that accompanies your software or to the applications' Help systems.

If you have a question or comment about any New Riders book, there are several ways to contact New Riders Publishing. We will respond to as many readers as we can. Your name, address, or phone number will never become part of a mailing list or be used for any purpose other than to help us continue to bring you the best books possible.

You can write us at the following address:

New Riders Publishing
Attn: Publisher
201 W. 103rd Street
Indianapolis, IN 46290

If you prefer, you can fax New Riders Publishing at:

317-817-7448

You also can send electronic mail to New Riders at the following Internet address:

dgibson@newriders.mcp.com

New Riders Publishing is an imprint of Macmillan Computer Publishing. To obtain a catalog, or information, or to purchase any Macmillan Computer Publishing book, call 800-428-5331 or visit our Web site at `http://www.mcp.com`.

Thank you for selecting *Unlocking Active Server Pages*!

CHAPTER 1

An Overview of Active Server Pages

Not long ago, programming web applications that really interacted with the user or retrieved live data from databases were a pain to create, deploy, and maintain. You didn't have many options for programming the site and it wasn't cost-effective: even the simplest changes to the layout of a single programmed page were expensive because you needed highly-skilled programmers to maintain the site.

This chapter tells you why Active Server Pages makes your life easier as a web developer—and how ASP helps you go online with your business with the best and most interactive site. I assume you can live without an elaborate history of the Internet, which I won't provide here. I'll touch on only the main problems you face when creating sites.

In this chapter, I'll take you on a guided tour of how Active Server Pages helps you create cool sites easily and I will contrast this method with the known technologies of today. This chapter explains the following topics:

◆ The challenges you face when developing for the World Wide Web

◆ How you can program your web server

◆ Why and how to use ASP

The Challenges of the World Wide Web

I promised to touch general Internet issues briefly. However, to make it clear why a powerful server-side technology is really important for the Internet business of today, I'll elaborate on the following topics:

◆ Limitations of the variety of browsers

◆ Bandwidth problems

◆ Developing an intranet site versus Internet sites

The Wide Variety of Browsers

The Hypertext Transfer Protocol (HTTP) is used for the World Wide Web to transfer any kind of data. Hypertext Markup Language (HTML) files are well-known; these documents are rendered in a web browser on the client's computer. One of the first browsers available was lynx on various flavors of UNIX, which was only capable of displaying text. With the browser named Mosaic, the Web jump-started because graphics and text could be displayed—multimedia on the Internet.

Today there are two major competitors in the marketplace for web browsers: Microsoft with its Internet Explorer (current version at time of this writing is 3.02, 4 is available in broad beta) and Netscape, with Communicator version 4. Both are capable of displaying standard HTML documents. However, both companies invented new extensions to HTML as the Web was growing and this caused problems. Some features may work well in one browser, and not at all in the other, or in the worst case, the other browser will interpret the features the wrong way and mess up the page.

Not only were new HTML tags introduced, new technologies were added as well, such as Java, JavaScript, ActiveX controls, Plug-Ins, VBScript, and many more. Some of these work on both browsers, some don't. This means that you have to maintain two different sets of source files for each browser, which isn't very effective.

To learn more about customizing HTML pages for different browsers, see "Using ActiveX Components," (Chapter 6).

Cross
Reference

Because client-side technology differs greatly between different browsers (and the platforms on which they run), Microsoft "activated" the web server to serve dynamic content, independently of the different capabilities of the browsers. The programming is transferred back to the server where you know the capabilities of your machine exactly—the client's browser only receives plain-vanilla HTML that you can even customize for the specific capabilities of the client's browser. No single line of server-side code is sent to the client, preserving your investment.

Bandwidth Considerations

Another crucial issue on the Internet is bandwidth. Creating interactive pages using a lot of client-side technology results in bigger HTML files transferred to the user. The average Internet user, however, if he or she isn't surfing from the office, uses a modem to dial the Internet. Roughly estimating a standard 28.8 line yields about 3 KB transferred per second—not very much when you put a bunch of multimedia pizzazz in your pages. It takes the user about 14 seconds to download and display a really simple page with 40 KB of text and images .

Letting your users decide whether they want to be bothered with large multimedia images or whether they want a simpler text-based version of your site is another use of ASP technology—serving dynamic, personalized content for your users. The user can decide what information he or she wants to be presented.

To see a full-featured personalization example, please refer to Chapter 17, "Adding Personalization to Your Site," p. 451.

Cross Reference

Intranet versus Internet

When you're developing a web site for an intranet, you're lucky. You have fewer problems with bandwidth and know which browser the user will use. Therefore, you can build a lot of client intelligence in your pages and create the richest user experience.

On the other hand, when you are developing for the Internet and its different browsers, you have to do most of the intelligence on the server side to ensure the broadest reach of your site. You will have to decide what kind of information will be sent to the user based on browser type—a graphic or multimedia animation, a static text, or an ActiveX control. You need a server technology that enables you to easily make these decisions and reach a high number of users without requiring you to be an expert C/C++ programmer.

Programming the Web Server

For a long time, the only way to maintain a presence on the Web was to use a UNIX computer with the operating system's various web servers. One of the most popular servers was httpd, because it was standard on these systems.

Netscape jumped into the server market with an impressive suite of servers and was able to maintain a very powerful position until Microsoft introduced a broad beta of Internet Information Server 1.0 that was given away at the Internet Professional Developers Conference in March 1996. There was one big difference between Netscape's and Microsoft's web servers: IIS was free.

Within a year, Microsoft blasted through two new versions and several add-ons. They now have version 3 of this very popular web server (version 2 shipped with Windows NT 4.0) and Microsoft shows no signs of slowing down. With this new version, Microsoft introduced a feature to IIS named Active Server Pages (ASP). ASP is a server-side programming technology, adding to the three that were already available—Common Gateway Interface (CGI), Internet Server API (ISAPI) and the Internet Database Connector (IDC). Figure 1.1 shows the differences between the four technologies in approachability and richness of content.

Figure 1.1

The approachability and richness of the different server-side programming options IIS offers.

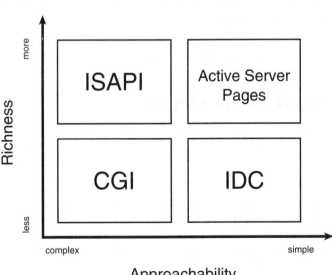

Each of these technologies is discussed in a following section, starting with the senior technology present in web servers—CGI.

Common Gateway Interface: CGI

This kind of support is built into almost every web server. On UNIX computers, most of the CGI applications are written using PERL (Practical Extraction and Report Language). A popular use is creating e-mail forms for feedback. Another language used for creating CGI applications is C, which enables developers to create fast and powerful applications. Unfortunately, applications created with C are hard to maintain, and debugging them is difficult.

A downside to using CGI is that for each request a new process has to be created. This takes a lot of server resources and processing time. However, by creating a WIN32 application, you can manipulate every part of the operating system directly. Figure 1.2 shows the dsnform tool that comes with IIS—it enables the creation of ODBC datasources on the web server directly from within any web browser.

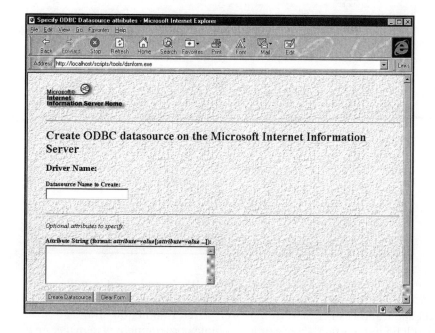

Figure 1.2

Using dsnform to create a new datasource.

Internet Server API

Using the Internet Server API (or ISAPI) is a way to circumvent one major disadvantage of CGI applications—the need to spawn a new process for every request. ISAPI is the programming interface used for creating two different types of ISAPI applications:

◆ **Filters:** These work transparent to the client and are used for monitoring requests, custom authentication schemes, on-the-fly data translation, and more.

Filters are loaded into the web server's process space at server-startup and stay in memory until the server is shut down.

◆ **Extensions**: Closely resembling the way CGI applications work—serving requests for specific users—ISAPI extensions are used for form processing, retrieving data from databases, performing business logic, and much more. Just like ISAPI filters, extensions are loaded into the process space of the web server. However, this occurs only when the first user requests a service from the extension, not when the server starts. Figure 1.3 illustrates that you also can use extensions to gain operating system level access.

Figure 1.3

Displaying Eventlog entries using an ISAPI extension DLL.

	Date	Time	Source	Event
ⓘ	05.05.97	15:47:46	EventLog	6005
ⓘ	05.05.97	15:42:13	Print	10
ⓘ	05.05.97	15:41:01	Print	9
ⓘ	05.05.97	15:35:33	Print	10
ⓘ	05.05.97	15:35:14	Print	9
ⓘ	05.05.97	15:32:28	Print	10
ⓘ	05.05.97	15:10:58	Print	10
ⓘ	05.05.97	11:42:45	Service Control Manager	7026
ⓘ	05.05.97	11:42:11	EventLog	6005
ⓘ	05.05.97	09:07:41	Service Control Manager	7026
ⓘ	05.05.97	09:07:05	EventLog	6005
ⓘ	05.05.97	05:32:47	Service Control Manager	7026
ⓘ	05.05.97	05:32:11	EventLog	6005
ⓘ	04.05.97	21:39:53	Service Control Manager	7026
ⓘ	04.05.97	21:39:13	EventLog	6005
ⓘ	04.05.97	18:33:27	Service Control Manager	7026
ⓘ	04.05.97	18:32:54	EventLog	6005
ⓘ	04.05.97	15:01:12	Service Control Manager	7026
ⓘ	04.05.97	15:00:31	EventLog	6005

Eventlog Extension © 1997 Christoph Wille - Microsoft Internet Explorer

Address http://194.8.136.102/EventLog/evlog.dll?List&source=system&target=_top&maxrec=60

By now I have mentioned more than once that ISAPI DLL's are loaded into the process space of the web server. The apparent downside of this method is that a badly written ISAPI application can crash the entire web server. Another disadvantage is that you are still bound to using a more or less complex programming language, such as C/C++ or Delphi. Enough about the disadvantages, what are the advantages? Why should you bother creating ISAPI filters or extensions? You can't re-create the functionality of filters with any other technology, and extensions are well-suited for dynamic web applications. However, this area is where ASP is taking over.

To learn more about creating ISAPI applications, please refer to *Inside ISAPI*, published by New Riders.

**Cross
Reference**

Internet Database Connector

A special feature of IIS since version 1 is the Internet Database connector (IDC). You can create pages that are dynamically filled with data coming from any database that is accessible with ODBC. Now it's easy to get at database data and present it to the client without having to create either a CGI application or an ISAPI extension.

SQL statements are used to retrieve data, and HTML templates are used to merge the results returned from the database with the layout you have decided for your results page. Figure 1.4 shows an example page that uses the returned information to create a dynamic form with checkboxes.

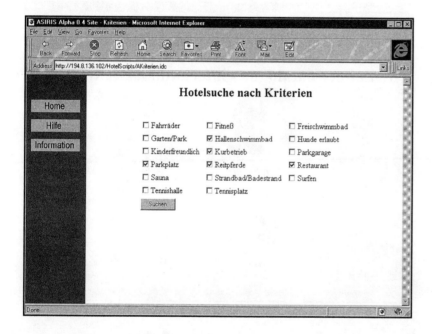

Figure 1.4

Creating a form using the Internet Database Connector.

One final note about the Internet Database Connector: database programming with querying or inserting information is now easy, but you are limited to database programming only.

Active Server Pages

Wouldn't it be great if the developer had access to all the best features of the previous technologies? Easy programming and database access such as IDC, powerful operating system access such as CGI or ISAPI, all combined with the speediness of ISAPI? And wouldn't it be a nice feature if it was additionally extensible by third-party tools? Microsoft thought it might be a good idea. That's why they developed Internet Information Server 3.0, ActiveX Server.

Microsoft Active Server Pages (ASP) provides an environment based on server-side scripting that is conducive to creating dynamic, interactive applications that don't consume enormous amounts of processing time. This is a breath of fresh air for the experienced web developer and the novice basement webster. Now the developer can build logic into his or her static web pages and can turn the corner from information to interaction.

Figure 1.5 shows an example of a product catalog page that is generated dynamically with database data. Additionally, the server-side script makes adjustments to the resulting HTML for the different browsers.

Figure 1.5

An online product catalogue generated dynamically.

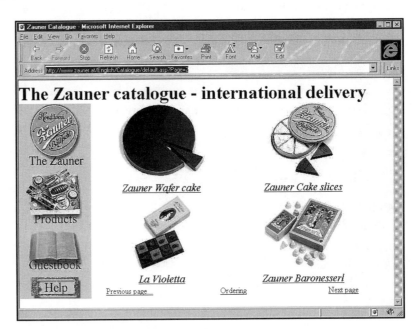

Activating the Server with ASP

What do I mean by "activating the server"? What are the advantages to using ASP instead of IDC, CGI, or ISAPI? What are its key benefits? This section is dedicated to answering these questions and giving you an overview of what you can do with ASP— or what ASP can do for you.

The nice thing is that the developer only needs a working knowledge of HTML to begin taking advantage of Active Server Pages technology. This is because ASP applications are completely integrated into your HTML pages.

ASP applications offer advantages over normal web applications that other web server products only wish they could support. The advantages of Active Server Pages over normal web applications are many, but here are four of the main ones:

◆ Approachability

◆ Openness

◆ Compile-free

◆ Browser-independence

One of the key benefits is of course approachability. By this I mean to say that an HTML author can start designing an ASP application and have a finished product in hours. There's a small learning curve if you're not familiar with a scripting language's syntax, but the ASP application designers have made it as easy as they can for those of you who do. The programmer isn't tied down to the two languages that come with the server, JScript and VBScript. Because the server uses the power of the ActiveX scripting interface, the developer can use the scripting language he or she is most familiar with as long as it conforms to the ActiveX scripting standards.

To learn more about using scripting languages and creating your first ASP pages, see Chapter 3, "Foundations for Creating Active Server Pages."

Part of openness—in addition to the freedom of choosing a scripting language—is that the core functionality provided by Active Server Pages can be extended by ActiveX Server Components, which are lightweight COM components designed for use with Active Server Pages.

The components that come with Active Server Pages are presented in Chapter 6, "Using ActiveX Components." If you to learn how to create ActiveX Server Components on your own, please see Chapter 12, "Extending Active Server Pages with Components."

Another benefit, and possibly the most crucial to the webmaster, is the fact that ASP applications don't need to be compiled. If you have ever programmed a CGI or ISAPI application, you know that you first have to compile your program, then, in the case of ISAPI, you have to stop the web server, copy the file to its storage location, restart the web server, and test it. Heaven forbid if an error is detected, because then you have to go through the process again. Even if you just want to change a simple HTML tag in the resulting output, you have to start the whole process over again. With ASP, this seemingly endless task of updating is a walk in the park. You can change whatever you want—layout, content, or logic—without ever disrupting service.

The biggest advantage ASP offers to the client is, of course, the fact that it is browser-independent. Because all the code resides on the server, you no longer have to worry about a browser's ability to run your scripts. Even if you still have some scripts that need to be run at the client level, you can let ASP tell you what a browser's capabilities are and then show the client content what will maximize the capabilities of his or her browser.

To learn more about customizing HTML pages for different browsers, see "Using ActiveX Components," (Chapter 6).

**Cross
Reference**

Summary

Active Server Pages is the newest level of web server technology. It is offered by Microsoft as an alternative to static web content and is a big enough breakthrough to change the way you think about web development from this day forth.

Before ASP, web content was static and pale. Until there was a way to keep content fresh, the Web was going to join the morass of every other information source we have today. Anyone can pick up a paper to get the day's news, but the chances of the paper having just the information you want and when you want it are slim to none. With the capabilities of Active Server Pages, you can publish the kind of dynamic content that users have been craving since they first started surfing the net. And the most amazing part of it all is that it doesn't take a rocket scientist to create this content.

The next chapters show you how to use ASP to create great content for your site in minutes. However, before you jump into the creation of ASP pages, the next chapter introduces concepts of site planning tailored to channel the power of ASP.

CHAPTER 2

Designing Active Server Pages

In this chapter, you are introduced to the issues you will face when you begin planning your ASP web site. Web design and development is moving from the realm of the hobbyist to the realm of the corporation. Web sites can quickly grow out of control, and if you don't plan properly you can find yourself unable to administer and maintain web sites you've developed for yourself and your customers.

By the time you finish this chapter, you should be able to do all of the following:

◆ Establish a logical and workable plan to implement your ASP web site

◆ Examine the problems and pitfalls of web design and development

◆ Identify problem areas in your current sites

◆ Learn how to plan your sites, while keeping leading edge web technologies in mind

Site Planning

Before you actually create your site, you need to consider how you will approach the design. Implementing an Active Server Pages (ASP) web site can be as simple as renaming all of the existing files with an .asp extension or as difficult as re-planning and reconstructing your entire site from scratch. Of course, creating a new ASP site involves the same issues: There are a number of things to think about, including site planning, navigation through the site, and the site's "look and feel."

Creating a web site is a lot like programming: Sometimes you will want to just sit down with Visual InterDev or your favorite HTML editor and get to work, but it's important to establish a plan and site structure before you start creating the actual pages. Making the correct site decisions early on can save you a lot of headaches later, when the growth of the site might make it difficult to implement even simple revisions. Of course, if you plan it properly, even complex revisions should be relatively straightforward.

This chapter provides the foundation you need for creating effective ASP web sites. Most of the concepts here, however, can be applied to any type of web site.

The first step in creating a web site is to plan the structure of the site. Site planning includes planning everything from the directory structure of the site to the files that make up the site. For a simple web site, it may be acceptable to leave all the files in the root, or upper-most, directory of the site. Typically, however, it makes sense to consider a more logical structure for your web site. This is especially important in the early planning stages of your site: You don't want to have to rearrange the structure after you've created a number of pages. This can lead to broken links and unhappy users.

A poorly-designed site also is a maintenance nightmare for the webmaster and developers. You should have a plan for the site structure before you start creating pages and adding images, with an eye toward future expansion and growth. If you're working in a team environment, the site structure should be universally understood and agreed upon before it's created. This way, you don't have one designer placing images in a different directory from the rest of the team, or a developer placing code in the wrong place.

Let's take a look at some of the site structure issues you should consider when beginning a new site.

Site Structure Issues

One obvious structural addition is an *images* directory. Typically, this is located in /images or similar. All of your image files should reside in this directory and references to images would then take this form:

```
<IMG SRC="images/someimage.gif">
```

Depending on the complexity of your site, you might have a different images directory for each section of the site, along with a global image directory that exists in the root site directory. Such a structure would resemble the one shown in Figure 2.1.

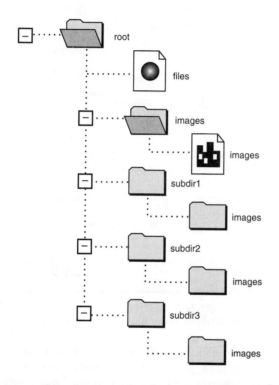

Figure 2.1

A simple web site might have a single images directory right off of the root.

With the sort of directory structure shown in Figure 2.1, you could reference global images (that is, images in the root images directory) as follows:

```
<IMG SRC="/images/someimage.gif">
```

Also, a file stored in the subdir1 directory shown in Figure 2.1 could reference images in its own subdirectory:

```
<IMG SRC="images/someimage.gif">
```

The arrangement of subdirectories in your site is dependent upon the site. Consider a site with four major sections: *News, What's New, Tools,* and *Information.* This sort of arrangement makes it easy to construct a site plan, because each section can logically get its own directory off of the root and image directory if necessary. It might look something like Figure 2.2.

Figure 2.2

Depending upon the complexity of your site structure, it may make sense to have separate image subdirectories for each directory in the site.

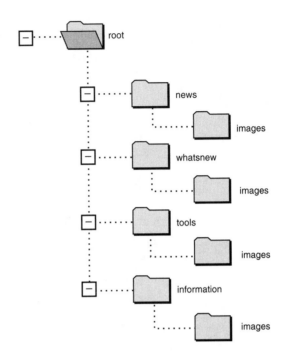

Of course, in the early planning stages, this sort of arrangement might not be obvious and you might not have come up with the sections, or departments, you wish to have in your site. The important thing to consider here is the effect your structure will have on your users as they navigate the site. If the site can't be easily navigated and doesn't have an obvious user interface, not many people will return. Create a logical structure for the content you know you will have, but leave the design open for future expansion.

Other Site Design Considerations

Other candidates for unique directories include external cascading style sheets, graphics for ad rotations, and files that are used in server-side includes. If you were to use all three of these features, for example, you might have the subdirectories in the root of your web site shown in Figure 2.3:

Warning   If you're using a database that is connected to your Active Server Pages with a system data connection, make sure you don't place the actual database in a directory that's directly accessible over the web.

Taking this precaution is especially important when you're working with Access databases, which are simple .mdb files that can easily be downloaded. ODBC is designed to establish a link with your database regardless of its location on your web or database server.

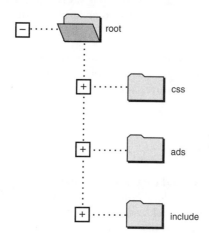

Figure 2.3

A full-featured site will need a more complex directory structure.

In short, never place a database in a directory that's accessible from the web.

 Optimally, you will have a separate database server located on a different machine on your network.

Navigation

Most web developers browse the web frequently and know the types of sites they like and wish to emulate. If a web site requires that you click link after link to get to the actual page you wish to visit, something is very wrong with the design of the site. A good web site is structured logically, but keeps the human element in mind: Real people are going to visit. Can they get in and out easily? Does it make sense? Is it obvious?

Navigation issues need to be resolved early in the design stage. Experiment with simple designs if necessary, but don't flesh out the design of individual pages until you have settled on a logical and usable site structure. The best way to test this is to beta test an early design of the site with people who aren't involved in the design phase. Too often, developers and designers are so familiar with the site that they aren't objective.

There are two approaches to designing the navigation style of your site. You can find a site you enjoy and attempt to duplicate its navigational prowess. You should be careful about that, however. For one thing, you don't want to blatantly steal another site's design, (although you should be keeping a watchful eye on the competition, and paying attention to the way they implement their sites). On the other hand, some sites are so bad, they're worth remembering just to ensure you don't make the same mistakes.

The second approach is to adopt a unique navigational style of your own. The goal is that it shouldn't be so different from what users expect that they don't understand how it works. A confused user is lost forever, so keep the navigation simple.

Site Look and Feel

A web site should have a consistent and clear style that extends to virtually every page in the site. Again, this style should be determined early on in the design process: don't start coding a site and then go back and fix every page periodically. Obviously this can't always be avoided, but a good design withstands the testing process.

It should be obvious to users that they are within, or have left, your site. One of the side benefits of this approach is element reuse: you should use the same graphical and text elements as often as possible. Navigational toolbars, text menus, and graphical elements that recur across several pages also can be inserted with server-side includes, making site management that much easier. This is good for you, but it's also good for the user because it provides a clear, consistent user interface that the user will be comfortable with.

 If you're using a frames-based design, don't open external links to your site within your own frameset. This can be maddening to the user, especially if the user wishes to bookmark the new page. It's just common courtesy; open external links in the full browser window.

Universal Design Ideas

The best web sites have a theme that repeats from page to page. Microsoft's web site, shown in Figure 2.4, features a simple black toolbar that runs across the top of most of the pages on their site, giving the user easy access to common areas, like their home and search pages. Frames-based sites, or sites that use tables and server-side includes feature some sort of navigational toolbar that enables the user to easily get around the site. These elements are now considered universal web design elements and you should use at least some of them in the design of your own sites.

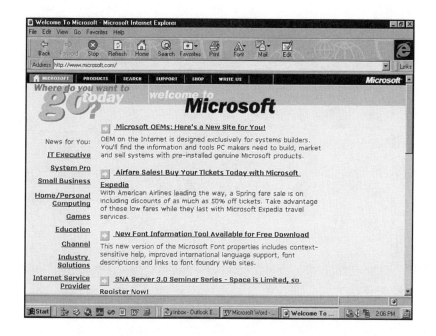

Figure 2.4

The Microsoft web site uses a navigational toolbar on each page for a consistent design.

Remember that web-based media isn't the same as books and magazines, or even multimedia CD-ROMs, though it's heading in that direction. The user interface paradigm used on the web involves simple navigation with single mouse-clicks on hyperlinks. This interface has proven so popular that Microsoft is now integrating it as a new view mode in upcoming versions of Windows and Windows NT. Existing Windows users can download Internet Explorer 4.0 to achieve this affect. With hundreds of millions of users, Windows sets the user interface standard and web-based navigation is where it's at. Internet Explorer's Web view is shown in Figure 2.5.

For thematic sites, it's okay to emulate the look and feel of legacy media, such as the USA Today site shown in Figure 2.6. Don't be too concerned about copying the layout of the New York Times for a news web site, however, it won't work on the Web. The web interface forces designers and developers to work with a type of media, so it's wise to take advantage of the things that work well.

For users, this means simplicity and ease of navigation. The greatest thing you can do for users is to make it easy and make it fast. Both of these things are inherent in the design of your site.

Figure 2.5

Internet Explorer 4.0 uses a "web view" in its user interface so that browsing the Web and browsing your local hard drive have a similar look and feel.

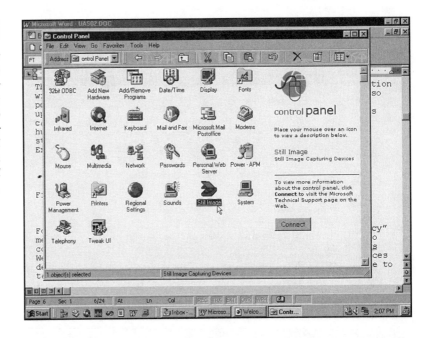

Figure 2.6

The USA Today web site emulates the print version of the newspaper.

The "Two Links" Rule

Remember the "two links rule": Put simply, don't make a user navigate more than two links to get to specific content. Nothing is more aggravating than getting lost in a monster web site that mindlessly forces you to click on hyperlink after hyperlink. These sites are driving users away in droves. If you're moving such a site to an Active Server Pages design, take the time to reorganize the site with a simpler design. Your few remaining users will thank you; new users will be more apt to visit again and again. If you're creating a new site, make sure to keep the design simple from Day One. It's generally better to have a few longer pages than numerous short pages: Try and group content simply and logically on fewer pages.

Site Maps and Directory Trees

Many times, web sites provide *site maps* and *directory trees* to aid navigation. A site map is simply a hierarchical layout of the site, shown graphically or with text. Site Maps can be organized in many ways, but are typically organized by subject. You also can provide a directory tree view, which shows the user the layout of the site as it appears in the actual file system. If you planned the site properly, a directory tree view should be logical and useable. If it isn't, you've probably done something wrong and may want to consider planning the site further.

The differences between a site map and directory tree can be minimal if you plan your site properly. Both provide the same sort of site overview that many users will appreciate. Figure 2.7 shows a typical site map menu from Microsoft's site.

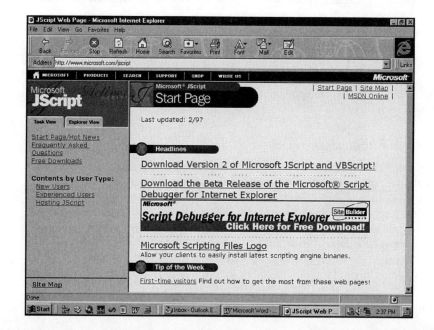

Figure 2.7

The JScript Web site uses a site map similar to a table of contents.

Microsoft uses a site map feature on many of its web sites that enables you to switch between Explorer and Site Map views. The Explorer view, shown in Figure 2.8, is simply a directory tree view, so Microsoft is probably confident that it's web site is logically arranged.

Figure 2.8

When you turn on Explorer view, the contents are replaced by a Windows Explorer-like hierarchical view of the site.

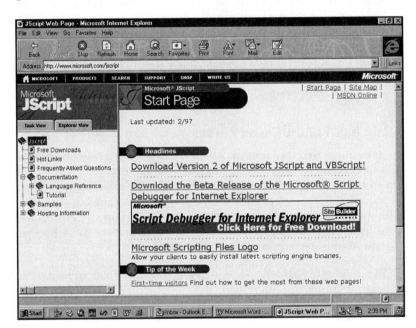

You also might decide to include a site map on a separate page, rather than in a navigational frame or table element. Microsoft does this with its VBScript page, shown in Figure 2.9. This is fine, but decide early on how (or if) you will implement such a feature. Some users love site maps and directory trees, but others aren't comfortable with this sort of site overview. Determine whether your users would use such a feature before adding it to your site.

Internet Explorer 4.0 Site Map

Internet Explorer 4.0, shown in Figure 2.10, was supposed to introduce a Site Map feature that allowed the browser to automatically create a site map view that would appear in the All Folders pane of Explorer. Unfortunately, the proposed standard was modified by the World Wide Web Consortium (W3C), the governing body responsible for the HTML specification, so Microsoft scrapped plans to include it with IE 4.0. However, a future version of Internet Explorer will likely include support for the finalized Site Map specification, which is currently being debated.

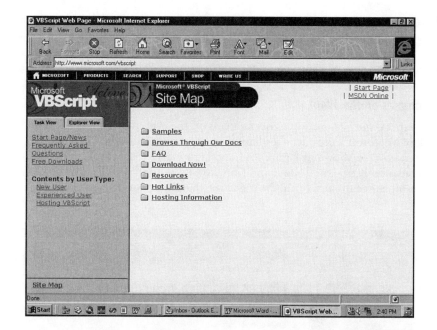

Figure 2.9

The VBScript web site includes a site map as a separate link off of the main page.

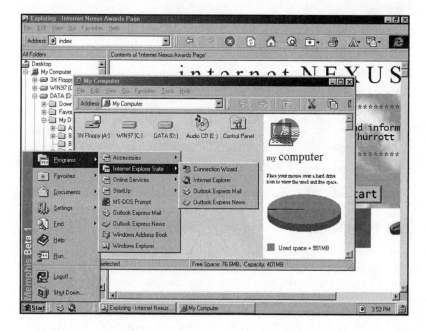

Figure 2.10

Internet Explorer 4.0 is the next generation web browser that incorporates the World Wide Web and your local desktop.

Until the W3C agrees on a Site Map specification and the most popular browsers support it natively, you will have to implement this feature manually. Popular web management programs like Front Page and Visual InterDev have wizards that create Table of Contents and site map-style pages for you automatically.

Site Map Examples on the Web

As you might expect, the best examples of site maps on the Web right now come from Microsoft. All of Microsoft's product sites have nice site maps. The Visual InterDev and Visual C++ web sites, shown in Figure 2.11 and Figure 2.12 respectively, are good examples of consistently designed site maps. Compare these to the earlier examples of other Microsoft site maps and I think you'll agree that they provide almost identical functionality.

Figure 2.11

The Visual InterDev web site is reminiscent of other sites for Microsoft development products.

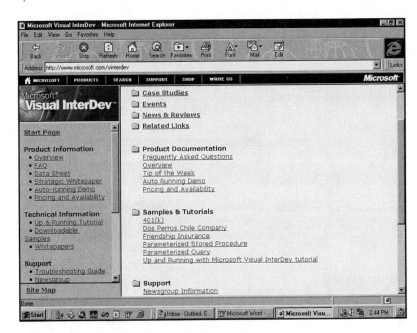

Simplicity Over Complexity

The most advanced multimedia features can't save your web page if the majority of your users are surfing the Web at 28.8 and less. As of today, most people don't have high-speed connections, so users are likely to reach for the Back button if your web site loads too slowly. In this day and age, simplicity rules over complexity, making your content the primary lure for the user. It's possible to design an aesthetically pleasing web site without resorting to Shockwave animations, soundtracks, and embedded AVI videos.

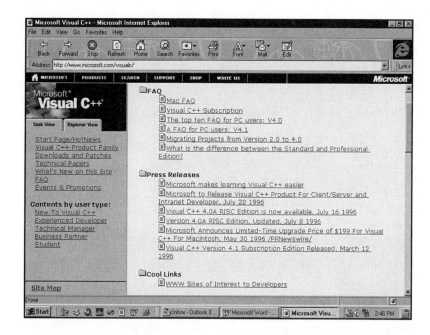

Figure 2.12

The Visual C++ web site, like the InterDev site, uses a site map that is consistent with other similar areas on the Microsoft web site.

The point here is that simplicity in the design, presentation, and structure of your web site will go a long way toward making your site a desirable destination. Not to discount content, of course, but the overabundance and misuse of Java applets, ActiveX controls, scrolling marquees, and blinking text on the Web today suggests a general misunderstanding of basic design fundamentals. Also, it's wise to adopt a general rule of keeping the total size of the content on any given page to 35-50K or less. This means that the combination of every graphic file, Java applet, etc., must weigh in under that range.

Content Ratings

The major browser manufacturers have teamed with the Recreational Software Advisory Council (RSAC), an independent, non-profit organization, to provide the public with a means to rate content on the Internet. The RSAC has helped Microsoft create a Contents filter in Internet Explorer, shown in Figure 2.13. It enables parents to filter out content based on a ratings system known as the RSACi—the Recreational Software Advisory Council on the Internet (RSACi). RSACi was specially developed as a *self-rating* system for web sites and other Internet content.

Web sites can register with RSAC and become rated. This information is stored in special HTML tags that identify your site to the Internet Explorer Web browser. To register your site, please visit the RSAC home page at `http://www.rsac.org/`. This site is shown in Figure 2.14.

Figure 2.13

Internet Explorer allows you to easily enable a contents rating system that reads special HTML tags embedded in participating web sites.

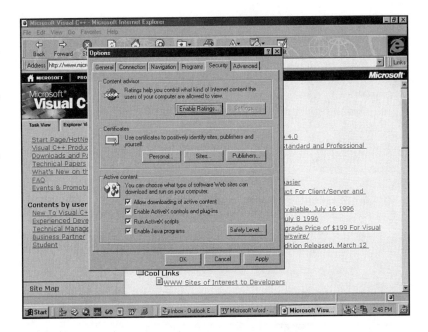

Figure 2.14

The RSAC web site is a central hub for information about the RSACi content ratings system used by Internet Explorer.

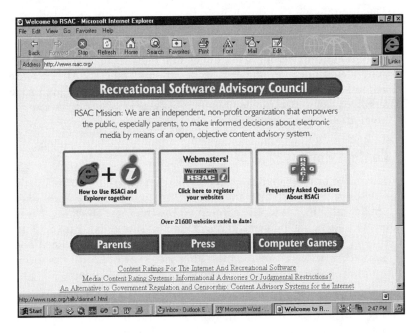

Personalization

Today's web sites have large numbers of customers with varying interests, needs, and wants. A challenge for any web site is to effectively service all of these customers in a meaningful, unique way. One of the most exciting recent developments in web design is the idea of *personalization*. A personalized web site gets your preferences the first time you visit and remembers them every time you come back. Of course, you can change these settings as well, at any time. The more advanced personalized sites don't require you to log in either, but use Cookies to store your customized user profile.

With Active Server Pages, you can roll your own personalization features using Cookies, but Microsoft also offers the Personalization System as part of its Microsoft Commercial Internet Systems (MCIS) server suite. The Personalization System is an Internet server that provides server-side ActiveX controls that determine how content is delivered, providing the user with his or her own personalized experience.

If you'd prefer to create your own personalization system, you can do so with ASP. Active Server Pages provide access to Cookies and server-side databases, both of which can be used to store user configuration information.

Allowing the User To Configure Your Site

Regardless of how you decide to personalize your site, you should provide a configuration screen the user can easily access if they wish to change their profile. The information the user can change will vary from site to site. A news web site, for example, like WinInfo (`http://www.internet-nexus.com/wininfo.asp`) might provide a list of news-related subjects the user could choose to be updated on each time he or she visits. Always provide a way out as well: If the user would prefer not to have a personalized experience, that also should be an option.

The point here is that the user should feel in charge. They also should regard your site as a unique and dynamic place they will want to visit often.

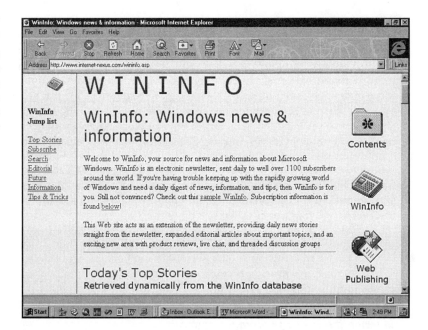

Figure 2.15

News sites such as WinInfo can be configured to display information that is customized for each visitor.

Navigational Concerns

When you're designing your web site, you need to make some decisions about the basic navigational structure. Will it be frames-based and if not, how will you replicate information across the various pages? What sorts of technologies will you use for navigation? In today's alphabet soup of web technologies, Java, JavaScript, ActiveX, and VBScript all have their pros and cons, but the final decision about what technologies you will implement should come down to your users. It won't matter that you have the coolest ActiveX control on the planet if the majority of your users browse the site with the America Online browser.

Frames

Frames provide a logical way to arrange your site but introduce some major problems. From a development standpoint, frames are harder to create and maintain because you will always have to worry about correctly targeting the frame. Keep the abilities of your development team in mind before you attack a frames-based site and always remember the alternatives—in most cases, it makes more sense to go with a simpler table-based design with no frames.

Most importantly, frames can be confusing to users, especially less-experienced users. Different browsers and browser versions handle the Back and Forward button differently with frames, and that can lead to headaches. Most importantly, users won't be able to bookmark specific pages within your site, and will end up bookmarking the frameset instead. This is very frustrating: When a user attempts to bookmark a specific page and returns later only to find out they bookmarked your entry page, they will be upset. This is probably the number one reason not to use frames.

 Tip If you must use frames, consider providing a non-frames version of your site for users who don't like that feature. It's more work, but the outcry against frames is strong enough that some users won't even enter a frames-based site.

Image Maps

In the dark days of just a few years ago, the only type of image map you could create required the use of CGI scripts on the server. Today, however, client-side images maps can easily be created and most browsers can handle them. The only real issue, then, with image maps, involves download time: Your users aren't going to be too happy if they have to download a one megabyte GIF image just to navigate your site. The Silicon Graphics web site (http://www.sgi.com) is a good example of a nice-looking site with an overly-large image map on the front page.

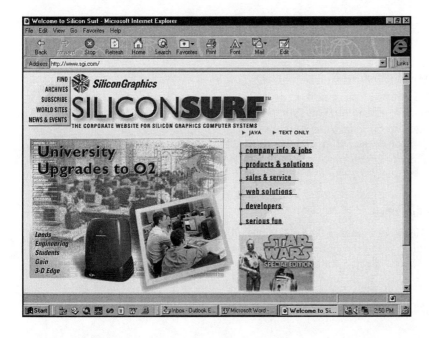

Figure 2.16

The Silicon Graphics web site uses a large image map that many users will not appreciate loading.

There are two alternatives to a graphics-heavy site like SGI. First, you could provide a text-only version of your web site that includes a text navigational menu bar.

Alternatively, you might include that text navigation feature along with the image map to ensure that text-only browsers, or users with graphics turned off, will be able to access your site. Figure 2.17 depicts the text-only version of SGI's web site.

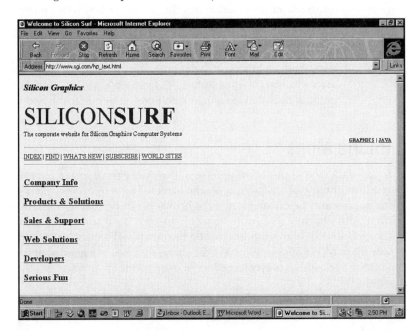

Links to Common Pages

Regardless of whether you choose to go with an image map, a frame-based navigational menu, or a text menu, you should provide an upper-level list of links to common pages on every page of your site. This list might include links to your home page, a search page, and other relevant links. The Big Tent web page (http://www.bigtent.com) uses a simple row of text links to the most common pages on the site, as shown in Figure 2.18.

Appear on All Pages

Make sure the list of common links is displayed on every page. It's important to give the user a quick way to navigate to major pages on the site quickly and not have to rely on clicking the Back button repeatedly. With the Big Tent web site, shown in Figure 2.18, the menu of common links is displayed on every page in the site, enabling you to navigate quickly back and forth between major site sections.

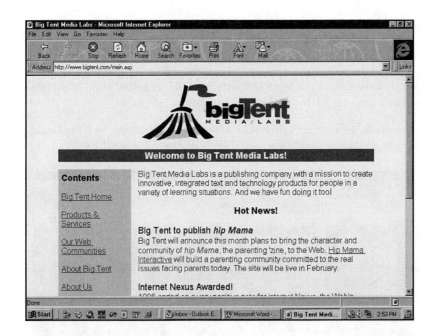

Figure 2.18

The Big Tent web site uses a text-based menu that appears on every page, providing a simple, consistent user interface.

Have Same Appearance

It goes without saying that the list of common links should look the same on every page. Don't put an image map on one page and then use a text menu on another. The easiest way to ensure this consistency is to place these navigational links within server-side includes. This has the additional benefit of enabling you to update only one document and not to perform a global search and replace across all of the pages in the site. A server-side include is a special file that is linked from most of the other pages on the site. If you change this file, the results will be seen on every page that references it. If you don't use server-side includes and wish to change text that appears on many pages, you will have to hand-edit each page or perform a search-and-replace across your whole web site if you're using a web tool that supports it.

Appear in Same Location on Each Page

The list of common links should be displayed in the same location on every page. If you have a menu bar at the top of one page, don't place it at the bottom of another. You're not trying to confuse the user, but rather are trying to make navigation of your site transparent so that the user can concentrate on the content.

Table of Contents Frame

Many web sites provide some sort of table of contents frame or table element. The goal is to repeat a common set of top-level links across every page in the site, making it easy for users to get from place to place. Microsoft, for example, uses a server-side include to re-create their navigational bar on every page. This takes two forms, depending on the page. The main navigational bar is a black band running across the top of each page. This provides the requisite links to the top-level pages at Microsoft's web site. Individual areas within the Microsoft web page, for example, the JScript area or the Windows area, provide their own level of navigational contents.

The "Stomped" web site uses a nice Table of Contents frame featuring an image map with links to all of the major pages on the site. This is shown in Figure 2.19.

Figure 2.19

This PC games web site uses a series of images in a small frame as a table of contents that is always visible.

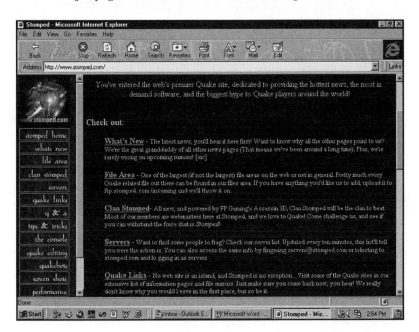

These second-level contents can occur in a frame or as a separate table element. In either case, there are two major areas to place such an aid.

Along the Side

You can place your table of contents or navigational toolbar along the right or left side of your web pages. This is the preferred approach because most web pages have more vertical than horizontal depth. Most users think nothing of scrolling up and down a page, but would be disconcerted if they had to scroll left and right.

Along the Bottom or Top

Another possibility is to place your navigational elements at the top or bottom of each page. The only problem with this approach is screen real estate: it's easy to take up too much space in the browser with this approach, so horizontal menu bars, tables of contents, and navigational toolbars should be as small as possible if you use this method. Microsoft's black TOC strip is a good example of a horizontal navigational aid that doesn't take up too much space.

Look and Feel

Regardless of where you place your site navigation aids, and whether you choose a frame-based design or not, it's important that each page in your site maintain a consistent look and feel. It's easy, as a web designer, to tweak your design as you fill out a site, but you should resist the urge and stick with a simple, clear design.

If you decide to update the design, update the entire site at the same time. Remember that users who visit your site are going to expect a transparent user interface: That means that they should be able to navigate your site without constantly wondering how to get from one page to the other. If your site is properly designed, users will be able to get around the site and view content freely. The key to providing this sort of experience is the look and feel of your site.

Consistency, Consistency, Consistency

It goes without saying that consistency is the first step to successful web page design. Don't use a vertical table of contents in one area of your site and a horizontal navigational toolbar in another. Obviously, you will want to test various visual styles while designing the site, but once a design is accepted, stick with it and fill out the site.

Consistent web sites have a transparent user interface. That is, your users quickly start navigating around the site without having to figure it out. Once they get past the first page, navigating further into the site should come naturally. By creating a consistent user interface throughout your site, you are enabling your users to concern themselves with the content in your site.

Choosing a Color Scheme (And Sticking with It)

The color scheme you choose provides a unique personality for your site. In the early days of the Web, black text on gray was the common color scheme (see Figure 2.20).

Later, black backgrounds with bright neon-colored lettering became common as masses of people flocked to the Web. Rise above the millions of inferior sites that exist out there and go with a professional mixture of muted background colors and dark text. There's no reason a web site can't look as professional as any trade publication or magazine. The Slate web site, shown in Figure 2.21, is a good example of this.

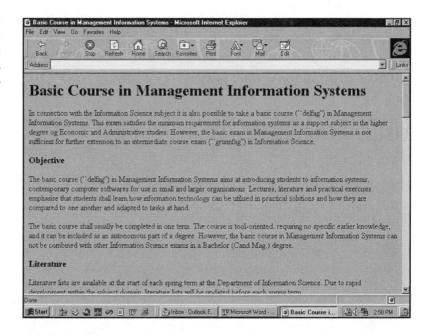

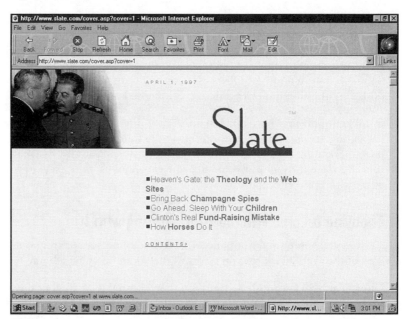

An important thing to keep in mind is the so-called Netscape palette of acceptable colors. This palette has 256 solid colors that can easily be described with an RGB triplet value in HTML. Stick with these colors for compatibility with the majority of browsers and you can be sure that your pages will load with solid (rather than dithered) colors on your user's browsers.

You can find a list of these solid colors and their hex values for insertion in HTML at the Microsoft Site Builder Workshop at `http://www.microsoft.com/workshop`.

Background

The use of glaring, bright background images or solid colors is a disturbing current trend in web page design. These types of backgrounds tend to obscure text, and the more inept home pages often use light, or even white text so that you can't even read the content. Needless to say, you should avoid this at all costs.

Solid, Soft Color

Any background color you specify for your site should be a solid, non-dithered soft color or plain white. This will contrast nicely with the text that is displayed on your pages. Light grays, tans, and yellows are preferable, although boxed areas of light green, light blue, light orange, and light purple are often used to highlight key areas of text.

Very Light Repetitive Watermark

One interesting approach is to use a light, delicate watermark image as a backdrop. The watermark should have a light palette and will need to be tileable, meaning that the edge of the image should not be apparent when it is tiled on the backdrop. As with a solid background color, any watermark image you use should contrast with the text that will be displayed above it.

Consistent Location Of Navigational Links

Your decision about navigational links will affect the look and feel of your site dramatically. As discussed previously, the location and persistence of your navigational links—regardless of the form they take—can make browsing your site transparent to the user.

Keeping the User Experience in Mind

The user experience should be at the forefront of every design decision you make for your site. Every minute change you make to the structure of your site will affect the way users view and use your site. Don't make these decisions lightly. In fact, any decision you make regarding the design of the site should be to improve the user experience. It's that simple: If it doesn't make it *better* for the user, don't do it.

What's "better" then? Real people are going to visit this site, so you have a few things to think about. First, you have to grab their attention immediately, or they will browse to a different page. This can be done with a compelling presentation (graphics, layout, and design), or by providing obviously useful content up front. Regardless of how you get the user's attention—and browsing time—to keep their attention, you must then make it easy to find information in your site and navigate around the site. Any changes you make to the site will affect these goals. If a change doesn't make it easier on the user, that is, positively affect the user experience, that change is not "better."

Choosing Fonts

Some day you will be able to embed font information in HTML documents just as you can now embed them in word processing documents. This way, even a user who doesn't have your vast selection of fonts will be able to see your documents the way you want them to be seen. The picture today, however, is a little less ideal.

Currently, font information is only *specified* in your HTML code. If the user doesn't have the font you specify, the browser will substitute a font (typically Times New Roman or Courier) so that your text at least displays. The only fonts you can be sure users have are Times and Courier. Windows users also have Arial, although many Macintosh users do not.

One thing you can do is request that users download free font collections. Microsoft, in particular, offers an excellent selection of free, downloadable fonts for both Windows and the Mac. These fonts include the following:

Table 2.1
Free TrueType Fonts from Microsoft

Column Heads
Arial
Arial Black
Comic Sans
Courier New
Georgia
Impact
Times New Roman

Column Heads
Trebuchet
Verdana

You can download these fonts from http://www.microsoft.com/truetype/fontpack/ default.htm. For the short term, this is a barely acceptable fix. Hopefully, the days of embedded font information aren't far off.

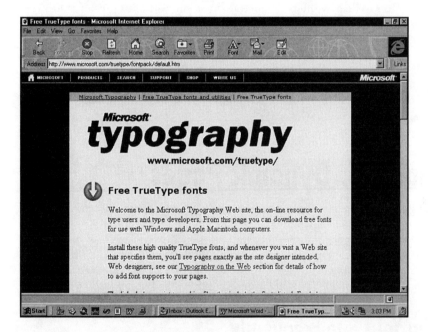

Figure 2.22

The Microsoft Typography web page is an excellent online resource for free fonts.

Screen Resolution Concerns

Like font issues, the screen resolution your users have is a problem. At the beginning of 1996, most people browsing the Web were still using a resolution of 640 × 480. The second largest group, curiously, is 1024 × 768, followed by 800 × 600. Before ASP, there were two ways you could approach the screen resolution issue.

Firstly, you can hard-code the width of your pages using tables. If you want to support the majority of users, you should code them at 600 to 620 pixels wide, which gives 640 × 480 users a little room for their scrollbars and window edges. This particular solution isn't optimal for 1024 × 768 users, but at least you can be sure that everyone viewing your site is seeing the same thing.

Another, more complicated approach, is to use relative table widths to set the width of your pages. Specifying percentage widths in your table tags does this. With this approach, you could have every user see your pages at the full width of their browser, for example. This may seem like the best way to approach the problem, but this can lead to many unexpected screen glitches and strange results. Also, you will have to test your pages at a variety of resolutions to make sure that they look right. It usually isn't worth the bother.

Active Server Pages introduces an interesting, if complicated, solution to this problem. With ASP, it's possible to determine the resolution of the user's browser. You can use this information to display the table and table column widths at pre-set values, which enables you to test a finite number of resolutions. A three column layout at 640×480, for example, might use equal column widths of 200 pixels, while the same page at 800×600 could use columns widths of 250. Because you are now using ASP to generate your web site, this is the suggested approach if you are worried about supporting multiple resolutions. Otherwise, consider hard-coding the width at something less than 640 pixels. Using relative table widths is more work than it's worth.

Personalized, Dynamic Pages

Once you've gotten a user to navigate around your site and bookmark it, the next step is getting them to come back again and again. Dynamic Web sites offer a clear advantage over static sites because the content changes often enough that users will want to keep visiting. There are a few interesting approaches to making a site dynamic: You can simply update the pages frequently or you can personalize the site and provide automatic updates, perhaps from a database.

Updating Your Site Frequently

The most obvious approach to creating a dynamic web site is frequent updates. Nothing will halt repeat visitors more quickly than not updating the site often enough. How many times have you browsed to a site that ominously reported that it was last updated in 1995?

Frequent manual updates may be an option if you have a large enough web team, but even that can turn into a logistical nightmare. One alternative, described in detail in the following section, is to store dynamic information in a database or text file—a single file can be changed and your ASP-powered web site can automatically update itself dynamically as new information is entered.

Keep the User Coming Back

If a user likes the site enough to bookmark and visit again a few days later, site updates can keep that user as a repeat customer. There's nothing more satisfying than revisiting a compelling site again and again to find that it has been updated each time. Depending on the nature of the site, your updates can be made daily, weekly, or even monthly. A news site might be updated throughout the day.

Updating your site gives value to your users and will keep them coming back. Just remember to set a schedule you can keep: don't promise daily site updates if you can only provide updates once every week or every few days. If your users know when to come back, they will, but don't disappoint them. If they have a few bad experiences, they won't bother trying again.

Facilitating Changes

The nature of your site determines how it is changed. Updating a site doesn't mean fooling around with the site structure or design, it means that you have added actual new content. You can change your site by manually changing the HTML in individual pages, but ASP opens up a more elegant approach: the actual data you display on your pages can be stored in text files or databases that can be updated without having to manually edit the site. This approach enables content developers to provide updates without synchronizing with the web designers and developers.

Store Current News in a Text File or Database

Active Server Pages enables you to easily add ODBC database integration to your sites. This lets co-workers add information to databases that automatically propagate new information across the site. This is the approach used by *Looking Out For Yourself* (*"LOFY"*)(http://www.lofy.com) and the *Internet Nexus* (http://www.internet-nexus.com), two web sites that use SQL Server databases with web front-ends. Both of these sites are automatically updated throughout the week as new news stories and resources are added to the databases associated with the sites. Figure 2.23 shows a typical news day at the Nexus web site.

Additionally, users also can modify the databases directly from web pages. LOFY uses this approach to enable user resource ratings. It's very cool, and compelling from a user's standpoint, because the site is updated so often it's like a living, breathing entity with a unique personality.

This type of site also is exciting for the web development team because it opens up new possibilities for dynamic sites that were simply impossible only a few short months ago.

Figure 2.23

The Internet Nexus is a dynamic web application with daily news stories that are drawn from a database.

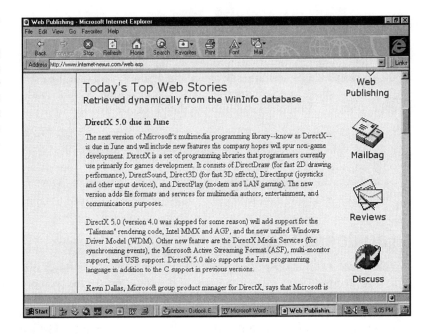

Personalization

Another important feature of a dynamic web site is *personalization*. This feature is discussed earlier in this chapter within the context of the site's look and feel, but personalization is an important feature to offer for other reasons as well. In addition to the unique visible changes personalization offers to your users, personalization is the best way to keep users coming back, especially if it's transparent enough.

Give the Users What They Want

The first goal of personalization is to give your users what *they* want. This means that they are able to make decisions about the content that your site displays and the way it is presented. Allow your users to choose between a frames and no-frames display, for example. Lots of sites do this already, but they require you to choose each time you visit the site. With personalization, you can save this setting in a Cookie and then display the correct version each time the user returns.

Personalization is another feature that really takes your site to the next level. Users will be excited about it, and will want to visit your site more often.

No Need To Search

Another obvious benefit of personalization is that users won't be forced to search for the information they want. Because the site is personalized to their preferences, they will be shown the content they want to see without any need to find it.

Of course, site search is still important, but personalization should eliminate the need to use this feature as often. A search feature can even be tailored to the preferences of your users—automatically—or be set to default to full search values if they desire.

How To Personalize Your Web Site

To remember preferences set by your users, you need to store some sort of persistent data. In general, there are a few good ways to do this using Microsoft-based solutions. You can store personalization information on the user's machine as a Cookie or in a database on the server using the Microsoft Personalization System. The next two sections take a quick look at both approaches.

Using Cookies

Active Server Pages script makes it easy to read and write Cookies and because Cookies don't require any sort of additional purchase on your part, they are an obvious solution. You can detect whether a user has visited before by first checking for the existence of your Cookie when the user arrives at any page in your site. If it doesn't exist, present the user with a special configuration page that enables the user to set their personal settings. Then, save the information in the Cookie and let the user proceed to the page they were attempting to access.

If the Cookie does exist, use the information in the Cookie to automatically provide that user with the settings they chose. The user won't need to visit the configuration page again, unless they want to. Make sure that your users *can* change their settings should they want to, by revisiting the configuration page. This page should be easily accessible from any point in your site.

Of course, people who use older browsers won't be able to fully take advantage of Cookies. ASP supports a server-side feature that can test the user's browser capabilities and determine whether they can use Cookies. If this capability isn't present, you can act accordingly. You also can use this as a warning to people who have disabled Cookies because they wrongly believe there might be a security risk.

Store Personalization Information on the User's Machine

So what types of information should the user be able to set? This is very dependent on your site and the level of customization you wish to provide. Some basic personalization information you should consider includes the following:

◆ User's name

◆ Login information for secure access

◆ User's address/physical location

- ◆ User's email address
- ◆ Color scheme for background, text, and hyperlinks
- ◆ Hyperlink underlining on or off
- ◆ Frames or no-frames
- ◆ Relative table width vs. hard-code table widths
- ◆ Screen resolution
- ◆ Include user in mailing lists that informs user about site changes?

Microsoft Personalization System (MPS)

An interesting alternative to using Cookies is to use a dedicated personalization server. Microsoft now offers the Personalization System (MPS), an Internet Server that works with Internet Information Server (IIS) to retain information about each user on the server itself. This information is stored in an SQL Server database and provides a dizzying array of customizable options. The main benefit to using this system is that you wouldn't need to hand-code the personalization with ASP yourself. If you know right away that you will be offering extensive personalization services, you should at least consider the MPS.

The Microsoft Personalization System home page, shown in Figure 2.24, is located at `http://backoffice.microsoft.com/product/personalization/system.asp`.

Figure 2.24

The MCIS Personalization web site provides whitepapers, FAQs, and a demo download of Microsoft's latest server.

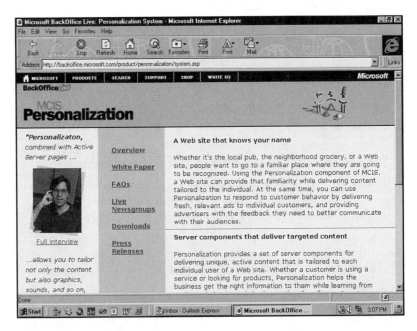

Store Personalization Information on the Server

MPS goes beyond simple user customization by using a server-side database that stores user information, customization options, preferences, and even usage history. You can use this information to determine how people are using your sites. This can aid in site expansion decisions and even help you target specific advertisements at different users. If you know a user is accessing a certain chat area frequently, for example, you can target applicable ads on each page that the user visits. This can be done on a user-by-user basis: each user can see a different ad on the same page.

The Personalization System includes the following benefits:

◆ **User Profile Store**—centrally located database for user preferences.

◆ **No registration process**—users simply access the web site and their preferences are seamlessly identified.

◆ **Voting**—a voting component enables users to give opinions and rate resources that are tallied in a database.

◆ **Mail connection**—users can receive mail automatically after visiting your web pages.

◆ **Browser independence**—like Active Server Pages, the MPS is browser-independent.

◆ **Easy administration**—the MPS is easy to set up and features a simple graphical administration tool.

◆ **Integrates with Conference Server**—this integration provides users with information about friends that might also be online.

Immediate Applications

Heady personalization features not withstanding, there are less complex ways to personalize your site. Just knowing the names of your users and some simple preferences enables you to provide cues that let the user know your site is something special.

In some cases, it may be wise to start off with these simpler personalization methods and work up to an MPS-based solution. Some users, however, may be put off by personalization and there is a fine line between elegant personalization and the form letter syndrome. If you're uncomfortable with the higher-end approaches, you might consider some of the less-intrusive baby steps into personalization discussed in the following sections.

Personalized Greetings Message

Once you have a user's name, it's a simple matter to place that name into personalized greetings messages. Avoid the form letter approach, where their name is used throughout the site, but a hearty "Welcome back, Paul!" can go a long way toward creating a friendly environment that the user will appreciate.

Obviously, you can use Cookies to store this simple information or you can simply ask users to enter their name when they arrive each time. This is a little inelegant, however, and most users won't be too excited about doing this. The goal of personalization is that it works in the background and doesn't confront the user each time they visit your site.

Good Morning, Good Afternoon, Good Evening

Another simple customization determines the time of day using scripting code and outputs the appropriate message, depending on the time. A user named Paul might be greeted with "Good morning, Paul!" if it's before noon, for example. This sort of greeting is trivial to code and provides that extra element of human contact so often missing from otherwise professional web sites.

 Tip   If you do set time of day using scripting code on the server, realize that the time is the server's time, not the user's. Even though it is afternoon where the server is in Chicago, it may still be morning in Seattle where the user is browsing.

Summary

Well, by this point you're probably itching to get to the fun part: coding your site and learning Active Server Pages. That's certainly understandable!

This chapter has stressed the fact that proper site planning goes a long way toward creating a memorable site. Always keep the goals of the site and the experiences of your users in mind as you design, implement, and maintain your web sites.

You should now feel comfortable with creating a logical plan to implement your ASP web site. You also should understand the problems and pitfalls of general web design and development and should be able to identify problem areas in your current sites if you will be porting them to ASP.

New enhancements to web design and development are available on an almost daily basis and it is a constant struggle just to keep up with today's technologies. Active Server Pages is the first step to the next generation of web technology and you made the right choice in a field crowded with possibilities. Your users will thank you for creating exciting, dynamic sites and you will thank yourself for making those sites easy to update and fun to create.

Foundations for Creating Active Server Pages

This chapter takes you on a tour of what Active Server Pages are and how they are processed on the ActiveX Server, the add-on to Microsoft's web servers for processing Active Server Pages. This chapter gives you in-depth coverage about the following topics:

- ◆ Creating an ASP application

- ◆ Managing state information for your clients

- ◆ Selecting a scripting language of your choice

- ◆ Creating simple active pages

Active Server Pages Overview

Active Server Pages are a very powerful and yet easy-to-learn server-side scripting environment for Internet Information Server for Windows NT Server, for Peer Web Server for Windows NT, and for Personal Web Server for Windows 95. This environment provides you with the ability to create a website that is dynamic, fast, and interactive, without requiring you to worry about the capabilities of your clients' browsers, which you have to do if you rely on client-side scripting.

The web server processes the Active Server Page and sends the resulting plain HTML to the browser that requested it. See Figure 3.1 for a schematic overview of how this processing is done.

Figure 3.1

Processing of an Active Server Page request.

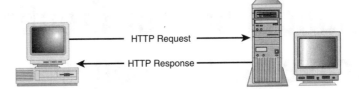

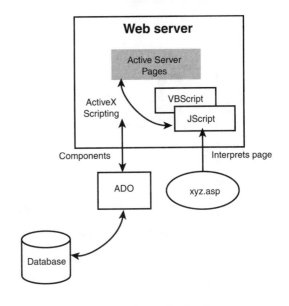

When the web server receives a request for a page xyz.asp, the script begins to run. The ActiveX Scripting Engine (described in the following section) executes each line of code and the resulting final HTML code is sent to the client.

The following list walks you, step-by-step, through what happens if the client requests the page xyz.asp:

1. The client request the page xyz.asp from the server. The web server checks the file extension to see whether a special program (in most cases an ISAPI extension DLL) has to be invoked to process the request. In this case, the web server determines that it should invoke ActiveX Server to process this page.

2. If this page has never been requested before or has changed since the last request, it has to be parsed, syntax checked, and compiled. Otherwise the page may be read from a cache of recently processed pages, which aids in performance. During the parse process, the HTML and Scripting code are separated. The ActiveX Scripting engine determines which language engine is responsible for the script and delegates the work of syntax checking and compiling to the language engine.

3. Now the code is executed. All objects that the language engine cannot handle are requested from the ActiveX Scripting Engine, which also is responsible for returning interface information for external COM objects that are created and used inside the script. If it too cannot supply the object, an error is generated.

4. Script output and static HTML code in the ASP file are merged.

5. The final HTML is sent back to the user.

ActiveX Scripting Engine

One of the big advantages of Active Server Pages is that it is language agnostic, meaning that the program isn't limited to the Microsoft-provided standard scripting languages. It can be extended by the scripting language of your choice, as long as this scripting language supports the ActiveX Scripting model.

This language independence is achieved by the same technology that was first presented with Microsoft Internet Explorer 3.0: the ActiveX Scripting Engine. By the way, Internet Explorer and the Active Server Pages use the identical engines for VBScript and JScript. Updating the scripting engines for one product affects the other (assuming you do this on the same machine).

> **Note** You can use this ActiveX Scripting model in your own applications too. If you support this model, you never have to invent a macro programming language of your own, and your customers can choose the scripting language of their choice to script your application.

Because you have a variety of possibilities for selecting a scripting language for your pages, an entire section named "Choice of Scripting Language" is dedicated to it. You can find it later in this chapter.

Objects and Components

The ActiveX Server supplies five built-in objects for request and response processing as well as for creating and managing a web application:

- **Application:** Stores application-wide state information.

- **Session:** Maintains information on a per-user basis in this object. Session is the personal storage of each user visiting your site.

- **Request:** Consists of all information that is passed to the server from the browser. Contains form/query data.

- **Response:** Writes HTML and various other information, including cookies and headers, back to the client.

- **Server:** Provides server functionality for use in Active Server Pages.

These objects are core parts of ActiveX Server and will be presented in full depth in Chapter 5, "Programming Active Server Pages."

In contrast, components can be added at your leisure to extend the basic functionality of ActiveX Server. Components that ship with Active Server Pages are as follows:

- **Ad Rotator:** Creates advertisement rotation on your web pages with a schedule set by you.

- **Browser Capabilities:** Helps you determine which capabilities each browser accessing your pages has—support of ActiveX controls, frame support, and more.

- **Database Access:** Provides a lightweight interface for any database supporting ODBC. These are the ActiveX Data Objects (ADO) which are built upon OLE/DB.

- **Content Linking:** Enables automatic linking of files in a sequential manner as well as the creation of a table of contents based on a content-linking file provided by the programmer.

◆ **File Access Component:** Accesses disk files on your server to store/load information.

The components shipping with ActiveX Server are discussed in Chapter 6, "Using ActiveX Components" and Chapter 7, "Database Access with ActiveX Data Objects" is entirely dedicated to ADO.

First Steps to Developing Active Server Pages

Now is the time to show how incredibly simple it is to create Active Server Pages. All you need to create these example pages is a text editor—my personal favorite is Notepad.

To run Active Server Pages scripts, you need a virtual directory on your server configured to enable read and execute operations (you do not technically need read permission on this directory unless you also have static HTML documents in the directory). The setup for Active Server Pages has created a virtual directory /aspsamp/ on your computer (if you chose to install the samples) where you can store the samples, or create a new directory.

The following numbered steps show you how to create a new virtual directory:

1. Create a physical directory on your server and grant access to the user account IUSR_Computername (your IIS user account).

2. Using Internet Service Manager, add a virtual directory to your server mapping the directory you just created to the new virtual directory (name it /unlock-samp/). It must have read and execute permissions set for Active Server Pages to work. See Figure 3.2 for an example of how entries in the Directory Properties dialog box should be filled out.

Figure 3.2

The Directory Properties dialog box.

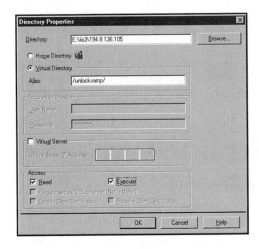

Hello World

It seems boring, doesn't it? Every programming book sports "Hello World" as its first example. But this simple example shows one very important part of any programming language; how to output results.

Start your favorite text editor and enter the following code snippet (or open it from the book's accompanying CD):

On the CD

LISTING 3.1 - HTML CODE FOR HELLO WORLD

```
01. <HTML>
02. <HEAD>
03. <TITLE>Chapter 3: Hello World</TITLE>
04. </HEAD>
05. <BODY>
06.
07. Hello World!
08.
09. </BODY>
10. </HTML>
```

So far this is still standard HTML with no active additions. But now, add a loop to it:

LISTING 3.2 - HELLO WORLD WITH A LOOP

```
01. <HTML>
02. <HEAD>
03. <TITLE>Chapter 3: Hello World</TITLE>
04. </HEAD>
05. <BODY>
06.
07. <%  for i=1 to 7 %>
08. <FONT SIZE=<%=i%>>Hello World!</FONT><BR>
09. <%  Next %>
10.
11. </BODY>
12. </HTML>
```

What has changed? In line 7 you'll notice that the code begins with <% and ends with %>. These are the so-called script delimiters, which tell the ActiveX Scripting Engine what to compile. Enclosed between the delimiters is a simple VBScript for statement, increasing the variable i in a loop from 1 to 7. The closing Next statement can be found on line 9.

The most interesting part happens on line 8. It looks like a standard HTML font tag. But included in it is the statement <%=i%>, which writes back the value of the variable i to the client browser. The resulting HTML that is sent to the client browser (after processing by the ActiveX Scripting Engine) is presented in Listing 3.3.

LISTING 3.3 - RESULTING HTML OF PROCESSED
HELLO WORLD PAGE

```
01. <HTML>
02. <HEAD>
03. <TITLE>Chapter 3: Hello World</TITLE>
04. </HEAD>
05. <BODY>
06.
07.
08. <FONT SIZE=1>Hello World!</FONT><BR>
09.
10. <FONT SIZE=2>Hello World!</FONT><BR>
11.
```

continues

Listing 3.3, Continued

```
12. <FONT SIZE=3>Hello World!</FONT><BR>
13.
14. <FONT SIZE=4>Hello World!</FONT><BR>
15.
16. <FONT SIZE=5>Hello World!</FONT><BR>
17.
18. <FONT SIZE=6>Hello World!</FONT><BR>
19.
20. <FONT SIZE=7>Hello World!</FONT><BR>
21.
22.
23. </BODY>
24. </HTML>
```

All of the scripting code that generated this HTML code is stripped off before it is sent to the client. From the client's point of view, it looks like any other static HTML it has requested from anywhere else. All the processing has been done on the server without any client intelligence needed.

Figure 3.3 shows how Internet Explorer views the Hello World example with its output.

Figure 3.3

The Internet Explorer view of our first Active Server Page.

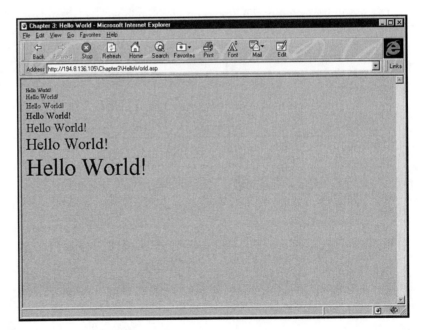

This completes the Hello World example. To show more basic programming techniques, the next section's example is a bit more sophisticated.

Countdown for Turn of the Millennium

With every day we get closer to a new millennium. It is a nice feature to provide a countdown on your page showing how many days are left until the first of January of 2000. Because there isn't much programming theory included, this section starts right off with the sample code. See Listing 3.4 for the countdown. Please notice that you have to change line 9's date format to your local date format before executing this page (for standard U.S. date format, change it to 1/1/2000). Otherwise you will receive a type mismatch error for this line.

LISTING 3.4 - COUNTDOWN FOR THE NEW MILLENNIUM

On the CD

```
01. <HTML>
02. <HEAD>
03. <TITLE>Chapter 3: Countdown</TITLE>
04. </HEAD>
05. <BODY>
06.
07. <%
08.   Dim nDaysto2000
09.   nDaysto2000 = DateDiff("d",Now,"1.1.2000")
10. %>
11.
12. <H1>Countdown 2000</H1>
13. <%=nDaysto2000%>  days left!
14.
15. </BODY>
16. </HTML>
```

In line 8, the variable *nDaysto2000* is declared, but it doesn't seem to have a datatype. This is because VBScript is a downsized version of Visual Basic and has only one datatype, *Variant*, so it doesn't need to be declared explicitly. You don't even need to include the Dim statement; the variable itself will be created when it is first referenced. The computation of days left is done in line 9, and the output is handled in line 13.

So far, there hasn't been much new in this example, but more will be added to it. What happens if this program runs longer than until the first of January, 2000? It would print rather dull results when you cross this date boundary: zero days left for the first of January, 2000. From that point on it would print negative numbers for the days left to the turn of the millennium.

To prevent this from happening, some more programmatic logic had been added to this program in Listing 3.5 (again, you have to change 1.1.2000 in line 9 to match your date format).

LISTING 3.5 - ENHANCED COUNTDOWN FOR THE NEW MILLENNIUM

```
01. <HTML>
02. <HEAD>
03. <TITLE>Chapter 3: Countdown enhanced</TITLE>
04. </HEAD>
05. <BODY>
06.
07. <%
08.    Dim nDaysto2000
09.    nDaysto2000 = DateDiff("d",Now,"1.1.2000")
10. %>
11.
12. <H1>Countdown 2000</H1>
13. <%  if nDaysto2000 > 0 then %>
14.        <%=nDaysto2000%>   days left!
15. <%  else %>
16.        <FONT SIZE=6 COLOR=red>Welcome in the new millenium</FONT>
17.        <%  if nDaysto2000 <  0 then %>  for now
      ➥<%=(1)*(nDaysto2000)%>   days!
18. <%      end if
19.    end if %>
20.
21. </BODY>
22. </HTML>
```

When you run this script today (assuming you're reading this before 2000), it will have the same output as the simpler first version of the countdown. What has been enhanced is the handling of the turn-of-the-millennium. This is first checked in line 13. If you still have some days left, the normal countdown will be displayed. If you have stepped into the new millennium (line 15), you will be greeted with a hearty red welcome message. And it will display how many days you have been living in this new millennium. To test this new logic for yourself, either stop reading until the year 2000 or change the year from 2000 to 1900 and see how many days it has been since the turn of the century!

This sample shows one of the problems of server-side scripting: because the Internet is a world-spanning network, there are many different time zones. When the people in Berlin are already celebrating a new year, the time in San Francisco will be 3pm. Be careful when dealing with date and time values computed on the server!

Choice of Scripting Language

In the examples so far only VBScript has been used as the scripting language; however, due to the fact that the ActiveX Scripting Engine is language agnostic, you can choose whatever scripting language you want. Of course, this language must support the ActiveX Scripting Engine.

Microsoft delivers two scripting languages for ActiveX Server; VBScript and JScript, Microsoft's version of JavaScript. By installation default VBScript is the standard scripting language for all pages.

How to Set the Scripting Language for Your Code

If you want to change the scripting language for your code, you are presented with three different choices:

- **Registry:** Change for all pages of your server

- **File Level:** Change only for current page

- **Function Level:** Set scripting language only for a specific function

Registry-Level Scripting Language Changes

By default, the standard scripting language is set to VBScript. If you plan to do most of your project using another scripting language, you should change the default.

To change the default to JScript, for example, follow these steps:

1. Open the Registry editor

2. Open the key `HKEY_LOCAL_MACHINE\SYSTEM\CurrentControlSet\ Services\W3SVC\ASP\Parameters`

3. Change the entry `DefaultScriptLanguage` from VBScript to JScript

4. Stop and restart IIS so changes take effect

When you're done with this, from this time on all your scripts will by default use the JScript engine.

File-Level Scripting Language Changes

If you have set a default scripting language in the Registry, you still may want to program some pages using a scripting language other than the default. An example for this would be using VBScript as default for the entire site, but using `PerlScript` for system level programming, a task for which `PerlScript` is exceptionally well-suited.

 There is still another more convincing argument for setting the scripting language on file level: distributing your files to a server where it's not guaranteed that the scripting language you have used is the default.

The syntax for setting the scripting language on file-level looks like this:

```
<% @ Language=ScriptingLanguage %>
```

Replace the `ScriptingLanguage` parameter with the name of the scripting language you will be using as default on this page. This statement has to be at the beginning of the file.

For example,

```
<% @ Language=JScript %>
```

sets the default scripting language for this page to JScript.

Function-Level Scripting Language Changes

You can even set the scripting language on a per function basis, overriding default and file-level scripting languages. The syntax for controlling scripting languages on function level is

```
<SCRIPT LANGUAGE=ScriptingLanguage RUNAT=SERVER>
....
</SCRIPT>
```

You may know the SCRIPT tags from client-side scripting. To distinguish server-side from client-side code, the server-side <SCRIPT> statement has the additional directive RUNAT=SERVER included. Replace ScriptingLanguage with the language of your choice. See the next section, "Mixing Scripting Languages," for a cool way to use this statement.

Mixing Scripting Languages

One of the neat things you can do with the ActiveX Scripting Engine is mix two or more different scripting languages on a page and call a function from JScript that was written in VBScript. You will have to use the <SCRIPT> tag to mix different languages on a single page.

Listing 3.6 shows a modified Hello World example, where a function written in VBScript is called from the default page scripting language JScript.

LISTING 3.6 - JSCRIPT CALLS VBSCRIPT FUNCTION

On the CD

```
01. <%  @ Language=JScript %>
02.
03. <HTML>
04. <HEAD>
05. <TITLE>Chapter 3: Hello World 2</TITLE>
06. </HEAD>
07. <BODY>
08.
09. <%
10.    PrintHello(3);
11. %>
12.
13. <SCRIPT  LANGUAGE=VBSCRIPT RUNAT=SERVER>
14. Sub PrintHello(i)
15.    For iIdx=1 to i
16.       Response.Write("Hello World #" & iIdx & "<BR>")
17.    Next
18. End Sub
19. </SCRIPT>
20.
21. </BODY>
22. </HTML>
```

The statement in line 1 changes the scripting language for this page to JScript. Enclosed in *<SCRIPT>* tags from line 13 to 19 is the VBScript function *PrintHello*, which is called from JScript in line 10 with the parameter 3. The VBScript function then prints "Hello World" and the number of iterations so far. For output, it uses the *Write* method of the *Response* object, which is one of the built-in ActiveX Server objects. In fact, this is nothing new: the statement <%=*someVar*%> is just a shortcut for *Response.Write*.

The output of this sample looks like Listing 3.7.

LISTING 3.7 - OUTPUT OF SCRIPT IN LISTING 3.6

```
01. <HTML>
02. <HEAD>
03. <TITLE>Chapter 3: Hello World 2</TITLE>
04. </HEAD>
05. <BODY>
06.
07. Hello World #1<BR>Hello World #2<BR>Hello World #3<BR>
08.
09. </BODY>
10. </HTML>
```

All the output from *Response.Write* is printed on a single line—line 7. This occured because a carriage return/line feed pair hasn't been inserted to make it more readable for the human (Internet Explorer does fine with this). However, if you have to trace the output of your Active Server Pages containing a larger amount of data for a subtle error, it helps if you have structured the output to build logical groups. Just change line 16 of Listing 3.6

```
Response.Write("Hello World #" & iIdx & "<BR>")
```

to include carriage return and line feed using the vbCRLF literal.

```
Response.Write("Hello World #" & iIdx & "<BR>" & vbCRLF)
```

Now all Hello World messages are displayed in the resulting HTML on a single line of their own (Listing 3.8).

LISTING 3.8 - OUTPUT OF HELLO WORLD LOOP USING THE CRLF MODIFICATION

```
01. <HTML>
02. <HEAD>
03. <TITLE>Chapter 3: Hello World 2</TITLE>
04. </HEAD>
05. <BODY>
06.
07. Hello World #1<BR>
08. Hello World #2<BR>
```

```
09. Hello World #3<BR>
10.
11. </BODY>
12. </HTML>
```

Active Server Pages Applications

By now you have seen how simple it is to incorporate script code in existing HTML code; however, you don't want to build only simple pages, you will want to group them together to form a logical group in order to build a web application.

Conventional applications like Microsoft Word are used on one computer by one person at a time. This application can very easily store information about the current user. Your Active Server Pages application, in contrast, will be used by different persons at the same time, each taking different actions. You need to be able to store information for each user and retrieve it when the user returns. The information stored for each user is dependent on the application he is currently using.

Setup of Applications

A web application is defined by a virtual directory, and its subsequent files and subdirectories. Your root directory also counts as a virtual directory, so it can be an application as well.

If you need to create an application from scratch, you first have to set up a virtual directory which will contain your application. The steps needed to create an application are as follows:

1. Create a physical directory on your server and grant access to the group of users you want to have access. If it's accessible for everyone, grant access to the user account IUSR_*Computername* (your IIS user account).

2. Using Internet Service Manager, add a virtual directory to your server, mapping the physical path to it. It must have execute permissions set for Active Server Pages to work (you additionally need read permissions when static HTML pages are contained in this directory too). See Figure 3.4 for a screenshot of how entries in the Directory Properties dialog box should be filled out.

Figure 3.4

*The Directory
Properties dialog
box.*

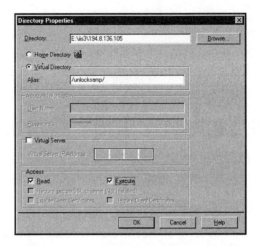

It's very simple to create an application, because creating one does not differ from creating a virtual directory. However, because it is so simple to set up applications, you could easily tap into the problems that can arise when setting up applications.

◆ One virtual directory is entirely contained in the other one. For example, the virtual directories /vroot and /vrootdemo could cause problems for the correct scope of user sessions, which use cookies to identify their storage. Cookies with deeper nesting (longer path) are returned first, so the sessions for the shorter path are not returned correctly.

◆ A virtual directory is stacked with another one. An example of this would be the virtual directory / (root) located in c:\webroot having a subfolder sales and a virtual directory /sales, which is created on exactly this subfolder. When you're running this configuration and requesting /sales/info.asp, the server doesn't know which application is responsible for this request—the root application or the /sales application.

The second case is checked for by the ActiveX Server. You can turn off this checking to improve the performance of your production server when you don't have any such collisions. You have to set the entry CheckForNestedVroots located under the Registry key HKEY_LOCAL_MACHINE\SYSTEM\CurrentControlSet\Services\W3SVC\ASP\Parameters to 0 to turn checking off.

When you're done with the setup of the application, you are ready to run it. You can now track information for each user hitting your application as if it were a "normal" Windows application and storing it as state information to the users session.

Storing State in Your Application

HTTP (Hypertext Transfer Protocol) was designed to be a stateless protocol, which means that you will not know whether a user has requested a page on your server before or not. And you will not receive notification when the user leaves your server.

So you're still wondering how to implement a shopping bag for your users? Maintain other information about your users? As always, someone came up with a solution—cookies. These cookies are sent to the browser, which stores them locally and sends the cookies to the server at each subsequent request. Presto—you know who is coming back to your site and you can track specific information for him or her on your server (like shopping bag information).

Programming cookies the normal way was a bit tricky and complicated, and associating it with more and more user information can be a challenge. But again, there is a solution—sessions.

Tracking User Sessions

Every time a new user hits an ActiveX Server application, a session is created for this user to store information for and about him or her. This information is only accessible to this user.

You can use the locker metaphor for sessions: each user gets a locker on the server on the first request and is sent the key, a cookie (a unique, non-continual ID). When a user comes back, he carries the key (cookie) with him to give the server access to his user information. When the user doesn't come back in a given time interval, the locker is cleared.

This brings up an interesting point: We don't know when a user has left the application entirely. The solution for this is to set a timeout before a session is considered abandoned.

 The standard Timeout value is 20 minutes. If you want to change the standard Timeout, you need to change the SessionTimeout entry in the Registry under the key HKEY_LOCAL_MACHINE\SYSTEM\CurrentControlSet\Services\W3SVC\ ASP\Parameters.

Another interesting point is that when a browser doesn't support cookies, no session object is created; however, the vast majority of browsers support cookies, so this isn't a considerable problem.

If you don't need session information for your users—no shopping bag or whatever—you can prevent the creation of sessions and speed up your server that way: simply set the `AllowSessionState` entry in the Registry to 0 (again, this is found under the `HKEY_LOCAL_MACHINE\SYSTEM\CurrentControlSet\Services\W3SVC\ASP\Parameters` key). You will have to restart your web server before this change takes effect.

Chapter 5 details how to use the `Session` object to store user information.

Tracking Application State

Why would you want to track application state? There is one very good reason: the application is shared among all sessions, so if you place any information in the application, it's readily available to all sessions. Everything you store in the application is available to all sessions, like global variables are for all functions of a module. A nice example is the count of currently active sessions on your application (see Chapter 5).

In the previous section, the `Session` object's lifespan was presented. The `Application` object has an even simpler lifespan: it's created when the first user requests any page (it must be a script page, because a simple HTML page won't cause the creation of the application) and is destroyed when the web server is shut down.

The `Application` object is presented at full length in Chapter 5, together with the `Session` object.

Creating Reusable Code Blocks

When you're designing your application, you will pinpoint some elements that are found on many pages throughout your application. Such elements can be navigation bars or a bottom line with the e-mail address of your webmaster. Other elements might be code-fragments to display the day, standard financial computations, and many more standardized pieces of HTML or Active Server Page code.

Because it's possible (financial calculations) or very likely (navigational bars) that these pieces change over time, it's a problem to promote these changes to all the pages they were incorporated in without missing some of the pages. You will have to change and verify many files.

One great way to work around this is to include the navigation bar with an include file in all your pages. If you have to change the bar, you only have to change it once—the changes are automatically incorporated in all pages that include it. You don't have any more work to do!

The same is true if you build code libraries using this mechanism. You simply include the file containing the functions you want to use in the current page and call the functions from this code library as if they were declared in the current page.

Now that you have seen the advantages of includes, it's time to switch from theory to practice. The general statement to include files is

```
<!--#INCLUDE FILE¦VIRTUAL="filename"-->
```

You can put this statement anywhere in your page, but you cannot change the *filename* parameter from a script, because files are included prior to script execution.

Virtual Includes

If you use the *VIRTUAL* keyword, the file is included from a virtual directory of your web server. An example for including a file in your script would be the following:

```
<!--#INCLUDE VIRTUAL="/common/inc/baseline.inc"-->
```

Microsoft recommends that you use the .inc extension for files to be included. This extension isn't vital for correct operation.

 If you include a file with server-side script code that has an .inc extension, it could be downloaded in non-executed form, thus revealing all your code. You can prevent this by sticking to the extension .asp, which is no problem to be included, but will execute on download. Also, you can prevent file reads by turning read permission off on your virtual directory.

File Includes

The *FILE* keyword includes files relative to the directory where the including file resides. You don't need to provide a fully qualified path relative to the root of your server, instead it is sufficient to provide a path relative to the path of the current page that includes the file.

```
<!--#INCLUDE FILE="orders/item44.asp"-->
```

This statement includes the item44.asp file from the directory orders into your file.

 If you want to use the syntax ../ for accessing directories below your current directory, you have to set the Registry entry *EnableParentPaths* to 1.

Summary

This chapter presented the basics of Active Server Pages and how they are processed by the ActiveX Server. You saw how you can select the scripting language of your choice down to the function level. You learned how an Active Server Pages application can be built and what challenges you may face when setting up and running this application. This chapter also covered server-side includes and how to use them to ease your development burden.

CHAPTER 4

Working Visual InterDev

T his chapter walks you through the basics of using Microsoft Visual InterDev. It addresses the creation of Web applications and the interaction with Microsoft SQL Server. It shows the tools, wizards, and design-time controls that help you save time by automating tedious work or by simply improving the approachability of certain technologies, like databases. With Visual InterDev, you can concentrate on the pieces that are relevant for your project. This chapter covers the following topics:

◆ The creation of a web application

◆ Working with databases

Creating a Web Application

When you're starting Visual InterDev for the first time, you're presented with the empty development environment. This development environment will look familiar to you if you have already used Visual C++ 4.x, FORTRAN Powerstation, or Visual J++ 1.0 (see Figure 4.1).

To learn how to install Visual InterDev, see Appendix A, "Installing Visual InterDev, " p. 477.

Cross Reference

Figure 4.1

The Visual InterDev development environment.

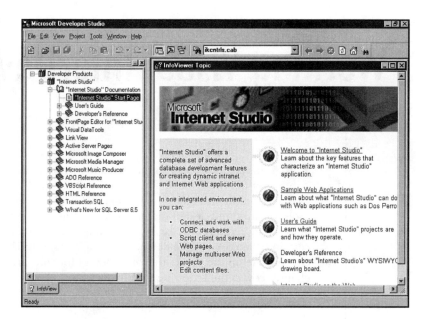

You can open files for editing by choosing Open from the File menu. However, most of the time you will be working on entire applications. To create a new application using Visual InterDev, you have to follow these steps:

1. Select the New command from the File menu.

2. The New dialog box is opened (see Figure 4.2). Switch to the Projects tab and select Web Project Wizard. Enter a project name, for example, **unlocking**. Leave the Create new workspace option checked.

You can use the Web Project Wizard only when you have a web server with FrontPage 97 Server Extensions installed. Please refer to Appendix A, "Installing Visual InterDev," to see how to set up a web server that can be used by Visual InterDev.

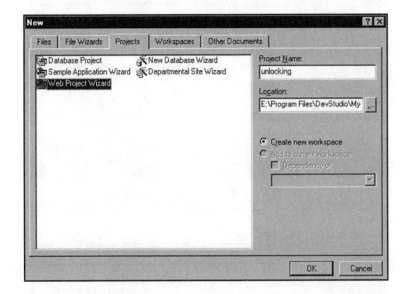

Figure 4.2

Creating a new web application.

3. The Web Project Wizard starts. Provide the name of the server or its IP address to allow Visual InterDev to contact it. Leave "Connect using SSL" unchecked. Figure 4.3 shows you how to fill out this dialog box.

4. Step 2 of the Web Project Wizard asks you whether you want to create a new application, or connect to an existing one. Leave Create a new Web checked and enter the name for the application as presented in Figure 4.4.

5. Visual InterDev now contacts your web server to create the new project and opens the project in the FileView tab of the Workspace window (see Figure 4.5).

Figure 4.3

*Web Project
Wizard Step 1.*

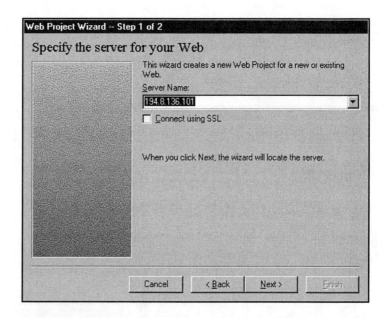

Figure 4.4

*Web Project
Wizard Step 2.*

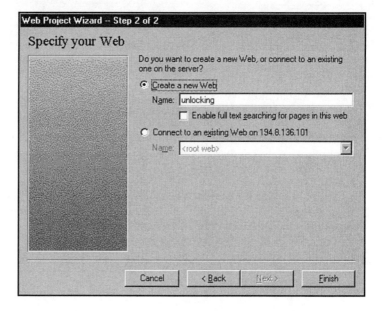

Now you have created your first application using Visual InterDev and its Web Project
Wizard. It contains a file named global.asa that will be used to store the event handlers for the application and user sessions as well as database connections, and an
empty directory named Images. Your project may also contain a file named

SEARCH.HTM if the Enable full text searching for pages in this web checkbox was checked on page 2 of the wizard.

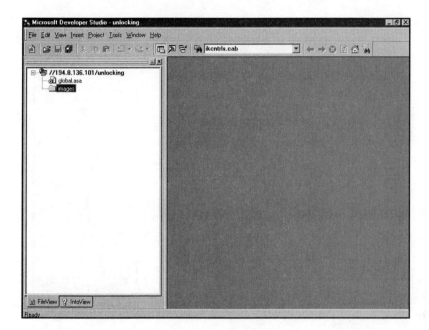

Figure 4.5

The application you just created is opened in Visual InterDev.

There is no Active Server Page in this project right now. Again, as in Chapter 3, the Hello World example is the first page that will be inserted in your first project. Follow these steps to create an Active Server Page for your project:

1. Select New from the File menu.

2. Choose Active Server Page to create and check Add to Project (see Figure 4.6). Enter a filename for the page. You don't need to include the .asp extension.

3. The file you have created is added to the project and opened in the code editor. The HTML and script code is syntax colored—you could see this in Figure 4.7 if this book were printed with colors.

4. To add scripting code to this page, replace the line

```
<!-- Insert HTML here -->
```

with the following scripting code:

```
<H1>Welcome from <%=Request.ServerVariables("REMOTE_ADDR")%>
➥</H1>
```

```
<%  For I = 1 To 7 %>
<FONT SIZE=<%=I%>>Hello World</FONT><BR>
<%  Next %>
```

Figure 4.6

Create an Active Server Page.

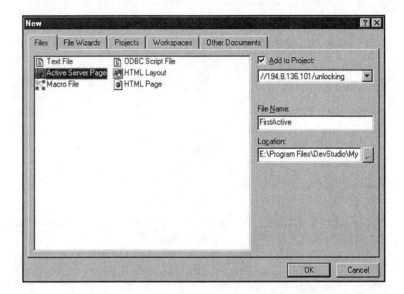

Figure 4.7

The standard body created for a new Active Server Page.

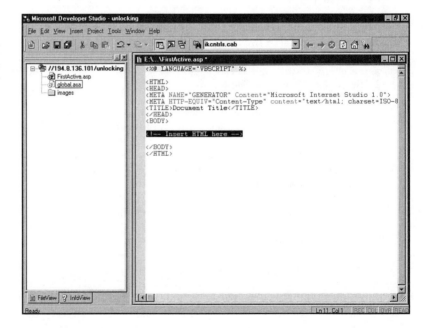

The code for this page should look like Figure 4.8 now. Save the file.

Figure 4.8

The final code for your first page created in Visual InterDev.

5. Right-click on FirstActive.asp in FileView to bring up the context menu shown in Figure 4.9.

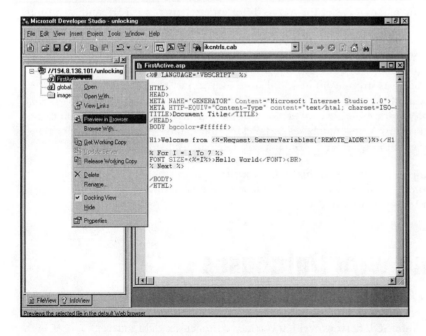

Figure 4.9

Context menu for files.

6. Select Preview in Browser to open the page in Internet Explorer.

Figure 4.10

*Use Internet
Explorer to
display the result
of your page.*

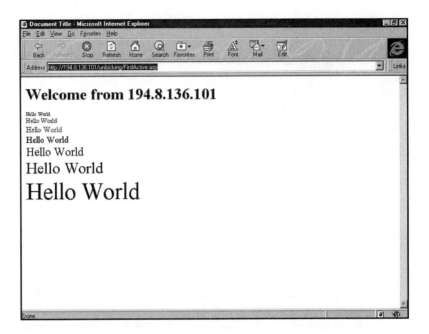

Congratulations, you have just created your first page using Visual InterDev. The syntax coloring makes it easier for you to differentiate between HTML and scripting code and helps to point out where you failed to close a code section with %>.

My main reason for working with Visual InterDev is its perfect integration with Microsoft SQL Server. You also can use Microsoft Access as a database for your web server, but Access is strongly limited: only one user can write to the database at a given time, and this isn't acceptable for medium- to heavy-load web servers. SQL Server can deal with multiple concurrent connections to one and the same database. And it outperforms Access databases by far. More on databases and their performance issues is presented in Chapter 7, "Database Access with ActiveX Data Objects."

All the examples that follow in this chapter assume that you have an SQL Server running somewhere in your network. If you don't, take a look at the following sections, and you will want one.

Working with Databases

Before you can work with a database in Visual InterDev, you have to add a data source to your project. The example presented here assumes that you have already created a database on your SQL Server to which you can connect the data source.

For adding a data source to your project, you must follow these steps:

1. Select the Data Connection command from the menu Project/Add to Project. This opens the Select Data Source dialog box. Switch to the Machine Datasource tab (Figure 4.11 shows the opened dialog box).

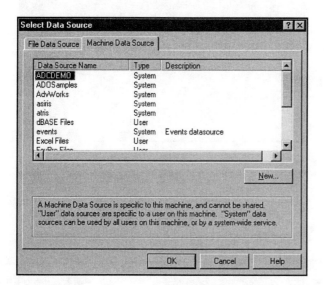

Figure 4.11

Machine Datasource tab in the Select Data Source dialog box.

Note You need to create a machine datasource because User datasources are specific to the current user account and cannot be used in the context of the web server. Machine datasources are available to all users and services on the local computer.

2. Click the New button.

3. The wizard for creating a new data source is opened. Select System Data Source as the type of data source you are creating. Figure 4.12 shows how this dialog box looks.

4. The next step (see Figure 4.13) presents you with a choice of drivers you can use to create the data source. Select SQL Server and click Next.

5. Step 3 asks you to confirm your selection of data source type and driver. Click Finish.

6. The ODBC SQL Server Setup dialog box is opened. Enter **unlocking** as the data source name, the name of the computer your SQL Server is running on, and under Options, enter the name of the database. Figure 4.14 shows how the finished Setup dialog box looks. When you're finished, click OK.

Figure 4.12

Select the type of data source.

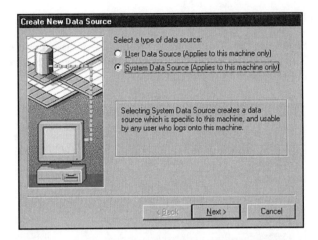

Figure 4.12

Select the type of data source.

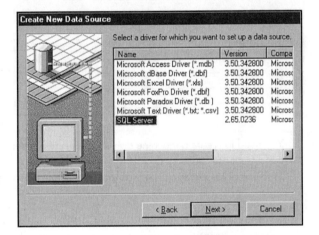

Figure 4.13

Select the driver for the data source.

7. Now you're back in the Select Data Source dialog box and your newly created data source is highlighted. Click OK to finish.

8. Enter the username and password of a valid SQL Server account.

The data source is added to your project and the DataView tab is now visible in the Workspace window.

Working in DataView

The DataView window is optimized for SQL Server. There are four groups of objects that are valid for SQL Server, but only a subset of these four is used by other data sources.

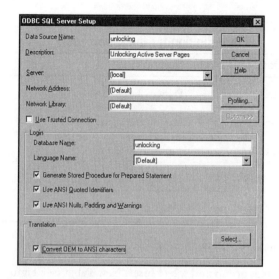

Figure 4.14

Enter information about the SQL Server database.

◆ **Database Diagrams:** Displays the tables of the data source with all the relationships. This feature is available only for SQL Server.

◆ **Tables:** Lists all tables that are contained in this data source.

◆ **Views:** Returns all views that are created on SQL server or all queries that were, for example, created using MS Access.

◆ **Stored Procedures:** Provides a list of all stored procedures in the database. Valid only for SQL Server.

When you're using SQL Server, you cannot only list these types of objects; you can create, edit, and delete them. You can even debug stored procedures. If you're using any database other than SQL Server, you won't be able to update or create any of these object types.

To provide a real-world example when presenting the database features of Visual InterDev, you will create an event calendar as the following section walks you through some of the most exciting features of Visual InterDev.

The example database has only one table: Events. This table has the following columns:

TABLE 4.1
Table Definition for the Events Table

Column name	Datatype	Description
EventId	int	Primary key index
EvDate	datetime	Date of the event
EvTime	datetime	Time of the event
Location	varchar(255)	Location where this event takes place
Description	varchar(255)	Descriptive text for the event

To create a table in DataView, follow these steps:

1. Right-click the Tables group and select Insert New Table (see Figure 4.15). The Choose Name Dialog Box is displayed. Type in **Events** as the table name and select OK. A new table design is opened.

Figure 4.15

The context menu for the tables group in DataView.

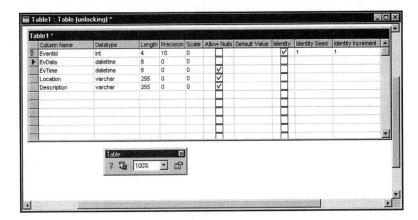

2. Enter the columns from Table 4.1. Disallow Nulls for EventId and EvDate. Select Identity for the EventId column. When you're through entering the columns, your table design should look like the one in Figure 4.16.

3. Click in the definition for the EventId column and make it a primary key by choosing Set Primary Key in the Table toolbar.

4. Close the table design window and save the table.

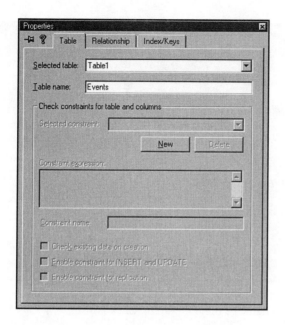

Figure 4.16
*The table design
for Events table.*

The table Events is now added to the Tables group, and double-clicking it opens it for data entry. Add some events to the table, but don't include values for the `EventId` column, because SQL Server will insert the values itself.

There is one thing left to do, namely, putting the information about these events on a page. The next section is dedicated to this task.

Presenting Database Data to the User

You have a table with data and want to make the live data available for the users? That's no problem with the Data Range Builder that comes with Visual InterDev. Follow these steps to create a list of the events without any programming.

1. Select File/New and add an Active Server Page named **Events** to your project. The file opens automatically.

2. Right-click over the Insert HTML here statement and select Insert HTML using Wizard from the context menu.

3. Select Data Range Wizard from the Choose Builder dialog box and click OK.

4. The Data Range Builder opens. Select Show only and leave ten for the amount of records to display at a time. Figure 4.17 shows the finished step 1 of the Data Range Builder dialog box. Click Next to go on to step 2.

Figure 4.17

Data Range Builder, Step 1.

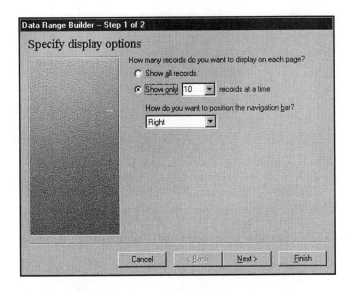

5. Enter **drange** for the name of the data range. Click Finish.

6. Now a lot of scripting code is inserted in your page. Your screen will look like Figure 4.18.

Figure 4.18

Data Range Builder has finished.

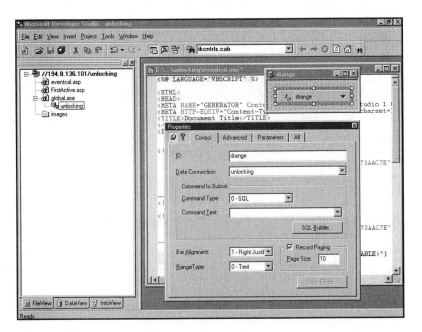

7. In the Control tab select unlocking from the Data Connection drop-down list.

8. Click the SQL Builder button to open the Query Builder.

9. Drag the Events table from the Tables group to the Query Builder window and drop it in the Diagram pane. Check the *(All Columns) checkbox in the Events table. Add another check to EvDate and remove the checkmark in the Output checkbox for EvDate in the Grid pane. Select Ascending for Sort Type. Your Query Builder window will look like the one shown in Figure 4.19.

Figure 4.19

Query Builder Window.

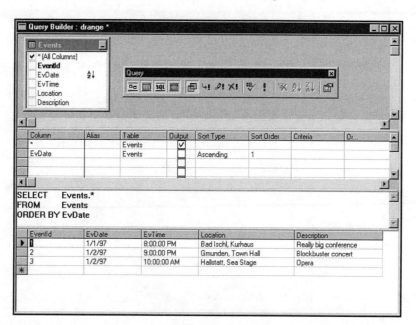

10. Click the Run button in the Query toolbar to preview the query results in the Results pane.

11. Close the Query Builder window and update the Data Range.

12. Close the Data Range design time control window. Move to the beginning of the file. Before the comment starting with METADATA, insert the following lines of code:

```
<TABLE CELLSPACING=10>
<TR><TH>Event</TH><TH>Location</TH><TH>Date</TH>
➥<TH>Time</TH></TR>
```

13. Press **Ctrl+F** and enter **endspan** as the search string. When you have found the first occurrence, go to the end of the line and press ENTER. Insert the following code at this position:

```
<TR>
<TD><%=drange("Description")%></TD>
<TD><%=drange("Location")%></TD>
<TD><%=drange("EvDate")%></TD>
<TD><%=drange("EvTime")%></TD>
</TR>
```

14. Save the file and preview it in the browser. It should look like Figure 4.20.

Figure 4.20

*The finished
events page.*

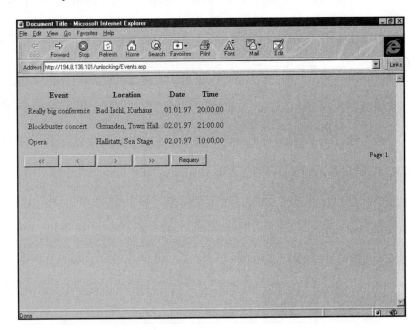

Of course you still have to insert a page title and a nicer background color; however, you have just created an event calendar without writing more scripting code than writing the database fields to the user.

Because you do not want to enter the events manually via Visual InterDev, it would be cool to create an online form that can add, update, and delete entries, and best, asks before taking any action. If you tried that on your own, that would be a challenge and a task for some hours, but Visual InterDev has a solution for this problem too—the Data Form Wizard.

Data Form Wizard

This tool saves you a lot of time and tedious work. You only have to answer some simple questions—and, presto—you're finished. The steps for creating such a form are even easier than the ones in the previous section. The following steps are needed to create a data entry form:

1. Choose File/New, switch to File Wizards, select Data Form Wizard, and enter a filename (**Event**).

2. In the first step you have to specify the datasource and the caption for the pages. Choose unlocking as the datasource and enter **Online Events** as the caption. Click Next when you're finished.

3. Step 2 asks for the type of database object to use for the form. Stick with table and click Next.

4. In the third step you have to select the table you want to use for the form. Select the Events table and add all fields except EventId to Selected Fields (see Figure 4.21). Click Next when you're done to go on to step 4.

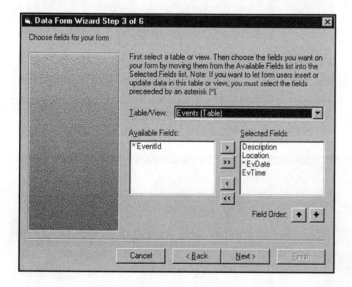

Figure 4.21

Choose these fields.

5. If you want to allow only specific operations to be performed by the users on this page, select the appropriate actions. For this example, all options are enabled. See Figure 4.22 for a look at which options you can select. Click Next when you're done.

6. Step five provides options for paging through the data, type of display, and status line. All options should be enabled.

7. The last step provides you with choices of themes for the pages. You can stick with the default—for this example, I chose Redside as the theme.

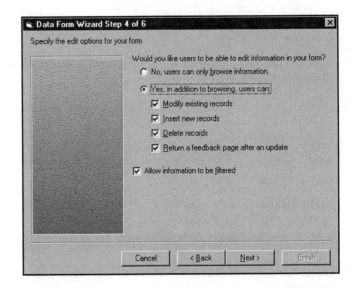

Figure 4.22

*Select all options
for the Events
data form.*

8. Click Finish.

When you're previewing the page EventForm.asp in the browser (Figure 4.23), you should notice that all features are implemented: Update, Delete, and New. You can preview the records either one at a time or in list view, and you can apply filters. And you didn't program a single line of code!

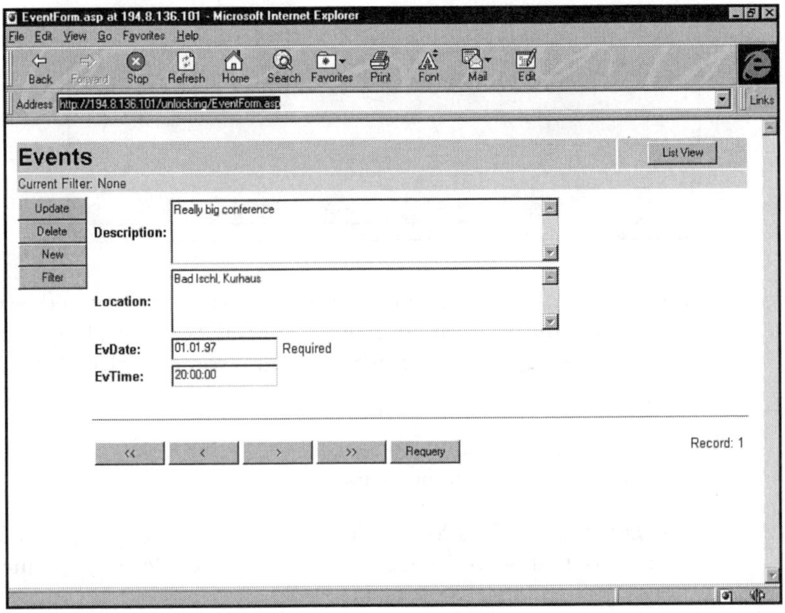

Figure 4.23

*Editing events
with the newly
created form.*

Summary

When it comes to working with databases (along with many other things!), your life definitely becomes easier when you're using Visual InterDev. If you have used the Microsoft SQL Server provided tools before, you have probably noticed that the tools Visual InterDev provides are much more powerful and easier to use than the ones that come with SQL Server. An overview of form design and other topics was presented in this chapter. In the chapters that follow, you will notice how much time Visual InterDev has saved in the creation of forms and pages.

I have provided only a small subset of the Visual InterDev features. The source control features, the FrontPage 97 editor, database diagrams, and many other topics weren't even discussed. If you want to learn more about these features, I'd suggest that you either start working with Visual InterDev or read its documentation (or simply read a good book about them).

CHAPTER 5

Programming Active Server Pages

C hapter 3 presented you with background information about Active Server Pages and web applications along with a brief introduction to scripting. This chapter takes a closer look at how to process forms, send data to the user, maintain state information for single users and the entire application, and examines the utility functionality that is provided by the Server object. This chapter covers the following topics:

- ◆ Active Server Pages Built-in Objects
- ◆ Utility Functionality Provided by the Server Object
- ◆ Processing Client-Provided Information
- ◆ Sending Data to the User
- ◆ Managing State for the Application and Users

Active Server Pages Built-in Objects

The Active Server Pages framework encapsulates the application and session state management, client request, server response, and server operations in five built-in objects dedicated to these tasks:

- Application
- Request
- Response
- Server
- Session

The Application and Session objects manage state, the Request and Response object are for receiving and sending data to the browser, and the Server object supplies server-side utility functionality.

These objects are part of the Active Server Pages framework, and are therefore available for scripting without the need to be created prior to use. The objects and their functionality are presented based on the concepts they introduce:

- Utility functionality provided by the Server object
- Processing client-provided information
- Sending data to the user
- Managing state for the application and users

Utility Functionality Provided by the Server Object

The Server object provides needed access to server functionality. The methods of this object serve as utility functions you will want to use in your scripts.

Setting the Timeout for Your Script

If you expect your script to take a great amount of time to run, you should adjust the maximum amount of time before the script times out. Set the `ScriptTimeout` property to the maximum time you want to allow this script to run. The default value of this property is set with the Registry (the *ScriptTimeout* entry), and its default value set by installation is 90 seconds.

Listing 5.1 shows you how to use this property:

LISTING 5.1 - USAGE OF SERVER.SCRIPTTIMEOUT

On the
CD

```
01. <HTML>
02. <HEAD>
03. <TITLE>Chapter 5: Testing ScriptTimeout</TITLE>
04. </HEAD>
05. <BODY>
06.
07. <%
08. Response.Write(Server.ScriptTimeout & "<BR>")
09. Server.ScriptTimeout = 120
10. Response.Write(Server.ScriptTimeout & "<BR>")
11. Server.ScriptTimeout = 10
12. Response.Write(Server.ScriptTimeout & "<BR>")
13. %>
14.
15. </BODY>
16. </HTML>
```

The output is, as you might expect, 90-120-10. But the statement in line 11 doesn't terminate the script after 10 seconds, because values set to be less than the default aren't accepted.

 Tip   If you set the `ScriptTimeout` property to −1, the script may run for an indefinite time.

Creating Objects

To create instances of components for use in your scripts, use the `CreateObject` method. By default, each object created with this method has only page scope. This means that it is automatically destroyed when the page is finished. The syntax for this method is as follows:

```
Set xObj = Server.CreateObject(ProgId)
```

ProgId is the human-readable counterpart for the ClassId (this nice 128-Bit globally unique identifier) of any OLE/ActiveX component. It is built the following way (items in square brackets are optional):

```
[Vendor.]Component[.Version]
```

If you want to instantiate for example the FileSystemObject that is part of Scripting, the command looks like the following:

```
Set fsObj = Server.CreateObject("Scripting.FileSystemObject")
```

You can now use this object in your script as if it were a native part of the scripting language you're using.

I mentioned earlier that the default scope is file. You can extend the scope to Session or Application when you create a property in these objects with the newly instantiated component assigned to it. They will persist until the session or application itself is destroyed or until you close the object yourself. Listing 5.2 demonstrates how to add an object as a property and how to delete it.

On the CD

LISTING 5.2 - USAGE OF SERVER.CREATEOBJECT

```
01. <HTML>
02. <HEAD>
03. <TITLE>Chapter 5: Testing CreateObject</TITLE>
04. </HEAD>
05. <BODY>
06.
07. <%
08. ' create the object
09. Set fsObj = Server.CreateObject("Scripting.FileSystemObject")
10.
11. ' use it, and when done with it, close the object
12. Set fsObj = Nothing
13.
14. ' set the object to be session-wide accessible
15. Set Session("SessionWideAvail") = Server.CreateObject("Scripting.
      ➥FileSystemObject")
16.
17. %>
18.
19. </BODY>
20. </HTML>
```

The FileSystemObject is created in line 9. From there on you could use it to access files on your server's hard disk. The code in line 12 shows how to immediately destroy an object and free its associated storage. And finally, in line 15, a property in the Session object is created and assigned a newly created object. There is more on session properties and accessing them later in this chapter, when the Session object is presented.

Applying HTML Encoding to Strings

Some characters have a special meaning in HTML as markups, for example less than (<) and greater than (>). If you want to incorporate them in your text with their mathematical meaning, they have to be encoded to be distinguishable from the markup characters. This encoding is supported by the HTMLEncode method supplied by the Server object.

The Internet has many computers running on a great variety of hardware platforms. Each has code pages that interpret each character code of your page into a different display character, except the standard characters. Extended characters (copyright sign, German special characters, and more) have to be encoded, so that the client browser can then assign the right display character to this HTML code.

Listing 5.3 shows how to use this feature to make the greeting for "Altötting near München" (Munich for non-Europeans) displayable worldwide on all computer platforms.

LISTING 5.3 - USAGE OF SERVER.HTMLENCODE

On the
CD

```
01. <HTML>
02. <HEAD>
03. <TITLE>Chapter 5: Testing HTMLEncode</TITLE>
04. </HEAD>
05. <BODY>
06. <H1>
07. <%
08. Response.Write(Server.HTMLEncode("Welcome to Altötting near München"))
09. %>
10. </H1>
11. </BODY>
12. </HTML>
```

The German special characters contained in the string in line 8 are converted to HTML codes, which the client browser on a different platform can display. The result is as follows:

```
Welcome to Alt&#246;tting near M&#252;nchen
```

The method HTMLEncode comes in handy when you're extracting information from a database. It's awkward to enter information with all of the encoding in it; it renders it almost unreadable and slows down the entire process of data entry. With the HTMLEncode method, you needn't care about characters that have to be encoded, you simply convert the strings you have extracted from the database with HTMLEncode before sending them to the user.

Mapping Virtual Paths to Physical Paths

When referencing (hyperlinking) files in standard HTML on your local server, you use paths relative to your server's root or your current path. This saves you from troubles if the entire site were moved from drive c: to, for example, drive f:.

If you have to access files on your disk for reading or writing, you need absolute paths to be able to open them. You could hard-code the file locations in your scripts, but you would have to update them if you move your file to another directory.

The solution for maintaining the advantages of relative path information when you need absolute paths is the method MapPath. It takes as a parameter the virtual path (either an absolute path or a path relative to the current file) and converts it to a physical path. It doesn't, however, check to see if the resulting path is a valid one. Listing 5.4 demonstrates how to convert relative paths to absolute ones.

On the CD

LISTING 5.4 - USAGE OF SERVER.MAPPATH

```
01. <HTML>
02. <HEAD>
03. <TITLE>Chapter 5: Testing MapPath</TITLE>
04. </HEAD>
05. <BODY>
06.
07. Physical Path for "/" is:
08. <%
09. Response.Write(Server.MapPath("/"))
10.
11. ' now a file that does not exist in this directory
12. Response.Write("<P> non-existing file in local directory: ")
13. Response.Write(Server.MapPath("grmblfix.asp"))
14. %>
15.
16. </BODY>
17. </HTML>
```

The Server.MapPath method returns converted paths, whether they exist or not. In the example in Listing 5.4, line 9's statement returns the physical path for the server's root; line 13's code, however, might return a path to a file that physically doesn't exist (when you do not have this one in the current directory).

Applying URL Encoding to Strings

URLs (Uniform Resource Locators) are used to locate files and information on the Internet. If you request information from a server, you're sending a URL. Fields contained in this URL are encoded for transport reasons (for example, spaces are converted to pluses). The Request object is responsible for decoding all fields in such a URL.

If you want to redirect from a certain page to another, you have to apply these URL encoding rules to the data you want to pass. Instead of doing this on your own, you should use the Server object's method URLEncode. It takes the string-to-convert as parameter and returns the encoded string. See Listing 5.5 for a how-to.

LISTING 5.5 - USAGE OF SERVER.URLENCODE

```
01. <HTML>
02. <HEAD>
03. <TITLE>Chapter 5: Testing URLEncode</TITLE>
04. </HEAD>
05. <BODY>
06.
07. <%
08. Response.Write(Server.URLEncode("test.asp?name= Christoph Wille&tag=<BR>"))
09. Response.Write("<P>")
10. Response.Write("test.asp?" & Server.URLEncode("name=
    ➥Christoph Wille&tag=<BR>"))
11. %>
12.
13. </BODY>
14. </HTML>
```

On the
CD

The output of this function is interesting. See Listing 5.6.

LISTING 5.6 - OUTPUT OF SAMPLE LISTING 5.5

```
01. test%2Easp%3Fname%3DChristoph+Wille%26tag%3D%3CBR%3E
02. test.asp?name%3DChristoph+Wille%26tag%3D%3CBR%3E
```

Line 1 of Listing 5.6 corresponds to the code from line 8, Listing 5.5. This URL isn't valid, because only the data has to be encoded, not the script name. Line 2 shows the correct form of a URL with data associated with it.

Final Example

The Server object is the first of five core Active Server Pages framework (built-in) objects, but you can already build a fully-functional page with it. There is only one component, the File Access component, that is needed in advance for this example.

On the CD

LISTING 5.7 - FINAL EXAMPLE FOR OBJECT SERVER

```
01. <HTML>
02. <HEAD>
03. <TITLE>Chapter 5: Server Object - final example</TITLE>
04. </HEAD>
05. <BODY>
06.
07. <%
08. Set fsObj = Server.CreateObject(
       ➥"Scripting.FileSystemObject")
09. Set txtFile = fsObj.OpenTextFile(Server.MapPath(
       ➥Request.ServerVariables("PATH_INFO")))
10. While Not txtFile.AtEndOfStream
11.    Response.Write(Server.HTMLEncode(txtFile.ReadLine)
       ➥& "<BR>")
12. Wend
13. %>
14.
15. </BODY>
16. </HTML>
```

A FileSystemObject is created in line 8, and the next line of code opens the current file. Between lines 10 and 12 a while loop begins that doesn't end until the end of the file. The code in line 11 outputs the HTML encoded (remember that?) line read from the file and appends a break; so you can view the entire sourcecode of this HTML file. The output of this page is simply the code of Listing 5.7.

Processing Client-Provided Information

Often, the main purpose of an ASP application is to get information from the user or get information about the user. You might think of information about the user being where the user is coming from or what browser the user is visiting your page with. Information from the user, however, is generally gained whenever the user submits a form inside your application. No matter what type of information you're interested in, the ASP built-in Request object makes accessing that information very easy. The Request object manages all information that was provided by the client's browser: Form data, certificates, cookies, and server variables. These are organized in collections; you don't have to bother with how to decode form data, cookies, or anything. It is all done by Active Server Pages for you—you just have to make the best of it.

Accessing Elements of the Request

The Request object has five collections that you can use to access the elements of the request. See Table 5.1.

Table 5.1
Collections

Collection	Description
ClientCertificate	Contains the fields of the client certificate that are sent when connecting to secure HTTP.
Cookies	This collection stores all values of cookies that are sent in an HTTP request.
Form	Contains the field/value pairs that are sent on a form POST.
QueryString	Contains the values that have been sent by a HTTP GET request. This is a parsed version of the server variable QUERY STRING.
ServerVariables	Lists the values of pre-determined environment variables.

There is a code construct each of these collections supports—iterating over all items. Listing 5.8 shows this for the Form collection.

LISTING 5.8 - ITERATING OVER ALL ITEMS IN REQUEST.FORM

```
<HTML>
<BODY>
 <%
 For Each key in Request.Form
    Response.Write(key & " - " & Request.Form(key) & "<br>")
 Next
 %>
<FORM METHOD=POST ACTION="<%=Request.ServerVariables
➡("PATH_INFO")%>">
  ID:<INPUT TYPE=TEXT SIZE=30 MAXLENGTH=30 NAME
➡="ID" VALUE=""><br>
  Password:<INPUT TYPE=PASSWORD SIZE=30 MAXLENGTH=30 NAME=
➡"PASSWORD" VALUE=""><br>
  <INPUT TYPE=SUBMIT VALUE="OK">
  <INPUT TYPE=RESET VALUE="Clear">
</FORM>
</BODY>
</HTML>


01. <%
02. For Each key in Request.Form
03.    Response.Write(key & " - " & Request.Form(key))
04. Next
05. %>
```

This code fragment helps you to dump all the elements of a collection.

Accessing Client Certificate Information

If you're running a secured site with SSL3.0/PCT1 enabled (you can recognize these sites by the HTTPS:// instead of HTTP://), the client is required to send a certificate. This certificate is stored in the ClientCertificate collection. If no certificate is sent, the collection returns EMPTY.

 Note Certificates are only sent on secured sites. You can enable client certificates on your server by selecting a directory and selecting Enable Client Certificates. If you require these certificates, also enable the Require Client Certificates checkbox.

You can retrieve the certification fields by using the collection with the following syntax:

```
Request.ClientCertificate(key[subkey])
```

Table 5.2 provides additional certification field information.

Table 5.2
Key Parameters

Value	Description
Certificate	Is a string containing the entire certificate content in binary form.
Flags	Set of flags that contain additional information for the client certificate. The flags are defined as constants in the files Cervbs.inc and Cerjavas.inc located in the directory \InetPub\ASPSamp\Samples.
Issuer	String containing information about the issuer of this certificate. If no subkeys are used, the string is returned in comma separated form.
SerialNumber	This string contains the serial number of the client certificate.
Subject	String with subkeys about the subject of this certificate.
ValidFrom	Date when this certificate becomes valid.
ValidUntil	Expiration date of this certificate.

The two keys "Issuer"" and "Subject"" have subkey fields, which are simply appended to the key, for example, "IssuerO"" to retrieve the issuer's organization name. The complete list of subkeys is provided in Table 5.3.

Table 5.3
Subkey Parameters

Value	Description
C	Name of country of origin
CN	Common name of user (part of "Subject" key)
GN	Retrieve given name
I	Set of initials
L	Defines locality

continues

Table 5.3, Continued
Subkey Parameters

Value	Description
O	Company or organization name
OU	Organizational unit name
S	State or province
T	Title of person or organization

You have already seen how to iterate over an entire collection. What is more interesting with client certificates is to know whether one has been presented to us, and if so, determining whether it is valid. See Listing 5.9.

On the CD

LISTING 5.9 - CLIENT CERTIFICATES

```
01. <HTML>
02. <HEAD>
03. <TITLE>Chapter 5: Client Certificates</TITLE>
04. </HEAD>
05. <BODY>
06.
07. <%
08. If 0 = Len(Request.ClientCertificate("Subject")) Then
09.    ' no client certificate
10.    Response.Write("Client did not provide a client certificate!")
11. Else
12.    ' check if it is valid
13.    If ((Request.ClientCertificate("ValidFrom") <= Now) And _
14.       (Request.ClientCertificate("ValidUntil") > Now)) then
15.      Response.Write("Thank you for providing a valid certificate!")
16.    End If
17. End if
18. %>
19.
20. </BODY>
21. </HTML>
```

In this listing one line is interesting besides the code for certificate authentication—the underline (_) in line 13. It tells VBScript that this line is continued on the next one. Use this method to break long statements.

Retrieving Cookies

A cookie is a piece of information that the server stores on the client computer for later retrieval. This ability hangs solely on the capabilities of the browser. Luckily, most of the newest browsers support cookies.

If you want to store information on the client computer about the client, then cookies are what you have been looking for. The cookies you initially send to the client (with the Response.Cookies collection) are retransmitted with every request to your server, so you can read the values.

Most popular uses for cookies are the creation of shopping bags, or the tracking of user preferences like high, medium, or low graphics version of the site (thus being a small personalization system). The Session object also is cookie-based.

To learn how to create a shopping bag, see Chapter 14, "Creating a Shopping Bag," p. 363.

Cookies can contain one piece of information or a number of key/value pairs that together form a cookie dictionary. All cookies are stored in the Cookies collection that's part of the Request object.

Cookies are referenced with syntax shown in Table 5.4.

Cross Reference

Table 5.4
Referencing Cookies

Syntax	Description
Request.Cookies(cookie)	Retrieve the information from a cookie that has no associated keys .
Request.Cookies(cookie)(key)	This references a cookie dictionary (this means that the cookie has keys). To determine whether a cookie has keys, use Request.Cookies(cookie).HasKeys.

If you want to dump all the cookie information, you have to take care of cookies with dictionaries (determined with the .HasKeys attribute). See Listing 5.10 for dumping all cookies.

```
<HTML>
 <HEAD>
 <TITLE>Cookies</TITLE>
 </HEAD>
 <BODY><CENTER>
```

```
<H1>The Session ID Value</H1>
<H3>HTTP_COOKIE has the value: <%=Request("HTTP_COOKIE")%></H3>
</CENTER>
 </BODY>
 </HTML>
```

On the CD

LISTING 5.10 - DUMPING ALL COOKIE INFORMATION

```
01. <HTML>
02. <HEAD>
03. <TITLE>Chapter 5: Cookies</TITLE>
04. </HEAD>
05. <BODY>
06.
07. <%
08.
09. For Each cookie in Request.Cookies
10.     If Not Request.Cookies(cookie).HasKeys Then
11.         ' cookie has only information, print it
12. %>
13.         <%= cookie %>  = <%= Request.Cookies(cookie)%>
14. <%
15.     Else
16.         'print the dictionary of this cookie
17.         For Each key in Request.Cookies(cookie)
18. %>
19.         <%= cookie %>  (<%= key %>) =
            ➥<%= Request.Cookies(cookie)(key)%>
20. <%
21.         Next
22.     End If
23. Next
24. %>
25.
26. </BODY>
27. </HTML>
```

There is one caveat: You can send cookies with the same name from different nesting levels of your application, for example /sales/ and /sales/boost/. If you have sent cookies with the same name from both directories, the Cookies collection returns only the cookie from the deeper path, in this case, /sales/boost/.

Processing Form Data

On your web server, forms are used for data entry like guest books as well as for data retrieval, as with search engines. These forms can contain checkboxes, list boxes, combo boxes, simple edit fields, and option fields. A sample form is presented in Figure 5.1.

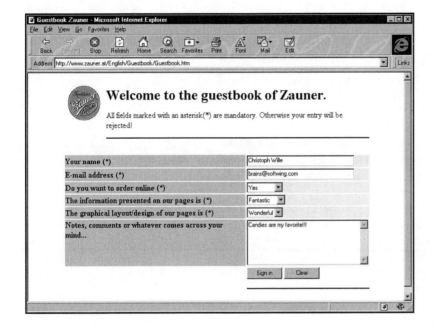

Figure 5.1

A sample Guestbook.

Forms can be sent to the web server by means of two different mechanisms:

◆ GET Request: the form data is part of the URL requested. It is limited in size. A sample URL could look like the following: `test.asp?action=lookup&dir=forward`.

◆ POST Request: the form data is separated from the URL. The URL simply contains the name of the processing page.

The Form collection retrieves values that were sent to the server using the POST method. GET is retrieved by the QueryString collection. Both collections have exactly the same syntax:

```
Request.collection(parameter)[(index)¦.Count]
```

Replace *collection* for either Form or QueryString. If a user sends information back from multiple select list boxes or checkboxes, you can reference the single values with an index. A Count property also is provided. Use it to determine whether or not there are multiple values available.

Listing 5.11 shows the HTML code for the form that will be submitted.

On the CD

LISTING 5.11 - HTML FORM

```
01.  <HTML>
02.  <HEAD>
03.  <TITLE>Chapter 5: Sample Form</TITLE>
04.  </HEAD>
05.  <BODY>
06.  <CENTER>
07.  <H1>Late-night programmers eating habits</H1>
08.  Check all that apply<P>
09.
10.  <TABLE><TR><TD ALIGN=LEFT>
11.  <FORM ACTION="form.asp" METHOD=GET TARGET="_top">
12.  <INPUT TYPE="CHECKBOX" NAME="chk" value="Pizza">Pizza<BR>
13.  <INPUT TYPE="CHECKBOX" NAME="chk" value="Coffee">
     ➥Coffee<BR>
14.  <INPUT TYPE="CHECKBOX" NAME="chk" value="Chips">Chips<P>
15.  <INPUT TYPE=SUBMIT VALUE="Submit">
16.  </FORM>
17.  </TD></TR></TABLE>
18.
19.  </CENTER>
20.  </BODY>
21.  </HTML>
```

It contains three checkboxes with the same name that ask for the eating habits of late-night programmers. The form data is submitted using the GET method to the form "form.asp," which is shown in Listing 5.12.

On the CD

LISTING 5.12 - THE FORM HANDLING LATE-NIGHT PROGRAMMERS REQUESTS

```
01.  <HTML>
02.  <HEAD>
03.  <TITLE>Chapter 5: Sample Form Processing</TITLE>
04.  </HEAD>
05.  <BODY>
06.  <CENTER>
07.  <H1>Late-night programmers eating habits</H1>
08.  Your choices<P>
```

```
09. </CENTER>
10.
11. <B>You like:</B><BR>
12. <%
13. For i=1 To Request.QueryString("chk").Count
14.   Response.Write(Request.QueryString("chk")(i) & "<BR>")
15. Next
16. %>
17.
18. <P>
19. <B>All entities:</B> <%=Request.QueryString("chk")%><BR>
20. <B>Shorthand:</B> <%=Request("chk")%><BR>
21.
22. </BODY>
23. </HTML>
```

Lines 13 to 15 retrieve all favorite meals that the late-night programmer has selected, one at a time. If you're retrieving the parameter, as in line 19, not caring about possible multiple values, all values are returned in a comma-separated string (very useful for SQL queries with the WHERE .. IN clause). Line 20 shows a shorthand, *Request(parameter)*, which searches all collections for a key match in all collections of the Request object.

 If you change the method from GET to POST in Listing 5.11, only the shorthand returns the correct data (try this!). If you're likely to change forms from GET to POST (or vice versa), use the shorthand Request(parameter), because it always returns the values, regardless of how the form was submitted.

Retrieving Environment Variables

If you need to retrieve the environment variables and headers for your current script, the ServerVariables collection comes in handy. If you have ever dealt with the standard HTTP_Headers, like HTTP_USER_AGENT and HTTP_SERVER_PORT, then you're already familiar with the ServerVariables collection. The main purpose of this collection is to provide simplified access to these variables from within an ASP script. Simply supply the name of the environment variable as the parameter and the ServerVariables collection returns a string containing its value. Table 5.5 lists the names of environment variables that can be retrieved.

Table 5.5
Environment Variables

Variable	Description
AUTH_TYPE	The authentication method the server uses when a client requests a protected script.
CONTENT_LENGTH	The length of the content as sent by the client.
CONTENT_TYPE	Type of content that was sent to the server. Returned as MIME types.
GATEWAY_INTERFACE	Version number of the CGI interface used by this server.
HTTP_<HeaderName>	Retrieve the value that is stored in the header HeaderName. All underscores are interpreted as dashes in the actual header.
LOGON_USER	The account the user is logged into. Only set when accessing protected scripts.
PATH_INFO	Extra path information given by the user.
PATH_TRANSLATED	The physical path corresponding to PATH_INFO.
QUERY_STRING	String following the question mark (?) in a URL. Contains the query information.
REMOTE_ADDR	Client's IP address.
REMOTE_HOST	Name of the host corresponding to REMOTE_ADDR. If this isn't available to the server, it is left empty.
REQUEST_METHOD	Method the request was made with. Most common methods are GET and POST.
SCRIPT_NAME	Virtual path to the script being executed. Use it to create self-referencing forms or for creating "Go back" links for scripts that can be accessed from different pages.
SERVER_NAME	Server name as used in the URL. Can be a hostname, IP address, or DNS alias.
SERVER_PORT	Port number to which the request was sent.

Variable	Description
SERVER_PORT_SECURE	Values of 0 or 1, depending on whether this request was made on a secured port (1) or not(0).
SERVER_PROTOCOL	Protocol information.
SERVER_SOFTWARE	Server software, for example "Microsoft-IIS/3.0"
URL	Base portion of the URL.

Internet Explorer 3.0 sends additional headers to your server that aren't supported by Netscape Navigator versions 2 and 3. These additional headers deal with the capabilities of each client's computer. See Table 5.6.

Table 5.6
Internet Explorer 3.0 Additional Headers

Header	Description
HTTP_UA_COLOR	Contains information about the color depth a client's computer is currently set to.
HTTP_UA_CPU	Returns the CPU type of the client's computer, for example, "x86" for all Intel compatible computers. You can use this information to decide which ActiveX control packages to send to this computer (Intel, Mac, Alpha, or Mips version).
HTTP_UA_OS	Reports the operating system under which the browser is running.
HTTP_UA_PIXELS	Returns the resolution the client's computer is set to.

A sample on dumping HTTP server variables is part of the Active Server Pages samples. It can be started with the URL `http://localhost/aspsamp/samples/srvvar.asp` and dumps all environment variables and HTTP headers.

Sending Data to the User

Whenever you need to send information back to the user, you need the `Response` object. It's responsible for the cookies being sent to the client, the type of content sent, the content itself, and its expiration date.

Setting Cookies

The `Cookies` collection in the `Request` object was read-only and contained the cookie information that was supplied by the client. The `Cookies` collection of the `Response` object is responsible for sending the cookies you want the client to receive.

If the cookie you assign a value to does not exist, it is created. If it exists, the old value is discarded and takes the new value.

> **Warning** If assigning a single value to a cookie that is a dictionary (multiple key/value pairs), all of this information is discarded. This also is true if you assign a key/value pair to a cookie containing only a single value: it is discarded and a cookie dictionary is created.

The syntax for setting cookie values is as follows:

```
Response.Cookies(cookie)[(key)¦.attribute] = value
```

The optional key parameter is used to create or set a key/value pair in a cookie that is a dictionary. The attributes you can set are shown in Table 5.7.

Table 5.7
Attributes

Attribute	Access	Description
Expires	Write-only	Specifies the date when the cookie expires.
Domain	Write-only	If specified, the cookie is sent only to requests to this domain.
Path	Write-only	If Path is set, this cookie is sent only when requesting pages from the path specified.
Secure	Write-only	Determines whether or not a cookie is secure.
HasKeys	Read-only	Returns the number of keys in a cookie.

Chapter 14, "Creating a Shopping Bag," demonstrates one application of cookies. Another useful application of cookies is to personalize the content of your pages for users. You can do this with a simple input form that gathers information about the user and his preferences for your site. Figure 5.2 shows the form the user is presented with.

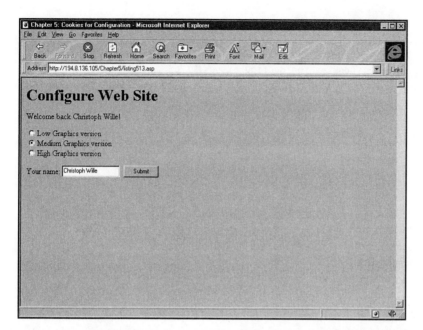

Figure 5.2

Sample personalization page.

This form takes input about the user's name and his preference for the amount of graphics he wants to be presented on your site. You can use this form for first-time users as well as for users coming back to reconfigure their profile. See Listing 5.13 for the implementation of the miniature personalization system.

LISTING 5.13 - USING COOKIES FOR PERSONALIZATION

On the CD

```
01. <%
02. strGraphCap = "hi" ' initially high graphics
03. strUsername = "" ' no user name
04.
05. If 0 = StrComp(Request("prefact"),"change") Then
06.    strGraphCap = Request("Graphics")
07.    strUsername = Request("UserName")
08.    Response.Cookies("UserInformation")("UName") =
       ➥strUsername
09.    Response.Cookies("UserInformation")("GraphCap") =
       ➥strGraphCap
10. End If
11. %>
12.
13. <HTML>
```

continues

LISTING 5.13, CONTINUED

```
14. <HEAD>
15. <TITLE>Chapter 5: Cookies for Configuration</TITLE>
16. </HEAD>
17. <BODY>
18.
19. <H1>Configure Web Site</H1>
20.
21. <%
22. If (Len(Request.Cookies("UserInformation")("UName")))
    ➥Then
23.    strUsername = Request.Cookies("UserInformation")
       ➥ ("UName")
24.    strGraphCap = Request.Cookies("UserInformation")
       ➥ ("GraphCap")
25.    Response.Write("Welcome back " & strUsername & "!<P>")
26. End If
27. %>
28.
29. <%
30. Dim chkArr(3)
31. Select Case strGraphCap
32. Case "lo"
33.    chkArr(1) = "CHECKED"
34.    chkArr(2) = ""
35.    chkArr(3) = ""
36. Case "md"
37.    chkArr(1) = ""
38.    chkArr(2) = "CHECKED"
39.    chkArr(3) = ""
40. Case else
41.    chkArr(1) = ""
42.    chkArr(2) = ""
43.    chkArr(3) = "CHECKED"
44.
45. End Select
46. %>
47.
48. <FORM ACTION="<%=Request.ServerVariables("SCRIPT_NAME")
    ➥%>" METHOD=POST>
49.    <input type=hidden name="prefact" value="change">
```

```
50.    <input type="radio" <%=chkArr(1)%>  name="Graphics"
    ➦ value="lo">Low Graphics version<BR>
51.    <input type="radio" <%=chkArr(2)%>  name="Graphics"
    ➦ value="md">Medium Graphics version<BR>
52.    <input type="radio" <%=chkArr(3)%>  name="Graphics"
    ➦ value="hi">High Graphics version<P>
53.    Your name: <input type=text name="UserName"
    ➦value="<%=strUsername%>">
54.    <input type=submit name="Submit">
55. </FORM>
56.
57. </BODY>
58. </HTML>
```

The listing already looks complicated, because the scripting code is now mixed with normal HTML code. The form you saw in Figure 5.2 is constructed between lines 48 and 55. It contains a hidden field *prefact* (preferences action), the *Graphics* radio buttons for selecting high/medium/low versions of the site, and the user name.

When this form is submitted, the prefact field is set to "change", which causes the statement in line 5 to evaluate to True. The user's name and graphics preferences are written to the cookie "UserInformation", which is sent to the user's browser for storing.

Lines 22 to 26 deal with a user coming back to reconfigure his profile. The information is simply read from the cookie and stored to local variables for further processing.

If you want to set a radio button to the checked state, you need to add the CHECKED statement to the <INPUT> tag. For a new user, this could be done with simple HTML, but you need to take care of users reconfiguring their profile. Therefore, this checkmark has to be set dynamically. This is achieved by creating an array with strings (lines 30 to 45) and writing the CHECKED string to the appropriate index, depending on the selected graphics resolution. The values of the arrays are inserted with the shorthand <%=chkArr(..)%> in lines 50 to 52.

Specifying the Type of Content Your Script Returns

If you want to send some content different from HTML, you can use the ContentType property to define the type of content that is sent back to the browser by your script. You can set it to any valid MIME type. If you don't specify ContentType, the default text/html is used. The most important types are listed in Table 5.8.

Table 5.8
Important MIME Types

MIME type	Description
text/html	Sets the type of information sent back to the client to be of type text, subtype HTML. The browser then knows to interpret the page as HTML.
text/plain	The content is plain text.
image/gif	An image of type GIF is sent.
image/jpeg	Same as image/gif; this time a JPEG will be sent.

The types listed in this table are only a small subset of types you can send, but these are the one you're most likely to find on an HTML page. If you want to take a look at which types the Microsoft Internet Information Server is capable of sending, open the Registry editor and navigate to HKEY_LOCAL_MACHINE\SYSTEM\CurrentControlSet\Services\InetInfo\Parameters\MimeMap. This is a good reference point for MIME types.

Adding Expiration Information to Your Pages

If you want to be sure that a user receives up-to-date content from your site, you either need to set an absolute expiration date or an expiration period to determine the amount of time a page should be cached by the client's browser. When the content expires, the client's browser requests the latest information from your server when the user again navigates to this specific page.

The Response object contains two properties that enable you to either set an expiration date or a time span. With the Expires property you set the number of minutes until a cached page expires. Use this when your page contains data that is changed on a regular basis.

```
Response.Expires = 24
```

ExpiresAbsolute sets an expiration date when the page should expire. The time is converted to GMT (Greenwich Meantime) before being sent to the client.

```
<% Response.ExpiresAbsolute=#July 29,1997 19:30:00# %>
```

Returning Processing Status

If you want to return special status information about the processing of the page, you can use the `Status` property. The status information consists of a three-digit number (the status code) and a brief explanation. For a list of all possible status codes, please consult the reference of a web server or the HTTP specification found at the W3C—the World Wide Web Consortium.

Adding HTTP Headers to Your Response

If you want to add customized or special headers to the response, use the `AddHeader` method to add your headers. You have to do this before any output is written to the client (or use the `Buffer` property to enable buffering so you can insert headers later in your script). Headers are written to the client as `name/value` pairs and new headers are always added, no matter if a header of the same name already exists. Headers will not be overwritten. Once you have added a header, you cannot remove it, so use headers only when other mechanisms like cookies aren't suitable for what you intend to do.

The syntax of this method is as follows:

```
Response.AddHeader name, value
```

If `name` contains dashes, please be aware that you have to replace the dashes with underscores when retrieving the header with `Request.ServerVariables(...)`.

Logging Information About the Request

If you need to log additional information about the current request to the IIS log, use the `AppendToLog` method. You can use it, for example, to store additional information about the page request for later analysis by a log analysis tool. Be aware that the length of the strings is limited to a maximum of 80 characters and that it shouldn't contain any commas, because if the log is stored to a file, the format for this file is CSV—Comma Separated Values.

> **Note**   To view the logfile, you first need to know where it is located. Open IIS Service Manager, double-click the web service for the server you want to view the logfile and then go to the Logging tab in the properties dialog box. Here you can find out where IIS stores logfiles to and how the files are named (this depends on the time interval set to create new log files). Please note that you might not see the most recent entries in the log because output to this file is buffered for performance reasons.

Listing 5.14 illustrates how to log the type of browser used to request this page.

On the
CD

LISTING 5.14 - ADDING INFORMATION ABOUT THE BROWSER TO THE LOG

```
01. <HTML>
02. <HEAD>
03. <TITLE>Chapter 5: Add information to the log</TITLE>
04. </HEAD>
05. <BODY>
06.
07. You are using <B><%=Request.ServerVariables(
    ➥"HTTP_USER_AGENT")%></B> for browsing!
08. <%
09. Response.AppendToLog(Request.ServerVariables(
    ➥"HTTP_USER_AGENT"))
10. %>
11.
12. </BODY>
13. </HTML>
```

Line 9 adds the information about the user agent (client's browser) to the log file. It is the last entry on the line of information about this request.

 When creating this example, I made an error (I omitted the `Request` object in line 7). On execution of the script I was presented with the error message `"Type mismatch"`. Error information also is appended to the server log, which contains the line number, error code, and a brief description. You can use the log to track errors on your production servers.

Buffering Page Processing Output

If you want to control whether all scripts are processed before any content is sent to the browser, you can do this by setting the `Buffer` property to either true or false. This property can only be set before any output is sent to the user. No output is sent to the user until completion of the script or calls to the `Flush` or `End` methods when buffering is enabled. If you enable buffering and a long script is running, the delay until the completed script is sent can be perceptible. The following line of code enables buffering for the current script:

```
01. <% Response.Buffer = True %>
```

Please note that the statement is in line 1. Because it has to appear before any output is sent to the client, line 1 is the best place for the statement.

The advantage of using buffering is that you can add HTTP headers anywhere in your script. In contrast, when no buffering is selected, you can set headers only at the top of your script, before any output is done.

Note   The registry entry BufferingOn controls how buffering is handled by default. By installation default, buffering is disabled. If you set it to 1, it is enabled. You don't need to restart the web server.

If you want to cancel all output done so far, use the Clear method. To send all output done so far to the client, use the Flush method. Both methods can only be used with buffered output. The End method, in contrast, can be used with buffered and non-buffered output to immediately terminate script processing. Listing 5.15 shows how these methods work.

LISTING 5.15 - CLEAR, END AND FLUSH IN ACTION

On the CD

```
01. <% Response.Buffer = True %>
02. <HTML>
03. <HEAD>
04. <TITLE>Chapter 5: Testing Buffering</TITLE>
05. </HEAD>
06. <BODY>
07.
08. Welcome to this page!<P>
09.
10. <% Response.Flush %>
11.
12. This is not intended to be seen by the client!!!
13.
14. <% Response.Clear %>
15.
16. Now back to business. We will omit the last two lines
17.
18. <% Response.End %>
19.
20. </BODY>
21. </HTML>
```

I have inserted blank lines in listing 5.15 for easier reading. Line 1 enables buffering, and the Flush statement in line 10 writes all output that was made up to this point to the client. Because the text in line 12 is not intended for the client, the buffer up to this point is cleared with the Clear statement in line 14. The End method found on line 18 then terminates the processing of this script, which causes the closing </BODY></HTML> tags to not be sent to the client.

Redirecting the User

Redirecting the user to another page from within the page that is currently being processed can happen for several reasons, for example, to redirect to a login page before the user can enter a specific area on your server. The Redirect method that is used to perform the redirection uses a header to notify the client that it has to request another page, therefore, no output must be done before a call to Redirect. To redirect to another page, use the following syntax:

```
Response.Redirect("/otherpages/newpage.asp")
```

The Redirect method takes one parameter—the file to which you want to redirect the client. You can do the redirection on your own if you add the following statement to a script:

LISTING 5.16 - "MANUAL" REDIRECT

```
01. <%
02. Response.Status="302 Object Moved"
03. Response.AddHeader "Location","/otherpages/newpage.asp"
04. %>
```

This listing results in the same effect as redirecting to "newpage.asp", but the Redirect method is surely the easier way. To see a more sophisticated example of how to use the Redirect method, take a look at Chapter 15, "Implementing a Search Wizard."

Writing Content to the Client

There are two ways to write textual content to the client: Using the Write method or its shorthand <%=%>. The general use is as follows:

```
<% Response.Write("some string") %>
```

You also can use the shorthand form:

```
<%="some string"%>
```

Both statements write the string "some string" to the client—nothing really new, so far. However, when you're using VBScript as your scripting language, you need to be aware of a limitation when using static strings. Static strings are limited to 1022 characters in VBScript. However, if you use a variable to create strings longer than 1022 characters, this is no problem.

If you want to send binary data to the client, you have to use the BinaryWrite method to be able to send nonstring information without character-set conversions. You have to set the content type to guarantee that the information will be interpreted in the right way. The syntax for this method is as follows:

```
Response.BinaryWrite(data)
```

 Don't try to use the TextStream component to read binary data and send it via BinaryWrite to the client, because TextStream doesn't read binary data correctly.

Managing State for the Application and Users

So far, I have presented objects for handling requests, writing back the response, and working with helper routines. These were the Request, Response, and Server objects. Two more are missing—Application and Session.

These two are designed to store properties ("state") for all users (the Application object) and properties for a single user (the Session object). The Application object's lifetime starts when the first page of the application is requested, and ends when the web server is shut down. The Session object, in contrast, is created when the user first requests a page and is destroyed when the user leaves your server (either by timeout or an explicit logoff from your server).

For managing housekeeping for both objects, you are informed via events when an Application or Session object is created or destroyed. You can load state information, make one-time initializations, and on destruction, make the information persistent by storing it to the server's hard disk.

All of the code handling these events has to be placed in a file named global.asa, which must reside at the root of your application. This file cannot be executed and an application can have only one global.asa file. Besides the events for the Application and Session objects, global.asa also can contain objects created with the <OBJECT> tag.

An entire section of this chapter, "Processing Application and Session events in the global.asa file," is dedicated to global.asa, however, the `Application` and `Session` objects are presented up front.

Managing Application State

The `Application` object represents the running instance of your web application. It is used to share information among all users currently connected to your application. You simply add properties to the `Application` object by using the following syntax:

```
Application("myProperty") = someVal
```

You can assign either values or objects. If you want to assign an object, the syntax is similar to assigning an object to a variable:

```
Set Application("myObj") = myObj
```

When accessing shared objects for writing, you need to guard the shared data. The `Application` object supports two methods, detailed in Table 5.9.

Table 5.9
Methods

Method	Description
Lock	Restricts other clients from modifying properties of the `Application` object.
Unlock	Enables other clients to modify `Application` object properties.

You need these methods to prevent the problems that arise out of multithreading: one user accesses a page, from which the code modifies the properties of the `Application` objects. This code is preempted and another piece of code run for another user modifies properties currently being modified by the other, preempted code. Data inconsistency is sure to happen.

Whenever modifying `Application` properties, use the `Lock` and `Unlock` methods to guard the modifying code. See Listing 5.17 for an example of how to protect `Application` object's properties.

LISTING 5.17 — GUARDING APPLICATION PROPERTIES

```
01. <%
02. Application.Lock
```

```
03. Application("Usercount") = Application("Usercount") + 1
04. Application.Unlock
05. %>
```

What would happen if the code on line 3 were unguarded? Take this hypothetical approach: User 1 runs to this line and execution is preempted when Application("Usercount") has been retrieved. The preemption has occurred for User 2, who also executes this line. This time, all execution takes place and Usercount is incremented by one. When User 1's code begins to run again, it has already retrieved the Usercount and doesn't know about his preemption, thus adding one to the Usercount before User 2's addition. You have just lost one user!

That is all for properties; however, the interesting part concerns the events. The Application object has two events for start and end, which you can handle to add initialization or shut down. These events have to be declared in the file global.asa. See Table 5.10.

Table 5.10
Events

Event	Description
Application_OnStart	Called by Active Server Pages when the first client requests an ASP file.
Application_OnEnd	Called when the server is shut down. Write all information that needs to be persistent to the disk for reloading when the application restarts.

Managing State Information for Users

Each user is represented by a Session object that's created when the user hits your application for the first time. You can use the session to store information and objects you need for further requests for this specific user. Examples include information about products the user has put in his shopping bag, whether the user's browser supports ActiveX controls, database connection strings, and more. The Session object is the personal locker of the user.

 You can store values in the Session object only when the user's browser supports cookies and the user didn't turn off the cookie support.

The Session object has two properties and one method. The properties are listed in Table 5.11, the method in Table 5.12.

Table 5.11
Properties

Property	Description
SessionID	Returns the session identification, which is only guaranteed to be unique as long as the web server isn't restarted. Don't use it for the creation of unique keys in databases!
TimeOut	Specifies the maximum time of user inactivity until the session is considered abandoned. This is measured in minutes.

Table 5.12
Method

Method	Description
Abandon	Call this method to immediately destroy the Session object and release its resources. Use this method when providing an explicit logout from your application. No parameters.

The Abandon method is useful if, for example, after the user has finished the payment process for the shopping, you provide the choices for starting a new shopping session or jumping to another site. When the user decides to leave, you can destroy the Session object, because you no longer need it.

A Session object has events for start and end like the Application object. These are fired when the user first requests an ASP page and are closed when the session either times out or you have called Abandon to destroy the Session object. See Table 5.13.

Table 5.13
Events

Event	Description
Session_OnStart	Called by Active Server Pages when the client requests an ASP page for the first time. Performs all one-time initialization here.
Session_OnEnd	Called when the session is closed. Happens when either the session times out or you have called the Abandon method.

Processing Application and Session Events in the global.asa File

All Application and Session events are handled in this file. All objects with scope Application or Session are created in this file. It is the Active Server Application file and is located in the root of your application. Listing 5.18 shows a global.asa with the event handlers inserted.

LISTING 5.18 - GLOBAL.ASA

```
01. <SCRIPT LANGUAGE=VBSCRIPT RUNAT=SERVER>
02.
03. Sub Application_OnStart
04. End Sub
05.
06. Sub Application_OnEnd
07. End Sub
08.
09. Sub Session_OnStart
10. End Sub
11.
12. Sub Session_OnEnd
13. End Sub
14.
15. </SCRIPT>
```

No code has been added to the event handlers. Listing 5.19 adds an overall user count because the application has started and a count for the number of users currently connected to the application has begun.

LISTING 5.19 - GLOBAL.ASA WITH USER COUNTING

On the
CD

```
01. <SCRIPT LANGUAGE=VBSCRIPT RUNAT=SERVER>
02.
03. Sub Application_OnStart
04.    Application("OverallUsers") = 0
05.    Application("OverallSince") = Now
06.    Application("CurrentUsers") = 0
07. End Sub
08.
09. Sub Application_OnEnd
10. End Sub
```

```
11.
12. Sub Session_OnStart
13.   Application.Lock
14.   Application("OverallUsers") =
      ↪Application("OverallUsers") + 1
15.   Application("CurrentUsers") =
      ↪Application("CurrentUsers") + 1
16.   Application.UnLock
17. End Sub
18.
19. Sub Session_OnEnd
20.   Application.Lock
21.   Application("CurrentUsers") =
      ↪Application("CurrentUsers") - 1
22.   Application.UnLock
23. End Sub
24.
25. </SCRIPT>
```

The event handler for Application_OnStart contains the code to initialize the user counts to zero. No state is maintained when the web server is shut down. The overall count refers to the start time of the application, maintained in the OverallSince property.

The session event handler OnStart increases both counts, while OnEnd only decreases the number of currently-connected users. These code blocks are guarded with calls to Lock and UnLock to prevent data consistency problems.

That is all you need to track the user information, but you probably want to present it to the users currently connected to the site. A simple example with automatic update is presented in Listing 5.20.

On the CD

LISTING 5.20 - PRESENTING THE USER COUNT TO THE USERS

```
01. <META HTTP-EQUIV="REFRESH" CONTENT="5;URL=
    ↪<%=Request.ServerVariables("SCRIPT_NAME")%>">
02.
03. <HTML>
04. <HEAD>
05. <TITLE>Chapter 5: Tracking user counts</TITLE>
06. </HEAD>
```

```
07. <BODY BGCOLOR=#ffffff>
08.
09. <CENTER>
10. There are currently <%=Application("CurrentUsers")%>
    ➥ users connected to this site.
11. The overall user count since <%=Application(
    ➥"OverallSince")%>  is <%=Application("OverallUsers")%>.
12. </CENTER>
13.
14. </BODY>
15. </HTML>
```

Line 1 tells the browser to update this page every 5 seconds, using the SCRIPT_NAME environment variable to enable the renaming of the file without breaking the code. Lines 10 and 11 simply give information about the user counts. When reading properties, you don't need to guard them.

So far these are simple properties, meaning date and string data types. However, sometimes you will want to attach an object as a session property (for example the Browser capabilities component for information about the each client's browser doesn't need to be recreated for every page). When instantiating components, you are presented with two different choices:

◆ **Server.CreateObject:** This method can be used for creating objects that have file scope, or by attaching these created objects to an Application or Session property, gaining Application or Session scope.

◆ **<OBJECT RUNAT=SERVER> Tag:** You can insert this tag only in global.asa. Objects created with this tag can only have Application or Session scope and creation is delayed until the object is first used in any page. They are treated like global variables that are available to all files.

The syntax for Server.CreateObject has already been presented in the section dealing with the Server object. The syntax for the <OBJECT> tag is as follows:

```
<OBJECT RUNAT=SERVER SCOPE=scope Id=name [ProgId¦ClassId]=></OBJECT>
```

You need to replace the *scope* for either Application or Session. The *Id* takes the name for the instance of the object. In contrast to CreateObject, you can use either a ProgId (human readable) or the ClassId (the string version of the GUID—globally unique identifier) to create the object. Listing 5.21 instantiates the BrowserCapabilities component using both methods:

On the CD

LISTING 5.21 - CREATING OBJECT WITH THE <OBJECT> TAG

```
01. <OBJECT RUNAT=SERVER SCOPE=SESSION ID=testProgId
    ➥PROGID="MSWC.BrowserType">
02. </OBJECT>
03.
04. <OBJECT RUNAT=SERVER SCOPE=SESSION ID=testClassId
    ➥CLASSID="Clsid:0ACE4881-8305-11CF-9427-444553540000">
05. </OBJECT>
```

Lines 1 and 4 create an object, `BrowserCapabilities`, with `Session` scope. When you first reference it, the object is created. The following line of code, for example, returns the browser type using the object created with the `ClassId`:

```
<%=testClassId.Browser%>
```

Summary

This chapter showed the concepts behind the use of the five ActiveX Server framework objects: form processing, sending data to the user, managing state information for the users and the application, and using the functionality that is provided by the `Server` object where it is appropriate. With the information provided in this chapter, you are now capable of fitting ASP scripts together for an application as well as service information for specific users.

The next chapter, "Using ActiveX Components," deals with the issue of using components to extend the basic functionality of Active Server Pages.

CHAPTER 6

Using ActiveX Components

With the basic objects provided by the Active Server Pages framework you can already build fairly sophisticated applications. However, Microsoft provides a way for you to extend the functionality of Active Server Pages: Components. This chapter covers the following topics:

◆ Instantiating the ActiveX Components

◆ Determining the Capabilities of the Client's Browser

◆ Working with File Data Using the `TextStream` Object

◆ Advertisement Rotation on Your Site

Instantiating the ActiveX Components

You can use the `Server.CreateObject` method or the `<OBJECT>` tag to create instances of components for use in your pages. The components (or component groups) that are part of ActiveX Server are shown in Table 6.1.

TABLE 6.1
Standard Components

Component	Description
Browser Capabilities	Determines type, version, and capabilities of a browser that enters your site.
File Access Component	Provides access to files on the web server for reading and writing.
Ad Rotator	Changes advertisements on your pages based on a rotation schedule.
Content Linking	Links pages in a sequential order based on a table of contents file.
Database Access (ADO)	Provides access to any ODBC-compliant databases. See Chapter 7, "Database Access with ActiveX Data Objects" for more information.

In a previous chapter it was mentioned that when presenting the `<OBJECT>` tag you can create the object either with its `ProgId` or `ClassId`. Because only `ProgId` is documented in Active Server Pages Roadmap, Table 6.2 details a mapping of `ProgId` to `ClassId` for ActiveX Server components.

TABLE 6.2
`ClassId` and `ProgId` for ActiveX Components

Component	Description
Browser Capabilities	ProgId: "MSWC.BrowserType" ClassId: "0ACE4881-8305-11CF-9427-444553540000"
File Access Component	ProgId: "Scripting.FileSystemObject" ClassId: "0D43FE01-F093-11CF-8940-00A0C9054228"

Component	Description
Ad Rotator	ProgId: "MSWC.AdRotator" ClassId: "1621F7C0-60AC-11CF-9427-444553540000"
Content Linking	ProgId: "MSWC.Nextlink" ClassId: "4D9E4505-6DE1-11CF-87A7-444553540000"

You may notice that I have omitted the Database Access objects in the preceding table. To learn more about them, see Chapter 7, p. xx.

Cross Reference

Determining the Capabilities of the Client's Browser

How many browser manufacturers do you know? How many different versions for various platforms of these browsers are around on the Internet? These questions aren't easy to answer, but one thing is sure: all available browsers have small differences in their capabilities.

You could help yourself by taking a closer look at the HTTP_USER_AGENT header, which contains information about manufacturer, name, platform, and version of the browser. Then you would still have to know whether this browser supports frames, ActiveX controls, tables, VBScript, JavaScript, cookies, and more.

The Browser Capabilities component that ships with ActiveX Server comes in handy: it takes the HTTP_USER_AGENT header and maps it to its table of browser capabilities, stored in the file browscap.ini, located under /%webserverdir%/ASP/Cmpnts. At the time this book was written, the information that could be returned about browser capabilities included the following, listed in Table 6.3.

TABLE 6.3
Browser Capabilities Determined

Property	Description
ActiveXControls	Specifies whether the browser supports ActiveX controls.
backgroundsounds	Specifies whether the browser is capable of playing background sounds.

continues

TABLE 6.3, CONTINUED
Browser Capabilities Determined

Property	Description
beta	Specifies whether the browser connecting to your site is Beta software.
browser	Specifies the name of the browser.
cookies	Specifies whether the browser supports cookies.
frames	Specifies whether the browser supports frames.
javaapplets	Specifies whether the browser is capable of running Java applets
javascript	Specifies whether the browser supports JavaScript.
majorver	Specifies the major version number of the browser.
minorver	Specifies the minor version number of the browser.
platform	Specifies the platform the browser is running on.
tables	Specifies whether the browser supports frames.
vbscript	Specifies whether the browser supports VBScript.
version	Specifies the version number of the browser consisting of major and minor version number.
Win16	Specifies whether this browser runs on a Win16 computer. Valid only for Microsoft Internet Explorers.

If any of these capabilities is not defined for the browser hitting your site, the string "UNKNOWN" is returned.

 Tip   Updates to the browscap.ini file. More browsers and capabilities can be found on the Internet Information Server page at Microsoft. The URL is: http://www.microsoft.com/iis/.

If you're creating a site that stores information—like a shopping bag's information—in the Session object, the client's browser must support cookies, because sessions are identified via cookies. The code in Listing 6.1 should be inserted on your start page to warn users of possible problems when using older browsers that don't support cookies.

On the
CD

LISTING 6.1 - DECIDING WHETHER SOMEONE CAN CREATE A SHOPPING BAG

```
01. <HTML>
02. <HEAD>
03. <TITLE>Chapter 6: Browser Capabilities</TITLE>
04. </HEAD>
05. <BODY>
06.
07. <%
08.    Set bc = Server.CreateObject("MSWC.BrowserType")
09.    If Not CBool(bc.cookies) Then
10. %>
11.    Sorry, your browser <B><%=bc.browser & " " & bc.version%></B>
       ➥does not support cookies,
12.    so no shopping bag could be created for you.
       ➥Please download a newer browser!
13. <% Else %>
14.    <H1>Welcome to our shopping site</H1>
15.    ...
16. <% End If %>
17.
18. </BODY>
19. </HTML>
```

In line 8, the Browser Capabilities object is created, and the code in line 9 checks for the capability of storing and sending cookies. If the browser isn't capable of using cookies, information about this fact is sent back to the user. In normal cases, the user is welcomed at this site.

If all the capabilities information provided with the browscap.ini file isn't sufficient, you can simply edit the browscap.ini file to add the capability information you need. When opening the file in any text editor (yes, Notepad will do the trick), you should notice that there are lots of browsers already defined. Internet Explorer 3.0 is used for the following presentation. The following steps take you to the code section I am referencing in Listing 6.2:

1. Open the file browscap.ini in your favorite text editor.

2. Search for the phrase **IE 3.0**.

Listing 6.2 shows you what you should see after following the preceding steps.

LISTING 6.2 - SNAPSHOT FROM BROWSCAP.INI

```
01. ;;ie 3.0
02. [IE 3.0]
03. browser=IE
04. Version=3.0
05. majorver=#3
06. minorver=#0
07. frames=TRUE
08. tables=TRUE
09. cookies=TRUE
10. backgroundsounds=TRUE
11. vbscript=TRUE
12. javascript=TRUE
13. javaapplets=TRUE
14. ActiveXControls=TRUE
15. Win16=False
16. beta=False
17. AK=False
18. SK=False
19. AOL=False
20.
21. [Mozilla/2.0 (compatible; MSIE 3.0; AOL; Windows 95)]
22. parent=IE 3.0
23. platform=Win95
24. AOL=True
```

Line 21 contains a value of HTTP_USER_AGENT enclosed in brackets. It uses exactly the same syntax that is used for initialization files: section names are enclosed in brackets, and key/value pairs are separated by an equal sign and comments beginning with a semicolon. So line 21 starts the definition section for a Microsoft Internet Explorer 3.0, customized for America Online (AOL). You can inherit capabilities for the browser you're currently defining by using the parent key and setting its value to another section's name. This is done in line 22 and references the browser definition in line 2. Incidentally, this definition is used as a parent definition for all different flavors of Internet Explorer 3.0.

One important entry is missing for Internet Explorer 3.0—its capability to use Cascaded Style Sheets (CSS). One can create the coolest design with simple fonts, but it will definitely look ugly when displayed on a non–CSS-capable browser. The only thing to do is to add a line after line 19 and insert CSS=TRUE. Save the file and enter Listing 6.3.

LISTING 6.3 - TESTING FOR THE CSS PROPERTY

On the
CD

```
01. <HTML>
02. <HEAD>
03. <TITLE>Chapter 6: Browser Capabilities extended</TITLE>
04. </HEAD>
05. <BODY BGCOLOR=#ffffff>
06.
07. <%
08.   Set bc = Server.CreateObject("MSWC.BrowserType")
09.   If ("True" = CStr(bc.CSS)) Then
10. %>
11.
12. <STYLE type=text/css>
13. <!--
14. .bigletter
15. {font-family:Arial;
16. font-size:160;
17. font-weight:bold;
18. line-height:100%;
19. color:slateblue;
20. margin-top:.3in;
21. text-align:center;
22. background:darkslateblue}
23.
24. .smalletter
25. {font-family:Arial;
26. font-size:30;
27. font-weight:bold;
28. line-height:100%;
29. color:white;
30. margin-top:-0.25in;
31. text-indent:.04in;
32. text-align:center}
33. -->
34. </STYLE>
35.
36. <span class=bigletter>CSS</SPAN><BR>
37. <span class=smalletter>cascaded style sheets</SPAN>
38.
39. <% Else %>
40. <H1>CSS - Cascaded Style Sheets</H1>
41. are cool, but your browser does not support 'em!
```

continues

LISTING 6.3, CONTINUED

```
42. <% End If %>
43.
44. </body>
45. </html>
```

One line is of special interest; line 9. The statement ("True" = CStr(bc.CSS)) instead of (True = bc.CSS) has to be used because this capability was only added to the definition of Internet Explorer and all other ones return the string Unknown, which doesn't quite work for a Boolean comparison. Therefore, bc.CSS has to be converted to a string before the comparison is done. The rest of the listing simply deals with cascaded style sheets. The output of the CSS definition is shown in Figure 6.1.

Figure 6.1

How Internet Explorer displays a page designed with CSS.

Accessing Files from ASP Pages

VBScript doesn't support direct access to any system components by itself; it has to be extended with components to gain this access. This was done because VBScript not only runs on servers, but also on a client's computer, where a malicious script that has access to the hard disk could destroy a lot. Then, of course, there's no need to mention the cool viruses you could write that run directly from a web page.

When you need access to files on the server's hard disk, two objects support this functionality: the FileSystemObject object for creating and opening files, and the TextStream object for reading from or writing to this file.

Opening and Creating Files with the `FileSystemObject` Object

The sole purpose of the `FileSystemObject` object is to attach a `TextStream` object to a file on the hard disk. You can create entirely new append to and read files. There are only two methods that are needed to support this functionality, defined in Table 6.4.

TABLE 6.4
`FileSystemObject` **Methods**

Method	Description
CreateTextFile	Creates a file with the specified name and returns a `TextStream` object for reading or writing.
OpenTextFile	Opens a file with the specified name and returns a `TextStream` object for reading and appending.

Before you can use any methods provided by the `FileSystemObject` object, you have to create an instance of it. This is achieved with the following line of code:

```
Set fsObj = Server.CreateObject("Scripting.FileSystemObject")
```

The code in the next sections references this instance of the `FileSystemObject` object.

`CreateTextFile` Method

The `CreateTextFile` method is used for creating a file and attaching it to a `TextStream` object for reading or writing. The syntax is as follows:

```
Set txtStreamObj = fsObj.CreateTextFile(name[,bOverWrite[,bUnicode]])
```

Only the `name` argument is mandatory, which tells the method the filename of the file to be created. Boolean flags tell the method whether to overwrite an existing file and whether this given file should be created as an Unicode file.

`OpenTextFile` Method

In contrast to `CreateTextFile`, the `OpenTextFile` method opens existing files for appending and reading. For opening a file, you have to use the following syntax:

```
Set txtStreamObj = fsObj.OpenTextFile(name[,iomode[,bCreate[,format]]])
```

The `name` parameter has the same meaning as `CreateTextFile`. The third and optional argument `bCreate` determines whether to create a given file or fail when it does not exist. If set to `True`, this is simply the behavior of `CreateTextFile` with the parameter `bOverWrite` set to `False`.

The remaining parameters are trickier. The `iomode` parameter—according to the documentation—can have the following values: `ForAppending` and `ForReading`. The `format` parameter should be a `Tristate` to denote whether to use ASCII, Unicode, or the default. When you use any of these symbolic constants, you will get an error. So there had to be another solution for this. Taking a look at the `AdventureWorks` example, I found out that the `format` parameter was used, as in `CreateTextFile` (hence a Boolean), and `iomode` was inserted as numeric values. To save you from figuring out all possible values, Listing 6.4 shows you the include file you can use.

On the CD

LISTING 6.4 - INCLUDE FILE FOBJVBS.INC

```
01. <%
02. Const ForReading = 1
03. Const ForWriting = 2
04. Const ForAppending = 8
05.
06. Const TristateTrue = -1
07. Const TristateFalse = 0
08. Const TristateUseDefault = -2
09. Const TristateMixed = -2
10. %>
```

The `Tristate` constants on lines 6 and 7 have the same values as `True` (Unicode) and `False` (ASCII) that are used in `CreateTextFile`. So it was safe to use `True` and `False` instead. But what about the constant `ForWriting` in line 3? If you use this in conjunction with `bCreate` set to `True`, `OpenTextFile` has the exactly same functionality that `CreateTextFile` offers with `bOverWrite` set to `True`. Listing 6.5 shows how to use this undocumented functionality to open a file.

On the CD

LISTING 6.5 - UNDOCUMENTED `OpenTextFile`

```
01. <HTML>
02. <HEAD>
03. <TITLE>Chapter 6: ForWriting parameter</TITLE>
04. </HEAD>
05. <BODY>
06. <!--#include file="fobjvbs.inc"-->
07. <%
```

```
08.    Set fs = CreateObject("Scripting.FileSystemObject")
09.    'open file c:\test.txt for writing, create if not exists and ASCII format
10.    Set a = fs.OpenTextFile("c:\test.txt", ForWriting, True, False)
11.    a.WriteLine("Using functionality that is not documented is dangerous")
12.    a.Close
13. %>
14. ready!
15. </BODY>
16. </HTML>
```

Line 11 uses the `TextStream` object, which is discussed in the next section.

Working with File Data Using the `TextStream` Object

The `FileSystemObject` object's methods create a `TextStream` object that facilitates sequential access to the file. As the name implies, it is best fit for accessing textual information in a file.

All properties the `TextStream` object exposes are read-only. They give information about the position in the file. Table 6.5 lists the properties.

TABLE 6.5
`TextStream` **Properties**

Property	Description
AtEndOfLine	Returns `True` if the file pointer has reached the end of a line. Applies only to files that have been opened for reading. Otherwise, an error is generated.
AtEndOfStream	Returns `True` if the file pointer has reached the end of a file. As for `AtEndOfLine`, this property applies only for files opened for reading.
Column	Returns the current column the file pointer has reached in a given line. Indexing of columns starts with 1.
Line	Returns the line to which the file pointer is currently set. Indexing of lines starts with 1.

You use these properties in conjunction with the methods provided by the `TextStream` object to read from and write to disk files. The methods are listed in Table 6.6.

TABLE 6.6
TextStream **Methods**

Method	Description
Close	Closes an open TextStream file.
Read	Reads the specified number of characters from the TextStream file.
ReadAll	Reads the entire TextStream. When dealing with large files, use other methods, like reading line by line.
ReadLine	Reads an entire line from the TextStream file and positions the file pointer to the next line. The newline character is skipped.
Skip	Skips the specified number of characters.
SkipLine	Skips an entire line in the specified TextStream file.
Write	Writes the specified string to the TextStream file.
WriteLine	Writes the specified string to the TextStream file and appends a newline character.
WriteBlankLines	Writes the specified number of newline characters to the TextStream file.

The methods for the TextStream object provide a rather narrow functionality and don't justify an entire section on its own. Instead, I will present two interesting examples that use TextStream object functionality that you can incorporate into your own sites.

Tip of the Day Example

This sample is taken from the AdventureWorks site, which is part of the Active Server Pages examples. It opens a file containing a given number of tips (10), creates a random number of which tip to present and skips number-1 lines and then reads the tip on the next line. The tip text is sent to the user. The surrounding code has been cut out to show only what is important for displaying the tip.

LISTING **6.6** - DISPLAYING THE TIP OF THE DAY

On the
CD

```
01. <HTML>
02. <HEAD>
03. <TITLE>Chapter 6: Tip of the Day from Adventure Works Welcome Center
        ➥</TITLE>
04. </HEAD>
05. <BODY BGCOLOR=#ffffff>
06.
07. <!--#include file="fobjvbs.inc"-->
08.
09. <%
10. ' Pick a tip between 1 and 10 to display in the page
11. Randomize
12. TipNumber = Int(Rnd*10)
13.
14. ' Open the file with the 10 tips in it
15. Set FileObject = Server.CreateObject("Scripting.FileSystemObject")
16. Set Instream = FileObject.OpenTextFile (Server.MapPath ("tips.txt"),
        ➥ForReading, False, False)
17.
18. ' Skip the tips before the tip you want to display in the page
19. For i = 1 to TipNumber -1
20.     InStream.SkipLine()
21. Next
22.
23. ' Assign the variable TipOfTheDay to the tip randomly selected above
24. TipOfTheDay = Instream.ReadLine
25. Instream.Close
26. %>
27.
28. <B><%= TipOfTheDay %></B>
29.
30.
31. </BODY>
32. </HTML>
```

The original code has been changed a bit. Line 7 includes the OpenTextFile constants, of which ForReading is used in line 16. The tips file (tips.txt) is located in the same directory as the script page. However, the Server.MapPath method has to be used to get the physical location of the file. You can use the tips.txt file that comes with the AdventureWorks example. Because there are exactly 10 tips in the file and the function Rnd (line 12) returns a number between 0 and 1, simply multiplying it with 10 returns a valid tip number in the tips file. Lines 19 to 20 skip to the right tip, and 24's statement reads it.

Visitors Count Example

This example is taken from AdventureWorks as well. It maintains a persistent visitor count that is read from a file on startup of the Application object and written back in intervals in the Session_OnStart event—so the count is at least somewhat current if power fails or something else happens that disallows a controlled shut down of the web server and thus invokes the Application_OnEnd event handler. This point is the last time that the count is written to disk. And this Application_OnEnd handler is the reason why this example is especially interesting.

When your OnEnd handler for the Application object gets called, the Server.MapPath method only returns garbage: it can't be used any more at this point. However, you have to write the user count to a physical file. What to do? The only practical solution is to store the physical path information at an earlier stage, preferably in the OnStart event handler, and add it as a property of the Application object. And that's exactly how the solution works. Listing 6.7 shows how the global.asa has to look.

On the CD

LISTING 6.7 - GLOBAL.ASA FOR ADVENTUREWORKS VISITOR COUNT

```
01. <SCRIPT LANGUAGE=VBScript RUNAT=Server>
02. Sub Application_OnStart
03.    VisitorCountFilename = Server.MapPath ("visitors.txt")
04.    Set FileObject = Server.CreateObject("Scripting.FileSystemObject")
05.    Set Out= FileObject.OpenTextFile (VisitorCountFilename, 1, False, False)
06.    Application("visitors") = Out.ReadLine
07.    Application("VisitorCountFilename") = VisitorCountFilename
08. End Sub
09.
10. Sub Application_OnEnd
11.    Set FileObject = Server.CreateObject("Scripting.FileSystemObject")
12.    Set Out= FileObject.CreateTextFile (Application("VisitorCountFilename"),
       ➥True, False)
13.    Out.WriteLine(Application("visitors"))
14.    Out.Close
15. End Sub
16.
17. Sub Session_OnStart
18.    Application.Lock
```

```
19.    Application("visitors")= Application("visitors") + 1
20.    t_visitors = Application("visitors")
21.  Application.Unlock
22.
23.    Session("VisitorID") = t_visitors
24.
25.    ' Periodically, save to file
26.    If t_visitors MOD 15 = 0 Then
27.    Set FileObject = Server.CreateObject("Scripting.FileSystemObject")
28.    Set Out= FileObject.CreateTextFile (Application("VisitorCountFilename"),
       ➥True, False)
29.    Application.Lock
30.    Out.WriteLine(t_visitors)
31.    Application.Unlock
32.    End If
33.  End Sub
34.  </SCRIPT>
```

Again, unnecessary code was stripped out. Lines 3 and 7 in the listing are responsible for mapping and storing the path information in the Application object so it can be reused in the Session_OnStart and Application_OnEnd event handlers. When you take a look at line 5, you should notice that I used the numerical value of ForReading here: You can't include any files in global.asa where the code is enclosed with <%...%> tags as it was used in the constants file (see Listing 6.4). Another implication of the usage of ForReading is that the file visitors.txt must exist—otherwise, the code on line 5 would generate an error.

The Session_OnStart event handler code beginning on line 17 has a lot of work to do—increasing the visitor count, and when it has reached a multiple of 15, writing it to disk, so disaster can strike without losing more than 15 users. Please take a look at how the visitor count that is stored as an Application property is protected with Lock/Unlock methods.

You may want to present the user with a counter. A very simple line of code achieves this:

```
You are visitor number <%=Session("VisitorID")%> of <%=Application("visitors")%>
```

You can insert this line of code in any file where you want to present the user with this information, or simply keep the visitor count for statistical analysis.

Advertisement Rotation on Your Site

Most popular web sites today have rotating advertisements on their pages. Why not put them on your site too? With the Ad Rotator component it is easy to add advertisement rotation to your pages. This component automates the rotation of a preset group of advertisements on a page. The component automatically places a new image on the page every time the page is opened or reloaded. The information about which ad to present—and therefore which image and link—is taken from the Rotation Schedule File.

Adding ad rotation to a page is very simple. Besides the line for creating an instance of the Ad Rotator object, there is only one line you must add to the script code of your page, line 2. See Listing 6.8.

LISTING 6.8 - ADDING ADVERTISEMENT ROTATION TO YOUR PAGE

```
01. Set adrot = Server.CreateObject("MSWC.AdRotator")
02. Response.Write(adrot.GetAdvertisement("/virtualpath
    ➥/RotScheduleFile.txt"))
```

The method GetAdvertisement inserts the image for the ad and the hyperlink. So the main work you have to do is create this rotation schedule file. However, before diving into this rotation schedule file, I present the properties of this component.

TABLE 6.7
Ad Rotator Properties

Property	Description
Border	Specifies the border thickness around the image for the advertisement. Overrides the default set in the Rotation Schedule file.
Clickable	Specifies whether the advertisement is a hyperlink to the advertiser's homepage.
TargetFrame	Specifies the frame the advertiser's homepage should be displayed in.

You must set these properties before a call to GetAdvertisement. See Listing 6.9.

On the
CD

LISTING 6.9 - SETTING PROPERTIES FOR THE AD ROTATOR

```
01. <HTML>
02. <HEAD>
03. <TITLE>Chapter 6: Ad Rotation</TITLE>
04. </HEAD>
05. <BODY>
06.
07. <%
08. Set adrot = Server.CreateObject("MSWC.AdRotator")
09. adrot.Border(3)
10. adrot.Clickable(True)
11. adrot.TargetFrame("_new")
12. Response.Write(adrot.GetAdvertisement("adrotfile.txt"))
13. %>
14.
15. </BODY>
16. </HTML>
```

Because the Ad Rotator component doesn't support named properties, you have set the arguments for the properties in parenthesis. See lines 9 through 11.

Rotation Schedule File

The Rotation Schedule file contains general information that is used to determine how to set up the advertisements on your pages, as well as information about all advertisements to be displayed. The general section is separated by an asterisk (*) from the information for the advertisements. The general syntax for this file is shown in Listing 6.10.

LISTING 6.10 - SYNTAX FOR ROTATION SCHEDULE FILES

```
01. [REDIRECT URL]
02. [WIDTH numWidth]
03. [HEIGHT numHeight]
04. [BORDER numBorder]
05. *
06. adURL
07. adHomePageURL
08. Text
09. impressions
```

The first four arguments are all optional. The asterisk (*) has to be present even if all of the first four arguments are missing. The next four arguments comprise an advertisement. When you don't have information for one, insert a dash (-) instead. Repeat these four lines for each advertisement, but don't include any lines for spacing. See Table 6.8.

TABLE 6.8
Rotation Schedule File Parameters

Parameter	Description
URL	Specifies the URL for the ISAPI extension or Active Server Page that performs the actual redirection. You can use this redirection file to count the number of hits for this advertisement.
numWidth	Specifies the width of the advertisement images.
numHeight	Specifies the height of the advertisement images.
numBorder	Specifies the thickness of the border around the advertisement image. Can be overridden with the Border property.
adURL	The URL to the image for this advertisement.
adHomePageURL	The URL to the homepage of the advertiser.
Text	The text to display when the browser either doesn't support images or the user has turned off graphics.
impressions	A number specifying the relative weight of this advertisement. All weights of all advertisements are added up and display time is determined on the percentage of overall weight this advertisement has.

A real-life example of how a Rotation Schedule file can look is the one shown in Listing 6.11.

LISTING 6.11 - EXAMPLE OF A ROTATION SCHEDULE FILE

```
01. REDIRECT adrot.asp
02. WIDTH 420
03. HEIGHT 150
04. *
05. /images/softwing_ad.gif
```

```
06. http://www.softwing.com
07. -
08. 80
09. /images/zauner_ad.gif
10. http://www.zauner.at
11. Welcome to the pastry shop Zauner
12. 20
```

I have specified two advertisements in the rotation schedule file, one with alternate text, the other without. Both impression values add up to 100, so most impressions will go for the first advertisement. And I did specify a redirection file, which leads us nicely into the next section.

Redirection File

If you didn't specify the REDIRECT parameter, the advertisement image hyperlink would contain the URL to the advertiser. In case the redirection file is specified, the following hyperlink is inserted:

adrot.asp?url=http://www.softwing.com/&image=/images/softwing_ad.gif

This enables you to store the number of successful impressions an advertisement has generated, because a page on your server has to redirect the user to the advertiser's homepage. The example in Listing 6.12 appends the impression information to the server log.

LISTING 6.12 - EXAMPLE OF A REDIRECTION FILE ADROT.ASP

On the
CD

```
01. <%
02. strAdvertiserURL = Request.QueryString("url")
03. Response.AppendToLog strAdvertiserURL
04. Response.Redirect(strAdvertiserURL)
05. %>
```

Line 2's statement retrieves the URL the user has to be redirected to, stores it in the log for analysis (line 3), and finally redirects to the advertisers homepage.

Automatically Linking Pages in a Sequential Manner

If you did link together pages with previous and next page functionality, you had to insert links manually for this to work. Whenever a page was added or inserted, you had to adjust links in two more files. This is tedious work, and can introduce errors in the order that the pages are linked together as well as with the table of contents. You still have to write it on your own. Figure 6.2 shows how pages are linked together sequentially. You need to maintain 2*(x-1) links, where x is the number of pages.

Figure 6.2

Linking together pages in a sequential manner.

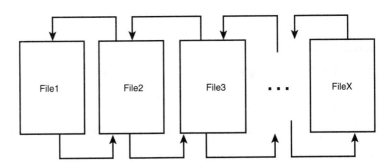

The Content Linking component makes life easier. It has a supporting text file where all page links are stored together with a descriptive text in the order the pages are linked together. You simply have to insert the URL and description once, and then you can create the table of contents and the links between the pages automatically. If you change a line, the changes are immediately reflected in the table of contents and link order. No need to update files manually.

The format for the supporting text file, the Content Linking List file, is very easy. First comes the URL, then a TAB character to separate it from the following description.

LISTING 6.13 - EXAMPLE OF A CONTENT LINKING LIST FILE

```
01. informations.asp<TAB>Informations about the product
02. personalinfo.asp<TAB>Personal information entry form
03. /legaldepartement/legalagreement.asp<TAB>Legal agreement
04. /download/downloadselect.asp<TAB>Select a product to download
```

The <TAB> in the preceding listing isn't a new HTML tag, it is a placeholder for a real TAB character you wouldn't see in print. You can reference any file on your local server, but URLs using the http:// syntax for accessing files not located on your local server aren't supported and won't be processed.

Warning You can run into serious trouble when inserting a page more than once. Take for example the sequence A-B-C-A-D. When you move from page C one forward, you are back at A. Instead of showing D as the next link, B is returned. This is because the Content Linking List file is read from the beginning.

That's all for the Content Linking List file. Which methods support you in creating navigational links and a table of contents? See Table 6.9 for a reference. The methods are listed by affiliation, not by alphabet. Each of these methods takes as its first parameter the virtual path to the Content Linking List file.

TABLE 6.9
Content Linking Component Methods

Method	Description
GetListCount	Returns the number of items in the Content Linking List file.
GetListIndex	Gets the index of the current page in the Content Linking List file. Zero (0) is returned when the page is not part of the list.
GetPreviousURL	This method returns the URL of the previous item in the list; if the current page isn't part of the list, the URL for the first page is returned.
GetPreviousDescription	Returns the description for the previous item in the list.
GetNextURL	Gets the URL of the next item in the list. If the current page isn't part of the list, the URL of the last item is returned.
GetNextDescription	Returns the description for the next item in the list.
GetNthURL	Gets the URL for the Nth item in the list. If there are less than N items in the list, the URL for the last item is retrieved.
GetNthDescription	Returns the description for the Nth item in the list.

This is a lot of functionality, but you're probably wondering how to create a table of contents with it. Listing 6.14 shows how to create a simple table of contents using an unordered list and an ordered list for Step-by-Step instructions. Both use the same Content Linking List file.

On the CD

LISTING 6.14 - EXAMPLE OF A TABLE OF CONTENTS

```
01. <HTML>
02. <HEAD>
03. <TITLE>Chapter 6: TOC</TITLE>
04. </HEAD>
05. <BODY BGCOLOR=#ffffff>
06.
07. <%
08.    Set NextLink = Server.CreateObject("MSWC.NextLink")
09.    nLinkCount = NextLink.GetListCount("nextlink.txt")
10. %>
11.
12. <H2>TOC - unordered list</H2>
13. <UL>
14. <%
15.    For i = 1 To nLinkCount
16. %>
17.    <LI><A HREF="<%= NextLink.GetNthURL ("nextlink.txt", i) %>">
18.    <%= NextLink.GetNthDescription ("nextlink.txt", i) %></A>
19. <%
20.    Next
21. %>
22. </UL>
23.
24. <H2>TOC - Step-by-Step instructions</H2>
25. <TABLE BORDER=0 CELLSPACING=0>
26. <OL>
27. <%
28.    For i = 1 To nLinkCount
29. %>
30.    <TR><TD>Step</TD><TD><LI><A HREF="<%= NextLink.GetNthURL
       ➥ ("nextlink.txt", i) %>">
31.    <%= NextLink.GetNthDescription ("nextlink.txt", i) %></A></TD></TR>
32. <%
33.    Next
34. %>
35. </OL>
36. </TABLE>
37.
38. </BODY>
39. </HTML>
```

From lines 15 to 20 the `GetNth`-methods are used to iterate over all items in the Content Linking List file and create a simple table of contents. The same is done for the Step-by-Step table of contents from lines 28 to 33, but I had to include a table to have the string `Step` and the list number on the same line. These are the two most common variants of TOCs.

There is one thing left: creating navigational links to the previous and subsequent page from the current one. In the example in Listing 6.15, the previous and next page links are only displayed if there is really a next or previous one. The heading for the page is taken from the description of the Content Linking List file.

LISTING 6.15 - EXAMPLE OF LINKING

On the
CD

```
01. <HTML>
02. <HEAD>
03. <TITLE>Chapter 6: Step X</TITLE>
04. </HEAD>
05. <BODY BGCOLOR=#ffffff>
06.
07. <%
08.    Set NextLink = Server.CreateObject ("MSWC.NextLink")
09.    nLinkIndex = NextLink.GetListIndex ("nextlink.txt")
10.    If (0 <> nLinkIndex) Then _
11.       Response.Write("<H1>" & NextLink.GetNthDescription("nextlink.txt",
           ➥nLinkIndex) & "</H1>")
12.    If (nLinkIndex > 1) Then
13. %>
14. <A HREF="<%=NextLink.GetPreviousURL ("nextlink.txt")%>">Previous Page</A>
15. <%
16.    End If
17.    If (nLinkIndex <> NextLink.GetListCount("nextlink.txt")) Then
18. %>
19. <A HREF="<%= NextLink.GetNextURL ("nextlink.txt") %>">Next Page</A>
20. <%
21.    End If
22. %>
23.
24. </BODY>
25. </HTML>
```

In the statement on line 10, a check is performed to see whether the current file is listed in the Content Linking List file. If it is, the description for this item is used as the page title. Line 12's check is for page one: a link to a previous page isn't included on the first one. The same happens between lines 17 and 21: the next link is only displayed when it isn't the last page.

Summary

Active Server Pages can be extended by the use of components. The components that ship with ASP provide access to files, enable you to create advertisement rotation, create sequentially-linked content and, finally, to determine the capabilities of the client's browser. The next chapter, "Database Access with ActiveX Data Objects," deals with a group of components that enable you to easily access data stored in a wide variety of database management systems. However, you aren't limited to using the provided components: you can create your own components to extend the functionality of ASP.

Cross Reference

To learn how to easily access data stored in a variety of database management systems, see Chapter 7 p. 149.

Cross Reference

To learn how to create components in different programming languages, see Chapter 12, "Extending Active Server Pages with Components," p. 293.

CHAPTER 7

Database Access with ActiveX Data Objects

Databases play a key role when you want to provide personalized and live content. You can use databases for any kind of information, from quotes of the day to full-featured online stores.

Microsoft provides access to databases with the ActiveX Data Objects (ADO), which build upon OLE DB. If you have already worked with Data Access Objects (DAO) or Remote Data Objects (RDO), the interfaces provided by ADO will be familiar to you and you shouldn't have any trouble switching.

This chapter is divided into four parts, which are designed to present an overview of ADO, showing how to use ADO in scripts, a reference of functionality, and a section on how to optimize the performance for database access. Each of these topics is presented in a section of its own:

◆ The architecture of ADO

◆ Working with ADO

- ◆ ADO objects reference

- ◆ Optimizing performance

The Architecture of ADO

When you're used to working on Windows platforms for a longer time—two years or more—you will know ODBC (Open DataBase Connectivity) and might already have used it to connect to databases on local or remote machines. ODBC is a single, well-defined interface for uniformly accessing different database management systems, regardless of the provider-specific interface. By simply changing the ODBC datasource name for database access you can switch from, for example, Access 97 to Microsoft SQL Server 6.5 without having to rewrite a single line of code.

So why is a new specification needed, namely OLE DB? OLE DB was developed (in contrast to ODBC) to build upon COM (Component Object Model) rather than C interface functions optimized for SQL-based data access, as ODBC uses. If you're programming in an OLE environment, OLE DB is the best choice, because it also includes an OLE DB driver manager that enables OLE DB consumers to talk to ODBC providers very efficiently.

That is why ADO is built upon OLE DB, which provides only a thin and efficient layer to OLE DB. It eliminates unnecessary objects and optimizes tasks that were somehow complicated in DAO or RDO. Also, it exposes everything a data provider can do and adds extra value by creating shortcuts for common operations.

However, some data providers don't provide the same level of functionality as others. For example, SQL Server can provide stored procedures, others, like Microsoft Excel, can't because of the limitations in their database functionality. ADO automatically adjusts itself to the provided functionality.

Figure 7.1 shows a diagram of how the objects provided by ADO relate to each other.

Please note that both the Errors collection and the Command object are optional. These, for example, are supported on the MS SQL Server, but not with Microsoft Excel.

The relation between the objects shows how they fit together, however, each object with the exception of Field and Error can be created on its own. It is possible to open a Recordset without opening a connection to the database first. This is done automatically when a Recordset is opened.

This diagram implies that there is no real hierarchy in the model—and this is true.

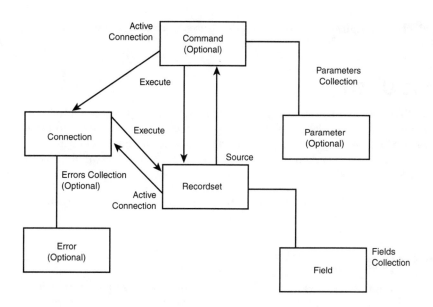

Figure 7.1

An ADO object model overview.

You don't have to create a connection before you open a Recordset. With this flexibility, you can attach, for example, a `Command` object to Connection A and attach it later to Connection B without having to rewrite the query string or change parameters. Simply rerun the `Command` to create a Recordset.

More in-depth coverage of each object is provided in the section "ADO Objects Reference." In this chapter, however, to give you a start for the next section "Working with ADO," (I know programmers like to learn along with examples) the next sections provide an overview of each object.

`Connection` Object

The `Connection` object represents the active connection to a database. You can use it to execute any command. If this command returns rows, a `Recordset` object is created automatically and returned. If you need to create more complex recordsets with cursors, create a Recordset, connect it to the `Connection` object and then open the cursor.

`Recordset` Object

The `Recordset` object's interface contains the most properties and methods of all objects. This is because all cursor management functionality is implemented in it. If you are used to the `Recordset` object provided by ADO or RDO, you will be up to speed very fast, because it is very similar to the one used in existing models today.

The Field object represents the columns in a Recordset. You can use it to read from or write to the database.

Command Object

The Command Object wraps a command, which can be either an SQL statement or a statement in a database access language the data provider understands. You can use it to execute plain SQL statements (or other language) that can both return or not return rows, or call stored procedures with input and output parameters that also can return rows or not.

The Parameter object that is part of the Parameters collection is used to specify the input and output parameters for parameterized commands.

Error Object

This is the second optional object in the ADO object model. Each single Error object found in the Errors collection represents an error returned from the data provider. It's useful when a provider can return multiple interesting errors for a single method call. An example for a data provider capable of returning multiple errors is SQL Server. When only a single error is returned, the COM method for raising errors is used.

Working with ADO

Before you can start working with databases, you first have to create the database and then add an ODBC system data source to access it via ADO.

Setting up a Database

The examples in this section use a sample table that has already been used in Chapter 4, "Working with Visual InterDev." It is a table that stores information about events. The definition for this table is presented in Table 7.1.

TABLE 7.1
Table Definition for the Events Table

Column name	Items in () are Access97 Datatypes	Description
EventId	`int`(autonumber)	Primary key index
EvDate	`datetime`(Date/Time)	Date of the event
EvTime	`datetime`(Date/Time)	Time of the event
Location	`varchar`(255)(Text(255))	Location where this event takes place
Description	`varchar`(255)(Text(255))	Descriptive text for the event

You can create the table with any database management system you want, however, I strongly recommend a dedicated database management system like Microsoft SQL Server 6.5, the performance of which is superior to a Microsoft Access based database, which is limited to one read or write operation at a given time. This isn't suitable for medium to heavy load servers, but is sufficient for the examples in this chapter or a small web server.

Creating an Access Database

If you're using Microsoft Access to create the table, follow these easy steps (assuming you have Access 97 installed):

1. Open Microsoft Access and select "Blank Database" in "Create new database using." See Figure 7.2.

Figure 7.2

Creating a new database using Access 97.

2. Select **unlocking** as the database name and store it in a location to which the anonymous web server user account has access (like the root of your web server).

Warning Although someone could download the database from your web server, this is okay for the examples.

3. Select Insert Table from the Insert menu. Select to view it in Design view.

4. Add all columns and set the EventId column to AutoNumber and add the primary index to it. Save the table as **Events**.

5. Go to Datasheet View and add some events. Then close Microsoft Access 97.

Figure 7.3

The finished Events table in Design view.

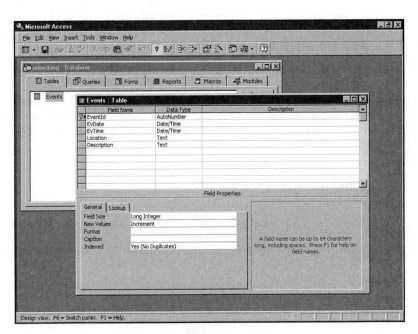

Now you have created the database and inserted some test values into the database. To be able to access the database from ADO and the web server, you need to add a system data source from ODBC pointing to the Access database. Steps to create the system data source are as follows:

1. Open the Control Panel on the server computer.

2. Open the ODBC control panel application by double-clicking the ODBC icon.

3. Switch to the System DSN tab and click Add.

4. Select Microsoft Access as the driver for your new data source. Click Finish.

5. The Microsoft Access 97 Setup dialog box opens. Select the database file in which you created the Events table. The completed dialog box should look like Figure 7.4, assuming that you have named the database and the data source **unlocking**.

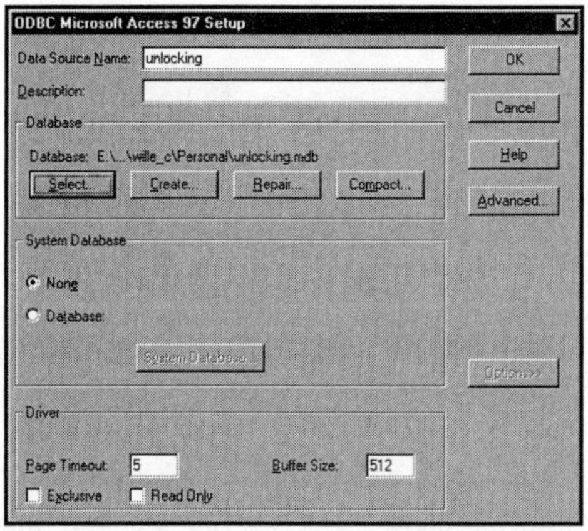

Figure 7.4

The completed Microsoft Access 97 Server Setup dialog box.

6. Click OK to add the newly created data source.

Now you're ready to start working with the database using ADO.

Creating a Microsoft SQL Server Database

When you're using Microsoft SQL Server, creating a database from scratch can be more complicated. However, the increased speed pays off in the long run. I'm assuming in this section that you are somewhat familiar with SQL Server.

You have to create a database device before you can put a database in it. If you can't create a database device on your own, please contact your database administrator to help you.

For this example, the database size doesn't need to exceed 2 megabytes of storage space, because it will hold only a little sample data. Create a database with the name **unlocking**, because all text and code will refer to this name later on.

Assuming that you have created a database named unlocking by now, start ISQL/w and connect to your database server. Switch to the unlocking database and run the following script:

LISTING 7.1 - SQL SCRIPT FOR THE EVENTS TABLE

```
01. /****** Object: Table dbo.Events Script Date: 20.02.97
    ➥12:15:21 ******/
02. if exists (select * from sysobjects where id =
    ➥object_id('dbo.Events') and sysstat & 0xf = 3)
03.     drop table dbo.Events
04. GO
05.
06. /****** Object: Table dbo.Events Script Date: 20.02.97
    ➥12:15:21 ******/
07. CREATE TABLE dbo.Events (
08.     EventId int IDENTITY (1, 1) NOT NULL ,
09.     EvDate datetime NOT NULL ,
10.     EvTime datetime NULL ,
11.     Location varchar (255) NULL ,
12.     Description varchar (255) NULL
13. )
14. GO
```

I obtained this script by using the Generate SQL Scripts command in the Enterprise Manager of Microsoft SQL Server.

Now that you have created the table, you still have to add events to the database. You can either use the SQL statement

INSERT INTO Events(EvDate,EvTime,Location,Description) VALUES (...)

or first create a data source and link the tables into a Microsoft Access database where you can easily edit the data. This method is convenient and provides you with the possibility of easily creating a front-end for data entry.

First add a system data source pointing to your SQL Server database:

1. Open the Control Panel on the server computer.

2. Open the ODBC control panel application by double-clicking the ODBC icon.

3. Switch to the System DSN tab and click Add.

4. Select SQL Server as the driver for your new data source. Click Finish.

5. The ODBC SQL Server Setup dialog box opens. Enter the information about the SQL Server and the database in which you have created the Events table. The completed dialog box should look like Figure 7.5, assuming that you have named the database and the data source unlocking.

If you have created the Access datasource before using unlocking as its name, you can't use it for this datasource again, because datasource names have to be unique.

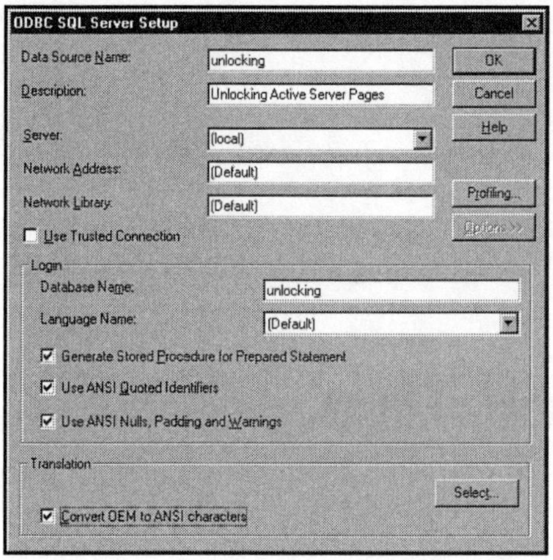

Figure 7.5

The completed ODBC SQL Server Setup dialog box.

6. Click OK to add the newly created data source.

This system data source can be used to connect to the database from ADO and the web server as well as from user databases, like the front-end for the Events database. To link tables into an Access database, follow these steps (assuming you have installed Microsoft Access 97):

1. Open Access 97 and create a new database named **frontend**.

2. Select Link Tables from File/Get External Data.

3. In the Link dialog box, select ODBC databases in the Files of Types drop-down box. The Select DataSource dialog box opens.

4. Switch to the Machine Datasources tab and select unlocking. Click OK.

5. You are now asked for your SQL Server login and password. Enter them and select OK.

6. The Link Tables dialog box opens. Select dbo.Events and click OK to insert it into the database.

7. The table is now linked to your database and you can start entering events by simply double-clicking the table and adding event data.

Figure 7.6

The Link Tables dialog box.

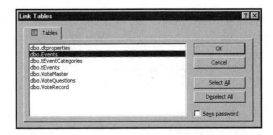

Now you have a high-speed back end and an easy-to-administer frontend for your database, and you are ready to start writing scripting code that brings your data to the Internet.

Your First ADO-Enabled Page

You have already complied with the prerequisites for creating pages that use ADO:

- ◆ You have created a database.

- ◆ You have added an ODBC system data source that points to this database.

Now you're ready to start coding your first page. The first page will simply retrieve all data from the Events table and put it into an HTML table. See Listing 7.2 for the code.

On the CD

LISTING 7.2 - RETRIEVING DATA FROM A DATABASE

```
01. <HTML>
02. <HEAD>
03. <TITLE>Chapter 7: First page</TITLE>
04. </HEAD>
05. <BODY BGCOLOR=#ffffff>
06. <!--#include file="adovbs.inc"-->
07.
08. <H1>Events</1>
09.
10. <%
11. Set Conn = Server.CreateObject("ADODB.Connection")
12. Conn.Open "unlocking","sa",""
13. Set rsEvents = Conn.Execute("SELECT * FROM Events
       ➥ORDER BY EvDate, EvTime")
14.
15. If rsEvents.EOF Then
```

```
16.         Response.Write "Sorry, no events in the database!"
17. Else
18. %>
19. <TABLE CELLSPACING=10 BORDER=1>
20. <TR><TH>Date</TH><TH>Time</TH><TH>Location</TH><TH>Description</TH></TR>
21. <%
22.    While Not rsEvents.EOF
23.       Response.Write "<TR><TD>" & rsEvents.Fields.Item("EvDate").Value &
          ➡"</TD>"
24.       Response.Write "<TD>" & rsEvents("EvTime").Value & "</TD>"
25.       Response.Write "<TD>" & rsEvents("Location") & "</TD>"
26.       Response.Write "<TD>" & rsEvents("Description") & "</TD></TR>"
27.       rsEvents.MoveNext
28.    Wend
29.    Response.Write "</TABLE>"
30. End If
31. %>
32.
33.
34. </BODY>
35. </HTML>
```

The file included in line 6 contains all constants that you need when dealing with ADO. Otherwise, you have to insert the numeric counterparts in your code. This file is located in the /InetPub/ASPSamp/Samples directory together with the include adojavas.inc for JScript.

The actual work done with ADO starts on line 11 with the creation of an instance of the Connection object. The statement to create a Connection object is as follows:

```
Set Conn = Server.CreateObject("ADODB.Connection")
```

Now you have a running instance, however, you must connect it to a real data source. This is done on line 12 by connecting to the unlocking SQL Server data source.

Warning   I am using the "sa user account without a password, which is standard by installation of SQL Server. For me, this is perfectly safe, because my computer isn't connected to a network. If you're running a production server that's connected to a network, always create user accounts specific for the databases. And use hard-to-guess passwords for all of your accounts!

Now that you're connected to the data source, you can execute any SQL statement against it. This example retrieves all data sorted by date and time. Line 15 checks to see whether there is any data returned by this query via the EOF property of the Recordset object that was returned through the Execute statement in line 13.

If you have already inserted data in the database table, an HTML table filled with the database results is generated. Line 23 shows the exact syntax to use when accessing a field value, and lines 25 and 26 show the shortcut to it. Because the entire result set is being iterated over, line 27 moves to the next record returned. The while statement on line 22 terminates when the last record is reached.

Submitting any SQL Command to the Database

When you have used ISQL/w that comes with SQL Server or the SQL pane of Microsoft Access, you know how easy it is to write SQL statements that can be tested against the database. So it would be useful if you have an HTML form where you can insert your SQL statement, press Submit, then have the statement execute and have results returned in tabular form. This is exactly what this example does: it presents a form where the user can enter any SQL command and returns the results that the SQL statement generates. See Figure 7.7.

Figure 7.7

SQL Query Builder form.

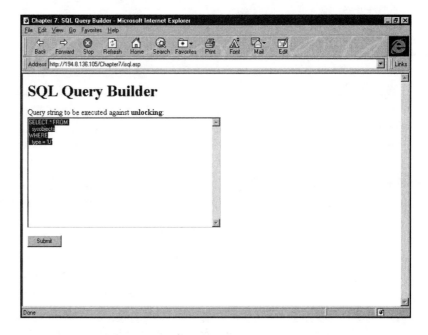

This page contains both the form data and the code that executes when the user submits an SQL statement. The code in Listing 7.3 contains error handling that is suitable for database management systems that either support COM error raising or the Errors collection of the Connection object.

LISTING 7.3 - SQL QUERY BUILDER

On the
CD

```
01. <HTML>
02. <HEAD>
03. <TITLE>Chapter 7: SQL Query Builder</TITLE>
04. </HEAD>
05. <BODY BGCOLOR=#ffffff>
06. <!--#include file="adovbs.inc"-->
07.
08. <H1>SQL Query Builder</H1>
09.
10. <%
11. On Error Resume Next
12. If Request.ServerVariables("Content_length")>0 Then
13.     Set Conn = Server.CreateObject("ADODB.Connection")
14.     Conn.Open "unlocking","sa",""
15.     Set rsQuery = Conn.Execute(Request.Form("sqlstmt"))
16.
17.     If Not IsObject(rsQuery) Then
18.       Response.Write "An error has occurred executing your statement:<P>"
19.       If Err.Number > 0 Then
20.        Response.Write Err.Description
21.       Else
22.         ' iterate over errors collection
23.         For Each dbError In Conn.Errors
24.           Response.Write dbError.Description & "<BR>"
25.         Next
26.       End If
27.       Response.End
28.     End If
29.
30.     If rsQuery.EOF Then
31.       Response.Write "Sorry, query did not return any rows!"
32.     Else
33.       Response.Write "<TABLE BORDER=1 CELLSPACING=10><TR>"
34.       For i = 0 to rsQuery.Fields.Count - 1
35.         Response.Write "<TH>" & rsQuery(i).Name & "</TH>"
36.       Next
37.       Response.Write "</TR>"
38.
39.       While Not rsQuery.EOF
40.         Response.Write "<TR>"
41.           For i = 0 to rsQuery.Fields.Count - 1
```

continues

LISTING 7.3, CONTINUED

```
42.              Response.Write "<TD>" & rsQuery(i) & "</TD>"
43.          Next
44.          Response.Write "</TR>"
45.          rsQuery.MoveNext
46.       Wend
47.        Response.Write "</TABLE>"
48.     End If
49. Else
50. %>
51. <FORM METHOD=POST ACTION="<%=Request.ServerVariables(
     ➥"SCRIPT_NAME")%>">
52. Query string to be executed against <B>unlocking</B>:<BR>
53. <TEXTAREA NAME="sqlstmt" cols=80 rows=15> Select * from Events
     ➥</TEXTAREA> <P>
54. <INPUT TYPE=SUBMIT NAME="Submit!">
55. </FORM>
56. <%
57. End If
58. %>
59. </BODY>
60. </HTML>
```

The listings tend to get longer now—even the error handling takes 11 lines of code in this one. Before I come back to error handling, I want to show the two big blocks of code—one that deals with what happens when the user has sent an SQL statement (beginning on line 13), and the other that sends the form to gather the SQL statement from the user starting on line 51. Because there's nothing special for the form, I will concentrate on the code found between lines 13 and 48.

Lines 13 and 14 contain nothing new—line 15, though, executes the statement that was passed to the page from the user. Because the database management system might not like the statement you have submitted and raise an error, you have to include On Error Resume Next to catch the error in your scripting code. Otherwise, script execution terminates and error and line information is sent to the user, which isn't good practice.

The error handling code between lines 17 and 28 works for database management systems that either raise an error with COM, or fill the Errors collection like Microsoft SQL Server does. Lines 19 to 22 deal with systems that prefer the first method, and lines 22 to 26 deal with systems that enter their error information into the `Errors` collection. For both, the description about the error is sent back to the user. When you're done dumping the errors, you normally should call `Conn.Errors.Clear` to remove all errors from the collection, however, because you are exiting immediately and not continuing processing, this can be omitted safely.

The check in line 30 for no results is necessary, because statements like `"CREATE PROCEDURE"` don't return any rows, but still execute successfully.

The last block of code in lines 33 to 47 iterates over all items found in the `Fields` collection and first creates table headers before simply dumping all rows that were returned from the query.

If you plan to generalize this example for accessing all data sources on your system, you only have to add three fields to the form, `DataSource`, `Username`, and `Password`, and change line 14 to

```
Conn.Open Request("DataSource"), Request("Username"), Request("Password")
```

Remember to check to see whether establishing the connection to the database succeeded or not.

Paging Through the Results

One of the drawbacks inherent to the solution in the previous section is that it can possibly return hundreds of rows or even more at once. To provide the user with an easy navigational aid, you can split the results into pages, which can be used to go back and forth in the result set.

For performance issues, you should execute the SQL command only once and store the results, the `Recordset` object, as a `Session` property for the user. So your page has essentially three purposes now:

1. Providing a user interface for entering and submitting the SQL statement.

2. Executing the SQL statement and storing the returned `Recordset` object.

3. Paging through the `Recordset`.

The user interface for entering the SQL statement is the same as for the example in the last section, so please refer again to Figure 7.7 for the input form. The code in Listing 7.4 doesn't include error handling, because that would have added another bunch of lines of code and made it more difficult to understand.

LISTING 7.4 - PAGING RESULTS

```
01. <HTML>
02. <HEAD>
03. <TITLE>Chapter 7: Paging results</TITLE>
04. </HEAD>
05. <BODY BGCOLOR=#ffffff>
06. <!--#include file="adovbs.inc"-->
07.
08. <H1>Paging results</H1>
09.
10. <%
11. If (Request.ServerVariables("Content_Length")>0) Then
12.     strSQLStmt = Request("sqlstmt")
13.     nPageTo = 1
14.
15.     If Len(strSQLStmt) > 0 Then
16.       ' a new query needs to be executed
17.       Set Conn = Server.CreateObject("ADODB.Connection")
18.       Set RS = Server.CreateObject("ADODB.RecordSet")
19.       Conn.Open "unlocking", "sa",""
20.       RS.Open strSQLStmt,Conn,adOpenKeyset,adLockReadOnly
21.       RS.PageSize = 5
22.       Set Session("RS") = RS
23.     Else
24.       ' we are paging
25.       strPageTo = Request("PageTo")
26.       If strPageTo <> "" Then
27.         nPageTo = CLng(strPageTo)
28.         If nPageTo <  1 Then nPageTo = 1
29.       Else
30.         nPageTo = 1
31.       End If
32.     End If
33.
34.     If Not IsObject(Session("RS")) Then
35.       Response.Write "Recordset not valid"
36.       Response.End
37.     End If
38.
39.     Set RS = Session("RS")
40.     RS.AbsolutePage = nPageTo
41. %>
42. Current page number: <%=nPageTo%><P>
```

```
43.  <TABLE BORDER=1 CELLSPACING=10><TR>
44.  <%
45.  For i = 0 To RS.Fields.Count - 1
46.     Response.Write "<TH>" & RS(i).Name & "</TH>"
47.  Next
48.  %>
49.  </TR>
50.  <%
51.  nRowCount = RS.PageSize
52.  While Not RS.EOF and nRowCount > 0
53.     Response.Write "<TR>"
54.     For i = 0 To RS.Fields.Count - 1
55.        Response.Write "<TD>" & RS(i) & "</TD>"
56.     Next
57.     Response.Write "</TR>"
58.     nRowCount = nRowCount - 1
59.     RS.MoveNext
60.  Wend
61.  Response.Write "</TABLE><P><TABLE><TR>"
62.  If nPageTo > 1 Then
63.  %>
64.     <TD><FORM METHOD=POST ACTION=" <%=Request.ServerVariables
        ➥("SCRIPT_NAME")%>">
65.     <INPUT TYPE=HIDDEN NAME="PageTo" VALUE=<%=nPageTo-1%>>
66.     <INPUT TYPE=SUBMIT VALUE="<<">
67.     </FORM></TD>
68.  <%
69.  End If
70.  If nRowCount = 0 Then
71.  %>
72.     <TD><FORM METHOD=POST ACTION="<%=Request.ServerVariables
        ➥("SCRIPT_NAME")%>">
73.     <INPUT TYPE=HIDDEN NAME="PageTo" VALUE=<%=nPageTo+1%>>
74.     <INPUT TYPE=SUBMIT VALUE=">>">
75.     </FORM></TD>
76.  <%
77.  End If
78.  Response.Write "</TABLE>"
79.  Else
80.  %>
81.     <FORM METHOD=POST ACTION="<%=Request.ServerVariables("SCRIPT_NAME")%>">
82.     Query string to be executed against <B>unlocking</B>:<BR>
```

continues

LISTING 7.4 - PAGING RESULTS

```
83.     <TEXTAREA NAME="sqlstmt" cols=80 rows=15>
        ➥Select * from Events</TEXTAREA> <P>
84.     <INPUT TYPE=SUBMIT NAME="Submit!">
85.     </FORM>
86. <%
87. End If
88. %>
89.
90. </BODY>
91. </HTML>
```

The block containing the code for the paging and creation of the `Recordset` is enclosed with lines 11 and 79. The code for the form for entering the SQL statement follows this line. The `recordset` is opened between lines 16 and 22. First the `Connection` and Recordset objects are created. Then a connection to the database is established and the `Recordset` is filled by a call to the `Open` method, which takes the following parameters:

```
rs.Open SQLStatement,ConnObj,CursorType, LockType, Options
```

The first two arguments are obvious, but the last three are more interesting. *CursorType* is used to tell the database which type of `Recordset` movements should be enabled for this recordset. Valid types are `ForwardOnly`, `Keyset`, `Dynamic`, and `Static`. You also can determine what type of locking—or concurrency—the database provider should use when returning the records, including read-only, pessimistic, optimistic, and batch-optimistic locking. The last parameter determines the type of command (the SQL statement) to be executed by the provider. More information on these parameters is provided in the "ADO Objects Reference" section in this chapter.

In line 21 the size of the pages is set to 5 records, and in the next line (22) the recordset is attached as a property to the user's `Session` object. A newly created recordset starts with page 1.

The code for retrieving the current page is between lines 24 and 31, which simply checks for valid pages. Lines 34 to 37 contain a safety check to determine whether the recordset is healthy.

The paging code starts on line 40, where the current page is set to the value passed to the page from the previous request. The table headers are written to the page, and on line 52 the iteration over the recordset starts. This time, there's an addition to the `while` condition. The `while` loop is exited either when there are no more rows in the recordset or when the maximum amount of rows to show per page has been retrieved.

Between lines 62 and 77 two forms are inserted for moving forward or backward in the recordset.

Inserting Values into the Database

Until now the examples presented only retrieved data. However, you might want to give the users the ability to submit events to the database so that they can participate and contribute to your site.

In production environments, you use a separate table to store the user-added events and check them before making them available online. But for this example, events are added directly to the table that is used to present events.

The input form contains four elements for date, time, location, and description. Before the events are added to the database, the user is asked to verify the event data. Only then is it added to the database. See Listing 7.5 for the page.

LISTING 7.5 - ADDING EVENTS TO THE DATABASE

On the
CD

```
01. <HTML>
02. <HEAD>
03. <TITLE>Chapter 7: Adding Events</TITLE>
04. </HEAD>
05. <BODY BGCOLOR=#ffffff>
06. <!--#include file="adovbs.inc"-->
07. <H1>Add Events to the database</H1>
08. <%
09. If Request.ServerVariables("Content_Length")>0 Then
10.     If "Insert" = Request("ActionType") Then
11.         ' no check for data validity done, the database
            ➥will return the errors...
12.         Set Conn = Server.CreateObject("ADODB.Connection")
13.         Set RS = Server.CreateObject("ADODB.RecordSet")
14.         Conn.Open "unlocking","sa",""
15.         RS.Open "Events", Conn , adOpenKeyset, adLockOptimistic
16.         RS.AddNew
17.         RS("EVDate") = Request("evdate")
18.         RS("EVTime") = Request("evtime")
19.         RS("Location") = Request("evlocation")
20.         RS("Description") = Request("desc")
21.         RS.Update
22.         Response.Write "Thank you for adding an event!"
23.     Else
```

continues

Listing 7.5, Continued

```
24. %>
25. You are going to insert an event on the <B><%=Request("evdate")%></B> at
    ➡<B><%=Request("evtime")%></B> o´clock.<BR>
26. The Location you have selected is <B><%=Request("evlocation")%></B>, your
    ➡event description is:<BR><I><%=Request("desc")%></I>.<P>
27. Do you want to insert it as shown?
28. <FORM METHOD=POST ACTION="<%=Request.ServerVariables("SCRIPT_NAME")%>">
29. <INPUT TYPE=HIDDEN NAME="evdate" VALUE="<%=Request("evdate")%>">
30. <INPUT TYPE=HIDDEN NAME="evtime" VALUE="<%=Request("evtime")%>">
31. <INPUT TYPE=HIDDEN NAME="evlocation" VALUE="<%=Request("evlocation")%>">
32. <INPUT TYPE=HIDDEN NAME="desc" VALUE="<%=Request("desc")%>">
33. <INPUT TYPE=HIDDEN NAME="ActionType" VALUE="Insert">
34. <INPUT TYPE=SUBMIT VALUE="Yes!">
35. </FORM>
36. <%
37.     End If
38. Else
39. %>
40. <FORM ACTION="<%=Request.ServerVariables("SCRIPT_NAME")%>" METHOD=POST>
41. <TABLE BORDER=0>
42. <tr><td>Date</td><td><INPUT TYPE=TEXT NAME="evdate" VALUE="<%=Date()%>">
    ➡</td></tr>
43. <tr><td>Time</td><td><INPUT TYPE=TEXT NAME="evtime" VALUE="20:00"></td>
    ➡</tr>
44. <tr><td>Location</td><td><INPUT TYPE=TEXT NAME="evlocation"></td></tr>
45. <tr><td>Description</td><td><TEXTAREA NAME="desc" COLS=80 ROWS=15>
    ➡</TEXTAREA></td></tr>
46. <tr><td><INPUT TYPE=SUBMIT VALUE="Submit"></td></tr>
47. </TABLE>
48. </FORM>
49. <% End If %>
50.
51. </BODY>
52. </HTML>
```

The verify page (lines 25 to 35) contains an additional field, "ActionType", that's used in line 10 to distinguish between data verification requests and database insertion requests. During verification, the sent data is presented to the user to give a chance to review the event data.

The code needed to insert the data into the database starts on line 11. A connection to the database is established and a recordset that's updateable is created as well. If you're familiar with DAO or RDO, the next lines don't present anything new to you: AddNew is called, the fields are assigned new values, and with Update, the new row is written into the database. However, when AddNew is used in this context, it should be replaced by the following:

```
RS.EditMode = adEditAdd
```

Without parameters, AddNew just expands to this statement. What are these parameters for AddNew? Exactly two, representing an array of fields and values:

```
RS.AddNew FieldsArray, ValueArray
```

So you can replace lines 16 to 21 with the following code that does exactly the same thing:

LISTING 7.6 - WORKING WITH ADDNEW PARAMETERS

On the CD

```
01.      Dim aFields(3)
02.      aFields(0) = "EVDate"
03.      aFields(1) = "EVTime"
04.      aFields(2) = "Location"
05.      aFields(3) = "Description"
06.      Dim aValues(3)
07.      aValues(0) = Request("evdate")
08.      aValues(1) = Request("evtime")
09.      aValues(2) = Request("evlocation")
10.      aValues(3) = Request("desc")
11.      RS.AddNew aFields, aValues
```

Notice that the arrays are declared using the upper bound (start with zero), not the actual number of elements.

If you like to work with SQL statements, you can even rewrite the insertion code to use an SQL INSERT INTO statement. You have to replace lines 12 to 21 with the following code fragment:

LISTING 7.7 - USING **INSERT INTO** FOR DATA INSERTION

On the CD

```
01.      Set Conn = Server.CreateObject("ADODB.Connection")
02.      Conn.Open "unlocking","sa",""
03.      strSQL = "INSERT INTO Events(EVDate,EVTime,Location,Description)
```

```
         ➥VALUES("
```

continues

```
04.        strSQL = strSQL & "CONVERT(DATETIME,'" &
           ➥Request("evdate") & "',4),"
05.        ' strSQL = strSQL & "'" & Request("evdate") & "',"
06.        strSQL = strSQL & "CONVERT(DATETIME,'" &
           ➥Request("evtime") & "',8),'"
07.        ' strSQL = strSQL & "#" & Request("evtime") & "#,'"
08.        strSQL = strSQL & Request("evlocation") & "','" &
           ➥Request("desc") & "')"
09.        Response.Write strSQL
10.        Conn.Execute(strSQL)
```

This code is written for SQL Server. Notice the two commented lines, 5 and 7. These contain the replacements for lines 4 and 6 when used in conjunction with Access databases. You have to write database-specific code, because the string is sent directly to the database engine.

When you're inserting date or time values, you have to convert them for SQL Server. I have used German date format (dd.mm.yy) and European time format (hh:mm:ss). You will have to look up the appropriate conversion formats for your locale in the SQL Server Books Online.

Prepared Statements

The SQL statement for inserting values in a table presented in the previous section is a rather small one. When you have to reuse one statement very often, for example retrieving events for specific locations, you get better performance by using prepared statements. This is because the SQL statement is syntax checked and compiled at the first execution and this compiled version is used for further requests.

There are two types of prepared statements:

♦ **SQL statements** are syntax checked and compiled before the first call. The compiled version is reused for subsequent requests with differing parameters. It can be used until the prepared statement is destroyed.

♦ **Stored procedures** (SQL Server) or **queries** (Access) are already syntax checked and compiled. Every call, even the first, uses the compiled version.

The best performance is achieved by using stored procedures, which also have another advantage: they are created and managed in a central location, not on a per script basis. A change made to the database reflects automatically in all scripts. With the other method, you have to check all files and adjust the scripts.

When you're using Microsoft Access, you can build queries, however, with Microsoft SQL Server you can create everything, from simple queries to large and complex business rules that reside on the server.

Again, I want to recommend Microsoft SQL Server, because it's much more powerful and fast when it gets to stored procedures. You have greater flexibility and a real programming language—Transact-SQL. All the examples in this section are built using stored procedures, however, you can recreate these on Microsoft Access very easily. The only exception is the next section's return parameters.

Stored Procedures

Stored procedures on Microsoft SQL Server have the following means of returning data:

◆ One or more result sets

◆ Explicit return value

◆ Output parameter

These are the return capabilities, but SQL Server also knows input parameters. They are handled in the same way as output parameters.

Return Values

Return values are the simplest and least powerful way of returning results from a stored procedure. They limit you to returning only integer values.

The example stored procedure in Listing 7.8 takes no parameters and returns the number of events in the database. It is used as a basis for the script page in Listing 7.9.

LISTING 7.8 - SCRIPT FOR THE STORED PROCEDURE

```
01. CREATE PROCEDURE sp_reteventcount AS
02.    declare @evcount int
03.    select @evcount=count(*) from Events
04.    return @evcount
05. GO
```

Use either ISQL/w or Enterprise Manager to add this stored procedure to the unlocking database. A third possibility is to use the SQL Query Builder form presented earlier in this chapter (it works quite well). Visual InterDev of course is another possibility.

On the CD

LISTING 7.9 - RETURN VALUES

```
01.  <HTML>
02.  <HEAD>
03.  <TITLE>Chapter 7: Prepared statements</TITLE>
04.  </HEAD>
05.  <BODY BGCOLOR=#ffffff>
06.  <!--#include file="adovbs.inc"-->
07.  <H1>How many Events</H1>
08.  <%
09.      Set Cmd = Server.CreateObject("ADODB.Command")
10.      Cmd.ActiveConnection = "dsn=unlocking;uid=sa;pwd=;"
11.      Cmd.CommandText = "{? = call sp_reteventcount}"
12.      Cmd.Parameters.Append Cmd.CreateParameter("numevents",
         ➥adInteger,adParamReturnValue)
13.      Cmd.Execute
14.      Response.Write "There are " & Cmd("numevents") & " in the database!"
15.  %>
16.  </BODY>
17.  </HTML>
```

Now, for the first time, the Command object is used. Notice that no Connection object is created. Instead, a string containing the database information is assigned to the ActiveConnection property of the Command object.

Line 11 contains the string that is used to call the stored procedure and tell the Command object how many parameters are used, and where they are to be inserted. Because there will be only a return parameter, only one question mark—the parameter placeholder—is inserted.

The next line is already a shortcut, so it needs to start reading that line from right to left. First, a Parameter object is created with the name "numevents", with the data type integer and direction set to indicate a return value. This newly created parameter is added to the Parameters collection. It contains the number of events found in the database after the call to Cmd.Execute in line 13.

Output Parameters

When you need to deal with more than one return value or want to return datatypes other than integers, you have to use output parameters.

The example stored procedure is a variation of the one in the section before. It simply returns the number of events as an output parameter.

LISTING 7.10 - SCRIPT FOR THE STORED PROCEDURE

```
01. CREATE PROCEDURE sp_eventcount
02.   @count int output
03. AS
04.   select @count=count(*) from Events
05. GO
```

The scripting code has only changed for the command text and the direction of the parameter that is supplied. See Listing 7.11.

LISTING 7.11 - OUTPUT PARAMETERS

On the CD

```
01. <HTML>
02. <HEAD>
03. <TITLE>Chapter 7: Prepared statements</TITLE>
04. </HEAD>
05. <BODY BGCOLOR=#ffffff>
06. <!--#include file="adovbs.inc"-->
07. <H1>How many Events</H1>
08. <%
09.    Set Cmd = Server.CreateObject("ADODB.Command")
10.    Cmd.ActiveConnection = "dsn=unlocking;uid=sa;pwd=;"
11.    Cmd.CommandText = "{call sp_eventcount(?)}"
12.    Set Param = Cmd.CreateParameter("numevents",adInteger,
       ➥adParamOutput)
13.    Cmd.Parameters.Append Param
14.    Cmd.Execute
15.    Response.Write "There are " & Cmd("numevents") & " in the database!"
16. %>
17. </BODY>
18. </HTML>
```

Notice that this time the newly created Parameter object was first assigned to a variable and then, on line 13, it was added to the Parameters collection.

Listing 7.12 is a nice example of mixing input and output parameters. It also shows that using database code can help you manage rules from a centralized location. It counts the number of events for a given day.

LISTING **7.12** - **INPUT AND OUTPUT PARAMETERS**

```
01. CREATE PROCEDURE sp_numofdailyevents
02.    @day varchar(255),
03.    @out int output
04. AS
05.    select @out=count(*) from Events where EVDate = convert(datetime,@day,4)
06. GO
```

The date conversion that takes place here is a fine example of centralized rule management. If you decide to change the date format for any reason, your changes need to be done only in this single stored procedure. All the pages calling it immediately use the new date format. In contrast when checking the validity of a date in every page before submitting to the database, you need to make date checking changes to multiple files.

The source code for the page that uses this stored procedure takes a different approach to filling the Parameters collection. See Listing 7.13.

On the CD

LISTING **7.13** - **INPUT AND OUTPUT PARAMETERS**

```
01. <HTML>
02. <HEAD>
03. <TITLE>Chapter 7: Prepared statements</TITLE>
04. </HEAD>
05. <BODY BGCOLOR=#ffffff>
06. <!--#include file="adovbs.inc"-->
07. <H1>Events for a specific day</H1>
08. <%
09. If Request.ServerVariables("Content_Length")>0 Then
10.     Set Conn = Server.CreateObject("ADODB.Connection")
11.     Conn.Open "unlocking","sa",""
12.     Set Cmd = Server.CreateObject("ADODB.Command")
13.     Cmd.ActiveConnection = Conn
14.     Cmd.CommandText = "{call sp_numofdailyevents(?,?)}"
15.     Cmd.Parameters.Refresh
16.     Cmd(0) = Request("evdate")
17.     Cmd(1) = 0
18.     Cmd.Execute
19.     Response.Write "There are " & Cmd(1) & " events for the "
        ➥& Request("evdate")
20. Else
21. %>
22. <FORM ACTION="<%=Request.ServerVariables("SCRIPT_NAME")%>" METHOD=POST>
```

```
23. <TABLE BORDER=0>
24. <tr><td>Events for date</td><td><INPUT TYPE=TEXT
    ➥NAME="evdate" VALUE="<%=Date()%>"></td></tr>
25. <tr><td><INPUT TYPE=SUBMIT VALUE="Submit"></td></tr>
26. </TABLE>
27. </FORM>
28. <% End If %>
29.
30. </BODY>
31. </HTML>
```

Notice that a `Connection` object is created and assigned to the `ActiveConnection` property of the `Command` object (line 13). The command text includes two question marks, one for the input parameter and one for the output parameter. Line 15's `Cmd.Parameters.Refresh` method call queries SQL Server to fill the `Parameters` collection. It now contains two `Parameter` objects—the first one is for the date, the second for the number of events. You don't have to specify either direction or data type information, because both are provided by the database management system.

 Tip   When you know what your parameters are in advance, avoid using the `Refresh` method of the `Parameters` collection. It takes a lot of time to retrieve the parameter information from the database you already have.

Returning Result Sets

One of the interesting things you can do with SQL Server is to build highly-sophisticated SQL queries that run on the server. You simply supply the parameters, and the result set is returned to you. You don't have to deal with building the SQL statement. An example of this is the stored procedure in Listing 7.14 that returns the events for a specific day—while simple, it conveys the concept.

LISTING 7.14 - RETURNING RESULT SETS

```
01. CREATE PROCEDURE sp_listdailyevents
02.    @day varchar(10)
03. AS
04.    declare @qday datetime
05.    select @qday = convert(datetime,@day,4)
06.    select * from Events where EVDate = @qday order by EVTime
07. GO
```

Listing 7.14 was optimized a little bit by accepting strings with only 10 characters maximum length and converting the textual date information first to a datetime value that is used in the query. The page in Listing 7.15 is basically the same as in Listing 7.13, except that it includes the code for displaying the result set in a table.

On the CD

LISTING 7.15 -WORKING WITH RESULT SETS RETURNED FROM STORED PROCEDURES

```
01. <HTML>
02. <HEAD>
03. <TITLE>Chapter 7: Prepared statements</TITLE>
04. </HEAD>
05. <BODY BGCOLOR=#ffffff>
06. <!--#include file="adovbs.inc"-->
07. <H1>Events for a specific day</H1>
08. <%
09. If Request.ServerVariables("Content_Length")>0 Then
10.     Set Conn = Server.CreateObject("ADODB.Connection")
11.     Conn.Open "unlocking","sa",""
12.     Set Cmd = Server.CreateObject("ADODB.Command")
13.     Cmd.ActiveConnection = Conn
14.     Cmd.CommandText = "{call sp_listdailyevents(?)}"
15.     Set param = Cmd.CreateParameter("day",adChar,adParamInput)
16.     Cmd(0) = Request("evdate")
17.     Set rsEvents = Cmd.Execute
18.     If rsEvents.EOF Then
19.       Response.Write "Sorry, no events in the database for the " &
          ➥Request("evdate")
20.     Else
21. %>
22. <H2><%=Request("evdate")%></H2>
23. <TABLE CELLSPACING=10 BORDER=1>
24. <TR><TH>Time</TH><TH>Location</TH><TH>Description</TH></TR>
25. <%
26.     While Not rsEvents.EOF
27.       Response.Write "<TD>" & rsEvents("EvTime").Value & "</TD>"
28.       Response.Write "<TD>" & rsEvents("Location") & "</TD>"
29.       Response.Write "<TD>" & rsEvents("Description") & "</TD></TR>"
30.       rsEvents.MoveNext
31.     Wend
32.     Response.Write "</TABLE>"
33.     End If
34. Else
35. %>
```

```
36. <FORM ACTION="<%=Request.ServerVariables("SCRIPT_NAME")%>" METHOD=POST>
37. <TABLE BORDER=0>
38. <tr><td>Events for date</td><td><INPUT TYPE=TEXT
    ➥NAME="evdate" VALUE="<%=Date()%>"></td></tr>
39. <tr><td><INPUT TYPE=SUBMIT VALUE="Submit"></td></tr>
40. </TABLE>
41. </FORM>
42. <%  End If %>
43.
44. </BODY>
45. </HTML>
```

The most important line is number 17, which contains the code for assigning the recordset that is returned from the stored procedure to a local variable. The rest of this listing is concerned with standard output of the recordset.

You can, of course, build much more sophisticated stored procedures that help you deploy your web site. However, I have covered all areas of accessing stored procedures with ADO. The next section describes how to create prepared statements from SQL statements at runtime.

Preparing Statements for Multiple Execution

When you need an SQL statement multiple times and only have a few parameters changing, pre-optimizing the statement at the first execution pays off in reduced execution time for the following requests. For Microsoft SQL Server, preparing a statement simply creates a temporary stored procedure in the tempdb database.

For this section's example, I rewrote last section's example to create a prepared statement instead of using a stored procedure from the beginning. See Listing 7.16.

On the CD

LISTING 7.16 - WORKING WITH RESULT SETS
RETURNED FROM PREPARED STATEMENTS

```
01. <HTML>
02. <HEAD>
03. <TITLE>Chapter 7: Prepared statements</TITLE>
04. </HEAD>
05. <BODY BGCOLOR=#ffffff>
06. <!--#include file="adovbs.inc"-->
07. <H1>Events for a specific day</H1>
08. <%
09. If Request.ServerVariables("Content_Length")>0 Then
```

continues

LISTING 7.16, CONTINUED

```
10.    If Not IsObject(Session("CmdExec")) Then
11.      Set Cmd = Server.CreateObject("ADODB.Command")
12.      Cmd.ActiveConnection = "dsn=unlocking;uid=sa;pwd=;"
13.      Cmd.CommandText = "SELECT * FROM Events WHERE
         ➥EVDate=CONVERT(datetime,?,4) ORDER BY EVTime"
14.      Cmd.Prepared = True
15.      Cmd.Parameters.Refresh
16.      Set Session("CmdExec") = Cmd
17.      Set Cmd = Nothing
18.    End If
19.
20.    Set Cmd = Session("CmdExec")
21.    Cmd(0) = Request("evdate")
22.    Set rsEvents = Cmd.Execute
23.    If rsEvents.EOF Then
24.      Response.Write "Sorry, no events in the database
         ➥ for the " & Request("evdate")
25.    Else
26. %>
27. <H2><%=Request("evdate")%></H2>
28. <TABLE CELLSPACING=10 BORDER=1>
29. <TR><TH>Time</TH><TH>Location</TH><TH>Description</TH></TR>
30. <%
31.    While Not rsEvents.EOF
32.      Response.Write "<TD>" & rsEvents("EvTime").Value & "</TD>"
33.      Response.Write "<TD>" & rsEvents("Location") & "</TD>"
34.      Response.Write "<TD>" & rsEvents("Description") & "</TD></TR>"
35.      rsEvents.MoveNext
36.    Wend
37.    Response.Write "</TABLE>"
38.    End If
39. Else
40. %>
41. <FORM ACTION="<%=Request.ServerVariables("SCRIPT_NAME")%>" METHOD=POST>
42. <TABLE BORDER=0>
43. <tr><td>Events for date</td><td><INPUT TYPE=TEXT
    ➥NAME="evdate" VALUE="<%=Date()%>"></td></tr>
44. <tr><td><INPUT TYPE=SUBMIT VALUE="Submit"></td></tr>
45. </TABLE>
46. </FORM>
```

```
47. <% End If %>
48.
49. </BODY>
50. </HTML>
```

The new code is in lines 10 to 18. It creates a new `Command` object when none exists for the current user and assigns the SQL statement that was contained in the stored procedure in the previous example as `CommandText`. The call to `Cmd.Parameters.Refresh` compiles the prepared statement and initializes the `Parameters` collection. From this point on, all code is identical to working with stored procedures.

Transactions

When you're building business applications today, you will already be familiar with transactions. Transactions are used to group together code statements that must either all be executed successfully or have no action performed at all. A good example of a transaction is an ATM, where you receive the money and the debit is processed by the system. While it would be wonderful to receive money without a debit, the other way round wouldn't be that funny. Both actions must take place or neither can take place at all. That is a transaction.

ADO supplies three methods in the `Connection` object for working with transactions: `BeginTrans`, `RollbackTrans`, and `CommitTrans`. Transactions are started with `BeginTrans` and successfully ended with `CommitTrans`. If you encounter an error condition, a call to `RollbackTrans` cancels all pending data changes made since the call to `BeginTrans`.

Listing 7.17 shows a nice transaction example. The page takes user input to add events to the database, but cancels the insert if the location is Sunnyvale. You could achieve the cancellation by simply testing this before doing any database insert, however, this is the situation. Yet another solution is to use an SQL Server trigger to cancel such inserts.

LISTING 7.17 - WORKING WITH TRANSACTIONS

On the CD

```
01. <HTML>
02. <HEAD>
03. <TITLE>Chapter 7: Adding Events with transactions</TITLE>
04. </HEAD>
05. <BODY BGCOLOR=#ffffff>
06. <!--#include file="adovbs.inc"-->
07. <H1>Add Events to the database</H1>
08. <%
```

continues

Listing 7.17, Continued

```
09. On Error Resume Next
10. If Request.ServerVariables("Content_Length")>0 Then
11.        ' no check for data validity done, the database
           ➥will return the errors...
12.        Set Conn = Server.CreateObject("ADODB.Connection")
13.        Set RS = Server.CreateObject("ADODB.RecordSet")
14.        Conn.Open "unlocking","sa",""
15.        Conn.BeginTrans
16.        RS.Open "Events", Conn , adOpenKeyset, adLockOptimistic
17.        RS.AddNew
18.        RS("EVDate") = Request("evdate")
19.        RS("EVTime") = Request("evtime")
20.        If Request("evlocation") = "Sunnyvale" Then Conn.RollbackTrans
21.        RS("Location") = Request("evlocation")
22.        RS("Description") = Request("desc")
23.        RS.Update
24.        Conn.CommitTrans
25.        Response.Write "Thank you for adding an event!"
26. Else
27. %>
28. <FORM ACTION="<%=Request.ServerVariables("SCRIPT_NAME")%>" METHOD=POST>
29. <TABLE BORDER=0>
30. <tr><td>Date</td><td><INPUT TYPE=TEXT NAME="evdate"
    ➥VALUE="<%=Date()%>"></td></tr>
31. <tr><td>Time</td><td><INPUT TYPE=TEXT NAME="evtime"
    ➥VALUE="20:00"></td></tr>
32. <tr><td>Location</td><td><INPUT TYPE=TEXT
    ➥NAME="evlocation"></td></tr>
33. <tr><td>Description</td><td><TEXTAREA NAME="desc"
    ➥COLS=80 ROWS=15></TEXTAREA></td></tr>
34. <tr><td><INPUT TYPE=SUBMIT VALUE="Submit"></td></tr>
35. </TABLE>
36. </FORM>
37. <% End If %>
38.
39. </BODY>
40. </HTML>
```

Lines 15 to 24 enclose the transaction I have opened. The check for Sunnyvale that terminates the transaction is on line 20. Because the Update statement on line 23 would cause an error when the transaction is canceled, I have included an On Error

`Resume Next` statement to skip over the error. Under normal circumstances, you should include error handling code.

Transactions are especially necessary for Active Server Pages, because the execution of these can be interrupted at any point the user chooses. Whenever you perform longer database insertions, use transactions!

ADO Objects Reference

The last sections provided hands-on experience for working with ActiveX Data Objects. This section is intended as your reference guide for all methods and properties of the ADO objects, and shows you how to use them in context.

As a helping guide, I have provided a model in Figure 7.8 for how the ADO objects interact and which collections they contain.

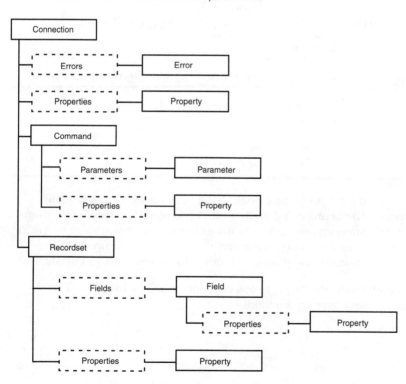

Figure 7.8

ADO Objects with their respective collections. Dashed boxes indicate collections.

Notice that the `Properties` collection is part of the three main objects; `Connection`, `Command`, and `Recordset`, and the `Field` object. Only the three main objects can be created directly with calls to `Server.CreateObject`. The `Error`, `Property`, `Field`, and

Parameter objects are accessed with the Errors, Properties, Fields and Parameters collections. As mentioned earlier in this chapter, the Errors collection may not be supported by every data provider, and the Command object may not be available for some providers.

Properties Collection

Because the Properties collection is part of each of the three main objects (as well as the Field object), its discussion goes first. The Property objects contained in the collection correspond to a characteristic of the ADO object that they describe that is specific to the provider.

The Properties collection itself doesn't contain any functionality other than iterating over and refreshing its contents. See Table 7.2.

TABLE 7.2
Methods and Properties of the Properties Collection

Name	Description
Count property	Returns the number of items in this collection
Item property	Returns the specified member of this collection either by name or ordinal
Refresh method	Requests updated information from the provider. Updates the objects in the collection

More interesting is the Property object itself. It contains the information about capabilities specific to the object it describes—for example, the capabilities a given Recordset object is offering; bookmarks, or moves permitted or capable of re-syncing. You can use this information to degrade gracefully when a specific provider doesn't support a given functionality using another method to achieve what you need.

The properties offered by the Property object are described in Table 7.3. The Property object doesn't have any methods.

TABLE 7.3
Properties of the Property Object

Name	Description
Attributes	Indicates the characteristics of the property specific to the provider. Its value can be a sum of any one or more of the XactAttributeEnum values. See the paragraph following this table for more information on these.
Name	String identifying the property
Type	Specifies the property data type
Value	Returns the value of the property

Each object that can be described with Property objects has specific values of the XactAttributeEnum enumeration. A complete reference of these values can be found in the ADO SDK documentation. This documentation is accessible via the ActiveX Server Roadmap. Look up the Attributes property.

To get a feeling for what you can do with the Properties collection, dump all properties in this collection and take a look at it. That is exactly the purpose of the example in Listing 7.18.

LISTING 7.18 - DUMPING PROPERTIES FOR CONNECTION AND RECORDSET OBJECT

On the
CD

```
01. <HTML>
02. <HEAD>
03. <TITLE>Chapter 7: ADO Properties</TITLE>
04. </HEAD>
05. <BODY BGCOLOR=#ffffff>
06. <!--#include file="adovbs.inc"-->
07. <H1>ADO Properties</H1>
08.
09. <H2>Connection properties</H2>
10. <TABLE BORDER=1><TR><TH>Property</TH><TH>Value</TH></TR>
11. <%
12.     Set Conn = Server.CreateObject("ADODB.Connection")
13.     Conn.Open "unlocking","sa",""
14.     For Each prop in Conn.Properties
15.       Response.Write "<TR><TD>" & prop.Name & "</TD><TD>"
```

continues

LISTING **7.18**, CONTINUED

```
16.     If VarType(prop) = vbBoolean Then
17.        Response.Write CStr(CBool(prop))
18.     Else
19.        Response.Write CStr(prop)
20.     End If
21.     Response.Write "</TR>"
22.   Next
23. %>
24. </TABLE>
25.
26. <H2>Recordset properties</H2>
27. <TABLE BORDER=1><TR><TH>Property</TH><TH>Value</TH></TR>
28. <%
29.   Set rs = Conn.Execute("Select * from Events order by EVDate,EVTime")
30.   For Each prop In rs.Properties
31.      Response.Write "<TR><TD>" & prop.Name & "</TD><TD>"
32.      If VarType(prop) = vbBoolean Then
33.         Response.Write CStr(CBool(prop))
34.      Else
35.         Response.Write CStr(prop)
36.      End If
37.      Response.Write "</TR>"
38.   Next
39. %>
40. </TABLE>
41. <%
42. Set rs = Nothing
43. Set Conn = Nothing
44. %>
45.
46. </BODY>
47. </HTML>
```

This listing contains two for…each loops for dumping the properties of the Connection
and Recordset objects. If you had created the Recordset object using a Command object
with a different CursorType, you would get slightly different results. You can use parts
of this listing to experiment with properties of the Field and Command objects.

Connection Object

The Connection object contains methods and properties in addition to the two collections, Properties and Errors. The Properties collection has already been discussed in the previous section, so it won't be repeated here.

Errors Collection

The Errors collection is optional and is only available from specific data providers, like SQL Server. The collection is especially useful when the execution of a statement or a method invocation returns more than one error. Please be aware that providers that don't support the Errors collection simply raise an error with COM mechanisms.

The Errors collection supports functionality for iterating and clearing the collection.

TABLE 7.4
Methods and Properties of the Errors Collection

Name	Description
Clear method	Removes all Error objects from the collection. Use this method when you have finished the error handling.
Count property	Returns the number of Error objects currently available in the collection
Item property	Returns a specific Error object

More interesting, of course, are the properties of the Error objects that are contained in the collection. They contain error-specific information that can be used to inform the users about the error condition. See Table 7.5 for a list of the properties.

TABLE 7.5
Properties of the Error Object

Name	Description
Description	A descriptive string for the Error that has occurred. Use this to report the error.
HelpContext	Indicates the help topic associated with the error
HelpFile	Indicates the help file associated with the error

continues

TABLE 7.5, CONTINUED
Properties of the Error Object

Name	Description
NativeError	Returns the provider-specific error code for the Error object.
Number	Returns the number to uniquely identify the Error object.
Source	Returns the name of the object or application that caused the error.
SQLState	Returns the SQL state for the Error object.

When you're only dealing with Web pages, the HelpContext and HelpFile properties might seem pretty useless. However, when you have to debug your scripts and need to find out more about an error, they come in pretty handy. The rest of the properties can be used to obtain more information about the error that occurred.

The example in Listing 7.19 provokes an error condition and returns the error description to the user, depending on whether the Errors collection is supported or the error is raised with COM.

On the CD

LISTING 7.19 - DUMPING ERRORS

```
01. <HTML>
02. <HEAD>
03. <TITLE>Chapter 7: Errors collection</TITLE>
04. </HEAD>
05. <BODY BGCOLOR=#ffffff>
06. <!--#include file="adovbs.inc"-->
07.
08. <H1>Errors Collection</H1>
09.
10. <%
11.     On Error Resume Next
12.     Set Conn = Server.CreateObject("ADODB.Connection")
13.     Conn.Open "unlocking","sa",""
14.     Set rsQuery = Conn.Execute("select a dummy from the database")
15.
16.     If Not IsObject(rsQuery) Then
17.       Response.Write "An error has occurred executing your statement:<P>"
18.       If Err.Number > 0 Then
19.         Response.Write Err.Description
20.       Else
21. %>
22. <TABLE BORDER=1><TR><TH>Description</TH>
```

```
➡<TH>NativeError</TH><TH>SQLState</TH></TR>
23. <%
24.      For Each dbError In Conn.Errors
25.          Response.Write "<TR><TD>" & dbError.Description & "</TD>"
26.          Response.Write "<TD>" & CStr(dbError.NativeError) & "</TD>"
27.          Response.Write "<TD>" & dbError.SQLState & "</TD></TR>"
28.      Next
29.      Conn.Errors.Clear
30.      Response.Write "</TABLE>"
31.    End If
32.  End If
33. %>
34.
35. </BODY>
36. </HTML>
```

Notice that this code works with all databases, whether they are supporting the `Errors` collection or not.

Methods of the Connection Object

With the exception of a single method, the methods supported by the `Connection` object have already appeared in the examples in this chapter. The entire list of methods is provided in Table 7.6. They are grouped by functionality and not listed by name.

TABLE 7.6
Methods of the Connection Object

Name	Description
Open	Establishes a connection to the data source that is specified
Close	Closes the Connection to the data source. A call to Set ConnObj = Nothing closes the connection as well.
Execute	Executes the specified SQL statement
BeginTrans	Begins a new transaction. If the provider supports nested transactions, the nesting level is returned.
CommitTrans	Commits a transaction and saves any changes made during this transaction
RollbackTrans	Cancels all changes made during the current transaction. Ends the current transaction.

The most typical cases of how to use these methods were included in the examples. The Execute method, however, has another interesting use:

```
Set rs = Conn.Execute(CommandText, RecordsAffected, Options)
```

CommandText is simply an SQL statement and the only mandatory argument to this method. This is how it was used in the examples. The two optional arguments can be used to retrieve the number of records that have been affected and determine what type of command is to be executed. Valid values for the Options parameter are adCmdText, adCmdTable, adCmdStoredProc, or adCmdUnknown, which is the default.

The example in Listing 7.20 makes use of the optional parameters to return the number of events deleted. The command that is executed, however, doesn't return a recordset, so the parentheses have to be omitted for the method invocation.

On the CD

LISTING 7.20 - USING THE OPTIONAL PARAMETER RECORDSAFFECTED TO RETURN THE NUMBER OF EVENTS DELETED FROM THE DATABASE

```
01. <HTML>
02. <HEAD>
03. <TITLE>Chapter 7: Execute optional parameters</TITLE>
04. </HEAD>
05. <BODY BGCOLOR=#ffffff>
06. <!--#include file="adovbs.inc"-->
07.
08. <H1>Execute optional parameters</H1>
09.
10. <%
11. Set Conn = Server.CreateObject("ADODB.Connection")
12. Conn.Open "unlocking","sa",""
13. Conn.Execute "delete from Events where Location='test'",
    ➥numrecords,adCmdText
14. %>
15.
16. Deleted <%=numrecords%>  entries in the Events table.
17. <%
18. Conn.Close
19. %>
20.
21. </BODY>
22. </HTML>
```

Properties of the `Connection` Object

The properties supplied by the `Connection` object can be used to set or retrieve connection information. Table 7.7 contains the complete reference of the properties.

TABLE 7.7
Properties of the `Connection` Object

Name	Description
`Attributes`	Set or get one or more characteristics of the connection. The attributes that can be set control the behavior of transactions.
`CommandTimeout`	Indicates the amount of time a command may take to execute before it's abandoned
`ConnectionString`	The connection string that's used to connect to the database
`ConnectionTimeout`	Indicates the amount of time it may take to establish a connection before the attempt is terminated
`DefaultDatabase`	Indicates the default database
`IsolationLevel`	Indicates the isolation level. Used in conjunction with transactions.
`Mode`	Indicates the permissions for modifying data
`Provider`	The name of the data provider
`Version`	Returns the version number of ADO

The examples in this chapter have so far used no properties. All connection information was specified in the `Open` method. When you need more control over `timeout` values, data modification permissions, and transactions, you need to deal with these properties.

Command Object

The `Command` object got a lot of attention in the section about prepared statements. You use the `Command` object when dealing with complex and/or recurring queries or stored procedures that may take any number of arguments. The arguments are supplied via the `Parameters` collection, which is the second collection besides the `Properties` collection that's contained in all major objects.

Parameters Collection

The collection is used to administer the Parameter objects that are needed to specify or retrieve the parameters for the queries or stored procedures. It contains the following methods and properties, as exhibited in Table 7.8.

TABLE 7.8
Methods and Properties of the Parameters Collection

Name	Description
Append method	Appends a Parameter object to the collection. You have to create the Parameter prior to adding it.
Count property	Returns the number of Parameter objects in this collection
Delete method	Deletes the specified Parameter object from the collection. Access is through index or name.
Item property	Returns the specified Parameter object
Refresh method	Updates the collection by querying the provider about the parameters this Command object takes. Time intensive.

You need to provide exactly the same number of Parameter objects in this collection as there are parameter placeholders in the Command object's command string.

The Parameter object itself is then used to specify data type, direction, and value of the parameter. With the exception of one method, there are only properties for the Parameter object.

TABLE 7.9
Properties of the Parameter Object

Name	Description
Attributes	Set or get one or more characteristics of the parameter. Use to indicate nullability, long data, or signed values.
Direction	Indicates return values, input, output, and input/output parameters. See the next section, "Methods," for a list of possible values.
Name	Indicates the name of the parameter
NumericScale	Sets or returns the number of decimal places a numeric value is resolved to

Name	Description
Precision	Sets or returns the number of digits to represent the value
Size	Indicates the maximum size of values in the `Parameter` object in bytes or characters
Type	Indicates the operational data type that this `Parameter` object is assigned to. The next section contains a list of the most common types. Please refer to the ADO SDK documentation for a complete reference of possible types.
Value	Sets or returns the value of the `Parameter` object

You can set the `Name`, `Attributes`, `Direction`, `Size`, and `Value` properties during the method call to `CmdObj.CreateParameter` or simply create an uninitialized object with this method and then set the properties in subsequent code.

The only method that is available for the `Parameter` object is `AppendChunk`, which is used to add large text or binary data. The syntax for this method is as follows:

```
Param.AppendChunk Data
```

Methods

There are only two methods supplied by the `Command` object, but they are very powerful ones. They are used to create `Parameter` objects and execute the command itself.

TABLE 7.10
Methods of the Command Object

Name	Description
CreateParameter	Creates a new `Parameter` object with the specified properties
Execute	Executes the command that you have associated with this `Command` object. Can be any SQL statement, table, or stored procedure.

The complete syntax for the `CreateParameter` method is as follows:

```
Set Param = Cmd.CreateParameter(Name, Type, Direction, Size, Value)
```

Only the `Name` parameter is mandatory—all others may be omitted. Use the `Type` parameter to specify the data type for Value, and Direction to indicate whether the parameter is a return value, input or output parameter, or both. Table 7.11 contains the complete list of Direction values, and Table 7.12 shows a list of the most common values for the Type parameter.

TABLE 7.11
List of Possible Direction Values

Name	Description
adParamInput	Indicates an input parameter. This is the default.
adParamOutput	Indicates an output parameter
adParamInputOutput	Indicates a parameter for input and output
adParamReturnValue	Indicates a return value from a stored procedure

TABLE 7.12
Most Common Values for the Type Parameter

Name	Description
adBoolean	A Boolean value
adChar	A fixed length string
adCurrency	A currency value
adDate	A date value
adInteger	An integer value
adNumeric	A numeric value
adVarBinary	A binary value
adVarChar	A variable length string

For a complete reference of Type values please refer to the ADO SDK documentation that is part of Active Server Pages documentation.

Properties

The Command object's properties are used to set or retrieve parameters of the active connection and command properties. Table 7.13 provides a list of all properties.

TABLE 7.13
Properties of the Command Object

Name	Description
ActiveConnection	Indicates the Connection object to which the Command object belongs. Set it with either a connection string or a Connection object.
CommandText	Contains the command text that is to be executed by the data provider
CommandTimeout	Indicates the amount of time the command is allowed to run before it is abandoned. Overrides the global value set in the Connection object. If set to zero, it never times out.
CommandType	Indicates the type of the current command. See Table 7.14 for a complete reference.
Prepared	Indicates whether the command is to be prepared and stored by the data provider for subsequent use on its first execution

You can optimize the evaluation of the CommandText property by the data provider by specifying the CommandType. A complete list of values is presented in Table 7.14.

TABLE 7.14
Values for CommandType

Name	Description
adCmdTable	Indicates that CommandText is a table
adCmdText	Indicates that CommandText is an SQL statement
adCmdStoredProc	Indicates that CommandText references a stored procedure
adCmdUnknown	Default. Indicates that the data provider should evaluate the type.

Recordset Object

Whenever you're dealing with data, you're dealing with the Recordset object. This object represents the records that are returned from invocations of the Execute method of either the Connection or Command object, or by calls to its own Open method. You use it to read, change, add, or delete data from a database.

To access the columns in a resultset, you use the `Field` objects that are grouped in the Fields collection.

Fields Collection

The `Fields` collection, like all other collections, only supplies a small functionality. The method and properties are listed in Table 7.15.

TABLE 7.15
Method and Properties for the `Fields` Collection

Name	Description
Count property	Returns the number of `Field` objects in this collection
Item property	Returns a specific `Field` object either by name or by ordinal number
Refresh method	Updates the `Fields` collection

You can use the collection to iterate over all columns (`Field` objects) in a given row of a recordset. If you want to retrieve data, you need to access it with the `Field` object.

The `Field` object supplies ten properties. The two methods are for appending and retrieving large text or binary data. The properties are listed in Table 7.16, the methods in Table 7.17.

TABLE 7.16
Properties of the `Field` Object

Name	Description
ActualSize	Indicates the actual size of the data stored in this field
Attributes	Specifies characteristics for this field
DefinedSize	Indicates the size of data the field can hold. It may be higher than `ActualSize`.
Name	Returns the name of the field

Name	Description
NumericScale	Indicates the numeric scale
OriginalValue	Contains the field value that existed before changes were made
Precision	Indicates the degree of precision for numeric fields
Type	Indicates the data type of the field. Please refer to the section "Properties of the Command Object" for the values.
UnderlyingValue	Returns the current value from the database. Includes changes made since you have opened your recordset.
Value	Indicates the value that is assigned to this field

If you have to deal with large text or binary data, you have to use the following two methods to insert it into or retrieve it from the database:

TABLE 7.17
Methods of the Field Object

Name	Description
AppendChunk	Appends large text or binary data to the field
GetChunk	Reads all or a portion of large text or binary data from a field

You could be tempted to store images in the database and use the GetChunk method to retrieve, and the BinaryWrite method to send them to the client. For speed reasons (needless traffic between the servers to send the image from the database server to the web server first before it is sent from there to the user), this isn't a very good idea. Use the database to store URLs to the images instead.

Methods

The methods that are supported by the Recordset object can be used to add, update, and delete data as well as page through the result set. Methods for cloning result sets, requerying, and re-syncing also are supported.

TABLE 7.18
Methods of the Recordset Object

Name	Description
AddNew	Adds a new row to the recordset. The recordset must be updateable to support this functionality.
CancelBatch	Cancels a pending batch update
CancelUpdate	Cancels a pending update operation prior to a call to the Update method
Clone	Creates a clone of the current recordset
Close	Closes the current recordset
Delete	Deletes the current row from the recordset
GetRows	Retrieves multiple rows at once into an array. You can specify the number of records to retrieve, the start row, and which fields to retrieve.
Move	Moves the position of the current record
MoveFirst	Moves to the first row in the result set
MoveLast	Moves to the last row in the result set
MoveNext	Moves to the next row in the result set. Sets the EOF property to True when the last row is reached.
MovePrevious	Moves to the previous record. Sets the property BOF to True when the first row of the result set is reached.
NextRecordset	Returns the next recordset by advancing in a series of commands separated by semicolons. The old recordset is cleared first.
Open	Opens a cursor. Cursors are discussed in more detail in the paragraphs following this table.
Requery	Updates the data in the recordset by re-executing the command on which the recordset is based
Resync	Updates the data in the recordset by querying for new values for the existing recordset

Name	Description
Supports	Returns the capabilities of the recordset. Use it to determine whether it is updateable, supports bookmarks, and more.
Update	Saves the changes made to the current row into the database
UpdateBatch	Saves all changes made during a batch update into the database

You can use the Supports method to determine the capabilities of a recordset you have opened. The most powerful and flexible way of opening a recordset is to use the Open method of the Recordset object in conjunction with a Command object to open a cursor. You are presented with four possible types of cursors you can create:

◆ **Static cursor:** Retrieves a static copy of a set of records you can use. Changes, additions, or deletions made by other users aren't visible to you.

◆ **Forward-only cursor:** Basically the same as the static cursor, but you can scroll only forward through the result set. This is the default cursor.

◆ **Dynamic cursor:** Changes, additions, and deletions made by other users are visible. You can move in any direction in the result set. Bookmarks are only available if the data provider supports them.

◆ **Keyset cursor:** As with the dynamic cursor, changes made by other users are visible. However, additions made by others are not visible and records deleted by others also are inaccessible.

The example presented in Listing 7.21 executes the same command four times using the different cursor types. The Supports method is used to view the possible record operations for each of the cursors.

LISTING 7.21 - POSSIBLE RECORD OPERATIONS
FOR THE DIFFERENT CURSOR TYPES

On the
CD

```
01. <HTML>
02. <HEAD>
03. <TITLE>Chapter 7: Different Cursortypes</TITLE>
04. </HEAD>
05. <BODY BGCOLOR=#ffffff>
06. <!--#include file="adovbs.inc"-->
07. <H1>Different Cursortypes</H1>
08. <%
```

continues

LISTING 7.21, CONTINUED

```
09.    Set Cmd = Server.CreateObject("ADODB.Command")
10.    Set rsEvents = Server.CreateObject("ADODB.Recordset")
11.    Cmd.Prepared = True
12.    Cmd.ActiveConnection = "dsn=unlocking;uid=sa;pwd=;"
13.    Cmd.CommandText = "SELECT * FROM Events ORDER BY EVDate,EVTime"
14.
15.    PrintCursorType rsEvents, Cmd, adOpenStatic, "Static Cursor"
16.    PrintCursorType rsEvents, Cmd, adOpenForwardOnly, "Forward-only Cursor"
17.    PrintCursorType rsEvents, Cmd, adOpenDynamic, "Dynamic Cursor"
18.    PrintCursorType rsEvents, Cmd, adOpenKeyset, "Keyset Cursor"
19. %>
20.
21. <SCRIPT  RUNAT=SERVER LANGUAGE=VBSCRIPT>
22. Sub PrintCursorType(rs,Cmd,nType,strType)
23.    rs.CursorType = nType
24.    rs.Open Cmd
25.    Response.Write "<H2>" & strType & "</H2>"
26.    PrintSupports rs
27.    rs.Close
28. End Sub
29.
30. Sub PrintSupports(rs)
31.    Response.Write "<TABLE BORDER=1><TR><TH>CursorOption</TH><TH>Supported
       ➥</TH></TR>"
32.    Response.Write "<TR><TD>AddNew</TD><TD>"
33.    Response.Write CStr(CBool(rs.Supports(adAddNew))) & "</TD></TR>"
34.    Response.Write "<TR><TD>ApproxPosition</TD><TD>"
35.    Response.Write CStr(CBool(rs.Supports(adApproxPosition))) & "</TD></TR>"
36.    Response.Write "<TR><TD>Bookmark</TD><TD>"
37.    Response.Write CStr(CBool(rs.Supports(adBookmark))) & "</TD></TR>"
38.    Response.Write "<TR><TD>Delete</TD><TD>"
39.    Response.Write CStr(CBool(rs.Supports(adDelete))) & "</TD></TR>"
40.    Response.Write "<TR><TD>HoldRecords</TD><TD>"
41.    Response.Write CStr(CBool(rs.Supports(adHoldRecords))) & "</TD></TR>"
42.    Response.Write "<TR><TD>MovePrevious</TD><TD>"
43.    Response.Write CStr(CBool(rs.Supports(adMovePrevious))) & "</TD></TR>"
44.    Response.Write "<TR><TD>Resync</TD><TD>"
45.    Response.Write CStr(CBool(rs.Supports(adResync))) & "</TD></TR>"
46.    Response.Write "<TR><TD>Update</TD><TD>"
47.    Response.Write CStr(CBool(rs.Supports(adUpdate))) & "</TD></TR>"
48.    Response.Write "<TR><TD>UpdateBatch</TD><TD>"
```

```
49.    Response.Write CStr(CBool(rs.Supports(adUpdateBatch))) & "</TD></TR>"
50.    Response.Write "</TABLE>"
51. End Sub
52. </SCRIPT>
53.
54. </BODY>
55. </HTML>
```

This example uses two subroutines to do the output for the different cursor types. Using subroutines saves you from duplicating code. The PrintCursorType subroutine takes four parameters, a recordset, a command, the cursor type, and the text that will be displayed as a header for the capabilities table. This subroutine calls PrintSupports to create the table with the supported operations for this cursor.

Properties

The properties that are provided by the Recordset object have appeared with the examples in the previous sections. Mostly, these were properties for finding or setting the position in the result set. The entire reference to all properties is in Table 7.19.

TABLE 7.19
Properties of the Recordset Object

Name	Description
AbsolutePage	Specifies the page to which you move the current record. The number of records per page is determined by the PageSize property.
AbsolutePosition	Moves to the record specified by the ordinal position.
ActiveConnection	Indicates to which connection the Recordsetobject currently belongs.
BOF	Returns True if the current record is the first in the result set.
Bookmark	Returns a bookmark that identifies the current record or sets the current record to the one identified by the bookmark.
CacheSize	Indicates the number of rows to be cached locally.
CursorType	Indicates the type of cursor for the current Recordset object. See the previous section for a list of possible cursor types.

continues

TABLE 7.19, CONTINUED
Properties of the Recordset Object

Name	Description
EditMode	Indicates the editing status for the row. Valid values are adEditNone, adEditInProgress, adEditAdd.
EOF	Returns False if the current record is the last in the result set.
Filter	Selectively screens out records in a Recordset object.
LockType	Indicates the locking strategy that is used by the data provider during record editing
MaxRecords	Indicates the maximum number of rows to return from a query
PageCount	Indicates the number of pages a recordset contains
PageSize	Indicates the number of rows that constitute a single page
RecordCount	Returns the number of records in a recordset
Source	Sets a string value or a Command object for the source of the recordset. Returns only string values.
Status	Returns the status of the current record. Please refer to the ADO SDK documentation for a complete reference of status codes.

The Filter property is very powerful. With it, you can selectively screen out records of the current recordset. This screening can be achieved by using three different methods:

♦ **Array of bookmarks:** Set the Filter property to an array of unique book-marks. These bookmarks must point to records in this Recordset object. All other records will be screened out.

♦ **Criteria string:** Set the Filter property to one or more Fieldname-Operator-Value clauses concatenated by "AND". Example is "Location='Seattle' AND Location='Mt. McKinley'". Valid operators are <, >, <=, >=, =, <>, and LIKE. Setting the Filter property to an empty string removes the filtering.

♦ **A FilterEnumGroup constant:** Set the filter to a constant that enables you to filter records being affected by different changes. Setting the Filter property to the adFilterNone constant removes the current filter. Using the adFilterPendingRecords constant views records that have been changed but not yet sent to the server. If you want to view records that were affected by the last call to either Delete, Resync, CancelBatch or UpdateBatch, use the adFilterAffectedRecords constant. The last constant, adFilterFetchedRecords, views the results of the last fetch from the database.

Immediately after an assignment to the Filter property, the filtering is applied to the current recordset.

Optimizing Performance

By now it should be obvious that I really prefer dedicated database management systems over file-based databases like Microsoft Access. There are good reasons for using dedicated database servers:

◆ They enable concurrent access to the database by multiple users

◆ They are easier to scale when more performance is needed

◆ They are faster and more powerful than other solutions

The biggest drawback to using Microsoft Access as a database for your web server is that only one operation can be performed at a time. Dedicated database systems are more powerful because multiple requests can be handled at the same time. So if you plan to deploy a medium to heavy-load server, you need to use a dedicated database server. If the server is expected to have only very little load, an Access database will be sufficient, as well.

When building a real web application, many different pages access the database. The examples in this chapter opened a new connection to the database for each request—with the one exception of the prepared statement that was stored as a Session property.

You may think it's a good idea to store a Connection object for each user as a Session property so that the database connection needs to be established only once. Unfortunately, sessions live longer than the user is really connected to your server, wasting memory and a connection. Imagine a server with hundreds of requests per minute. You would run out of connections shortly.

So there must be another way of achieving the goal of speedy database access for everyone while preserving server resources. The solution is connection pooling. This feature was introduced with ODBC 3.0 and enables multiple users to share a connection. Whenever a connection is needed, the connection pool is examined for idle connections. If there is one, the idle connection is used for this request, otherwise, a new connection is established. When the connection is no longer used, it is returned to the pool. If a given connection in the pool isn't reused within a specified time, it's closed.

Connection pooling is disabled by default for Active Server Pages. If you want to take advantage of connection pooling, open the Registry key HKEY_LOCAL_MACHINE\SYSTEM\CurrentControlSet\Services\W3SVC\Parameters and set the entry StartConnectionPool to 1. You have to restart the IIS web service for the change to take effect.

The next question is, of course, how to put this connection pooling to work. Implement the following easy steps to incorporate connection pooling into your web application:

1. Create a property in the Session object that will take the connection string. Place this code in the Session_OnStart event handler in global.asa:

```
Session("DbConn") = "dsn=unlocking;uid=sa;pwd="
```

2. On every page that needs access to this database, insert the following code before any other database access code:

```
Set Conn = Server.CreateObject("ADODB.Connection")
Conn.Open Session("DbConn")
```

3. A connection is taken from the pool and you can start working with your database code.

4. At the end of the page, insert the following line of code:

```
Conn.Close
```

It isn't mandatory that you store the connection string in the Session object, but when you need to change the string, the changes are promoted automatically to all pages doing database access. With this approach, connections can be shared across multiple user sessions. This solution reduces the time needed to access the database while preserving server resources.

 If you're using the connection pooling feature with Microsoft Access, you must have the NT 4.0 Service Pack 2 or later installed or your system may crash when the IIS service is shut down.

Summary

This chapter dealt with the most important feature for creating really "active" pages—database access. You should now have a firm understanding of what ADO is and how you can use it in your own pages. The architecture of ADO provides fast and powerful access to any ODBC datasource without much overhead through its object model.

This chapter provided a lot of downsized real world examples of pages you can reuse for your projects. Because not all cases fit in the examples, the references section of this chapter enables you to look up more information on every method and property of the ADO objects. The last section was dedicated to optimizing performance, which is extremely critical for high-traffic web sites.

CHAPTER 8

Converting IDC Applications to Active Server Pages

I n the early days of Internet Information Server—only about a year ago now—programmers already had the ability to publish data from databases in a very convenient way. The Internet Database Connector (IDC) enables you to issue SQL statements against any ODBC datasource and provides a powerful mechanism to merge the results returned from the queries with a pre-created template.

Many of us have created great sites by using the IDC mechanism. However, to harness the additional power that comes with Active Server Pages, you have to move to the new environment. You have to convert all of the old source code from IDC to the new platform: Active Server Pages and ActiveX Data Objects.

You can perform this move by recoding every single page using ASP syntax or by using a tool provided by IntraActive Software: the IDC2ASP conversion tool. It automatically generates ASP code based on your IDC/HTX files—you only have to fine-tune the code that was generated. To prove how easy and fast this conversion can be, this chapter showcases a sample IDC application that is converted to the new ASP platform using the IDC2ASP tool. The chapter then goes into how to fine-tune the resulting code. This chapter covers the following topics:

◆ Creating an IDC application to convert to ASP

◆ Converting IDC applications to ASP using the IDC2ASP tool

◆ Fine-tuning the tool-generated ASP code

◆ Adapting the tool to your needs

A Sample IDC Application

When I began working with a beta of Internet Information Server 1.0, I was fascinated by how easy it was to bring databases to the Internet by using the Internet Database Connector. I created many small applications before I moved on to larger projects in which the IDC played a major role.

To show how to convert IDC applications to ASP, I dug out an example from that time that is still useful today—a list of favorite URLs to which other users can submit their own favorites. The list was monitored by an administrator who had to validate and check submitted URLs before they were visible to all users. I decided to showcase this IDC application because it used features of IDC that create the need to fine-tune the ASP code generated by the IDC2ASP conversion tool. I'll explicitly point to these features in the listings of the IDC application in this section.

Before discussing the listings, a look at the design of this application is necessary. The next section explains which pages are needed to implement the URL Favorites example and how they interact with each other.

Designing the Application

Figure 8.1 contains a diagram that illustrates the overall design and shows the interconnections of the pages in this application.

Figure 8.1

Overview of the IDC application.

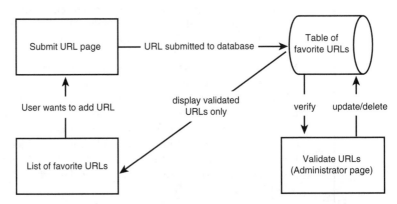

There are only three pages necessary for implementing all the functionality of the URL Favorites application. The main page that's first presented to the users is the list of all favorite URLs that have been submitted and validated (lower-left corner). If the user wants to add his or her favorite URLs, there's a separate page that contains a form for submitting the new URL to the database. However, at this time, the URL won't be visible in the favorite list because the administrator hasn't validated it yet. For this purpose there is a separate page where the administrator can test the link and modify the description for this URL. If the URL is accepted, it's updated in the database and made available to all users. If the URL is rejected, it's deleted from the database in this page as well.

Implementation

I've mentionedthe word database a lot. Actually, there's only one single table needed to implement the entire application (see Table 8.1 for its definition).

TABLE 8.1
Table Definition for the tFavURL Table

Column name	Datatype	Description
URL	varchar(255)	Primary key index. An URL can be contained in the list only once.
Description	text	A descriptive text about what this URL is pointing to.
Contributor	varchar(128)	The name or email address of the contributor.
Validated	bit	A Boolean value indicating whether this URL has already been validated by the Administrator.

For this example, I use SQL Server specific tricks only in a single place, so creating the table in any database system will do. Listing 8.1 contains the script to generate this table in SQL Server.

LISTING 8.1 - SQL SCRIPT USED TO GENERATE THE tFavURL TABLE

```
01. CREATE TABLE dbo.tFavURL (
02.      URL varchar (255) NOT NULL ,
03.      Description text NULL ,
04.      Contributor varchar (128) NOT NULL CONSTRAINT
         ➥DF_FavURL_Contributor DEFAULT ('nobody'),
05.      Validated bit NOT NULL CONSTRAINT
         ➥DF_FavURL_Validated DEFAULT (0),
06.      CONSTRAINT PK_tFavURLPrimKey PRIMARY KEY NONCLUSTERED
07.      (
08.            URL
09.      )
10. )
```

Before you can access a database or its tables from within an IDC application, you need to create an ODBC datasource the same way you would for Active Server Pages. The IDC scripts presented in this section use the unlocking datasource.

Cross Reference

For more information about creating ODBC datasources, please refer to "Creating a Microsoft SQL Server Database," p. 155 (Chapter 7) or "Creating an Access Database," p. 153 (Chapter 7).

Listing the URLs

Each IDC page consists of two files—an IDC file and a template file. The IDC file contains all information about the datasource, the SQL statement, and connection parameters. The template file is used to merge the results from the SQL statement into an HTML page.

Therefore, you need to create two files in order to create a listing page of favorite URLs. The IDC file is presented in Listing 8.2, and the template file is presented in Listing 8.3.

On the CD

LISTING 8.2 - THE IDC FILE FOR CREATING THE LIST OF FAVORITE URLs (LISTURL.IDC)

```
01. Datasource: unlocking
02. Username: sa
03. Password:
04. Expires: 900
05. Template: listurl.htx
06. SQLStatement:
07. + SELECT * from tFavURL where Validated=1 order by URL
```

One line that is interesting when converting to ASP is line number 4.

```
04. Expires: 900
```

The expiration period of thispage is set to 900 seconds. This means that once the SQL statement has been executed and the results merged with the template, the resulting HTML page is cached for 15 minutes. All further requests for the IDC page are fulfilled using the cached version without ever querying the database again during this time period. When you use this IDC file, the cached page is available for all users, which is impossible when you use ASP. This issue is discussed in more detail when the converted code is presented (see the section "The List of URLs Page").

The template file, which also is used during conversion, is presented in Listing 8.3. The code for iterating over the entire result set is produced by the SQL statement in the IDC file and then formats the columns into a HTML table is enclosed by the `begindetail` and `enddetail` directives.

LISTING 8.3 - THE TEMPLATE FILE FOR CREATING THE LIST OF FAVORITE URLs (LISTURL.HTX)

On the CD

```
01. <HTML>
02. <HEAD>
03. <TITLE>Favorite URL</TITLE>
04. </HEAD>
05. <BODY bgcolor="#FFFFFF">
06.
07. <CENTER>
08. <A HREF="favurl.htm">Add URL´s to this list</A><P>
09.
10. <TABLE BORDER>
11. <%begindetail%>
12. <%if CurrentRecord EQ 0 %>
13. <TR>
14. <TH><B>URL</B></TH><TH><B>Description</B></TH><TH>Contributor</TH>
15. </TR>
16. <%endif%>
17. <TR>
18. <TD><A HREF="<%URL%>" TARGET="_top"><%URL%></A></TD>
19. <TD ALIGN=RIGHT><%Description%></TD>
20. <TD><%Contributor%></TD>
21. </TR>
22. <%enddetail%>
23. <P>
```

continues

LISTING 8.3, CONTINUED

```
24.  </TABLE>
25.  </CENTER>
26.
27.  <P>
28.  <%If CurrentRecord EQ 0 %>
29.  <I><B>No URL's found!</I></B>
30.  <P>
31.  <%endif%>
32.
33.  </BODY>
34.  </HTML>
```

There's some code in this listing that needs special attention during the conversion to ASP. Two blocks use the built-in variable CurrentRecord to add specific information depending on the number of the current record.

The first block is between lines 12 and 16 and adds the table headers when the first row of results is processed:

```
12.  <%if CurrentRecord EQ 0 %>
13.  <TR>
14.  <TH><B>URL</B></TH><TH><B>Description</B></TH><TH>Contributor</TH>
15.  </TR>
16.  <%endif%>
```

The second block, after the detail section, prints a no-records message when no records were returned by the query:

```
28.  <%If CurrentRecord EQ 0 %>
29.  <I><B>No URL's found!</I></B>
30.  <P>
31.  <%endif%>
```

That is all the code presentation for the listing page. More interesting code is presented in the next section; inserting user-supplied URLs into the database.

Adding URLs to the Database

Listing 8.3 of the template file contained a link to a page for adding favorite URLs to the list (line 8).

```
08.  <A HREF="favurl.htm">Add URL's to this list</A><P>
```

This is only a simple HTML page that contains a form for submitting URL information. The form opens another IDC file that's responsible for inserting the new URL to the table tFavURL. After conversion of the IDC file to ASP, you could merge both the form and converted insert page to a single ASP page. The HTML form page for gathering information about the user's favorite URL is shown in Listing 8.4.

LISTING 8.4 - THE PAGE CONTAINING THE FORM FOR
SUBMITTING NEW FAVORITE URLS (FAVURL.HTM)

On the
CD

```
01. <HTML>
02. <HEAD>
03. <TITLE>Add URL</TITLE>
04. </HEAD>
05. <BODY bgcolor="#FFFFFF">
06.
07.
08. <CENTER>
09. <H1>Add your favorite URL</H1>
10. <P>
11. <FORM ACTION="addurl.idc" method="post">
12. <TABLE>
13. <TR><TD>WWW address</TD><td><input name="newurl"
    ➥value="http://" size=50></td></tr>
14. <TR><TD>Description</TD><td><TEXTAREA NAME="desc"
    ➥ROWS=8 COLS=54></TEXTAREA></td></tr>
15. <TR><TD>Contributor</TD><td><input name="contr" value="" size=50></td></tr>
16. </TABLE>
17. <INPUT TYPE="SUBMIT" VALUE="Add to our database!">
18. </FORM>
19. </CENTER>
20.
21. </BODY>
22. </HTML>
```

The information gathered in this form is sent to the addurl.idc script (Listing 8.5), which is responsible for inserting the data into the table.

LISTING 8.5 - ADDING A NEW URL TO THE TABLE (ADDURL.IDC)

On the
CD

```
01. Datasource: unlocking
02. Username: sa
03. Password:
```

continues

```
04. Template: addurl.htx
05. SQLStatement:
06. +insert into tFavURL (URL,Description,Contributor)
07. + values ('%newurl%','%desc%','%contr%')
```

Notice that the IDC file in the listing contains only an insert statement, which returns no results. The values for URL, description, and contributor, are enclosed in single quotes to denote string values that are inserted into the database.

To provide the user with feedback about the submission, the template file uses the parameters passed to the IDC file (Listing 8.6).

On the CD

LISTING 8.6 - PROVIDING FEEDBACK TO THE USER ABOUT THE SUBMISSION (ADDURL.HTX)

```
01. <HTML>
02. <HEAD>
03. <TITLE>Thank you</TITLE>
04. </HEAD>
05. <BODY bgcolor="#FFFFFF">
06.
07. <CENTER>
08. <H1>Thank you <%idc.contr%> for submitting your URL!</H1>
09. <P>
10. Your link will be validated before it is added to the
    ➡<A HREF="listurl.idc">list of our favorite ones</A>.
11. However, you can <A HREF="favurl.htm">add another URL</A>
    ➡ to our list!
12. <P>
13. Your entry for <%idc.newurl%>
14. <%  If Not "" EQ idc.desc %>
15.   with the description<BR><I><%idc.desc%></I>
16. <%EndIf%>
17. has been added to our database!
18. </center>
19.
20. </BODY>
21. </HTML>
```

All the information that's reported to the user is taken from the parameters that were submitted to the IDC file. These are referenced with *idc.*, which is equal to *Request("")* in ASP code. No further action is taken on this page.

Now the newly added URL is in the database, however, it isn't visible to everyone because the administrator hasn't okayed it yet to make it publicly available. The next section presents the administrators page used to validate the user-added URLs.

Administration of the Application

Because of the default on the Validated column, all newly inserted URLs have set this column to 0, which means that they aren't viewed on the list page (see the SQL statement in Listing 8.2). Therefore, this column has to be toggled by the administrator, who checks the information provided for the URL first, before deciding that this URL is to be added to the favorite list.

As it is surely the case that some information provided is invalid, the administrator must be presented with the ability to change the values for URL, description, and contributor as well as the ability to delete URLs that don't fit. Given these requirements, the check URLs page needs to provide functionality to list new URLs, update them, and delete them. For a better understanding of what's going on in the IDC files, I have decided to present the template file first. Just imagine that the query results that are used for this page consist of non-validated URLs (Listing 8.7).

LISTING 8.7 - THE TEMPLATE FILE CONTAINING FORMS FOR ALL NON-VALIDATED URLs (CHECKURLS.HTX)

On the CD

```
01. <HTML>
02. <HEAD>
03. <TITLE>Favorite URL</TITLE>
04. </HEAD>
05. <BODY BGCOLOR="FFFFFF">
06.
07. <BR>
08. <TABLE BORDER=0>
09. <%if CurrentRecord EQ 0 %>
10. <TR>
11. <TH COLSPAN=2><B>Edit Record</B></TH>
12. </TR>
13. <%endif%>
14. <%begindetail%>
15. <TR><TD COLSPAN=2><HR></TD></TR>
16. <FORM ACTION="checkurls.idc">
17. <TR><TD>
18. <A HREF="<%URL%>" TARGET="_top"><%URL%></A><BR>
19. <input TYPE=HIDDEN name="oldURL" value="<%URL%>">
20. <input name="URL" value="<%URL%>" size=60><BR>
```

continues

LISTING 8.7, CONTINUED

```
21. <input name="contr" value="<%Contributor%>" size=60><BR>
22. <input type="radio" name="Add" value="1" checked>
    ➥Update and mark validated
23. <input type="radio" name="Add" value="0">Delete<P>
24. <input type="SUBMIT" value="Execute!">
25. </TD><TD VALIGN=TOP>
26. Description:<BR>
27. <TEXTAREA NAME="desc" ROWS=5 COLS=58><%Description%></TEXTAREA>
28. </TD></TR>
29. </FORM>
30. <%enddetail%>
31. </TABLE>
32.
33. </center>
34. <P>
35. <%if CurrentRecord EQ 0 %>
36. <I><B>No URL´s have been added since last check!</I>.</B>
37. <%end if%>
38.
39. </BODY>
40. </HTML>
```

For each non-validated URL, a form is created (lines 16 to 29) that is used to either update and validate the URL (Add=1) or delete the URL from the table (Add=0).

The form contains two fields that are filled with the value of the URL from the database. The visible input field (line 20) is provided for the administrator to change the URL. The hidden oldURL field on line 19 is needed because when the administrator decides to change the URL, not having the original URL would break updates to the table because it is the primary key.

The update and validate, deletion and listing of non-validated URLs is handled by the SQL statement that's contained in checkurls.idc, which is presented in Listing 8.8.

On the
CD

LISTING 8.8 - LISTING, UPDATING, AND DELETING URLs
(CHECKURLS.IDC)

```
01. Datasource: unlocking
02. Username: sa
03. Password:
04. Template: checkurls.htx
05. DefaultParameters: Add=2
```

```
06. SQLStatement:
07. +set nocount on
08. +If %Add% = 0
09. +begin
10. + DELETE FROM tFavURL where URL = '%oldURL%'
11. +End
12. +If %Add% = 1
13. +begin
14. + UPDATE tFavURL SET URL='%URL%', Description='%desc%',
15. + Contributor = '%contr%', Validated=1 WHERE URL='%oldURL%'
16. +End
17. + select * from tFavURL where Validated = 0 order by URL
```

I have to use the `DefaultParameter` statement on line 5 because this page might be called without parameters:

```
05. DefaultParameters: Add=2
```

This means the only action to be performed should be listing all non-validated URLs (line 17):

```
17. + select * from tFavURL where Validated = 0 order by URL
```

In the SQL statement, there are two `if` blocks that trigger either an update or a deletion of a specific record. After this, the table is re-queried for non-validated URLs and the results are again merged with the template file presented in Listing 8.7.

Now the entire IDC application with pages for listing, adding, and verifying URLs is completed and you can deploy it on your site. This application uses the most common IDC parameters that are used in larger applications. It contains interesting code and is useful besides. Now, though, it's time to move this cool little IDC application to ASP—and the next section shows you how to do this with very little effort.

Converting the Application to ASP

You have a large IDC application—which is up and running and took a lot of time and money to develop—and you want to move it to ASP. How could you achieve this with little effort? You can take two approaches when converting an application to ASP: either re-code all the pages yourself, or use the IDC2ASP tool. It's very time-consuming to do all the coding manually. In contrast, using the IDC2ASP conversion tool to perform the basic conversion and then fine-tuning the resulting pages is a much easier and faster way. And this section is dedicated to proving this.

To download the IDC2ASP tool (for free), point your Internet browser to `http://www.microsoft.com/iis` and go to the area called "Developer Tools and Samples."

The IDC2ASP tool is available in two flavors, both of which are contained in the IDC2ASP package:

1. A command line utility

2. An ActiveX component

There are nine command line switches for the utility, which make the second choice more attractive because you can use this component in an ASP page and in any other programming language capable of using `Automation` objects (like Visual Basic for Applications found in Office applications, Borland Delphi, Visual C++ and many more). You also can create the user interface after your ideas when you decide to use the ActiveX component solution.

 The IDC2ASP utility can convert IDC pages only to VBScript ASP pages. If you use any other programming language for these pages, this tool might be of no use to you. You have to create all pages from scratch.

Writing the Conversion Utility

The heading might be misleading, therefore I have to clarify: I am using the ActiveX Server Component (of IDC2ASP) to write a nice wrapper with a user interface around it. This is then the conversion utility used to convert the IDC application presented in this chapter.

The first solution that came to my mind was to create an ASP page that would gather all input for the component (creating a custom user interface with this page) and pass this to the ActiveX component which would then convert the IDC pages based on this input. The output of the conversion would also be displayed in the page.

There are some situations where a Web-based solution isn't practical, that is, when there's no possibility of accessing the files that need to be converted from the web server. In this situation, a standalone application is great. However, an application with a user interface would be best. So I decided to port the code from the ASP page to a Visual Basic 5 application.

The next section starts by showing you how to implement the user interface in an ASP page, and the section following moves on to show you how to create the user interface in Visual Basic 5.0.

Leveraging the ActiveX Component in an ASP page

This book is about Active Server Pages, therefore it is most natural that the ActiveX component is used in this context. An ASP page enables you to bundle both the input form and the processing code in a single page. To know which information to provide input fields in the form, you must first know which functionality is offered by the IDC2ASP component. The entire conversion behavior of this component is controlled by ten properties, which are described in Table 8.2.

TABLE 8.2
Properties of the IDC2ASP Component

Property name	Description
ASPPath	Specifies the path where the generated ASP pages should be stored. The logfile containing the processing results is located there also.
CheckRequest	Preprocesses IDC/HTX parameters to catch stray server tag names. Default is False.
ConnectionString	Specifies whether to use a session-wide defined connection string. If set to False, connection information with username and password is inserted in every page. Otherwise, the Session variable ConnectionString is used (must be defined in global.asa). The default is False.
FixIDCLinks	If set to True, links to .idc files are replaced with links to .asp files. By default, this replacement is not enabled.
IgnoreErrors	If set to True, stops multiple files conversion processing if any errors were encountered.
IDCPath	Specifies the path where the IDC files that will be converted reside.
IDCPrefix	Specifies the prefix that is used for IDC parameters that would otherwise translate into illegal VBScript variable names. The default is "I_", which is preceded by the variable name.
IDCSource	Specifies the source files that are to be converted. Wildcard characters are allowed (like *.idc).
Overwrite	Enables overwriting of existing files. Default is to disable it.

continues

TABLE 8.2, CONTINUED

Property name	Description
SQLBatch	Turn SQL batch commands processing on by setting this property to True. When enabled, ASP code for processing multiple Recordsets returned by batch SQL statements is inserted in the resulting ASP page.

Three of these properties are used to define the source path, source files, and destination path (IDCPath, IDCSource, ASPPath). The others do have influence on the conversion, like SQLBatch, which allows specific handling for multiple queries (more on this later). When all properties are set, a call to

```
lResult = idc2asp_obj.Convert()
```

converts all files specified with the options set. Before discussing the source code for the conversion page, take a look at the finished input form in Figure 8.2.

Figure 8.2

The Web front-end for the IDC2ASP ActiveX component.

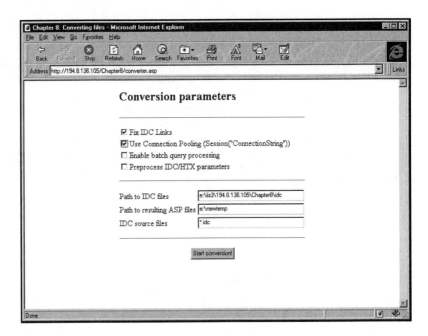

There are three properties omitted here—IgnoreErrors, Overwrite, and IDCPrefix. You can go with the defaults for these three most of the time. When all input is finished, a click on the Start Conversion button submits the form information. This information is then passed to the IDC2ASP component to perform the actual conversion. Listing 8.9 contains the source code for the conversion page.

LISTING 8.9 - CONVERTING IDC APPLICATIONS TO ASP (CONVERTER.ASP)

On the
CD

```
01. <!--#include file="fobjvbs.inc"-->
02. <HTML>
03. <HEAD>
04. <TITLE>Chapter 8: Converting files</TITLE>
05. </HEAD>
06. <BODY BGCOLOR=#ffffff>
07.
08. <%
09. If Request.ServerVariables("Content_Length") > 0 Then
10.     Set obj = Server.CreateObject("IntraActive.IDC2ASP")
11.
12.     obj.IDCPath = Trim(Request("IDCPath"))
13.     obj.ASPPath = Trim(Request("ASPPath"))
14.     obj.IDCSource = Trim(Request("IDCSource"))
15.
16.     If Request("SQLBatch") = "on" Then
17.         obj.SQLBatch = True
18.     End If
19.     If Request("FixIDCLinks") = "on" Then
20.         obj.FixIDCLinks = True
21.     End If
22.     If Request("CheckRequest") = "on" Then
23.         obj.CheckRequest = True
24.     End If
25.     If Request("ConnectionString") = "on" Then
26.         obj.ConnectionString = True
27.     End If
28.
29.     lResult = obj.Convert()
30.     Set obj = Nothing
31.
32.     ' now read the log file that was generated
33.     On Error Resume Next
34.     Set FileObject = Server.CreateObject("Scripting.FileSystemObject")
35.     Set Instream = FileObject.OpenTextFile(Request(
    ➥"ASPPath") & "\idc2asp.log", ForReading, False, False)
36.
37.     While Not Instream.AtEndOfStream
38.         Response.Write Instream.ReadLine & "<BR>" & vbCRLF
```

continues

LISTING 8.9, CONTINUED

```
39.      Wend
40.      Instream.Close
41. Else
42. %>
43.
44. <CENTER>
45. <FORM METHOD=POST ACTION="<%=Request.ServerVariables("SCRIPT_NAME")%>">
46. <TABLE>
47. <TR><TD COLSPAN=2><H2>Conversion parameters</H2><HR>
48. </TD></TR><TR><TD COLSPAN=2>
49. <INPUT TYPE=CHECKBOX NAME="FixIDCLinks">Fix IDC Links
50. </TD></TR>
51. <TR><TD COLSPAN=2>
52. <INPUT TYPE=CHECKBOX NAME="ConnectionString">
    ➥Use Connection Pooling (Session("ConnectionString"))
53. </TD></TR>
54. <TR><TD COLSPAN=2>
55. <INPUT TYPE=CHECKBOX NAME="SQLBatch">Enable batch query processing
56. </TD></TR>
57. <TR><TD COLSPAN=2>
58. <INPUT TYPE=CHECKBOX NAME="CheckRequest">Preprocess IDC/HTX parameters
59. </TD></TR>
60. <TR><TD COLSPAN=2><HR></TD></TR>
61.
62. <TR><TD>Path to IDC files</TD>
63. <TD><INPUT TYPE=TEXT NAME="IDCPath" VALUE=
    ➥"e:\iis3\194.8.136.105\Chapter8\idc" SIZE=40>
64. </TD></TR>
65. <TR><TD>Path to resulting ASP files</TD>
66. <TD><INPUT TYPE=TEXT NAME="ASPPath" VALUE="e:\newtemp" SIZE=40>
67. </TD></TR>
68. <TR><TD>IDC source files</TD>
69. <TD><INPUT TYPE=TEXT NAME="IDCSource" VALUE="*.idc"
    ➥SIZE=40>
70. </TD></TR>
71. <TR><TD COLSPAN=2><HR></TD></TR>
72. <TR><TD COLSPAN=2><CENTER><INPUT TYPE=SUBMIT VALUE=
    ➥"Start conversion!"></CENTER></TD></TR>
73. </FORM>
74. </CENTER>
75.
```

```
76. <%  End If %>
77.
78. </BODY>
79. </HTML>
```

The form for gathering conversion information is located between lines 45 and 73. However, the more interesting part of this page is surely the invocation of the conversion component IDC2ASP. This code starts on line 10 and ends on line 40. Most of the code is dedicated to extracting form data. The invocation of the Convert method is located on line 29. Another interesting piece of code starts on line 34: it reads the logfile created by the IDC2ASP component and displays it in the browser. This enables you to monitor success or failure of the conversion.

The ASP page is now finished—you can already convert your existing IDC applications to ASP code. As I have mentioned earlier, to use this approach the IDC application's files you want to convert must be accessible from the web server this ASP page is executed on. To be able to convert the IDC application on any computer (no web server installed), the next section presents a standalone solution programmed in Visual Basic 5.0.

Writing a Conversion Application in Visual Basic

After creating the ASP page, I switched gears and launched Visual Basic 5.0 to create a standalone application for converting IDC applications to ASP.

 The entire source code for this application is available on the accompanying CD. The name of the utility is VB5_IDC2ASP.exe.

 On the CD

This section isn't intended as a Visual Basic programmer's workshop—I only want to show the marginal differences between using ActiveX components in VBScript and Visual Basic. The first difference, of course, is in the user interface (Figure 8.3).

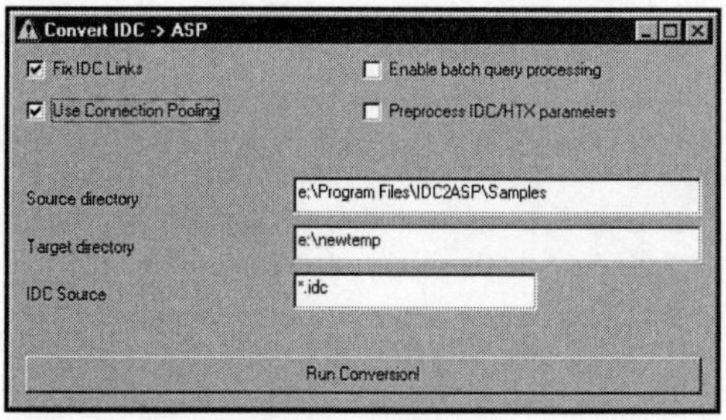

Figure 8.3

The user interface of the Visual Basic created conversion utility.

Pressing the Run Conversion button is equivalent to submitting the form for the ASP solution. The code that is triggered by clicking this button is shown in Listing 8.10.

LISTING 8.10 - VB SOURCECODE THAT'S TIED TO THE RUN CONVERSION BUTTON

```
01. Private Sub cmdRunConversion_Click()
02. On Error GoTo ErrConvError
03.
04.     Dim obj As New CIDC2ASP
05.     Dim lResult As Long
06.
07.     obj.IDCPath = Me.IDCPath
08.     obj.ASPPath = Me.ASPPath
09.     obj.IDCSource = Me.IDCSource
10.     If 1 = Me.FixIDCLinks Then obj.FixIDCLinks = True
11.     If 1 = Me.CheckRequest Then obj.CheckRequest = True
12.     If 1 = Me.SQLBatch Then obj.SQLBatch = True
13.     If 1 = Me.ConnectionString Then obj.ConnectionString = True
14.
15.     lResult = obj.Convert()
16.     lResult = Shell("notepad " & Me.ASPPath & "\idc2asp.log",
        ➥vbNormalFocus)
17.     Exit Sub
18.
19. ErrConvError:
20.     MsgBox Err.Description
21.     Exit Sub
22.
23. End Sub
```

The big differences are that I can use typified access to the IDC2ASP conversion object (the CIDC2ASP object found on line 4).

```
04.     Dim obj As New CIDC2ASP
```

With the exception of the fact that I'm using Notepad here to view the logfile, most of the source code should look familiar to the VBScript programmer.

You could easily extend this program by adding directory selection dialog boxes to it and by viewing the resulting logfile directly in the application. However, this program is already easier to use than the command line utility!

Performing the Conversion

This section discusses how to convert the example IDC application created in this chapter using the IDC2ASP tool. It's your choice whether to use the ASP or the Visual Basic front-end to this tool. However, be sure to check Fix IDC Links. You have to provide the source path to the IDC files and the destination path where the tool should create the ASP pages. If all goes well, the logfile presented to you should look like the one I received for the conversion presented in Listing 8.11:

LISTING 8.11 - THE LOGFILE GENERATED BY THE IDC2ASP COMPONENT

```
01. <========== Starting IDC2ASP Conversion ==========>
02. Date: 4/2/1997 Time: 18:1
03. e:\iis3\194.8.136.105\Chapter8\idc\ADDURL.IDC OK
04. e:\iis3\194.8.136.105\Chapter8\idc\checkurls.idc OK
05. e:\iis3\194.8.136.105\Chapter8\idc\LISTURL.IDC OK
06. Copied ADOVBS.inc to e:\iis3\194.8.136.105\Chapter8\idc\ADOVBS.inc
07. Copied IASUtil.asp to e:\iis3\194.8.136.105\Chapter8\idc\IASUtil.asp
08. <========== Completed IDC2ASP Conversion ==========>
```

All three files were converted without errors, which doesn't mean that the resulting ASP code is error-free. Notice that on lines 6 and 7 additional include files are copied to the target directory. The first one, adovbs.inc, is the include file that comes with ASP and contains the constants declarations for ADO. The second one, which comes with the IDC2ASP tool, IASUtil.asp, contains four additional helper functions:

- ◆ **CheckNextRS:** Checks Recordset for multiple Recordset processing using the NextRecordset method.

- ◆ **CheckRequest:** Validates IDC parameters.

- ◆ **CheckRS:** Validates the current Recordset.

- ◆ **SQLEncode:** Preserves single quotes in input strings.

These functions are used in the code generated by the conversion tool. Now take a look at what the conversion tool has generated!

The List of URLs Page

I wouldencourage you to open the converted listurl.asp page in the browser before taking a look at its source code. Did you see the flaw? Due to the choice of column name for storing the URL, I introduced a problem for the conversion program: it mistook the `<%URL%>` statement in the template file as an HTTP environment variable of the same name instead of assuming that it's part of the `Recordset`. This needs to be fixed and gives me a chance to discuss the generated output (see Listing 8.12).

On the CD

LISTING 8.12 - THE CONVERTED PAGE (LISTURL.ASP)

```
01. <%@ LANGUAGE="VBScript" %>
02. <!--#include file="ADOVBS.inc"-->
03. <!--#include file="IASUtil.asp"-->
04. <%
05.        Set Connection = Server.CreateObject("ADODB.Connection")
06.        Connection.Open "DSN=unlocking; UID=sa; PWD="
07.        SQLStmt = "SELECT * from tFavURL where Validated=1order by URL "
08.        Set RS = Connection.Execute(SQLStmt)
09.        Response.Expires = 15
10. %>
11. <HTML>
12. <HEAD>
13. <TITLE>Favorite URL</TITLE>
14. </HEAD>
15. <BODY bgcolor="#FFFFFF">
16.
17. <CENTER>
18. <A HREF="favurl.htm">Add URL´s to this list</A><P>
19.
20. <TABLE BORDER>
21. <%
22.        CurrentRecord = 0
23.
24.        Do While CheckRS(RS)
25.        If CurrentRecord = 0 Then %>
26. <TR>
27. <TH><B>URL</B></TH><TH><B>Description</B></TH><TH>Contributor</TH>
28. </TR>
29. <%        End If %>
30. <TR>
31. <TD><A HREF="<%= Request.ServerVariables("URL") %>"
    ➥TARGET="_top"><%= Request.ServerVariables("URL") %></A></TD>
32. <TD ALIGN=RIGHT><%= RS("Description") %></TD>
33. <TD><%= RS("Contributor") %></TD>
34. </TR>
```

```
35.  <%         RS.MoveNext
36.             CurrentRecord = CurrentRecord + 1
37.     Loop
38.  %>
39.  <P>
40.  </TABLE>
41.  </CENTER>
42.
43.  <P>
44.  <%      If CurrentRecord = 0 Then %>
45.  <I><B>No URL´s found!</I></B>
46.  <P>
47.  <%      End If %>
48.  </BODY>
49.  </HTML>
50.  <%      Connection.Close %>
```

The erroneous code is located on line 31: simply replace
`Request.ServerVariables("URL")` with `RS("URL")` and you're done. Please recall the
original IDC file and that there, `Expires` was set to 900. Line 9's `Response.Expires` is
the equivalent in minutes that was created by the conversion tool. However, this is
only for the current user—it is impossible to cache pages for all users.

Of course, all the `CurrentRecord` stuff is no longer needed and should be replaced by
other constructs. However, it doesn't hurt anything by being non-functional. Just
imagine how long it would have taken you to rewrite the entire page from scratch and
how much faster this approach is. An additional feature you could add is the capability to page through the records.

To learn how to add the feature that enable the user to page through records, see
"Paging Through the Results," p. 163 (Chapter 7).

Cross
Reference

The Adding URLs Page

The page created by the conversion tool is fully functional, but no input page exists
(remember, it was separate and still links to the IDC file). As with other examples
presented so far, it's a good idea to incorporate the form in the same page as the
processing code. This is what I did for Listing 8.13; the other code generated by
the tool is left untouched. To make it easier to distinguish new code, I made it all
uppercase.

On the
CD

LISTING 8.13 - THE NEW PAGE WITH SOME MODIFICATIONS APPLIED (ADDURL.ASP)

```
01. <%@ LANGUAGE="VBScript" %>
02. <!--#include file="ADOVBS.inc"-->
03. <!--#include file="IASUtil.asp"-->
04. <%
05. IF REQUEST.SERVERVARIABLES("CONTENT_LENGTH") > 0 THEN
06.      newurl = SQLEncode(Request("newurl"))
07.      desc = SQLEncode(Request("desc"))
08.      contr = SQLEncode(Request("contr"))
09.
10.      Set Connection = Server.CreateObject("ADODB.Connection")
11.
12.      Connection.Open "DSN=unlocking; UID=sa; PWD="
13.
14.      SQLStmt = "insert into tFavURL (URL,Description,Contributor) "
15.      SQLStmt = SQLStmt & "values ('" & newurl & "','" &
         ➥desc & "','" & contr & "') "
16.
17.      Set RS = Connection.Execute(SQLStmt)
18. %>
19. <HTML>
20. <HEAD>
21. <TITLE>Thank you</TITLE>
22. </HEAD>
23. <BODY bgcolor="#FFFFFF">
24.
25. <CENTER>
26. <H1>Thank you <%= Request("contr") %>  for submitting your URL!</H1>
27. <P>
28. Your link will be validated before it is added to the
    ➥<A HREF="listurl.asp">list of our favorite ones</A>.
29. However, you can <A HREF="<%=Request.ServerVariables(
    ➥"SCRIPT_NAME")%>">add another URL</A> to our list!
30. <P>
31. Your entry for <%= Request("newurl") %>
32. <% If Not "" = Request("desc") Then %>
33.   with the description<BR><I><%= Request("desc") %></I>
34. <% End If %>
35. has been added to our database!
36. </center>
```

```
37. <%  Connection.Close
38.
39. ELSE
40. %>
41. <CENTER>
42. <H1>Add your favorite URL</H1>
43. <P>
44. <FORM ACTION="<%=Request.ServerVariables("SCRIPT_NAME")
    ➥%>" method="post">
45. <TABLE>
46. <TR><TD>WWW address</TD><td><input name="newurl" value=
    ➥"http://" size=50></td></tr>
47. <TR><TD>Description</TD><td><TEXTAREA NAME="desc"
    ➥ROWS=8 COLS=54></TEXTAREA></td></tr>
48. <TR><TD>Contributor</TD><td><input name="contr" value=""size=50></td></tr>
49. </TABLE>
50. <INPUT TYPE="SUBMIT" VALUE="Add to our database!">
51. </FORM>
52. </CENTER>
53. <%  END IF %>
54.
55. </BODY>
56. </HTML>
```

I added the section from line 39 to 53, which is taken directly from favurl.htm, except that the script name is now added dynamically. This change also has been incorporated into line 29. There was only one error from the conversion tool to correct in this page: lines 32 to 34 were entirely garbage in terms of VBScript code. The rest of the page is left as it was generated by the tool. The code is fully functional.

Only one page is missing, then the entire IDC application is rebuilt using ASP code. The next section presents how to make adjustments to the converted administration page.

The Administration Page

This page is worth a look before you apply any changes to it. There's one conversion error we didn't encounter before, however, there's a more subtle programming problem inherent to this page that just didn't show up with IDC and isn't caused by the conversion tool. Now, with ASP and ADO, it does show up. Take a look at line 29 of Listing 8.14 and recall problems you might have already had with ADO and BLOB (binary large objects) fields.

LISTING 8.14 - THE ADMINISTRATOR PAGE RIGHT
AFTER THE CONVERSION

```
01. <%@ LANGUAGE="VBScript" %>
02. <!--#include file="ADOVBS.inc"-->
03. <!--#include file="IASUtil.asp"-->
04. <%
05.      Add = Request("Add")
06.      desc = SQLEncode(Request("desc"))
07.      contr = SQLEncode(Request("contr"))
08.      oldURL = SQLEncode(Request("oldURL"))
09.
10.      ' Perform IDC style DefaultParameter processing.
11.      If IsEmpty(Request("Add")) Or Request("Add") = "" Then
12.          Add = 2
13.      End If
14.
15.      Set Connection = Server.CreateObject("ADODB.Connection")
16.
17.      Connection.Open "DSN=unlocking; UID=sa; PWD="
18.
19.      SQLStmt = "set nocount on "
20.      SQLStmt = SQLStmt & "If " & Add & " = 0 "
21.      SQLStmt = SQLStmt & "begin "
22.      SQLStmt = SQLStmt & "DELETE FROM tFavURL where
         ➥URL = '" & Request.ServerVariables("URL") & "' "
23.      SQLStmt = SQLStmt & "End "
24.      SQLStmt = SQLStmt & "If " & Add & " = 1 "
25.      SQLStmt = SQLStmt & "begin "
26.      SQLStmt = SQLStmt & "UPDATE tFavURL SET URL='" &
         ➥Request.ServerVariables("URL") & "', Description='" & desc & "', "
27.      SQLStmt = SQLStmt & "Contributor = '" & contr &
         ➥"', Validated=1 WHERE URL='" & oldURL & "' "
28.      SQLStmt = SQLStmt & "End "
29.      SQLStmt = SQLStmt & "select * from tFavURL where
         ➥Validated = 0 order by URL "
30.
31.      Set RS = Connection.Execute(SQLStmt)
32. %>
33. <HTML>
34. <HEAD>
35. <TITLE>Favorite URL</TITLE>
36. </HEAD>
```

```
37. <BODY BGCOLOR="FFFFFF">
38.
39. <BR>
40. <TABLE BORDER=0>
41. <%        If CurrentRecord = 0 Then %>
42. <TR>
43. <TH COLSPAN=2><B>Edit Record</B></TH>
44. </TR>
45. <%        End If
46.
47.       CurrentRecord = 0
48.
49.       Do While CheckRS(RS)%>
50. <TR><TD COLSPAN=2><HR></TD></TR>
51. <FORM ACTION="checkurls.asp">
52. <TR><TD>
53. <A HREF="<%= Request.ServerVariables("URL") %>" TARGET=
    ➥"_top"><%= Request.ServerVariables("URL") %></A><BR>
54. <input TYPE=HIDDEN name="oldURL" value="<%= Request.
    ➥ServerVariables("URL") %>">
55. <input name="URL" value="<%= Request.
    ➥ServerVariables("URL") %>" size=60><BR>
56. <input name="contr" value="<%= RS("Contributor") %>" size=60><BR>
57. <input type="radio" name="Add" value="1" checked>Update and mark validated
58. <input type="radio" name="Add" value="0">Delete<P>
59. <input type="SUBMIT" value="Execute!">
60. </TD><TD VALIGN=TOP>
61. Description:<BR>
62. <TEXTAREA NAME="desc" ROWS=5 COLS=58><%= RS("Description") %></TEXTAREA>
63. </TD></TR>
64. </FORM>
65. <%          RS.MoveNext
66.            CurrentRecord = CurrentRecord + 1
67.       Loop
68. %>
69. </TABLE>
70.
71. </center>
72. <P>
73. <%        If CurrentRecord = 0 Then %>
74. <I><B>No URL´s have been added since last check!</I>.</B>
75. <%= RS("end") Then %>
```

continues

LISTING 8.14, CONTINUED

```
76.
77. </BODY>
78. </HTML>
79.
80. <%        Connection.Close %>
```

The problem is that ADO requires that all BLOB columns like the Description column that are of type text are the last columns returned in a Recordset. When you used the exact same table definition I used, the Validated column comes after the text column, which results in a runtime error issued by ADO. You can circumvent this problem by using

```
"SELECT URL, Contributor, Description FROM tFavURL WHERE Validated = 0 ORDER
➥BY URL"
```

instead of line 29's SQL statement.

The conversion error I mentioned is located on line 75.

```
75. <%= RS("end") Then %>
```

The conversion of <%endif%> failed and the solution to this problem is to replace the line with a VBScript End If statement:

```
75. <% End If %>
```

A second error is that the problem of the URL environment variable and column name shows up in this page again:

```
54. <input TYPE=HIDDEN name="oldURL" value="<%= Request.ServerVariables
       ➥("URL") %>">
```

A major issue of this page is that the SQL statements shown in lines 19-31 were once the only way in IDC times to add, delete, and retrieve rows in a single page. Now this method is outdated and can be solved in a more simple and elegant way, which is shown in Listing 8.15.

Given the minor conversion errors and the now outdated constructs introduced by the SQL statements that are in this page, you might ask "How long does it take to rewrite this code to make a cool ASP page out of it?"

I sat down in front of my computer with a stopwatch and it took me only about 4 minutes to come up with the following solution (Listing 8.15).

LISTING 8.15 - THE ADMINISTRATOR PAGE RECODED
TO BE MORE LIKE A REAL ASP PAGE

```
01. <%@ LANGUAGE="VBScript" %>
02. <!--#include file="ADOVBS.inc"-->
03. <!--#include file="IASUtil.asp"-->
04. <HTML>
05. <HEAD>
06. <TITLE>Favorite URL</TITLE>
07. </HEAD>
08. <BODY BGCOLOR="FFFFFF">
09. <%
10. Set Connection = Server.CreateObject("ADODB.Connection")
11. Connection.Open "DSN=unlocking; UID=sa; PWD="
12.
13. If Request.ServerVariables("CONTENT_LENGTH") > 0 Then
14.        desc = SQLEncode(Request("desc"))
15.        contr = SQLEncode(Request("contr"))
16.        newURL = SQLEncode(Request("newURL"))
17.        oldURL = SQLEncode(Request("oldURL"))
18.
19.        If ("0" = Request("Add")) Then
20.             ' url is primary index for the table
21.             Connection.Execute "DELETE FROM tFavURL where URL='" & oldURL
                   ➥& "'"
22.        Else
23.             strSQL = "UPDATE tFavURL SET URL='" & newURL & "',
                   ➥Description='" & desc & "', "
24.             strSQL = strSQL & "Contributor = '" & contr &"',
                   ➥Validated=1 WHERE URL='" & oldURL & "' "
25.             Connection.Execute strSQL
26.        End If
27. End If
28.
29. strSQL = "select URL, Contributor, Description from tFavURL where Validated
       ➥= 0 order by URL "
30. Set RS = Connection.Execute(strSQL)
31. %>
32. <BR>
33. <% If IsObject(RS) And Not RS.EOF Then %>
34. <TABLE BORDER=0>
35. <TR>
```

continues

LISTING 8.15, CONTINUED

```
36. <TH COLSPAN=2><B>Edit Record</B></TH>
37. </TR>
38. <%  While Not RS.EOF %>
39. <TR><TD COLSPAN=2><HR></TD></TR>
40. <FORM ACTION="<%=Request.ServerVariables("SCRIPT_NAME")%>" METHOD=POST>
41. <TR><TD>
42. <A HREF="<%= RS("URL") %>" TARGET="_top"><%= RS("URL")%></A><BR>
43. <input TYPE=HIDDEN name="oldURL" value="<%=RS("URL")%>">
44. <input name="newURL" value="<%=RS("URL")%>" size=60><BR>
45. <input name="contr" value="<%= RS("Contributor") %>" size=60><BR>
46. <input type="radio" name="Add" value="1" checked>Update and mark validated
47. <input type="radio" name="Add" value="0">Delete<P>
48. <input type="SUBMIT" value="Execute!">
49. </TD><TD VALIGN=TOP>
50. Description:<BR>
51. <TEXTAREA NAME="desc" ROWS=5 COLS=58><%= RS("Description") %></TEXTAREA>
52. </TD></TR>
53. </FORM>
54. <%    RS.MoveNext
55.     Wend
56. %>
57. </TABLE>
58.
59. <%  Else %>
60. <I><B>No URL´s have been added since last check!</I>.</B>
61. <%  End If %>
62.
63. </BODY>
64. </HTML>
65. <%  Connection.Close %>
```

The main changes are visible between lines 9 and 31. All checking for adding or deleting is now done in ASP code, no longer as a comparison that is executed on SQL Server. This yields a far faster execution and is definitely easier to maintain (you don't need a database guru any longer). I cleaned up the remaining code a little, but most was provided already by the tool.

If you compare rewriting the entire pages yourself and using this tool, the problems with minor errors that slip into the converted code are far outweighed by the time you save. The pages from the IDC application provided a fair sampling of challenges in converting IDC scripts to ASP and only left a few minor questions unanswered, all of which are dealt with in the next section.

Other Conversion Scenarios

The IDC mechanism allows much more control over the output with advanced parameters and you can create more sophisticated IDC/HTX code than that presented in the URL Favorites example. This section points to common areas you have to take special care of that weren't covered by the sample pages of the IDC application conversion, such as the following:

◆ Translation files

◆ Batch queries

◆ Converting trickier code

Translation Files

Translation files were used to convert data retrieved from the database into strings that could be displayed on every system on the Internet, independent of the code page or language used on these systems. Actually, this was achieved by replacing certain characters with their HTML code equivalents. The IDC2ASP conversion tool simply ignores the `TranslationFile` directives in the IDC file, but you can rebuild the functionality provided by this file by adding

```
Server.HTMLEncode()
```

around every column you're retrieving from the database. This bit of code applies HTML encoding to every string and ensures that the strings can be viewed on any system.

Batch Queries

You could execute multiple SQL statements in a single IDC file that then was merged into the template file. You used as many `<%begindetail%>` and `<%enddetail%>` directives as there were SQL statements in the IDC file to output the query results. Listing 8.16 shows an IDC file with two `SELECT` statements.

LISTING 8.16 - BATCH SQL STATEMENTS IN AN IDC FILE

```
01. Datasource: unlocking
02. Username: sa
03. Password:
04. Expires: 900
05. Template: multiple.htx
06. SQLStatement:
07. + SELECT * from tFavURL where Validated=1 order by URL
08. + SELECT * from tFavURL where Validated=0 order by URL
```

When you're converting such a page to ASP, you have to set the `SQLBatch` property to `True`, because the IDC2ASP tool creates specialized code that enables you to deal with these multiple statements using the `NextRecordset` functionality provided by the `Recordset` object. The code generated by the IDC2ASP utility for batch queries is perfectly usable—only minor modifications are needed. You can try this on your own!

Converting Trickier Code

By trickier code I mean hacks that you included in your IDC files. For example, what I did was switch template files based on some parameter submitted, which then looked like this sample IDC file (line 4 of Listing 8.17):

LISTING 8.17 - SWITCHING TEMPLATES BASED ON FORM PARAMETERS

```
01. Datasource: unlocking
02. Username: sa
03. Password:
04. Template: %templatename%.htx
05. SQLStatement:
06. + SELECT * from tFavURL
```

When you have programmed the Internet Database Connector using such tricks, I suppose that it's no problem for you to sort this out before converting it with IDC2ASP. Remove all tricks and the conversion runs without problems. In the preceding example you have to duplicate the IDC file (with different names of course) as many times as there are possible different templates. Replace line 4's code with:

```
04. Template: oneofthetemplates.htx
```

With this fix, the conversion is performed without problems. Depending on what you were trying to achieve with the code in Listing 8.17, you might copy the resulting ASP pages into a single page or do some other fine tuning.

Summary

This chapter showed you how to move existing Internet Database Connector applications to the new Active Server Pages platform without too much extra effort. The tool that is presented in this chapter, IDC2ASP, provides you with a starting point—and I want to emphasize *starting* point—for you to move IDC code to ASP code. You don't need to convert IDC code to ASP code manually. All you need to do is use the conversion tool and clean up the generated code and make adjustments where the converted code is no longer state of the art.

For more information about creating state of the art ASP code for accessing databases, please refer to Chapter 7, "Database Access with ActiveX Data Objects."

**Cross
Reference**

CHAPTER 9

The Microsoft Personalization System

This chapter shows you how to create sites that attract users to come back regularly. Part of the trick to ensuring that users return is making them "feel at home" on your site (because of the information provided). And how do you make someone feel at home? By letting users create the home! This chapter shows you how to achieve this goal by creating personalized content using the Microsoft Personalization System (MPS). This chapter covers the following topics:

◆ Personalizing content for users

◆ Providing the user with feedback via e-mail

◆ Gathering feedback from the user

Overview of MPS

The MPS is part of the Microsoft Commercial Internet System (MCIS), which is a family of servers that you can either install individually or as a whole. The eight servers constitute the newest addition to the Microsoft BackOffice family, and can be found in the following list:

◆ Address Book and Internet Locator Server

◆ Content Replication System

◆ Information Retrieval Server

◆ Internet Chat Server

◆ Internet Mail Server

◆ Internet News Server

◆ Membership System

◆ Personalization System

With these servers, you can set up an entire Internet business. However, the only member of this family that's discussed here is the Microsoft Personalization System. The MPS adds three server components that help you create personalized content for your users, as well as easier feedback and communication. These components are the following:

◆ User Property Database (UPD) component

◆ SendMail component

◆ Voting component

The Microsoft Personalization System leverages the component architecture to extend Active Server Pages with its own components. See Figure 9.1 for an overview of this architecture.

The browser connecting to this server doesn't need to perform any special tasks to take advantage of the three MPS components.

◆ The SendMail component can be used to send e-mail for feedback purposes from pages or to create an e-mail gateway. It uses an SMTP server to deliver e-mail.

◆ If you're creating personalized content, the User Property Database is the component you will be working with most of the time. It is used to store and retrieve user preferences.

◆ With the Voting component, you can hold ballots. The questions and values are stored in an ODBC database for later retrieval.

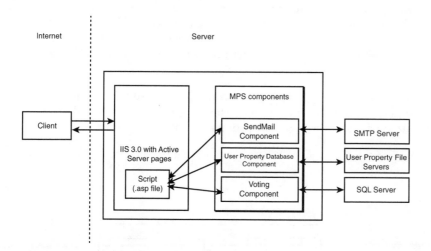

Figure 9.1

The architecture of MPS.

If you want to learn how to set up the entire MPS on your web server, please refer to the Microsoft Personalization System Operations Guide. This chapter discusses MPS from the web page author's point of view.

User Property Database

When you wanted to create personalized content in the past, you probably used cookies to store the personalization information on the computers of your clients. If you allowed them to personalize a lot, large cookies resulted, which in turn slowed down the response times. Some web caching proxies didn't like large cookies, which cut them off. Another drawback was that you had to use PERL or C to create CGI or ISAPI applications that could read the cookies and create the personalized content.

Today it's easier to use cookies to store information on the client's computer. The example in Chapter 5's section about the Cookies collection of the Response object uses this approach. However, the problems inherent with large cookies still exist.

See "Setting Cookies" p.108 (Chapter 5, "Programming Active Server Pages") to review how to use cookies to personalize a page.

Cross Reference

The solution to this problem is to send only one cookie to identify the user and then look up the user preferences on the server side. Now there is the problem of how to store the user preferences on your server. Perhaps a database? Good idea, but what will happen if you need to add some preferences? Your database schema will have to be changed every time you add or delete preferences. That is the point where the MPS User Property Database comes in handy: it takes care of all properties storage and retrieval. However, cookies are used to identify each single user in the UPD as well.

The User Property Database component is the properties store you can use to store and retrieve properties about the current user. This information can be used to create personalized pages for the user. The process flow of MPS is shown in Figure 9.2.

Figure 9.2

The process flow of MPS.

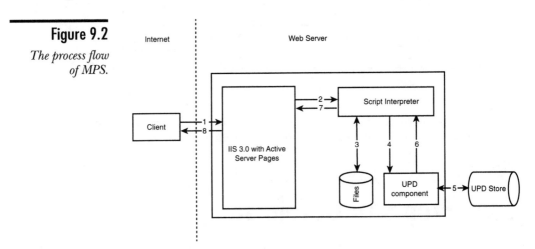

The process begins with the web browser requesting a page from the web server.

1. The web browser requests an active page from the web server.

2. The Internet Information Server passes the request to the Script Interpreter.

3. The Script Interpreter loads the appropriate script and starts executing it.

4. When the script contains code that uses an instance of the User Properties Database component, the cookie used to identify the user is extracted from the request.

5. The UPD component queries its properties store for the properties stored for the user identified by the cookie.

6. The UPD component returns the properties for the current user.

7. The Script Interpreter finishes execution of the script. Here you add the personalization of the page.

8. Internet Information Server returns the resulting personalized HTML code to the web browser.

Implementing steps 4 and 6 of this process in your pages is very easy because this simply invokes the User Properties Database component. However, before you can start working with the User Properties Database, there are two problems to address:

◆ Page Buffering

◆ Web Proxies

Because the User Property Database component modifies the HTTP headers, you have to either turn on page buffering or place all header-modifying scripting code before any HTML code. You can turn on buffering using two approaches:

1. Turn on buffering using the `Response.Buffer` property set to `True` on top of the page. Insert the following line as the first line in your page:

```
<% Response.Buffer = True %>
```

2. Simply instantiate the User Properties Database component. It will enable buffering automatically. It still has to be displayed before any HTML code.

```
<% Set upd = Server.CreateObject("MPS.PropertyDatabase") %>
```

Possibility two of enabling page buffering shows how to create an instance of the User Properties Database component.

There is one problem left to solve—web proxies. Proxy servers are used to cache information from various Internet sources to speed up browsing and decreasing the network load. For images and other static content this behavior is great, but for personalized content it isn't. Other users, for example, might receive a page personalized for someone else some time ago just because the proxy "remembered" this page. To prevent this from happening, you can tell the proxy not to cache the page:

```
<% Response.Expires = 0 %>
```

This statement sets the expiration time to zero, which means that the page is out of date immediately, even when clicking the Back button of your browser when you go back from a deeper nesting level. This implies that the page will have to be reloaded every time it is accessed, but it has advantages too—the user receives the latest data and the proxy doesn't return pages created for other users.

That's all of the prerequisites for creating personalized content with the User Properties Database. In this chapter the examples go first, and the discussion of the properties and methods follows.

First Steps with the UPD

In Chapter 5 there is an example of a small customization that only contains the Name and preferences about the graphics resolution of the pages. This cookie-based example is a good starting point for showing the differences between client-side stored personalization information and server-side stored personalization information. Figure 9.3 shows the personalized page.

To see the code for the cookie-based example, see Listing 5.13, p. 109 (Chapter 5).

Cross Reference

Figure 9.3

Cookie-based personalization.

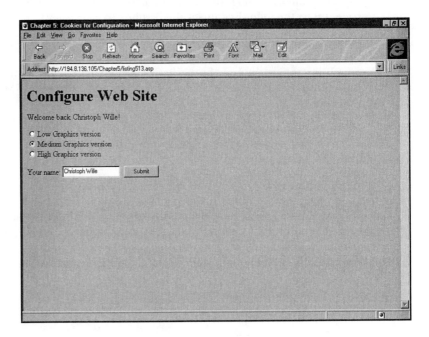

The code for the UPD-based example is shown in Listing 9.1.

LISTING 9.1 - PERSONALIZATION USING UPD

On the
CD

```
01. <%
02. Set upd = Server.CreateObject("MPS.PropertyDatabase")
03.
04. If Len(Request.Form)>0 Then
05.    upd.LoadFromString(Request.Form)
06. End If
07. %>
08.
09. <HTML>
10. <HEAD>
11. <TITLE>Chapter 9: MPS for Configuration</TITLE>
12. </HEAD>
13. <BODY>
14.
15. <H1>Configure Web Site</H1>
16.
17. <%
18. If Len(upd("UserName")) > 0 Then
19.   Response.Write "Welcome back " & upd("UserName") & "!<P>"
20. Else
21.   Response.Write "Please customize this page!<P>"
22. End If
23. %>
24.
25. <%
26. upd.Defaults "Graphics=hi"
27.
28. Dim chkArr(3)
29. Select Case upd("Graphics")
30. Case "lo"
31.    chkArr(1) = "CHECKED"
32.    chkArr(2) = ""
33.    chkArr(3) = ""
34. Case "md"
35.    chkArr(1) = ""
36.    chkArr(2) = "CHECKED"
37.    chkArr(3) = ""
38. Case else
39.    chkArr(1) = ""
40.    chkArr(2) = ""
41.    chkArr(3) = "CHECKED"
```

continues

LISTING 9.1, CONTINUED

```
42.
43. End Select
44. %>
45.
46. <FORM ACTION="<%=Request.ServerVariables("SCRIPT_NAME")%>
      ➥" METHOD=POST>
47.    <input type=hidden name="prefact" value="change">
48.    <input type="radio" <%=chkArr(1)%>  name="Graphics"
      ➥ value="lo">Low Graphics version<BR>
49.    <input type="radio" <%=chkArr(2)%>  name="Graphics"
      ➥ value="md">Medium Graphics version<BR>
50.    <input type="radio" <%=chkArr(3)%>  name="Graphics"
      ➥ value="hi">High Graphics version<P>
51.    Your name: <input type=text name="UserName"
      ➥ value="<%=upd("UserName")%>">
52.    <input type=submit name="Submit">
53. </FORM>
54.
55. </BODY>
56. </HTML>
```

This listing is shorter than the one for the cookies, though an extra welcome has been added for users who haven't yet personalized this page (lines 17 to 23). The syntax for accessing properties is similar to that for accessing user-defined properties in the Application and Session objects.

Line 26 is again interesting. Because this page is used for displaying to new users and ones that have already personalized it, the new user doesn't have any preferences for the graphics resolution the code in line 29 is checking for. To supply default values, you have to use the Defaults property, which takes a URL encoded string for all values you want to have defaults.

The only differences left are at the top of the listing, lines 1 to 7. First the User Property Database object is created and page buffering is turned on automatically. Line 4's code checks to see whether the page is called with parameters, and if True, stores the information provided in the UPD. The statement for storing all name/value pairs is as follows:

```
upd.LoadFromString(Request.Form)
```

You also could store the information on a one-by-one basis, adding each property explicitly to the database:

```
upd("UserName") = Request("UserName")
```

From an ease-of-use standpoint, the first method seems to be better, but from a security standpoint the second method is far superior. With the first method, any data is stored to the property database—you are open to a malicious attack to fill up your UPD with useless garbage. Method two's advantage is that the only properties that are added are ones you have decided to place into the database.

Multiple Value Properties

If you want to store information that is grouped, you can use multiple value properties. Examples of grouped information are favorite movies and preferred news. The multiple value properties work the same way that multiple values are returned, for example, from the `Request.Form` collection. The general syntax for retrieving multiple value properties is as follows:

```
strValue = upd(propertyname)(index)
```

If you want to iterate over the set of values, use the following piece of code:

```
For I = 1 To upd("Movies").Count
  Response.Write("Movie " & upd("Movies")(I) & " is a favorite<BR>")
Next
```

If you want to add values to the set of values, use the Append method. For deleting, use the Remove method.

```
upd("Movies").Append("Evita")
upd("Movies").Remove(1)
```

Please note that you can remove values only with their index in the set. If the index is greater than Count, an exception is generated.

A nice feature for a customized page and multiple value properties is providing the user with a list of his or her favorite links. You have to provide functionality for adding and removing links. See Figure 9.4 to see what the final page looks like.

Figure 9.4

*Creating a list of
favorite links.*

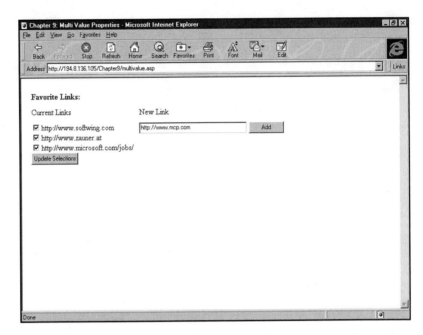

To provide the functionality of adding and removing links, two forms must be
incorporated in the page. Both forms contain a list of current links. The form for
adding links doesn't show these because they're hidden. The form for deleting links
shows them with checkboxes you have to uncheck when you want to remove the link
from the set. Again, all functionality is provided in a single page. The source code for
this page is shown in Listing 9.2.

**On the
CD**

LISTING 9.2 - CREATING A LIST OF FAVORITE LINKS

```
01. <%
02. Set upd = Server.CreateObject("MPS.PropertyDatabase")
03.
04. If (Request.ServerVariables("Content_Length")>0) Then
05.    upd.LoadFromString(Request.Form)
06. End If
07. %>
08.
09. <HTML>
10. <HEAD>
11. <TITLE>Chapter 9: Multi Value Properties</TITLE>
12. </HEAD>
13. <BODY BGCOLOR=#ffffff>
```

```
14.
15. <TABLE CELLSPACING=10>
16. <TR><TD COLSPAN=2><B>Favorite Links:</B></td></TR>
17. <TR><TD>Current Links</TD><TD>New Link</TD></TR>
18. <TR><TD VALIGN=BOTTOM>
19. <FORM METHOD=POST ACTION=<%=Request.ServerVariables("SCRIPT_NAME")%>>
20. <%
21. Response.Write "<INPUT TYPE=HIDDEN NAME=""FavURL""
    ➥Value=""none"">" & Chr(13)
22. For i = 1 To upd("FavURL").Count
23.    If (upd("FavURL")(i) <> "none") Then
24.       Response.Write "<INPUT TYPE=CHECKBOX NAME=""FavURL""
          ➥Value=""" & upd("FavURL")(i) & """ CHECKED>"
25.       Response.Write upd("FavURL")(i) & "<BR>" & vbCRLF
26.    End If
27. Next
28. %>
29.
30. <INPUT TYPE=Submit VALUE="Update Selections">
31. </FORM></TD>
32. <TD VALIGN=BOTTOM>
33. <FORM METHOD=POST ACTION=<%=Request.ServerVariables("SCRIPT_NAME")%>>
34.
35. <%
36. For i = 1 To upd("FavURL").Count
37.    If (upd("FavURL")(i) <> "none") Then %>
38.       <INPUT TYPE=HIDDEN NAME="FavURL" VALUE="<%=upd("FavURL")(i)%>">
39. <% End If
40. Next
41. %>
42.
43. <input TYPE=Text NAME="FavURL" SIZE=40>
44. <input TYPE=Submit name="Action" value="Add">
45. </FORM>
46. </TD></TR></TABLE>
47.
48. </BODY>
49. </HTML>
```

The form for removing links from the set is created between lines 19 and 31. All URLs are inserted using checkboxes. Please note that the double quotes are used to create single quotes in a string. A special URL with the value "none" is inserted on line 21. This one is needed because of the insertion method `LoadFromString` used in line 5. If you don't include this dummy URL, you won't be able to delete the last URL in the list. It would reappear every time because there would be no data posted to the server and thus nothing would be removed from the list.

If you only want to add URLs, you don't need this trick. The scripting code for creating the form in lines 33 to 45 is straightforward. It inserts all URLs that are already added in hidden fields and adds a single textbox to add a new URL.

Why did I use the `LoadFromString` method when I stated that it's potentially unsafe? Out of idleness, because you don't need to address how to determine which URL is added and which one is to be removed.

Intranet Scenario

If you're creating personalized content on an intranet, you could add some functionality that isn't possible when creating personalized content for the Internet.

- ◆ Prevent proxy caching but allow browser caching

- ◆ Change the ID of the user

Prevent Proxy Caching

If you're working with an HTTP/1.1 specification-compliant proxy server on your intranet, you can disable the proxy caching but allow browser caching. With this feature, each user receives the personalized content and the proxy doesn't cache it. However, the browser can cache pages locally for a given period of time. You have to add the Cache-Control header in your pages to achieve this.

```
Response.AddHeader "Cache-Control", "private"
Response.Expires = 15
```

The first line tells the proxy server not to cache this page, and the second line enables caching of this page on the browser for 15 minutes.

Change the User ID

In the Internetcase, the IDs that are attached to the cookies and the User Property Database for a specific user are created as globally unique identifiers. If you're working on an intranet project, you can use the NT logon accounts to identify the cookies and entries in the UPD. You must have disabled the anonymous account on your web server to receive the header `LOGON_USER`, which contains the username. See Listing 9.3.

LISTING 9.3 - CHANGING THE USER ID

```
01. <%
02. Set upd = Server.CreateObject("MPS.PropertyDatabase")
03.
04. If Len(Request.ServerVariables("LOGON_USER")) > 0 Then
05.    upd.ID = Request.ServerVariables("LOGON_USER")
06. End If
07. %>
```

You must set the ID before any access in the UPD.

Methods and Properties

Most of the properties and methods have already been shown in previous examples. A list of all properties is displayed in Table 9.1.

TABLE 9.1
Properties of the User Property Database Component

Property name	Description
Defaults	Set the defaults for the properties that might not be specified. Requires the data to be formatted as a URL.
ID	Retrieve or change the user's ID.
PropertyString	Returns all properties for the user from the User Properties Database in a URL.
ReadOnly	Set the UPD to read-only for pages that only perform read operations on the UPD.

The ID and Defaults property were already parts of examples. The ReadOnly property speeds up pages that only retrieve properties, but don't write to them. If you need access to all properties stored in the UPD for a specific user, use the PropertyString property to retrieve all properties in a URL-encoded string. Because the UPD doesn't support for...each looping over all properties, this is the only way to retrieve all properties. See Listing 9.4 for a way you should not retrieve all properties (but for dumping, it's adequate).

LISTING 9.4 - RETRIEVING ALL PROPERTIES

```
01. <% Response.Buffer=True %>
02.
03. <HTML>
04. <HEAD>
05. <TITLE>Chapter 9: Outputting all data; version 1</TITLE>
06. </HEAD>
07. <BODY BGCOLOR=#ffffff>
08.
09. <%
10. if (Len(Request.ServerVariables("Query_String"))>0) Then
11.    Response.Write("<TABLE>" & Chr(13))
12.    For Each key in Request.QueryString
13.      Response.Write("<TR><TD>" & key & "</TD><TD>" &
         ➥Request.QueryString(key) & "</TD></TR>" & Chr(13))
14.    Next
15.    Response.Write("</TABLE>")
16. Else
17.    Set mpsobj = Server.CreateObject("MPS.PropertyDatabase")
18.    mpsobj.ReadOnly=True
19.    Response.Redirect(Request.ServerVariables(
         ➥"SCRIPT_NAME") & "?" & mpsobj.PropertyString)
20. End If
21. %>
22.
23. </BODY>
24. </HTML>
```

The idea behind this example was to find a way to dump all properties stored in the UPD. Because the UPD stores the information in a URL-encoded string, one solution is very compelling—reading the PropertyString and calling the page again with the properties as a query string. This is what happens between lines 17 and 19. The dumping of properties between lines 11 and 15 is the same method used to dump all Form parameters. If you need to retrieve all properties in a page without using this approach, you have to URL-decode the string manually.

The User Property Database component supports only two methods:

TABLE 9.2
Methods

Method	Description
LoadFromString	Inserts user properties in the database directly from a QueryString or Form request.
Item	For reading and writing the user's properties.

The Item method can be used to explicitly reference the items stored in the user property database. However, lines 1 and 2 in the following listing are equal to lines 3 and 4. They are simply shortcuts to the Item method.

LISTING 9.5 - THE ITEM METHOD

```
01. upd("Movie")
02. upd("Movie")(1)
03. upd.Item("Movie")
04. upd.Item("Movie").Item(1)
```

The Item object for multiple value properties supports the following methods and properties.

TABLE 9.3
Methods and Properties

Name	Description
Append method	Appends an item to multiple value user properties.
Count property	Returns the number of items in multiple value properties.
Item property	Returns a specific item from multiple value properties.
Remove method	Removes the item at the specified position from multiple value properties.

The use of all these properties and methods has already been demonstrated in the examples of the previous sections.

SendMail Component

Active Server Pages or Internet Information Server don't come with built-in support for sending e-mail. The Microsoft Personalization System contains the `SendMail` component that enables you to send e-mail directly from your web pages. You can use this component to send automatic receipts from pages, mail information based on some form, or simply to build an e-mail gateway in your Web pages.

> **Tip**   The SMTP Server that this component uses to deliver e-mail is determined at Setup time. If you want to change it later, open the Registry key `HKEY_LOCAL_MACHINE\Software\Microsoft\MPS\SendMail` and change the entry "SMTP Server" to the desired server.

This e-mail gateway interface is shown in Figure 9.5. It contains four fields: From, To, Subject, and Body.

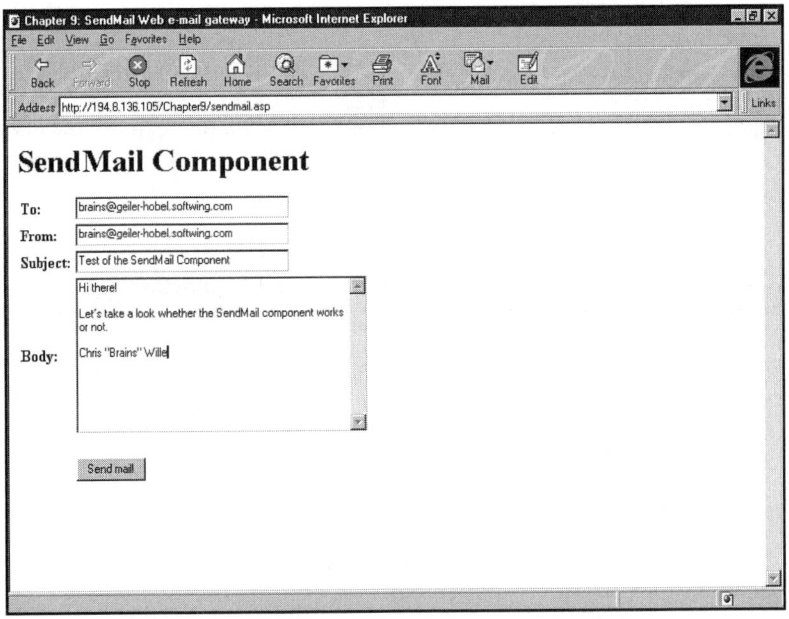

Figure 9.5

SendMail Web e-mail gateway.

The e-mail is sent using the only method supplied by the `SendMail` component: `SendMail`. This method takes four parameters:

- ◆ **Sender's address:** The sender's address. It must be an valid e-mail account.

- ◆ **Recipient's address(es):** A single recipient's address or a list of recipients separated by semicolons.

◆ **Subject:** The subject of this message. The subject is displayed in the subject field of the message header.

◆ **Body:** The message body. If you're creating a message from single strings, don't forget to insert `newline` characters using the `Chr(13)` statement.

With this information, the e-mail gateway is built very quickly. The source code for the sample gateway shown in Figure 9.5 is in Listing 9.6.

LISTING 9.6 - SendMail WEB EMAIL GATEWAY

On the CD

```
01. <HTML>
02. <HEAD>
03. <TITLE>Chapter 9: SendMail Web e-mail gateway</TITLE>
04. </HEAD>
05. <BODY BGCOLOR=#ffffff>
06.
07. <H1>SendMail Component</H1>
08.
09. <%
10. On Error Resume Next
11. If (Request.ServerVariables("Content_Length")>0) Then
12.    Set sm = Server.CreateObject("MPS.SendMail")
13.    retCode = sm.SendMail(Request("emailfrom"),
14. Request("emailto"),_Request("emailsubj"),Request("emailbody"))
15.    If True = retCode Then
16.      Response.Write "Thank your for using our e-mail gateway!"
17.    Else
18.      Response.Write "Failed to send your e-mail due to the following
         ➥error:<BR>"
19.      Response.Write "<B>" & Err.Description & "</B><P>"
20.    End if
21. Else
22. %>
23.    <TABLE>
24.    <FORM METHOD=POST ACTION="<%=Request.ServerVariables("SCRIPT_NAME")%>">
25.    <tr><td><B>To:</B></td>
26.    <td><input type=text name="emailto" size=40></td></tr>
27.    <tr><td><B>From:</B></td>
28.    <td><input type=text name="emailfrom" size=40></td></tr>
29.    <tr><td><B>Subject:</B></td>
30.    <td><input type=text name="emailsubj" size=40></td></tr>
```

continues

LISTING 9.6, CONTINUED

```
31.   <tr><td><B>Body:</B></td>
32.   <td><TEXTAREA COLS=60 ROWS=10 NAME="emailbody"></TEXTAREA></td></tr>
33.   <tr><td></td><td> <BR><input type=submit value="Send mail!"></td></tr>
34.   </FORM>
35.   </TABLE>
36. <% End If %>
37.
38. </BODY>
39. </HTML>
```

One single line of code is responsible for sending e-mail—line 13. It contains the method call to send mail. It doesn't check to see whether there is a subject or a body, but it works fine.

If you're sending receipts or any other form of e-mail feedback to the user, you will be passing strings that you have created instead of the user-provided information this e-mail gateway uses.

Voting Component

The last of the three MPS components is the Voting component. You can use this component to gather opinions from users, store them in an ODBC database, and show the results online. The information is grouped in ballots, so you can create multiple forms for different voting scenarios.

When working with the Voting component, you need to set up a database to store the results. You can use any ODBC-accessible database management system, including Microsoft Access, however, I would strongly recommend a dedicated database server like Microsoft SQL Server.

Creating a Voting Database on Microsoft SQL Server

The Microsoft Personalization System ships with a script file for SQL Server that you can use to create the database objects needed from scratch. This file, ssovdb.sql, is located in the /MPS/bin folder on the server computer running MPS.

When you're creating the database for a production server, you need to calculate the database size first. It makes a big difference whether you are only tracking the votes for each question or if you are storing the information on a per-user basis, which has the advantage of restricting the user to voting only once, but has the drawback that you have to store the ID of the user, which takes 32 bytes of extra storage space.

The outlined procedure assumes that you have—or your database administrator has—created a database on a Microsoft SQL Server that you can use to test-drive the Voting component. The database size doesn't matter a great deal—5 megabytes of storage is sufficient.

1. Open Microsoft ISQL/w and connect to your database server.

2. Select the appropriate database, for example the "unlocking" database used in Chapter 4, "Working with Visual InterDev."

3. Open the script ssovdb.sql in the Query pane with File/Open. The file is located in the /MPS/bin folder. Your ISQL/w window should now look like Figure 9.6.

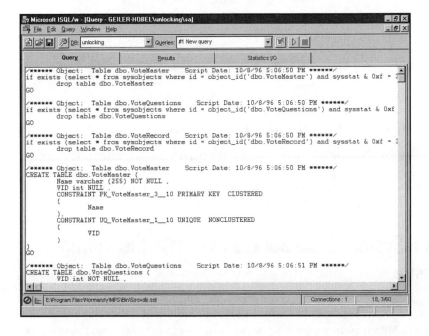

Figure 9.6

The ISQL/w window with the opened script ssovdb.sql.

4. Select the menu command Query/Execute to start the creation of the Voting component tables.

5. When the execution of the script is finished, there should be only one line of output:

```
This command did not return data, and it did not return any rows
```

6. Close ISQL/w.

This script has created three tables that are required for the Voting component: the VoteMaster, VoteQuestions, and VoteRecords tables.

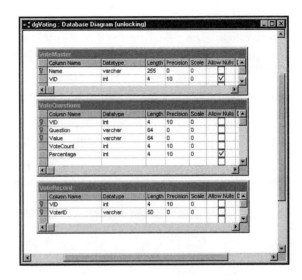

Figure 9.7

*The VoteMaster,
VoteQuestions,
and VoteRecords
tables.*

This database diagram shows that there are no relationships defined between these tables. This is done for speed reasons and it can be done safely, because only the Voting component is (or should be) accessing these tables.

The Votemaster table stores information about the ballots that were held. The actual status information of each question that was presented in the ballot is stored in the VoteQuestions table. The VoteRecord table is used only when you decide to track the users that have voted in a single ballot (remember, this takes a lot of storage space).

Adding a System Data Source to Access the Voting Database

To use the database you have created for the Voting component, you have to set up a System data source with the ODBC control panel application on the computer the web server with MPS is running on. Use the following steps to create this System data source:

1. Open the Control Panel on the server computer.

2. Open the ODBC control panel application by double-clicking the ODBC icon.

3. Switch to the System DSN tab and click Add.

4. Select SQL Server as the driver for your new data source. Click Finish.

5. The ODBC SQL Server Setup dialog box opens. Enter the information about the SQL Server and the database in which you created the Voting tables. If you have used the unlocking database, the completed dialog box should look like Figure 9.8.

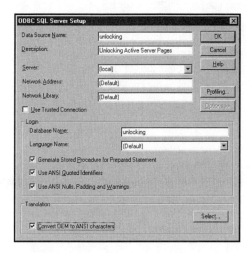

Figure 9.8

The completed ODBC SQL Server Setup dialog box.

6. Click OK to add the newly created data source.

Now that you have created all necessary database connections, you can start to create your ballots.

Using the Voting Component

The example ballot is about the user's favorite web server. The user can choose from three different servers. The page used for gathering information is used as a results page as well. See Listing 9.7 for the source code.

LISTING 9.7 - VOTE FOR YOUR FAVORITE SERVER

On the
CD

```
01. <HTML>
02. <HEAD>
03. <TITLE>Chapter 9: Voting component - Insert information</TITLE>
04. </HEAD>
05. <BODY BGCOLOR=#ffffff>
06.
07. <H1>Voting Component</H1>
08.
```

continues

```
09. <%
10. If (Request.ServerVariables("Content_Length")>0) Then
11.     Set vtc = Server.CreateObject("MPS.Vote")
12.     If True = vtc.Open("unlocking","sa","") Then
13.       retCode = vtc.SetBallotName("Favorite Servers")
14.       retCode = vtc.Submit("Favorite", Request("FavServer"))
15.       Response.Write "Thank you for submitting your vote!<P>"
16.       Response.Write vtc.GetVote("Favorite")
17.     End if
18. Else
19. %>
20.     <H2>Choose your favorite Web server</H2>
21.     <FORM METHOD=POST ACTION="<%=Request.ServerVariables("SCRIPT_NAME")%>">
22.       <input type=radio name="FavServer" value="Microsoft">Microsoft<BR>
23.       <input type=radio name="FavServer" value="Zauner">Pastry Shop Zauner<BR>
24.       <input type=radio name="FavServer" value="MCP">Macmillan Publications<P>
25.       <input type=submit value="Vote!">
26.     </FORM>
27. <% End If %>
28.
29. </BODY>
30. </HTML>
```

When the page is requested without the form data, the input form is displayed to gather the user's opinion. After the user has submitted the information, a Voting component object is instantiated. In line 11 the System data source that has been created in the previous section is used to establish a connection to the SQL Server. The next line sets the active ballot and in line 14 the user's choice of server is inserted in the database. Before returning to the user, a table with the ranking of the servers is presented to the user. This table is generated with the GetVote method.

Voting Component Methods

There are five methods provided by the Voting component. Two of these are used to retrieve user votes, and two are used for establishing connections to ballots and one for inserting votes into the database.

TABLE 9.4
Methods

Name	Description
GetVote	Returns the results of an entire ballot, for a single question, or a specific value that could be provided for a question. The results are formatted in an HTML table, including columns for the items, the total votes, and percentages.
GetVoteCount	Returns the number of votes submitted per ballot, question, or value.
Open	Opens the database connection that the Voting component should use for storage.
SetBallotName	Specifies the ballot on which the vote should be counted.
Submit	Inserts a vote in the database.

The methods are discussed in more depth in the next sections.

Open Method

Use this method to specify the ODBC connection the Voting component should use to store the voting results. The syntax for this method is as follows:

```
vtc.Open(SystemDSN,Username,Password)
```

Supply a valid System data source, *Username,* and *Password* to connect to the desired database. If the method succeeds, True is returned. Otherwise, False is returned, indicating an error.

SetBallotName Method

With the SetBallotName method you set the ballot the voting is stored to or retrieved from. The ballot name shows up when you display vote results, so choose a user-friendly string. You have up to 255 characters!

```
vtc.SetBallotName(BallotName)
```

This method returns True for successfully setting the appropriate ballot; False is unsuccessful.

Submit Method

The name already implies that this method adds a vote to the data source. It inserts a question/value pair into the database. Optionally, you can specify the User ID to disallow multiple votes from a single user. The syntax for the method is as follows:

```
vtc.Submit(Question, Value[,voterID])
```

Return values for this method are True and False, and the *Question* and *Value* parameters are strings up to 255 characters. The voterID is optional and can be obtained from the User Property Database. The next line of code shows how you could use it:

```
vtc.Submit("Favorite flavor of icecream","Yogurt",upd.ID)
```

GetVote Method

This method returns a formatted HTML table that includes the information about voting: item, totals, and percentage. The syntax for this method is as follows:

```
vtc.GetVote([question],[value])
```

Both arguments are optional. The return value of this method is HTML code. The resulting HTML depends on how many arguments you have specified:

- ◆ **No arguments:** Returns a table containing all questions of the current ballot.

- ◆ **Question:** Returns a table for the specific question in the ballot.

- ◆ **Question and value:** Returns the vote count for the specific question in the ballot.

In Listing 9.7 I have specified the Question argument, so the resulting HTML looks like Listing 9.8.

LISTING 9.8 – HTML CODE FOR GETVOTE("FAVORITE")

```
<table border=1>
<tr><th>Favorite</th><th>Number of Votes</th><th>Percentage
➥</th></tr>
<tr><td>Zauner</td><td ALIGN=CENTER>4</td><td ALIGN=CENTER>
➥57%</td></tr>
<tr><td>Microsoft</td><td ALIGN=CENTER>2</td>
➥<td ALIGN=CENTER>28%</td></tr>
<tr><td>MCP</td><td ALIGN=CENTER>1</td><td ALIGN=CENTER>
➥14%</td></tr>
</table>
```

`GetVoteCount` Method

If you need more control over the look and feel of the results table, you can use the `GetVoteCount` method and format the results yourself. This method returns the number of votes submitted per ballot, question, or value. The syntax for this method is as follows:

```
vtc.GetVoteCount([question],[value])
```

Both arguments are optional. The return value of this method is the number of votes for a ballot, question, or value. This depends on the number of arguments you have specified.

◆ **No arguments:** If the voters' IDs are tracked, it returns the number of voters that have voted for a given ballot. Otherwise, it returns 0.

◆ **Question:** Returns the number of votes submitted for the specified question in the ballot.

◆ **Question and value:** Returns the number of votes for a particular value of the specified question.

Listing 9.9 shows how to use the `GetVoteCount` method to create a customized table.

LISTING 9.9 - A CUSTOMIZED TABLE USING THE `GetVoteCount` METHOD

On the CD

```
01. <HTML>
02. <HEAD>
03. <TITLE>Chapter 9: Voting component - Results</TITLE>
04. </HEAD>
05. <BODY BGCOLOR=#ffffff>
06.
07. <H1>Voting Component Results</H1>
08. <%
09.    Set vtc = Server.CreateObject("MPS.Vote")
10.    If True = vtc.Open("unlocking","sa","") Then
11.      retCode = vtc.SetBallotName("Favorite Servers")
12.      nServerCount = vtc.GetVoteCount("Favorite")
13.      If (nServerCount > 0) Then
14. %>
15. <TABLE>
16. <tr><th>Server</th><th>Total</th></tr>
17. <TR><TD>Microsoft</TD>
```

continues

LISTING 9.9 - CONTINUED

```
18. <TD><%=vtc.GetVoteCount("Favorite","Microsoft")%>
    ➥</TD></TR>
19. <TR><TD>Pastry Shop Zauner</TD>
20. <TD><%=vtc.GetVoteCount("Favorite","Zauner")%></TD></TR>
21. <TR><TD>Macmillan Publications</TD>
22. <TD><%=vtc.GetVoteCount("Favorite","MCP")%></TD>
23. </TR></TABLE>
24. <%
25.     End If
26.   End if
27. %>
28.
29. </BODY>
30. </HTML>
```

This table doesn't contain any percentages of total, but this can be added easily with the following line of code:

```
((vtc.GetVoteCount("Favorite", "Zauner")/nServerCount)*100)
```

Summary

This chapter provided coverage of the Microsoft Personalization System with its three components—the User Property Database, the SendMail component, and the Voting component. It showed you how to create personalized content, how to communicate with the users, and how to gather opinions from the users. Chapter 13 uses the Voting component to gather feedback from users, and in Chapter 17, "Adding Personalization to Your Site," a site is created that can be personalized by users.

CHAPTER 10

Security

Security has always been one of the big issues on the Internet. This chapter gives you directions on how to secure your site and gives pointers on where to obtain more information about specific topics.

It provides in-depth coverage of three areas of security you will encounter when setting up a web business:

◆ Protecting your servers against intruders

◆ Secure data transmissions to and from your customers

◆ Creating communities on your server with access to members only

Protecting Your Server

This issue received a lot of attention when severe security bugs were discovered in Microsoft Internet Information Server in mid-February of 1997. The bugs allowed even the most unsophisticated hacker to download ASP source code and thus possibly SQL Server passwords and more from your computers. This again brought up the issue of how to secure Active Server Pages applications.

Securing Active Server Pages Applications

In the documentation for the first release of Active Server Pages, Microsoft recommended that you put ASP pages together with HTML and multimedia files in the same directory. In contrast to the other file types, ASP pages are executed prior to being sent to the user. When you mixed those file types, the directory had to be set in IIS to both Read and Execute. And that was precisely the reason why the bug showed up: you simply had to append special characters at the end of a URL referencing an ASP page and presto—you received the unexecuted ASP source code instead of the result of its execution. This was because IIS didn't recognize that the file had to be processed by a special engine. It still mapped it to the right physical file.

This bug is fixed now, but it showed that mixing different types of files can be extremely dangerous. If you're creating an ASP application, consider splitting your directories to Read and Execute only. Stick with this outline for creating a web directory structure:

◆ The virtual root is set to Execute, for example, /aspapplication contains only ASP pages. You also can put other execute-only files in this directory, like PERL files, or files for the Internet Database Connector.

◆ Create a separate virtual directory for your multimedia files, for example, /multimedia, and set it to Read only. Create subdirectories for images, movies, animations, and more.

◆ If you're still using HTML files, create a directory for them and assign Read permissions. An example for the name could be /staticcontent.

User Access

Internet Information Server enables access to resources only after the user's access privileges have been verified. Figure 10.1 shows the security checks performed before a user is permitted to access a requested page.

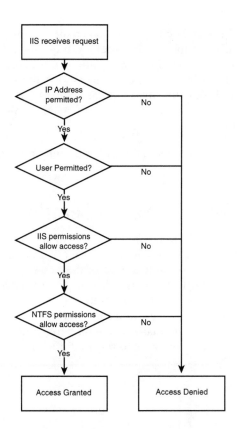

Figure 10.1

An overview of the security process.

You can set up the IIS web service to enable only users on computers in a given range of IP addresses to access files on this server. This enables you to put additional security on your intranet web server by disabling all IP addresses other than the local ones. It also is possible to disallow specific IP addresses for the web server, for example, addresses you know hacking attempts were made from.

The next level of access control comes into play when you have set your server with Secure Sockets Layer (SSL) to require Client Certificates. This security option is available only on secured servers. You will recognize secured servers by the `https://` protocol instead of `http://`. With this option enabled, only users that have a valid certificate are granted access to this server. There is another option for an intranet solution: you can open it to the Internet, but only your workers can access it via their certificates. And best, data is sent encrypted.

You can lock access to files with the Execute and Read access settings provided by IIS.

The last and most powerful security check is the NTFS file permissions. You can set access permissions for entire groups or single users. You can use it to grant access to administrative areas of the web server for Administrators only. For intranets, set file permissions to the group Domain Users to grant access only to users of your company (assuming that you have only one domain). This also is an option for creating members-only areas. There is more on this topic in the section "Members-only areas on your server" later in this chapter.

When all security checks have succeeded, the user is permitted to access the requested file.

SQL Server and MPS File Server Security

The best way to protect computers would be to lock them away with no connections to the outside world. Because you are providing information to the user over the public Internet, you cannot do this—at least not for the web server. For the other servers that do not communicate with the user directly (only via the web server, which relies on data provided by these servers), you can use a concept named firewalls to protect them. Firewalls are used to secure your local network from intruders that try to break into your systems. There are many very good books about firewalls; however, to illustrate a firewall's use, I will show a small version for a Web farm. Take a look at Figure 10.2.

Figure 10.2

Securing your web farm.

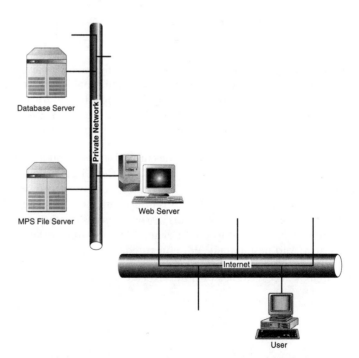

The cheapest and most effective means, though, is to insert a second network adapter in the web server. The network adapter for the Internet requests is bound to the TCP/IP protocol, and the adapter used for talking to the database and MPS file servers is bound to, for example, NetBEUI. No one can access the servers behind this firewall. If you prefer to use the TCP/IP protocol internally as well, simply disable IP routing on the web server to achieve the same level of security.

Secure Data Transmissions

Asking customers to transfer credit card information over the Internet without offering any safety for this data on its way from the customer to the web server isn't acceptable. The Secure Sockets Layer (SSL) protocol was invented to provide a means of security. It uses cryptography to secure the data transmissions to and from the customer.

Before you can offer SSL secured transmissions on your server, you have to acquire a security certificate from a certification authority like VeriSign. The following procedure outlines all the necessary steps for acquiring and then installing a security certificate on your server.

1. First you have to generate a key pair file and a request file. Open the Key Manager program located in the Microsoft Internet Server group for this. Select to create a new key and provide all the information needed.

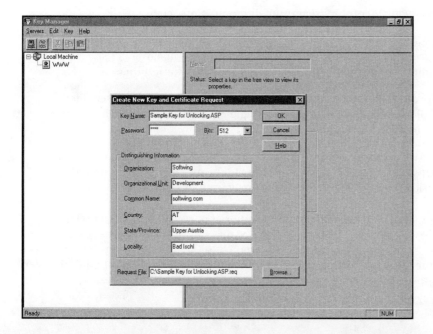

Figure 10.3

Create a new key using Key Manager.

2. Click OK. You are asked to verify the password and to enter an administrators email address and phone number. When you're done, select "Commit changes now" from the Servers menu. The key you have just created isn't valid for use on the Internet until you install a signed certificate from a certification authority.

3. To receive a valid certificate, send the certificate request file generated to a certification authority like VeriSign. VeriSign's Internet address is http:// www.verisign.com. Information about how to apply for a certificate can be obtained there.

4. When you have received the signed certificate from the certification authority, use Key Manager to install it on your server. Select Install Key Certificate from the Key menu. Open the file you have received and commit the changes to the web server.

5. Now you can SSL-enable directories on your server. Simply choose to edit a directory in Internet Service Manager and check the Require secure SSL channel checkbox. Now your data transmissions are secured for this directory.

Don't forget that now URLs must use https:// instead of http:// to reference files in this directory.

Members-Only Areas on Your Server

You can create members-only areas using different approaches:

♦ Use NTFS file security to enable access to the members area only for specific user accounts or groups. The disadvantage is that you have to create an NT user account for every member. This is a good solution for intranets.

♦ Create an ISAPI filter that implements a custom authentication scheme. Multiple members are mapped to a single NT user account which is granted access to a specific members area on your server.

♦ Create a custom authentication based on Active Server Pages. Every user is validated before access to any resources in the member area is allowed. The downside is that only .asp files can be protected by this mechanism.

Because this book is about ASP, the ASP solution is of course presented in-depth here. You have to provide a central login page that can be accessed from everywhere in your system. It's the first page that is presented to the user. However, because users can enter the area from any page they want, every page has to check whether the user has already been validated. Figure 10.4 shows how the validation process works.

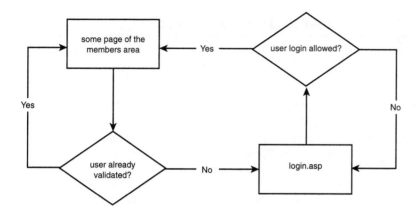

Figure 10.4

The user validation process.

The members validation system is based on a Microsoft SQL Server table and a stored procedure to validate the membership of a user trying to log in. The advantage to using a database is the easy maintenance of member information. The table that contains the members information is very simple; you can add more columns when you need to do so.

TABLE 10.1
Table Definition for the PrivateGroup Table

Column name	Datatype	Description
Userlogin	varchar(32)	User logins must be unique. Primary key index.
Password	varchar(32)	Password for this account. Required.
Fullname	varchar(255)	User's full name. Required.

Create this table in SQL Server using the script presented in Listing 10.1. This section's example assumes that you reuse the unlocking database presented in earlier chapters.

LISTING 10.1 - SQL SCRIPT FOR THE PRIVATEGROUP TABLE

```
01. CREATE TABLE dbo.PrivateGroup (
02.     Userlogin varchar (32) NOT NULL ,
03.     Password varchar (32) NOT NULL ,
04.     Fullname varchar (128) NOT NULL ,
05.     CONSTRAINT PK_PGroupPrim PRIMARY KEY NONCLUSTERED
06.     (
```

continues

LISTING 10.1, CONTINUED

```
07.        Userlogin
08.     )
09. )
10. GO
```

You can create a front-end to this database with either Microsoft Access or even an HTML-based member management. Add some members to the table. When you're done with it, create the following stored procedure in SQL Server:

LISTING 10.2 - SQL SCRIPT FOR THE sp_validateuser STORED PROCEDURE

```
01. CREATE PROCEDURE sp_validateuser
02.     @username varchar(32),
03.     @passwd varchar(32),
04.     @userfullname varchar(255) output
05. AS
06.   DECLARE @validuser int
07.   SELECT @validuser = COUNT(*), @userfullname=Fullname FROM PrivateGroup
08.     WHERE Userlogin=@username AND Password = @passwd GROUP BY
          ➥Userlogin,Fullname
09.   RETURN @validuser
10. GO
```

The return value is used to indicate whether the user is validated successfully and the full name is returned via an output parameter for the welcome message. This is all you need to do in SQL Server.

The example member area is based on an Active Server Pages application to show the usage of connection pooling. For such an application you need a global.asa file. For this example, Listing 10.3 shows its contents.

On the CD

LISTING 10.3 - GLOBAL.ASA FOR THE MEMBER-AREA EXAMPLE

```
01. <SCRIPT  LANGUAGE="VBScript" RUNAT="Server">
02. Sub Session_OnStart
03.     Session("PrivateGroupDSN") = "dsn=unlocking;uid=sa;pwd="
04.     Session("PGUFullname") = ""
05.     startPage = "/Chapter10/login.asp"
06.     currentPage = Request.ServerVariables("SCRIPT_NAME")
07.     If strcomp(currentPage,startPage,1) Then
08.       Response.Redirect(startPage & "?GoTo="
          ➥& Server.URLEncode(currentPage))
```

```
09.    End If
10. End Sub
11.
12. Sub Session_OnEnd
13.    'Insert script to be executed when a session ends
14. End Sub
15.
16. Sub Application_OnStart
17.    'Insert script to be executed when the application starts
18. End Sub
19.
20. Sub Application_OnEnd
21.    'Insert script to be executed when the application ends
22. End Sub
23. </SCRIPT>
```

The data source string that is used for connecting to a Connection object from the connection pool is added to the Session object in line 3. The next line's Session property contains the Fullname for the user from the database, however, to indicate users that aren't validated, it is set to an empty string.

For users that are requesting a different page than login.asp for their first request, the originally requested page is added as a QueryString to the redirection to login.asp. For the first request, every user ends up at the login page. The code for this login page is shown in Listing 10.4.

LISTING 10.4 - THE LOGIN PAGE

On the
CD

```
01. <!--#include file="adovbs.inc"-->
02. <%
03. If Request.ServerVariables("Content_Length")>0 Then
04.    Set Conn = Server.CreateObject("ADODB.Connection")
05.    Conn.ConnectionString = Session("PrivateGroupDSN")
06.    Set Cmd = Server.CreateObject("ADODB.Command")
07.    Cmd.ActiveConnection = Conn
08.    Cmd.CommandText = "{? = call sp_validateuser(?,?,?)}"
09.    Cmd.Parameters.Append Cmd.CreateParameter
       ➥("uservalid",adInteger,adParamReturnValue)
10.    Cmd.Parameters.Append Cmd.CreateParameter("userlogin",
       ➥adChar,adParamInput,32,Request("user"))
11.    Cmd.Parameters.Append Cmd.CreateParameter("password",
       ➥adChar,adParamInput,32,Request("passwd"))
12.    Cmd.Parameters.Append Cmd.CreateParameter("fullname",
       ➥adChar,adParamInputOutput,255,"dummy")
```

continues

LISTING 10.4, CONTINUED

```
13.    Cmd.Execute
14.    If Cmd(0)=1 Then
15.      Session("PGUFullname") = Cmd(3)
16.      If Len(Request("GoTo"))>0 Then
17.        Response.Redirect Request("GoTo")
18.      Else
19.        Response.Redirect "default.asp"
20.      End If
21.    End If
22. End If
23. %>
24.
25. <HTML>
26. <HEAD>
27. <TITLE>Chapter 10: Log in private group</TITLE>
28. </HEAD>
29. <BODY BGCOLOR=#ffffff>
30. <H1>Log in private group</H1>
31.
32. <FORM METHOD=POST ACTION="<%=Request.ServerVariables
    ➥("SCRIPT_NAME")%>">
33. <TABLE>
34. <TR><TD>Username</TD><TD><INPUT TYPE=TEXT NAME="user">
    ➥</TD></TR>
35. <TR><TD>Password</TD><TD><INPUT TYPE=PASSWORD NAME="passwd">
    ➥</TD></TR>
36. </TABLE>
37. <INPUT TYPE=HIDDEN NAME="GoTo" VALUE="<%=Request("GoTo")%>">
38. <INPUT TYPE=SUBMIT VALUE="Enter">
39. </FORM>
40.
41. </BODY>
42. </HTML>
```

A Connection object is created and the ConnectionString property is assigned the value of Session("PrivateGroupDSN"), the data source for this web application. The Command object that is used to call the stored procedure is initialized with its parameters between lines 8 and 12. This stored procedure uses a return value, input parameters, and an input/output parameter. All Parameter objects that are added to the Parameters collection are fully initialized with the CreateParameter method.

When the user with the given password exists in the database, then the first parameter contains 1 (because of the unique index on this column, there cannot be more). This indicates successful authentication and the user is redirected to the page he originally requested. Otherwise, he will be presented with the login form again. You can easily add a counter for how many times a user tried to log in and deny access to the login form after a specified number of unsuccessful retries.

The method presented so far has only one flaw: the user is automatically redirected to the login page from his first request, however, when the user decides to request another page in the members area, access is granted. To prevent this problem, I have created an include file, redirect.asp, that checks for successful user validation.

LISTING 10.5 - REDIRECT.ASP FOR THE VALIDATION CHECK

```
01. <%
02. If "" = Session("PGUFullname") Then
03.    Response.Redirect "login.asp?GoTo="
       ➥& Server.URLEncode(Request.ServerVariables("SCRIPT_NAME"))
04. End If
05. %>
```

You simply have to include this file in every page of your member area. From this time on, only validated members will be able to access pages in this area, as, for example the main page presented in Listing 10.6.

LISTING 10.6 - MAIN PAGE FOR THE PRIVATE GROUP

```
01. <!--#include file="redirect.asp"-->
02. <HTML>
03. <HEAD>
04. <TITLE>Chapter 10: Logged in to private group</TITLE>
05. </HEAD>
06. <BODY BGCOLOR=#ffffff>
07. <H1>Logged in to private group</H1>
08.
09. Welcome <%=Session("PGUFullname")%>  to our private area on our server!
10.
11. </BODY>
12. </HTML>
```

The first line includes the validation check from redirect.asp presented in Listing 10.5 in the current file. Now it is obvious why you should use only Active Server Pages files, because you can't protect other file types with this validation mechanism. However, the single line that is needed to make the mechanism work should justify renaming your other files.

Summary

This chapter showed you how to protect your servers against intruders because server security is getting more crucial as more and more internal data is used for a company's Internet presence. Another important topic that was covered was the security of transactions over the Internet. Providing clients with a secure means of transmitting credit card information over the Internet is mandatory today for creating online stores. Finally, you learned about creating private groups on your server that are open for members-only. The hands-on lesson presented how to create such private groups on your server with login validation.

CHAPTER 11

Troubleshooting Active Server Pages

The first thing that comes across a developer's mind when thinking about troubleshooting is the following procedure: read the reported error, track it, and fix it. This is an end-of-pipe technology. The most powerful solution is to actually avoid errors in the first place.

With the first release of Active Server Pages you can't actually debug your code line-by-line. Instead, you have to wait until an error stops the execution of your script. This is a very compelling reason to write the scripting code as cautiously as possible.

This chapter is backed by my knowledge of the examples (and the errors I made when creating them!) that I have presented throughout the book. I think it represents a good sampling of the errors that are most common when dealing with ASP scripts. Therefore, this chapter covers the following topics:

◆ Interpreting the Error Information

◆ Debugging Active Server Pages

Interpreting the Error Information

As I mentioned in the introduction to this chapter, you cannot really debug ASP scripts the way you can debug C source code, in which you can set breakpoints, step through the code line by line, change a variable's value, and perform other nice features that make debugging a snap. Debugging with ASP, in contrast, means that you can only find an error when it shows up, because then the execution of your script is terminated. The error message is sent to the browser with the line number on which it occurred. Only then can you start looking at the code and trying to guess why the error has shown up.

Because interpreting error information—and finding the code that caused it—is so important for fixing bugs in ASP scripts, this section is dedicated to explaining the parts of the error message you receive and how to find the code that caused it.

Error information looks like Listing 11.1.

LISTING 11.1 - SAMPLE ERROR INFORMATION

```
01. Microsoft VBScript runtime error '800a01a8'
02. Object required: 'Session(...)'
03. /chapter11/testlisting.asp, line 4
```

The page that generated this error is presented later in this chapter. The parts that comprise an error message are as follows:

◆ The scripting language that generated the error is the first part of the error message (see Listing 11.1, line 1)

◆ The error number

◆ A brief error description

◆ The name of the file the error occurred in with the line number on which the erroneous code is located

◆ For some errors you receive extended information, for example, critical errors that occur when executing stored procedures in SQL Server

All error messages are appended to the IIS log too, however, in an abbreviated version. A sample entry to the log file for an invalid CLng() conversion in an ASP script is presented in the following section.

```
1.1.1.1, -, 04.01.97, 18:14:17, W3SVC, W3_SRV_SOFTWING,
➥ 193.154.1.101, 21471, 288, 2002, 200, 0, GET,
➥ /DasHausZauner/default.asp,
➥ |ASP|49|800a000d|Type mismatch: 'CLng'
```

Of course I changed the IP address of the client's computer that requested the page. The error information is the last column to this log entry:

```
|ASP|49|800a000d|Type mismatch: 'CLng'
```

It contains the line number (49) on which the error occurred, the error number (800a000d), and a short description for the error itself (Type mismatch: `'CLng'`).

> **Tip**
>
> Searching log files for errors can be invaluable for production servers. The preceding log entry is taken from such a server and is the only chance to find hard-to-spot errors that occur only for specific configurations.
>
> To find out where the log files are stored and how they are named, open the Properties dialog box for the WWW Service in the IIS Service Manager. In the Logging tab you can view the directory in which the log files are stored and how the names for these are generated (depends on how many times new logs are created).

Debugging Active Server Pages

When you're debugging ASP pages, you open them in an editor and go to the line to which the error message's line information is pointing. Of course, you could use Notepad and count the number of lines until you reach the suspect line, however, using an editor that is capable of line numbering makes life much easier. Editors that support line numbers are, for example, HomeSite from Allaire, or Microsoft Visual InterDev.

> **Warning**
>
> Don't use word wrapping in the editor because this could mess up line numbering.
>
> Don't use the `On Error Resume Next` statement during development of your pages. If you use it in your source code, the error messages won't show up in the log file or on-screen. However, on production servers it is not intended that the user can see the error message. You can either turn error messages completely off (see Appendix C, "Configuration Tips for Active Servers," section "Error handling") or you have to handle error cases inline through the scripting code. For adding this inline error handling code when dealing with ADO (where it is most important), see the section "Submitting any SQL Command to the Database" in Chapter 7, "Database Access with ActiveX Data Objects."

Tracking the Actual Bug

What do I mean by *actual bug*? An example might help. Let's say that you are retrieving the version number of the user's browser using the `BrowserCapabilities` component in the following statement

```
nBrowserVersion = m_objBC.majorver
```

Because all variables are Variant in VBScript, `nBrowserVersion` might as well contain the string `"UNKNOWN"` in case the user requesting the page is using a browser that isn't defined in browscap.ini. Now, in some lines below, you are doing the following conversion:

```
nBrowserVersion = CLng(nBrowserVersion)
```

With the user's browser unknown, this line generates a conversion error as presented in the snapshot of the log file. The bug is introduced by the first statement, but the second one causes the bug to show up. There are many such scenarios when the bug that shows up for line X is caused by code on line Y, which might be located some lines before line X, or in an entirely different file. However, to reassure you, in most cases the bug is in the code on the same line it is reported for.

The next sections present common bugs. Sometimes these bugs occur because of an oversight; sometimes they are inherent to the implementation. Errors such as a missing `then` statement, typographical errors, or something like this are not presented. These are obvious to track.

Bugs Introduced by the Set Statement

The `Set` statement is used in conjunction with assignment of objects to variables. A typical use of this statement is the creation of an object, in this example, the creation of an ADO Connection object:

```
Set Conn = Server.CreateObject("ADODB.Connection")
```

Another common use is to assign such a newly created object to a session variable to be able to access it from any subsequent page. Typically, the assignment of session variables is implemented in the `Session_OnStart` event handler in global.asa. To more drastically show the error that can be introduced, I have put the code for object creation, assigned it to a session variable, and then reused this variable in Listing 11.2 on subsequent lines:

LISTING 11.2 - CREATING SESSION VARIABLES

```
01. <%
02.    Set Conn = Server.CreateObject("ADODB.Connection")
03.    Session("TheDBConn") = Conn
04.    Set objReuseHere = Session("TheDBConn")
05. %>
```

Notice the assignment of the newly created object to the session variable `TheDBConn` on line 3. I have omitted the `Set` statement intentionally to introduce the bug that creates the error message in Listing 11.3:

LISTING 11.3 - THE ERROR MESSAGE THAT LISTING 11.2 CREATES

```
01. Microsoft VBScript runtime error '800a01a8'
02. Object required: 'Session(...)'
03. /chapter11/testlisting.asp, line 4
```

This is the error message that I presented earlier in the chapter when depicting an error message's parts. The error description (line 2) means that the session variable that is accessed on line 4 in Listing 11.2 does not contain a valid object. With the knowledge that there is an assignment error—objects need to be assigned to variables using the `Set` keyword—on line 3, you can find the cause easily; it's obvious. It would be much more difficult to find the cause of such an error if lines 2 and 3 of Listing 11.2 were located in the global.asa file in the `Session_OnStart` event method and if line 4 were located in some page accessing this variable. It's too easy to fail to notice that only the `Set` keyword is missing.

To avoid such a nasty error message on a production server, you should always check for the validity of the object before you access any methods or properties exposed by the object. The code you need to avoid this error (by sanity-checking the object before accessing it) is presented in Listing 11.4.

LISTING 11.4 - SANITY CHECKING OBJECT VARIABLES

```
01. <%
02.    Set Conn = Server.CreateObject("ADODB.Connection")
03.    Session("TheDBConn") = Conn
04.    If Not IsObject(Session("TheDBConn")) Then
05.      Response.Write "Sorry, internal error occurred."
06.      Response.End
07.    End If
08. %>
```

Instead of simply terminating the script processing, you also could log the error information or send an e-mail to the web server administrator. You also could redirect the user to a page that explains in more detail that the requested page couldn't be opened due to some error.

Cross Reference

To learn how to automatically present the user with a customized error message when an unhandled error occurs, see Appendix C, "Configuration Tips for Active Servers," section "Error handling," p. 498.

Comments in ASP Pages

"What can be wrong with comments?," you might ask. Until recently, if someone told me that I could introduce bugs in a program with its comments, I surely would have laughed at him. Such a bug caught me. It took me some time to figure it out; I wasn't able to do so until I switched from Notepad to Visual InterDev. Visual InterDev, with its syntax coloring feature, immediately pointed me to the cause of the error.

To illustrate how one can introduce a bug with a comment, I have created Listing 11.5 for you. At first look it seems perfectly okay.

LISTING 11.5 - COMMENTS ALSO CAN INTRODUCE BUGS

```
01. <%
02.    x = 2  ' <%=5%>
03.    x = 5
04. %>
```

The comment in line 2 would look innocent if this section weren't about bugs. When you execute the script, it surprises you with an actual return:

```
x = 5 %>
```

This means that code starting with line 3 doesn't get executed. Therefore, the error must be located on line 2, and there it is! VBScript interprets ' <%=5 correctly as a comment, however, the %> following it is identified as the end of code statement by the Active Server Pages engine. When I started up Visual InterDev and opened this file, I immediately saw the problem because of InterDev's syntax coloring feature. However, using Notepad, I hunted this bug without luck.

To avoid bugs like these there is one piece of advice: never put any code in the comment that the scripting engine could misinterpret, like end of code statements, <SCRIPT> tags, or comment tags (<!--). The best way to avoid such errors without having to remember these tags is to use an editor that supports syntax coloring like Visual InterDev. You will see immediately where the correct code ends.

Problems with Databases

The variety of different databases you can access also creates some problems for developers. One very common problem is that the database cannot be accessed. This section includes solutions for both SQL Server and Microsoft Access. If you don't use either of these, I'm sure some of the solutions work for your database management system.

Connection to a SQL Server Fails

This error shows up when the web server and the SQL Server are installed on different machines on your network. I assume that the computers are integrated in a domain and that the web server isn't running on the Primary Domain Controller (a very safe assumption). Figure 11.1 illustrates this scenario.

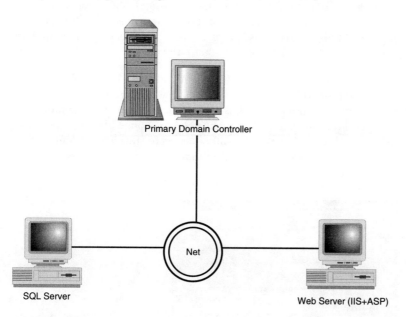

Primary Domain Controller

SQL Server

Net

Web Server (IIS+ASP)

Figure 11.1

A scenario in which a web server runs on a different machine from the SQL Server.

Regardless of whether you have set up the system datasource correctly, the following error message is displayed every time you try to access the database located on the remote SQL Server with Conn.Open:

LISTING 11.6 - FAILING TO CONNECT TO THE SQL SERVER

```
01. Microsoft OLE DB Provider for ODBC Drivers error '80004005'
02. [Microsoft][ODBC SQL Server Driver][dbnmpntw]ConnectionOpen (CreateFile()).
```

This error, however, is nothing especially new for ActiveX Data Objects. It is a problem of the default installation of Internet information. It also shows up when you're using the IDC/HTX mechanism.

This error occurs because of the installation of IIS. During installation, a logon account for anonymous access to resources on the web server is created. This account is created on the local computer and not on the domain server. This account's location is exactly the problem: the local account doesn't have sufficient rights to access the SQL Server with the network, therefore, SQL Server refuses the request to establish the connection.

You can resolve this problem by implementing the following steps (you need to have administrative rights for the domain):

1. Create a new user account in the domain database using User Manager For Domains. You need to grant the right Logon Locally to this account for the web server computer. Choose usernames and passwords for this account that are hard to guess (the best are mixed character-number passwords).

2. Open the Service Properties dialog box for the World Wide Web Publishing service that runs on the web server and enter the new account in the form *Domainname\Accountname* (the backslash is required). Enter the new password as well. Figure 11.2 shows an example. You may need to change file access permissions for your web server's directories to allow access for this new account the same way IUSR_*computername* had. If you don't know how to do this, ask your system administrator.

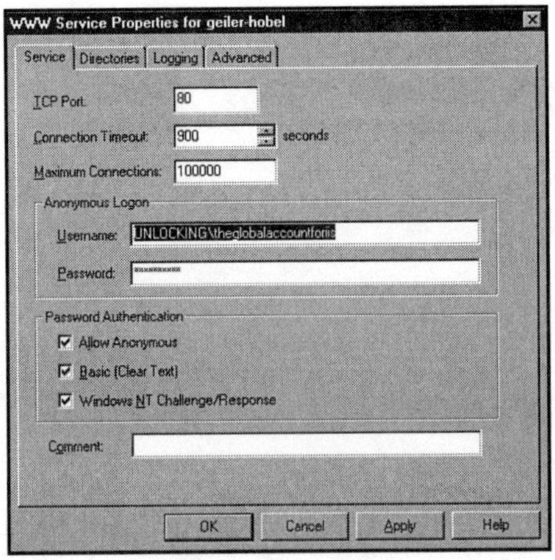

Figure 11.2

Changing the anonymous account from local computer to domain scope.

Now the anonymous account has the appropriate rights to access the SQL Server with the network, and your problems are gone.

Problems Accessing an Access Database

Security problems also occur when you're dealing with data stored in Microsoft Access databases. The .mdb file must be located in a directory that has both read and write permissions set for the anonymous IIS service account (or, if you are requiring logon to your server, the users accounts) to enable Access to create the .ldb file. This file is used to store locking information for the database and is created on the first use of the database.

When the directory containing the Access database hasn't set up security properly (read and write access for the account the current user is logged in to), you receive the following error message:

```
[Microsoft][ODBC Microsoft Access '97 Driver] Couldn't lock file.
```

The need for read and write access to the directory containing the file implies that it shouldn't be located in a directory that's part of the directory structure of your web site. Place it in a separate directory away from the site where you can (relatively) safely allow read and write access.

Apostrophes in Insertion Strings

When you're creating forms that enable users to search for specific records in your database, you're creating the SQL query string on the fly using a SELECT statement. To illustrate such a SQL statement creation see Listing 11.7, which uses input from the user to query the database.

LISTING 11.7 - QUERYING THE DATABASE
FOR USER ENTERED CRITERIA'S

```
01. <!--#include file="adovbs.inc"-->
02. <%
03.   Set Conn = Server.CreateObject("ADODB.Connection")
04.   Conn.Open "unlocking","sa",""
05.
06.   Set rs = Server.CreateObject("ADODB.Recordset")
07.   strSQL = "SELECT * FROM Events WHERE Description='"
      ➥& Request("DescQryString") &"'"
08.   rs.Open strSQL, Conn, adOpenKeyset, adLockReadOnly
09.     ' do something
10.   rs.Close
11.   Conn.Close
12. %>
```

Line 7's code generates the SQL statement that is issued against the database on line 8. The `DescQryString` form variable is used to query the `Description` column in the `tEvents` table. The string needs to be enclosed in apostrophes to be recognized as a correct string argument. If you supply, for example, `"Sample Description"` to `DescQryString`, the query executes with no problems. However, if the user wants to query for `"The band's history"`, the page terminates with the error message shown in Listing 11.8.

LISTING 11.8 - THE ERROR YOU WILL RECEIVE WHEN QUERYING FOR "THE BAND'S HISTORY"

```
01. Microsoft OLE DB Provider for ODBC Drivers error '80040e14'
02. [Microsoft][ODBC SQL Server Driver][SQL Server]Line 1:
    ➥Incorrect syntax near 's'.
03. /chapter11/last10.asp, line
```

The problem is that the SQL statement that is generated on line 7 of Listing 11.7 evaluates to the following string for `"The band's history"`:

```
strSQL = "SELECT * FROM Events WHERE Description='The band's history'
```

SQL Server thinks that the string to be queried for is only `"The band"` and doesn't know what to do with the rest. However, if you need to query for strings that might contain apostrophes, you simply have to double them to make SQL Server and others recognize them as single apostrophes and not the string delimiter. You have to modify line 7 of Listing 11.7 only slightly to change the apostrophes in a string to double apostrophes:

```
strSQL = "SELECT * FROM Events WHERE Description='" &
➥Replace(Request("DescQryString"),"'"," ''") &"'"
```

The VBScript Replace function escapes all single apostrophes, meaning it replaces all single quotes with double quotes. Now the script works as expected.

Using Wildcards

If you don't want to search for an exact match of a string in a field, you can use wildcard characters. The problem with wildcards is that the different database management systems use different characters as the wildcard character. For example, SQL Server uses the percent sign (%), and Microsoft Access uses the asterisk (*).

When you're writing database code that uses wildcards, you have to remember that you can't easily switch to another database management system. If you have to, you need to change every single occurrence of the wildcard character in the SQL statements. You won't necessarily receive an error message due to the wrong wildcard character (for example, when the wildcard character from database management system A is treated like a normal character in system B) when switching systems. To make you more flexible with different database management systems, use an Application variable to store the wildcard character and append it to the search strings when needed. This makes changing database management systems easy because you only have to change a single line of code.

Storing Data to Large Text Fields

When you're dealing with large amounts of textual information, you usually store it to text columns (SQL Server) or to give another example, memo fields in Access. Dealing with this data type is tricky because every system handles it in a slightly different fashion. This section is intended as a guide to avoid errors when dealing with this data type.

For the examples in this section, I use a very simple and in fact totally useless demo table named `TextFieldTest`. It contains an index column, a second column to add more value, and the text column.

TABLE 11.1
Table Definition for the `TextFieldTest` Table

Column name	Datatype	Description
IdCol	int	Primary key index
SomeColumn	varchar(50)	Just another column.
SomeText	text	A memo.

Again, for the users of SQL Server, I have provided the script to generate the table in Listing 11.9.

LISTING 11.9 - THE SCRIPT FOR GENERATING THE `TextFieldTest` TABLE

```
01. CREATE TABLE dbo.TextFieldTest (
02.       IdCol int IDENTITY (1, 1) NOT NULL ,
03.       SomeColumn varchar (50) NULL ,
04.       SomeText text NULL ,
```

continues

```
05.      CONSTRAINT PK_textfieldtest PRIMARY KEY NONCLUSTERED
06.      (
07.           IdCol
08.      )
09. )
10. GO
```

To test insertion behavior, I have created a simplistic form that handles it. There is only a <TEXTAREA> in the form to enter the text information. Listing 11.10 contains both the form and the database insertion code.

On the CD

LISTING 11.10 - INSERTING INFORMATION INTO THE DATABASE

```
01. <!--#include file="adovbs.inc"-->
02. <HTML>
03. <BODY BGCOLOR=#ffffff>
04. <%
05. If Not Request.ServerVariables("Content_Length")>0 Then
06. %>
07. <FORM ACTION="<%=Request.ServerVariables("SCRIPT_NAME")%>" METHOD=POST>
08. <TEXTAREA NAME="test" COLS=80 ROWS=10></TEXTAREA>
09. <INPUT TYPE=SUBMIT VALUE="Submit">
10. </FORM>
11. <%
12. Else
13.    Set Conn = Server.CreateObject("ADODB.Connection")
14.    Set RS = Server.CreateObject("ADODB.RecordSet")
15.    Conn.Open "unlocking","sa",""
16.    RS.Open "TextFieldTest", Conn , adOpenKeyset, adLockOptimistic
17.
18.    RS.AddNew
19.    RS("SomeColumn") = CStr(Request.ServerVariables("REMOTE_HOST"))
20.    RS("SomeText") = CStr(Request("test"))
21.    RS.Update
22.
23.    RS.Close
```

```
24.   Conn.Close
25. End If
26. %>
27. </BODY>
28. </HTML>
```

There is no spectacular code in this listing, only the code to insert the form data into the database (lines 18–21). The problem with this example is that as long as you provide information in the form field, the code to insert the information into the database works perfectly well. If you don't enter any information, you'll get the following error message:

LISTING 11.11 - THE ERROR MESSAGE YOU RECEIVE WHEN NO DATA IS SUPPLIED FOR THE TEXT COLUMN

```
01. ADODB.Recordset error '800a0d5d'
02. Data type conversion error.
03. /chapter11/texterrneous.asp, line 21
```

First of all, line 21 contains only RS.Update, which doesn't necessarily point to the problem of a zero-length text field. It took me some time to realize this problem was related to zero-length strings and not to some other possibly stranger thing. This problem is inherent to both SQL Server and Access.

However, there is a workaround to this problem that works for all scenarios. Simply replace line 20 with the three lines of Listing 11.12.

LISTING 11.12 - HOW TO WORK AROUND THE TEXT FIELD PROBLEM

```
01.   If Len(Request("test"))>0 Then
02.     RS("SomeText") = CStr(Request("test"))
03.   End If
```

Now, with the rewrite presented in Listing 11.12, the problem that arises when trying to insert empty strings into text fields is solved and the code works just fine.

Tracing Program Flow

Because you cannot step through your ASP code line-by-line, you cannot take a look at the variables the way you can with a debugger. Again, I can offer only workarounds to you for tracing the values of variables and paths of execution:

◆ Insert Response.Write statements in the code to dump the values of variables into the response that is sent to the browser.

◆ Open a `TextStream` and write the information to the disk.

The method with `Response.Write` is easy to apply and has worked very well for me. You can use this approach, for example, to check SQL statements that you create on the fly in your code. When you're done testing your scripts, you can comment the line or remove it entirely from your script.

If you want to create a log of errors or just don't want to dump into the response, you can create a `TextStream` object and write error information to the disk. Because this solution is a bit more complicated than `Response.Write`, I'll supply a small example of how you could use it for your purposes (see Listings 11.13, 11.14, 11.15).

The solution I present here takes the approach of creating an include file that contains all program logic for opening and closing the log file as well as for writing to it. The design is targeted at tracking log information for single users—in other words, this means that the output file is attached as a session variable.

The include file for the logging routines doesn't contain very much code; you can extend or modify it to fit your needs. Listing 11.13 is intended as a starting point for your logging extensions.

On the
CD

LISTING 11.13 - THE INCLUDE FILE LOGGING.ASP CONTAINS ALL LOGIC FOR OPENING, CLOSING, AND LOGGING ITSELF

```
01. <SCRIPT  LANGUAGE=VBSCRIPT RUNAT=SERVER>
02.
03. Sub InitializeLog(strLogfilename)
04.    Set FileObject = Server.CreateObject("Scripting.FileSystemObject")
05.    Set Out = FileObject.CreateTextFile (Server.MapPath (strLogfilename),
       ➥True)
06.    Out.WriteLine("Log created on " & Now())
07.    Set Session("Logfile") = Out
08. End Sub
09.
10. Sub CloseLog()
11.    If IsObject(Session("LogFile")) Then
12.      Session("LogFile").WriteLine("Log close on " & Now())
13.      Session("LogFile").Close
14.    End If
15. End Sub
16.
17. Sub Log(strLogText)
```

```
18.    If IsObject(Session("LogFile")) Then
19.      Session("LogFile").WriteLine(strLogText & " - logged at " & Now())
20.    End If
21. End Sub
22.
23. </SCRIPT>
```

A status line is automatically written to the log at the start and the end of the logging with timestamp information for later analysis. The output that you decided to write to the log with the Log method also is appended with timestamp information.

Now it's up to you to decide when to initialize a logging session. You can do this with a form with which you provide the location of the log, or you can enable logging for all users. To achieve this, you have to put the initialize and close methods into the OnStart and OnEnd event methods for the Session object. The filename is created using the SessionId and it is stored to the server root (not the best idea). Listing 11.14 contains the code that is necessary to get up and running for the global.asa file. It implements the approach of opening a new log file for each user.

On the CD

LISTING 11.14 - HOW GLOBAL.ASA COULD LOOK
WHEN YOU ARE LOGGING FOR EVERY USER

```
01. <!--#include file="logging.asp"-->
02. <SCRIPT  LANGUAGE=VBScript RUNAT=Server>
03. Sub Application_OnStart
04. End Sub
05.
06. Sub Application_OnEnd
07. End Sub
08.
09. Sub Session_OnStart
10.    strTest = "/" & CStr(Session.SessionId) & ".txt"
11.    InitializeLog strTest
12. End Sub
13.
14. Sub Session_OnEnd
15.    CloseLog
16. End Sub
17. </SCRIPT>
```

First you have to include logging.asp to be able to access the initialize and close methods for the log. There are only three lines of code needed to open and close the log for each user. The first two are located in `Session_OnStart` for creating a log file for the user (lines 10 and 11): the third one is used to close the log in `Session_OnEnd` (line 15).

The only thing you have to do to use the logging features on your pages is to include the logging.asp file and invoke the `Log` method wherever you want. To illustrate this, I have taken an example that was presented earlier and added the logging feature to it. Listing 11.15 contains its source code.

On the CD

LISTING 11.15 - LOGGING INFORMATION ABOUT THE
DATABASE CONNECTION FAILURE

```
01. <!--#include virtual="/logging.asp"-->
02. <%
03.   Set Conn = Server.CreateObject("ADODB.Connection")
04.   Session("TheDBConn") = Conn
05.   If Not IsObject(Session("TheDBConn")) Then
06.     Log "Could not open the connection to the database!"
07.     Response.Write "Sorry, internal error occurred."
08.     Response.End
09.   End If
10. %>
```

Notice that the file logging.asp is included with the virtual keyword, which means that it's located in the server's root directory (you have to adjust this if you want to store this include file in another location). The second line that is added here is number 6. You could write any other information to the log here.

Note | File output is buffered with the `TextStream` component, so you might not be able to view the contents of the log file before the session is abandoned.

If you want to log information in a single file for all users, you need to modify the code to store a file object in the `Application` object. However, if you decide to do so, be aware that you must guard access to this variable with the `Lock` and `Unlock` methods to prevent some side effects that could arise when two or more users are trying to access the variable at once.

Summary

Debugging Active Server Pages version 1.0 is definitely not very easy because you can only look at the line of code ASP tells you it didn't like. You cannot step through your code line-by-line, as you can other programming language's debuggers. Perhaps this will be a feature of the next version.

This chapter also included a wealth of tips about which traps to avoid. Take this chance to learn from errors others have made. If you need to trace the program flow of your ASP pages, there also is a solution for it: saving the output to a disk file. This precaution, however, is not a replacement for being careful when you program.

To learn more about problems others have already solved, navigate with your browser to Stephen Genusa's brilliant web site dedicated to Internet Information Server. The FAQ database is located under `http://www.genusa.com/asp/`. You can find links to online resources, free tools, and more on this site as well.

Cross
Reference

To learn how to present users on production servers with a customized error message when an unhandled error occurs, see Appendix C, "Configuration Tips for Active Servers," section "Error handling," p. 498.

CHAPTER 12

Extending Active Server Pages with Components

Active Server Pages doesn't have much power by itself, instead gaining its power by the components that extend it. The components shipping with ASP include the ActiveX Data Objects, the Ad Rotator component, the Browser Capabilities component, and more. These components extend the reach of ASP to databases and encapsulate functionality in a well-defined object.

If you want to create ActiveX Server components to add specific functionality, you can do so with any programming language that's capable of creating Automation servers. This chapter shows how to use the following programming languages to extend Active Server Pages:

- ◆ **Visual Basic 5.0:** This is the easiest and fastest way to create ActiveX Server components. It has the lowest learning curve of all programming languages when you are using ASP with VBScript.

- ◆ **Visual J++:** Using Visual J++ gives you the power and flexibility of Java. You could use it when you're more familiar with programming Java than Basic.

- ◆ **Visual C++ 5.0 and MFC:** If you have already used Visual C++ and MFC (Microsoft Foundation Classes), this is the way to create very powerful and fast components in a short time.

- ◆ **Visual C++ 5.0 and ATL:** With ATL (ActiveX Template Library), you create the fastest and most lightweight components. You need to be familiar with the foundations OLE and using template libraries in C++.

The next section deals with issues that are applicable to all programming languages.

Programming Considerations

You have to consider some issues before you start designing or coding your component. These considerations include the following:

- ◆ Packaging

- ◆ Threading models

- ◆ Using Page-Level event methods

Packaging

When you're familiar with OLE, you already know the two possible methods of implementing components:

- ◆ In-process, implemented as a DLL (Dynamic Link Library)

- ◆ Out-of-process, implemented as an executable (EXE)

The fastest method, of course, is implementing the component as an in-process component. This is because it runs in the process of the client using the component, which, in contrast to the out-of-process method, doesn't incur marshaling between processes.

When implementing an in-process component you should always be aware of the fact that buggy code in your component could crash the client, in this case, the web server.

Threading Models

It's not just the packaging of the components that impacts the performance of your web application. The choice of threading model for your component also greatly influences the performance. Basically, there are four threading models:

- **Single-Threaded:** Not recommended.

- **Apartment-Threaded:** Recommended, however, you can't store the object in the `Application` object. Objects created with application scope using the `<OBJECT>` tag lock the server down to one service thread, resulting in a performance penalty.

- **Free-Threaded:** Not recommended for use with Active Server Pages.

- **Objects marked as Both:** Highly recommended—you are able to store the object in the application. It does not come with a performance penalty when you create objects for application or session scope.

Depending on the programming language you're using, you are presented with the ability to choose the threading model. Objects marked as Both are only supported by the ATL (ActiveX Template Library), so if you plan to create high-performance components, there is no way around ATL.

Using Page-Level Event Methods

The components you create don't have to support any special methods, however, there are two optional methods you can implement: `OnStartPage` and `OnEndPage`.

The `OnStartPage` method is called before the component is first used on a page. This method is passed a `ScriptingContext` object, which can be used to obtain the `Application`, `Session`, `Request`, `Response`, and `Server` objects. With these, you can perform the same actions you could in ASP code.

When all scripts on the page have finished processing, your component's `OnEndPage` method is called. Use it to perform any clean-up you may need to perform (free memory, release interface pointers, and so on).

If you're instancing components for application scope in global.asa, obviously, these methods will never be called. When designing your component, you have to take care of this scenario and degrade gracefully when you do not receive the `ScriptingContext` object.

Creating Components with Visual Basic 5.0

This section presents the basics of creating components with Visual Basic with the Hello World example. This section's second example shows you how to rapidly create a useful and yet easy-to-implement component everyone has been waiting for: the `DirectoryBrowser` component.

This section assumes that you're familiar with the object concept and programming model in Visual Basic.

Hello World

The Hello World example is presented in two variations here—very basic, to show the minimum requirements for a component, and a second, more advanced version to show how to incorporate the ActiveX Server objects in your component's code.

Creating a Simple Component

The component presented in this section has only one method that can be called from an ASP page. However, you aren't limited to invoking it from ASP—any scripting container can make use of the component.

Implement the following steps to create the `HelloWorld` component.

1. Start Visual Basic 5.0. Select ActiveX DLL in the New Project dialog box.

Figure 12.1

Select ActiveX DLL as the new project.

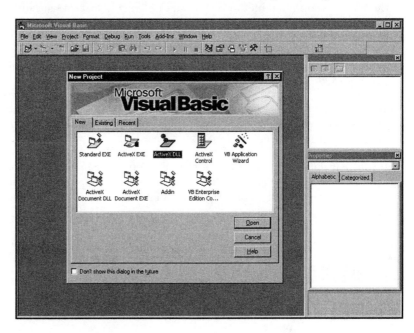

2. A new project named `Project1` and a class named `Class1` are created. Rename `Project1` to `Unlocking` and `Class1` to `VB5_HelloWorld` by selecting it in the Project window and then changing the name in the following Properties window.

3. Add the following code lines to your class file:

LISTING 12.1 - THE HELLOWORLD FUNCTION

```
01. Public Function HelloWorld() As String
02.    HelloWorld = "Hello World"
03. End Function
```

This inserts a function named `HelloWorld` that is accessible from a scripting language. It simply returns "Hello World".

4. Now your workspace window should look like Figure 12.2.

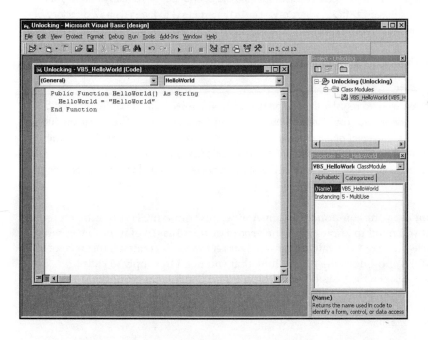

Figure 12.2

The workspace for the finished project.

5. Save your project to disk.

6. Select `File/Make` and enter the location for the resulting DLL. Select your project folder as target and name the file `unlocking.dll`.

7. Congratulations, you have created your first component in Visual Basic!

Creating the component isn't the final step. Before you can use the component, you have to register it on the computer on which the web server is running. The following steps assume that you're running the web server on the local machine where you are doing the component development.

1. Open File Manager and go to the project directory where you have saved the component's DLL.

2. Select the component's DLL and execute the `File/Run` command from the menu.

3. Enter **regsvr32** before the name of the DLL component in the Run dialog box. Click OK.

> **Note** This step assumes that the component registration utility regsvr32.exe is already in the path. If you receive an error that the file cannot be found, copy it from your Visual Basic CD-ROM (directory \tools\regutils\) to the system32 directory of your Windows installation.

4. When the registration has finished, you receive a completion message.

> **Tip** If you want to register the component on a web server where no Visual Basic 5 component was registered before, you need some additional DLLs to successfully execute the component. The easiest way is to create an installation disk set with Visual Basic for this component that adds all DLLs to the set that are needed for this component to execute (see the Visual Basic documentation for information about creating installation disks).

Now you can use your component in any ASP scripts you want. To instantiate the component you need to know either the `ProgId` or the `ClassId` of it, however, most often you use the `ProgId` in calls to `Server.CreateObject` to create an instance of the component. But how does the `ProgId` look that you need to supply to calls to `Server.CreateObject` for Visual Basic projects? The general syntax of `ProgIds` for Visual Basic components is as follows:

```
Projectname.Classname
```

For the project we have created, the `ProgId` is

```
Unlocking.VB5_HelloWorld
```

With this information, you can create an object of class `HelloWorld` and access its public function `HelloWorld`. See Listing 12.2 for the ASP code to access the new component.

LISTING **12.2** - ACCESSING THE NEWLY CREATED **HelloWorld** OBJECT   On the CD

```
01. <HTML>
02. <HEAD>
03. <TITLE>Chapter 12: VB 5 Hello World</TITLE>
04. </HEAD>
05. <BODY>
06.
07. <%
08. Set hworld = Server.CreateObject(
    ➥"Unlocking.VB5_HelloWorld")
09. Response.Write hworld.HelloWorld
10. %>
11.
12. </BODY>
13. </HTML>
```

The result, as expected, is Hello World. This is a very basic example and it isn't restricted to be used only with ASP scripts. It is a component you can use in any other tool that allows scripting of OLE Automation servers. The next section extends this example to write the information directly to the client using ActiveX Server objects.

Using OnStartPage and OnEndPage Event Methods

The big advantage of incorporating the OnStartPage and OnEndPage event methods into your component is that you are notified when the processing of an ASP script begins and when the processing of a page is finished. Also, with OnStartPage, you gain access to the built-in ActiveX Server objects, so you can perform any action you could in ASP and have the power of your programming language—in this case, Visual Basic 5.0.

The first step to use the ActiveX Server objects in your Visual Basic project is to add a reference to the Microsoft Active Server Pages Object Library. You add it with the Project/References command. Simply check the library in the References dialog box. See Figure 12.3 for this dialog box.

Now you can use the Application, Session, Request, Response, and Server objects in your Visual Basic source code. To access these objects, you need to implement the OnStartPage method and retrieve the object you need from the ScriptingContext object that is passed to this method. Listing 12.3 implements a sample OnStartPage method that retrieves the Response object, which can later be used to write directly to the client from within the component.

Figure 12.3

Adding the reference to the ASP Object Library.

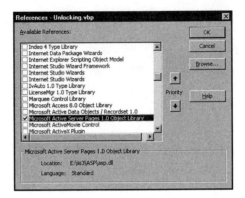

LISTING 12.3 - USING **OnStartPage** TO ACCESS THE ACTIVEX SERVER OBJECTS

```
01. Public Function OnStartPage(objSC As ScriptingContext)
02.    Set m_objResponse = objSC.Response
03. End Function
```

Of course, you could save a reference to the ScriptingContext object as well, and access the underlying objects when you need to do so. However, the approach presented in Listing 12.3 enables you to save references to objects you need. When you no longer need the object, it's good practice to release the object by setting it to Nothing. The last possibility for this is the OnEndPage method. See Listing 12.4 to learn how to release the Response object you referenced in Listing 12.3.

LISTING 12.4 - USING **OnEndPage** TO RELEASE REFERENCES TO OBJECTS

```
22. Public Function OnEndPage()
23.    Set m_objResponse = Nothing
24. End Function
```

The extended Hello World example takes advantage of exactly these implementations of the OnStartPage and OnEndPage event methods. Simply replace all existing code in the VB5_HelloWorld class with Listing 12.5 to reuse the existing component project. Don't forget to add the reference to the ASP object library!

LISTING 12.5 - HELLO WORLD WRITING DIRECTLY TO THE CLIENT

On the
CD

```
01. Option Explicit
02.
03. Private m_Greeting As String
04. Private m_objResponse As Response
05.
06. Public Property Let Greeting(ByVal strNewValue As String)
07.     m_Greeting = strNewValue
08. End Property
09.
10. Public Property Get Greeting() As String
11.     Greeting = m_Greeting
12. End Property
13.
14. Public Function HelloWorld()
15.     m_objResponse.Write m_Greeting
16. End Function
17.
18. Public Function OnStartPage(objSC As ScriptingContext)
19.     Set m_objResponse = objSC.Response
20. End Function
21.
22. Public Function OnEndPage()
23.     Set m_objResponse = Nothing
24. End Function
25.
26. Private Sub Class_Initialize()
27.     m_Greeting = "Hello World"
28. End Sub
```

Another thing has changed for this example—there's a newly added property named Greeting that simply contains the text string that is written to the client. Secondly, the HelloWorld function no longer returns a string. Instead, line 15 is used to write the string to the client the same way that you would have done in ASP code. All objects and their methods and properties work in exactly the same way that they work in ASP code—your learning curve for using Visual Basic to create components is very low.

When you choose File/Make now, you receive an error message stating that the resulting DLL can't be written to—given that you didn't restart IIS since the build of the first Hello World example. This happens because ASP caches components. As a result, you have to stop IIS, make the DLL, register it, then restart IIS.

This component now contains one property that is read/write, as well as the function HelloWorld, to write the property string to the client. Listing 12.6 shows how to use this component in your scripts and how to access its properties and methods.

On the CD

LISTING 12.6 -USING THE NEW HelloWorld COMPONENT IN AN ASP SCRIPT

```
01. <HTML>
02. <HEAD>
03. <TITLE>Chapter 12: VB 5 Hello World 2</TITLE>
04. </HEAD>
05. <BODY BGCOLOR=#ffffff>
06. <H1>Visual Basic component</H1>
07. <%
08.    Set hworld = Server.CreateObject(
       ➥"Unlocking.VB5_HelloWorld")
09.    hworld.HelloWorld
10.    Response.Write "<BR>"
11.    hworld.Greeting = "Welcome to the universe of
       ➥components!"
12.    hworld.HelloWorld
13. %>
14.
15. </BODY>
16. </HTML>
```

The first call to hworld.HelloWorld prints the value of the Greeting property that was set in the Initialize method of the HelloWorld component in line 27 of Listing 12.5. Line 11 sets the property to a new string, and the next line writes it to the client.

Of course, this is only a brief overview of what you can do with the ActiveX Server objects. Because the use of these objects is identical to their use in ASP code, the next section's example for Visual Basic focuses on a topic that is very important for "cool" components—collections.

The DirectoryBrowser Component

Checking for the existence of a single file is possible from within ASP, however, a feature that is missing in the ASP core components is the capability to enumerate files in a directory (with any wildcards you like). Returning an entire directory listing is an interesting challenge, and one for which collections come in handy. The component retrieves the file names and inserts them into the collection. From within the ASP script you can access the files that were enumerated with the for...each statement.

You must have Visual Basic 5.0 Enterprise Edition installed on your computer to use the Class Builder Utility that is used in this section to create the component. However, the final sample code compiles on all editions of Visual Basic 5.0.

The DirectoryBrowser example in this section contains two objects and one collection. See Figure 12.4 for the object model.

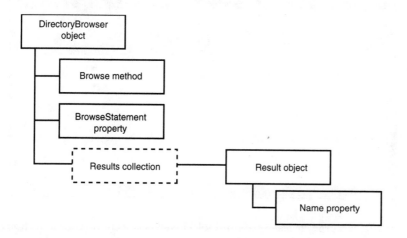

Figure 12.4

The object model for the DirectoryBrowser *component.*

Only the DirectoryBrowser object itself will be capable of being created from outside. The Results collection and Result object are managed internally by the DirectoryBrowser object.

When you're creating collections manually, you have to add some functions like Add, Remove, Count, Item, and _NewEnum that look mostly the same for all collections. To save you from this work—and other tedious object creation work—you can use the Class Builder Utility that comes with the Visual Basic Enterprise Edition. It helps with the creation of objects and collections, as well as their methods, events, and properties. See Figure 12.5 for an example of how the Class Builder shows the finished Directory-Browser component project.

Implement the following steps to create the skeleton for the DirectoryBrowser component.

1. Create a new ActiveX DLL project and delete Class1 from it with the Project/ Remove command. Name the project **unlocking**.

2. Select Add-Ins/Class Builder to open the Class Builder Utility. If it isn't available, you have to add it with the Add-In manager in this menu.

3. Select File/New/Object to create a new object. Name it **DirectoryBrowser** and leave MultiUse selected. Click OK. Now a class has been added to the Classes list of the Class Builder Utility.

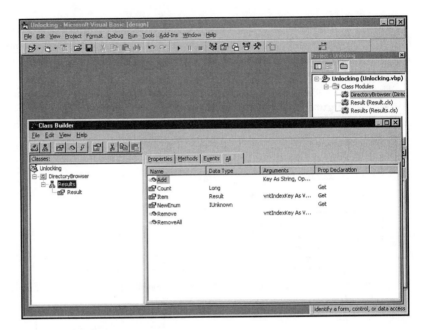

4. Right-click the DirectoryBrowser class and select New/Collection. The Collection Builder dialog box opens. Enter **Results** as the name of the collection and select Public Not Creatable for Instancing. Select New Class for Collection Of and enter **Result** as the name for the new class. Your Collection Builder dialog box should now look like Figure 12.6.

5. Click New Class Properties and change MultiUse to Public Not Creatable and then close the Class Module Builder dialog box. Close the Collection Builder dialog box.

6. Now the collection `Results` and the `Result` object are added to your project with standard implementations of the most common methods. Now you need to fine-tune the methods and properties to meet your needs.

7. Select the `DirectoryBrowser` class and add a new property. Name it `BrowseStatement`, change its data type to String, and make it the default property.

8. Add the Browse method to the `DirectoryBrowser` class. This method has no arguments and does not have a return value.

9. Select the `Results` collection and add a method named **RemoveAll** with no arguments and no return value.

10. Go to the `Result` class and add a property **Name**, making it the default property, and set the data type to String.

11. Click on File/Update Project and all classes and collections with standard implementations of properties and methods are created for you.

Most of the work for this project has been done now! Save your work. If you have ever implemented collections in straight C++, this recipe for creating collections might sound like a fairy tale. However, it is that easy.

Due to the implementation decision of the `Result` object, there are some corrections to make to the Class Builder generated code. The original source code is in Listing 12.7.

LISTING 12.7 - ORIGINAL SOURCE CODE FOR THE RESULT CLASS

```
01. Public Key As String
02.
03. Private mvarName As String 'local copy
04. Public Property Let Name(ByVal vData As String)
05. ' used when assigning a value to the property,
06. ' on the left side of an assignment. Syntax: X.Name = 5
07.     mvarName = vData
08. End Property
09.
10. Public Property Get Name() As String
11. 'used when retrieving value of a property, on the right
12. ' side of an assignment. Syntax: Debug.Print X.Name
13.     Name = mvarName
14. End Property
```

Notice that all the code needed for handling the Name property has been inserted. However, there also is a variable Key of type String contained in this class. This key is used to identify the object instances in the Results collections. Because file names are also unambiguous in a directory, the Key variable can be reused for the file name. Listing 12.8 shows the new code with the set method for the Name property omitted. This can be safely done because it is of no use for the client of the object to alter the name of the file—especially because this collection is intended for returning file names and nothing else.

LISTING 12.8 - FINAL CODE FOR THE RESULT CLASS

```
01. Public Key As String
02.
03. Public Property Get Name() As String
04.     Name = Key
05. End Property
```

Now the code for the Result class is shorter and simpler and you're done with this class! The next class to customize is the Results collection. For this class, we added the RemoveAll method with Class Builder Utility that needs to be implemented. It will provide the functionality of removing all elements from the collection. Listing 12.9 shows how to implement it.

LISTING 12.9 - CODE FOR THE RemoveAll METHOD

```
01. Public Sub RemoveAll()
02.     Dim Num
03.     For Num = 1 To mCol.Count
04.         mCol.Remove 1
05.     Next Num
06. End Sub
```

The Add method that was created by the Class Builder Utility for the Results collection has to be changed entirely, because it doesn't need the Name argument to be passed, nor does it need to be public or return the created Result object. Simply replace the Class Builder generated function with the code provided in Listing 12.10.

LISTING 12.10 - CODE FOR THE NEW ADD SUB

```
01. Sub Add(Key As String, Optional sKey As String)
02.     'create a new object
03.     Dim objNewMember As Result
04.     Set objNewMember = New Result
```

```
05.
06.          'set the properties passed into the method
07.          objNewMember.Key = Key
08.
09.          If Len(sKey) = 0 Then
10.              mCol.Add objNewMember
11.          Else
12.              mCol.Add objNewMember, sKey
13.          End If
14.
15.          Set objNewMember = Nothing
16. End Sub
```

These were all the changes or additions that had to be applied to the Results collection. The only class that still needs to be visited is the DirectoryBrowser class. In this class, you only need to add the following code to the Browse method:

LISTING 12.11 - CODE FOR THE **Browse** METHOD

```
01. Public Sub Browse()
02.      Dim strRet As String, rResults As Results
03.
04.      Set rResults = Me.Results
05.      rResults.RemoveAll
06.
07.      strRet = Dir(mvarBrowseStatement)
08.
09.      Do While "" <> strRet
10.          strRet = Dir
11.          rResults.Add strRet
12.      Loop
13. End Sub
```

Notice that the Results collection is referenced using the Me.Results statement. This is due to the implementation the Class Builder inserted for the Results collection. The collection isn't created before it's referenced for the first time, so it could happen that the variable representing the Results collection in the DirectoryBrowser object isn't initialized when you try to access it directly. To avoid this behavior, you have to use this type of referencing to guarantee that you will get an initialized collection. The rest of the code is used to enumerate all files that match the statement supplied with the BrowseStatement property.

Now you're done with customizing the code that the Class Builder Utility has provided. You got the for...each support for free and more. The only thing missing is the ASP code that makes use of this directory browsing component. Don't forget to build and register the DLL first!

Cross Reference

To learn how to register Visual Basic components, please refer to the section "Creating a Simple Component" on p.296 in this chapter.

The ASP source for enumerating the files in the root of your web server is contained in Listing 12.12.

On the CD

LISTING 12.12 - ASP PAGE FOR BROWSING THE CURRENT WEB SERVER'S ROOT

```
01. <HTML>
02. <HEAD>
03. <TITLE>Chapter 12: VB 5 Directory Browsing</TITLE>
04. </HEAD>
05. <BODY BGCOLOR=#ffffff>
06. <H1>Visual Basic Directory Browsing Component</H1>
07. <%
08.    Set myobj = Server.CreateObject(
          ➥"Unlocking.DirectoryBrowser")
09.
10.    myobj.BrowseStatement = Server.MapPath("/") & "\*.*"
11.    myobj.Browse
12.    For Each dirobj In myobj.Results
13.       Response.Write dirobj.Name & "<BR>"
14.    Next
15. %>
16. </BODY>
17. </HTML>
```

Now you can browse all your directories on the web server with this simple but very powerful component!

Creating Components with Visual J++

This section is dedicated to creating components with Visual J++, Microsoft's blend of Java compiler. With J++, you're working directly with the COM interfaces of the ActiveX Server components. Table 12.1 contains the list of interfaces for all ActiveX Server objects and how they map to the objects you already know.

TABLE 12.1
Interfaces of ActiveX Server Objects

Interface	Description
IScriptingContext	Returns interface pointers to the five built-in objects of ActiveX Server.
IApplicationObject	Call methods and properties of the Application object.
ISessionObject	Call methods and properties of the Session object.
IRequest	Call methods and properties of the Request object. Access the collections contained in this object.
IResponse	Call methods and properties of the Response object. Access the collections contained in this object.
IServer	Call methods and properties of the Server object.
IReadCookie	Retrieve the values of the Cookies collection from the Request object. Read-only.
IWriteCookie	Set the values for cookies in the Cookies collection of the Response object.
IStringList	Retrieve values stored in the ServerVariables, or the Form or Request collections.
IRequestDictionary	Use this to query all collections contained in the Request object.

If you need more information about each interface (because not all will be presented in this section), refer to the Active Server Pages roadmap, section Programmer's Reference (point your browser to http://localhost/IASDocs/ASPDocs/roadmap.asp to access it).

Hello World

The Hello World example presented for Visual J++ contains more basic functionality than the first example for Visual Basic. It has a property for the greeting message and displays information about the client's IP address. Implement the following steps to create the Hello World project.

1. Start Visual J++ and select File/New/Project Workspace. The New Project Workspace dialog box opens. Select the Java Workspace and name the project **JHelloWorld**. See Figure 12.7.

Figure 12.7

*Create a new Java
Workspace named*
JHelloWorld.

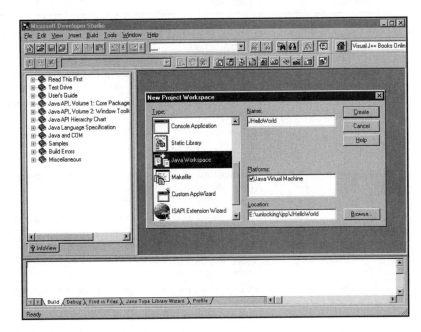

2. The new workspace is created. You need to insert a class. To do this, choose Insert/New Java Class. In the Create New Class dialog box enter **JHelloWorld** as the class name. Leave all other options untouched.

Figure 12.8

*Insert the new
class*
JHelloWorld.

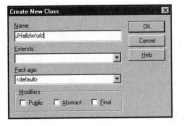

3. The file JHelloWorld.java is created and added to the project. To be able to access the ActiveX Server objects, you need to add the ASP object library to the project. To do this, choose Tools/Java Type Library wizard. Select the ASP object library.

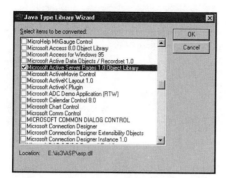

Figure 12.9

Add the ASP object library to the project.

4. Import the following packages to your project: `com.ms.com.*` and `asp.*`.

5. You are ready to start coding.

The preceding steps need to be performed for any Java project that uses the ASP object library, so I did not include the actual code specifics for the Hello World example. The code for it is in Listing 12.13.

LISTING 12.13 - THE JHELLOWORLD JAVA COMPONENT

```
01. /*
02.  *
03.  * JHelloWorld
04.  *
05.  */
06.
07. import com.ms.com.*;
08. import asp.*;
09.
10. class JHelloWorld
11. {
12.      String Greeting = "";
13.
14.      IResponse m_iResponse = null;
15.      IRequest m_iRequest = null;
16.
17.      public void OnStartPage(IScriptingContext
     ➥objContext)
18.      {
19.       m_iResponse = objContext.getResponse();
```

continues

```
20.        m_iRequest = objContext.getRequest();
21.    }
22.
23.    public void OnEndPage()
24.    {
25.     m_iResponse = null;
26.     m_iRequest = null;
27.    }
28.
29.    public void HelloWorld()
30.    {
31.     IRequestDictionary serverVariables =
       ➥m_iRequest.getServerVariables();
32.     Variant hname = new Variant();
33.     hname.putString("REMOTE_HOST");
34.     Variant v = serverVariables.getItem(hname);
35.     hname.putString(Greeting+"<P>Welcome from "+
       ➥v.toString());
36.     m_iResponse.Write(hname);
37.    }
38. }
```

The property I mentioned, *Greeting*, is created with a single line of code—line 12. It is a read and write property of type string, initialized to an empty string. The *OnStartPage* method looks similar to the one in Visual Basic, with the exception that you have to write *scriptcontext.getResponse()*. All properties have the prefix get for retrieval, and put for setting values. This is because the properties themselves are implemented with get and put methods, however, Visual Basic is capable of masking it to a single access for get and set. The implementation of OnEndPage simply sets the interface pointers to null, which is equal to Visual Basic's Nothing.

The HelloWorld method that starts on line 29 first retrieves a pointer to the IRequestDictionary object of the ServerVariables collection contained in the Request object. It is needed to retrieve the IP address (or host name if supplied) of the client's computer. Together with the greeting message it is sent to the user on line 36. Notice that you can't use a string directly, you have to work with Variants. This is why the com.ms.com.* package was imported.

Before you can use the Java component in your ASP pages, you need to register it. For the registration of the class you need the javareg.exe utility, located in the bin folder of your J++ installation. After registration, you have to copy the class file to the %SystemRoot%\Java\TrustLib folder on your computer. Listing 12.14 contains a batch file you can customize for the registration of your Java components.

LISTING 12.14 - THE REGISTRATION FILE FOR YOUR JAVA COMPONENTS

```
01. e:\msdev\bin\javareg /register /class:JHelloWorld
    ➥/progid:Unlocking.JHelloWorld
02. copy JHelloWorld.class %SystemRoot%\Java\TrustLib
```

This registration file is already customized for the JHelloWorld example. You have to change the path to the javareg utility to resemble your installation.

Note You will encounter similar, yet not exactly the same, problems that you did with Visual Basic when re-registering components that are currently in use with ASP. In contrast to being unable to access the DLL file during the make process, you will receive no error message with Visual J++. However, your new code isn't executing, it is still the old one. So every time you change the .class file, you need to stop and restart IIS before the changes take effect.

Now that you have registered the component, you can use it on your ASP pages. It provides the same functionality as the HelloWorld component written in Visual Basic and therefore the ASP page accessing the component doesn't need to be rewritten very much. See Listing 12.15 to see how to instantiate the component and work with its properties and methods.

LISTING 12.15 - USING THE **JHelloWorld** COMPONENT ON YOUR PAGES

On the
CD

```
01. <HTML>
02. <HEAD>
03. <TITLE>Chapter 12: J++ Hello World</TITLE>
04. </HEAD>
05. <BODY BGCOLOR=#ffffff>
06. <H1>Visual J++ component</H1>
07. <%
08.    Set hworld = Server.CreateObject(
       ➥"Unlocking.JHelloWorld")
09.    hworld.Greeting = "Welcome to the universe of
       ➥components!"
10.    hworld.HelloWorld
11. %>
12.
13. </BODY>
14. </HTML>
```

Notice that it takes longer for the first invocation of the component than it took for the Visual Basic components. This is because the VB 5 components were compiled to native code and the Java components run with the Java VM, which initializes on the first invocation of a Java program.

Creating a Calendar Component in Java

Programming nice monthly calendars on web pages was complicated before ASP came along. Now it's possible to create them with scripting languages, however, building a component that is capable of creating a monthly calendar would be really great. The result looks like Figure 12.10, and the necessary source code is in Listing 12.17.

Figure 12.10

All monthly calendars for 1997 on a single page.

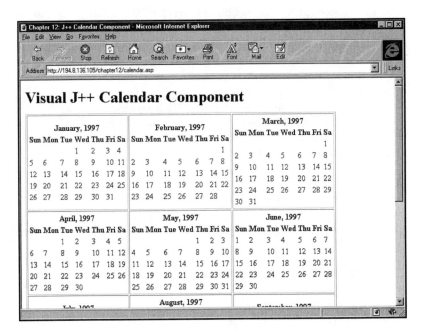

When you take a look at the source code for the Java component in Listing 12.16, notice that this code doesn't rely on the functionality "take the first of March and subtract 1 and you get the last day of February" to decide whether February has 28 or 29 days. The code uses the real calculation for leap years instead (lines 29 to 45). Before you start coding this calendar component, you need to follow the steps for creating a Java component project in the previous section "Hello World."

LISTING 12.16 - THE JAVA SOURCE CODE FOR THE `CalendarMaker`
COMPONENT

On the
CD

```java
01. /*
02.    * CalendarMaker
03.    */
04. import com.ms.com.*;
05. import asp.*;
06. import java.util.Date;
07.
08. class CalendarMaker
09. {
10.        private IResponse m_objResponse;
11.        private String astrMonths[] = new String[12];
12.
13.        public void OnStartPage(IScriptingContext
           ↪objScriptContext)
14.        {
15.              m_objResponse = objScriptContext.
                 ↪getResponse();
16.              astrMonths[0] = "January";
                 ↪astrMonths[1] = "February";
17.              astrMonths[2] = "March";
                 ↪astrMonths[3] = "April";
18.              astrMonths[4] = "May";
                 ↪astrMonths[5] = "June";
19.              astrMonths[6] = "July";
                 ↪astrMonths[7] = "August";
20.              astrMonths[8] = "September";
                 ↪astrMonths[9] = "October";
21.              astrMonths[10] = "November";
                 ↪astrMonths[11] = "December";
22.        }
23.
24.        public void OnEndPage()
25.        {
26.              m_objResponse = null;
27.        }
28.
29.        private boolean IsLeapYear(int nYear)
30.        {
31.              if ((nYear % 4) == 0)
```

continues

```
32.            {
33.                if ((nYear % 100) == 0)
34.                {
35.                    if ((nYear % 400) == 0)
36.                        return true;
37.                    else
38.                        return false;
39.                }
40.                else
41.                    return true;
42.            }
43.
44.        return false;
45.    }
46.
47.    public void PrintMonthlyCalendar(int nYear,
    ➡ int nMonth)
48.    {
49.        Variant vResponse = new Variant();
50.        int nDays,nCurrentDay, nColStart, nFirstDay;
51.
52.        if (nYear <  1900 || nYear > 2500 ||
    ➡nMonth <  1 || nMonth > 12)
53.        {
54.            vResponse.putString("<B>Invalid date
            ➡values entered!</B><P>");
55.            m_objResponse.Write(vResponse);
56.            return;
57.        }
58.
59.        nDays=31;
60.        switch (nMonth)
61.        {
62.        //case 1:case 3:case 5:case 7:case 8:case 10:
            ➡case 12:
63.        // nDays = 31;
64.        case 4:case 6:case 9:case 11:
65.            nDays = 30; break;
66.        case 2:
67.            if (IsLeapYear(nYear))
68.                nDays = 29;
69.            else nDays = 28;
```

```
70.            }
71.
72.            Date firstDay = new Date(nYear-1900,
               ➥nMonth-1,1);
73.            String strCalendar;
74.
75.            nFirstDay = firstDay.getDay();
76.            strCalendar = "<TABLE><TR><TH COLSPAN=7>"+
               ➥astrMonths[nMonth-1] + ", ";
77.            strCalendar += nYear + "</TH></TR>";
78.            strCalendar += "<TR><TH>Sun</TH><TH>Mon</TH>
               ➥<TH>Tue</TH><TH>Wed</TH>";
79.            strCalendar += "<TH>Thu</TH><TH>Fri</TH>
               ➥<TH>Sa</TH></TR>";
80.
81.            nCurrentDay = 1;
82.
83.            while (nCurrentDay <= nDays)
84.            {
85.                strCalendar += "<TR>";
86.
87.                if (1 == nCurrentDay && nFirstDay > 0)
88.                {
89.                    nColStart = nFirstDay;
90.                    strCalendar += "<TD COLSPAN=" +
                       ➥ (nColStart) + "></TD>";
91.                }
92.                else nColStart = 0;
93.
94.                for (int nCol=nColStart;nCol <  7;nCol++)
95.                {
96.                    strCalendar += "<TD>"+nCurrentDay+
                       ➥"</TD>";
97.                    if (++nCurrentDay > nDays) break;
98.                }
99.                strCalendar += "</TR>";
100.           }
101.           strCalendar += "</TABLE>";
102.
103.           vResponse.putString(strCalendar);
104.           m_objResponse.Write(vResponse);
105.       }
106. }
```

The method `PrintMonthlyCalendar` is used to print a tabular calendar for a given month in a year. The method begins on line 47, checks for valid dates, and computes the number of days in the given month. The process for creating the HTML table starts on line 76. First the headers are created, and lines 83 to 100 enclose the loop for inserting each day in the table for the right weekday. Notice that the first day of the month gets special attention, because you need to indent the right number of table columns. The finished table is written to the client on line 104.

The only thing you need to do now (besides registering the component) is to create a script that creates the calendar as shown in Figure 12.10. The ASP page that created this output is shown in Listing 12.17.

LISTING 12.17 - PRINTING THE CALENDAR FOR 1997

```
01. <HTML>
02. <HEAD>
03. <TITLE>Chapter 12: J++ Calendar Component</TITLE>
04. </HEAD>
05. <BODY BGCOLOR=#ffffff>
06. <H1>Visual J++ Calendar Component</H1>
07.
08. <%
09.    Set myobj = Server.CreateObject(
          ➥"Unlocking.CalendarMaker")
10.    Response.Write "<TABLE BORDER=1>"
11.    For i=1 To 12
12.      If (i Mod 3) = 1 Then Response.Write "<TR>"
13.      Response.Write "<TD>"
14.      myobj.PrintMonthlyCalendar 1997,i
15.      Response.Write "</TD>"
16.      If (i Mod 3) = 0 Then Response.Write "</TR>"
17.    Next
18. %>
19.
20. </BODY>
21. </HTML>
```

This page creates a table with three columns and fills each column with the output of calls to `PrintMonthlyCalendar`. This is a very good example of where componentization is useful.

Of course you can create more sophisticated components using Java, however, that would be out of the scope of this book. This section is only intended as an appetizer for what you can do with components.

Creating Components with Visual C++ 5.0 and MFC

The two languages presented so far don't dig very deeply into the foundations of components. However, if you choose to write your components using C++ and MFC, you need to have a more solid understanding of the workings of COM (Component Object Model) on which the ASP components build. This section assumes that you're already familiar with the basics of creating OLE Automation components.

There are some advantages when you write components using MFC:

◆ MFC provides a great deal of additional functionality.

◆ Components created with MFC support most COM threading models (single, apartment, but not free).

◆ MFC is easy to use and easy to get up and running—in contrast to using the ATL (ActiveX Template Library).

◆ You can leverage existing MFC code.

The nice thing about using MFC with Visual C++ is how easy it is to create Automation code. You are supported by the `ClassWizard` to generate the declarations and stub implementations of the properties and methods for your component. The next section's example shows how easy (in terms of C++) it is to create a component.

Creating the Hello World Example

The functionality presented in this example matches the Hello World example of Java. It has a property named `Greeting` and a method called `SayHello` that writes the greeting message to the client. To get this functionality, the `OnStartPage` and `OnEndPage` methods need to be implemented in the component.

With this said, implement the following steps to start creating the component:

1. Open Visual C++ 5.0 and choose File/New. In the New dialog box switch the Project tab and select MFC AppWizard(DLL). Enter **HelloWorld** as the project name. Now the New dialog box should look like Figure 12.11.

Figure 12.11

Filling in the information about the component project.

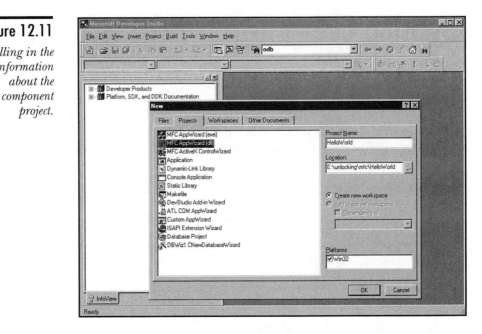

2. The MFC `AppWizard` opens. Here you can choose to either link MFC statically or dynamically. Leave dynamic linkage checked and check the Automation option to gain support for the Automation features of MFC. Figure 12.12 shows the wizard with all information entered.

Figure 12.12

Providing additional information for the project.

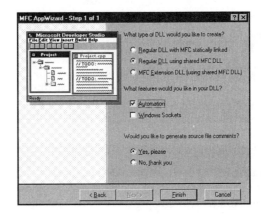

3. Click Finish and create the project. These are the steps you need for every component project.

4. Until now, there are no creatable components in this project. To add a component to the project, open `ClassWizard`. You can do this either by selecting View/

ClassWizard or pressing CTRL+W. Switch to the Automation tab and click the Add Class button. Enter the name of the class in the New Class dialog box. Select `CCmdTarget` as base class for it (you need `CCmdTarget` as base class for all Automation-enabled classes) and check the Creatable by type ID option. Enter **Unlocking.MFCHelloWorld** as the ProgId that will be used to instantiate objects of this class. With all this information entered, the New Class dialog box looks like Figure 12.13.

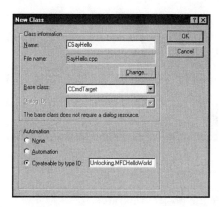

Figure 12.13

Adding the `SayHello` component to the project.

5. Now you are back in the Automation tab of the `ClassWizard`, the new `SayHello` class is selected. Because you need the interface pointer to the `Response` object, the `OnStartPage` and `OnEndPage` methods need to be implemented. Select Add Method and create a method `OnStartPage` with return type long and a parameter of type `LPDISPATCH` (pointer to the `ScriptingContext` interface). The Add Method dialog box is shown in Figure 12.14.

Figure 12.14

Adding the `OnStartPage` method to the project.

6. Add the method `OnEndPage` to the class. It takes no parameters and returns long.

7. Add an additional method `SayHello`, no parameters, no return value.

8. Create a new property named **Greeting**. Use the Add Property dialog box to provide the information. This property is of type BSTR and is accessed via Get and Set methods. See Figure 12.15 for an example of how to fill in the dialog box.

Figure 12.15

Creating the
Greeting
property.

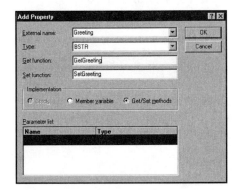

9. Now you have added all methods and properties that you need for the SayHello component. Click OK in the ClassWizard to save the modifications to the project. You could already compile the project without errors.

10. To enable access to the ASP objects and their interfaces, you have to include the file asptlb.h in the header file of the SayHello component (the SayHello.h file). You also need to include the file initguid.h. This file must be included in the implementation file before the include statement of the SayHello.h header—otherwise an error is generated.

11. Now you can start coding and using the ASP objects interfaces.

With the exception of steps 7 and 8 this process is valid for any component that you create using MFC.

The include file asptlb.h doesn't ship with Visual C++. It is included with ASP and located under %InstallDir%/ASP/Cmpnts, where %InstallDir% is the location you chose to install ASP to. Copy this file to the include folder of your Visual C++ installation so it can be included successfully in your component projects.

The ClassWizard has provided a skeleton framework of the SayHello component for you. The only thing to add is the real work code. Because the Greeting property is implemented with Get/Set methods, you need to declare an additional variable to hold the actual greeting message. Furthermore, a variable to store the interface pointer for the Response is needed.

There is a single method that I want to introduce in advance before taking a look at the final code (see Listing 12.19) for this component—the _ReleaseSCPointers method. It is used to release references to interfaces you have used. Table 12.2 contains the list of interfaces of ASP objects (you'll remember these from this chapter's section on Java).

TABLE 12.2
Interfaces of ActiveX Server Objects

Interface	Description
IScriptingContext	Returns interface pointers to the five built-in objects of ActiveX Server.
IApplicationObject	Call methods and properties of the Application object.
ISessionObject	Call methods and properties of the Session object.
IRequest	Call methods and properties of the Request object. Access the collections contained in this object.
IResponse	Call methods and properties of the Response object. Access the collections contained in this object.
IServer	Call methods and properties of the Server object.
IReadCookie	Retrieve the values of the Cookies collection from the Request object. Read-only.
IWriteCookie	Set the values for cookies in the Cookies collection of the Response object.
IStringList	Retrieve values stored in the ServerVariables, or the Form or Request collections.
IRequestDictionary	Use this to query all collections contained in the Request object.

The header file SayHello.h is presented in Listing 12.18 and contains the declarations for the methods and properties I have mentioned so far.

LISTING 12.18 - THE HEADER FILE SayHello.h FOR THE HelloWorld COMPONENT

```
01. #ifndef __SAYHELLO_H__
02. #define __SAYHELLO_H__
03.
04. // SayHello.h : header file
05. //
06.
07. #include <asptlb.h>
08.
09. /////////////////////////////////////////////////////////////
10. // CSayHello command target
11.
12. class CSayHello : public CCmdTarget
13. {
14.         DECLARE_DYNCREATE(CSayHello)
15.
16.         CSayHello(); // protected constructor
17.
18. // Attributes
19. public:
20.
21. // Operations
22. public:
23.
24. // Overrides
25.         // ClassWizard generated virtual function overrides
26.         //{{AFX_VIRTUAL(CSayHello)
27.         public:
28.         virtual void OnFinalRelease();
29.         //}}AFX_VIRTUAL
30.
31. // Implementation
32. protected:
33.         void _ReleaseSCPointers();
34.         IResponse* m_piResponse;
35.         CString m_strGreeting;
36.         virtual ~CSayHello();
```

```
37.
38.         // Generated message map functions
39.         //{{AFX_MSG(CSayHello)
40.             // NOTE - the ClassWizard will add and remove
                ➥member functions here.
41.         //}}AFX_MSG
42.
43.         DECLARE_MESSAGE_MAP()
44.         DECLARE_OLECREATE(CSayHello)
45.
46.         // Generated OLE dispatch map functions
47.         //{{AFX_DISPATCH(CSayHello)
48.         afx_msg BSTR GetGreeting();
49.         afx_msg void SetGreeting(LPCTSTR lpszNewValue);
50.         afx_msg long OnStartPage(LPDISPATCH isc);
51.         afx_msg long OnEndPage();
52.         afx_msg void SayHello();
53.         //}}AFX_DISPATCH
54.         DECLARE_DISPATCH_MAP()
55.         DECLARE_INTERFACE_MAP()
56. };
57.
58. /////////////////////////////////////////////////////////////
59.
60. //{{AFX_INSERT_LOCATION}}
61. // Microsoft Developer Studio will insert additional
       ➥declarations immediately before the previous line.
62.
63. #endif // __SAYHELLO_H__
```

The asptlb.h include that's needed for the declaration of the ASP objects interfaces is on line 7. Lines 48 to 52 contain the declarations for the methods and properties that were created with ClassWizard for the Automation interface. The only lines that need to be inserted manually are lines 33 to 35, containing the declaration for the interface release method, the member variables for the greeting message, and the interface pointer to the Response object.

The code for the implementation of the behavior of this component is located in the SayHello.cpp file, which is presented in Listing 12.19.

On the CD

LISTING 12.19 - THE IMPLEMENTATION OF THE HelloWorld COMPO-NENT USING MFC

```
01. #include "stdafx.h"
02. #include "HelloWorld.h"
03. #include <initguid.h>
04. #include "SayHello.h"
05.
06. IMPLEMENT_DYNCREATE(CSayHello, CCmdTarget)
07.
08. CSayHello::CSayHello()
09. {
10.       EnableAutomation();
11.
12.       m_strGreeting = _T("Hello World!");
13.       m_piResponse = NULL;
14.
15.       AfxOleLockApp();
16. }
17.
18. CSayHello::~CSayHello()
19. {
20.       AfxOleUnlockApp();
21. }
22.
23. void CSayHello::OnFinalRelease()
24. {
25.       _ReleaseSCPointers();
26.       CCmdTarget::OnFinalRelease();
27. }
28.
29. BEGIN_MESSAGE_MAP(CSayHello, CCmdTarget)
30.       //{{AFX_MSG_MAP(CSayHello)
31.             // NOTE - the ClassWizard will add and remove
                ➥ mapping macros here.
32.       //}}AFX_MSG_MAP
33. END_MESSAGE_MAP()
34.
35. BEGIN_DISPATCH_MAP(CSayHello, CCmdTarget)
36.       //{{AFX_DISPATCH_MAP(CSayHello)
37.       DISP_PROPERTY_EX(CSayHello, "Greeting",
          ➥GetGreeting, SetGreeting, VT_BSTR)
```

```
38.        DISP_FUNCTION(CSayHello, "OnStartPage",
           ➥OnStartPage, VT_I4, VTS_DISPATCH)
39.        DISP_FUNCTION(CSayHello, "OnEndPage", OnEndPage,
           ➥ VT_I4, VTS_NONE)
40.        DISP_FUNCTION(CSayHello, "SayHello", SayHello,
           ➥ VT_EMPTY, VTS_NONE)
41.        //}}AFX_DISPATCH_MAP
42. END_DISPATCH_MAP()
43.
44. static const IID IID_ISayHello =
45. { 0x814f342d, 0x9928, 0x11d0, { 0xbd, 0x2e, 0x0, 0x20,
    ➥0xaf, 0xd8, 0x1b, 0x6d } };
46.
47. BEGIN_INTERFACE_MAP(CSayHello, CCmdTarget)
48.        INTERFACE_PART(CSayHello, IID_ISayHello, Dispatch)
49. END_INTERFACE_MAP()
50.
51. IMPLEMENT_OLECREATE(CSayHello, "Unlocking.MFCHelloWorld",
    ➥0x814f342e, 0x9928, 0x11d0, 0xbd, 0x2e, 0x0, 0x20,
    ➥0xaf, 0xd8, 0x1b, 0x6d)
52.
53. long CSayHello::OnStartPage(LPDISPATCH isc)
54. {
55.        if (isc == NULL)
56.            return E_POINTER;
57.
58.        IScriptingContext *pContext = NULL;
59.        HRESULT hr;
60.
61.        hr = isc->QueryInterface(IID_IScriptingContext,
           ➥ (void**) &pContext);
62.        if (SUCCEEDED(hr))
63.            hr = pContext->get_Response(&m_piResponse);
64.
65.        return hr;
66. }
67.
68. long CSayHello::OnEndPage()
69. {
70.        _ReleaseSCPointers();
71.        return S_OK;
72. }
```

continues

Listing 12.19, Continued

```
73.
74. BSTR CSayHello::GetGreeting()
75. {
76.         return m_strGreeting.AllocSysString();
77. }
78.
79. void CSayHello::SetGreeting(LPCTSTR lpszNewValue)
80. {
81.         m_strGreeting = lpszNewValue;
82. }
83.
84. void CSayHello::SayHello()
85. {
86.         if (NULL == m_piResponse) return;
87.         m_piResponse->Write(COleVariant(m_strGreeting));
88. }
89.
90. void CSayHello::_ReleaseSCPointers()
91. {
92.         if (m_piResponse != NULL)
93.             m_piResponse->Release();
94.         m_piResponse = NULL;
95. }
```

You are now looking at 95 lines of code, however, only 21 of those lines were not created by the ClassWizard (remember, the stubs of the methods were already inserted for you!). The first important step for avoiding errors is to insert the include statement for initguid.h before the one for the header of the component (lines 3 and 4). The greeting message is initialized in the constructor of the class, and the interface pointer is set to NULL.

The OnStartPage method starts on line 53. First a pointer check is performed to catch the most obvious error—an uninitialized pointer. The return value for this method should now be clear: it is used to return the status of the method's execution (like every method in COM interfaces). Next, the interface pointer that was passed to the method is queried for the IScriptingContext interface. If this was successful, the Response interface pointer is retrieved from the ScriptingContext. The result of the execution is returned to the caller (ASP scripting engine).

The OnEndPage method following on line 68 simply invokes _ReleaseSCPointers and returns S_OK. The actual work of releasing the interfaces is done in this method. It starts on line 90 and simply performs cleanup that is needed for COM objects (again,

I assume that you are familiar with the concepts of COM interfaces). This method is called from the `OnFinalRelease` method to ensure that the pointer is definitely released.

The code presented for `OnStartPage` and `OnEndPage` can be used in any project for creating components, but the code presented from now on is specific to the `HelloWorld` component. The `Get` and `Set` methods for the `Greeting` property are implemented between lines 74 and 82 and simply set or return the value of the greeting message. Even the `SayHello` method is very simple, because besides the sanity check for the interface pointer of the `Response` object, it contains only a single line of code for writing the greeting message to the user. This line looks exactly the same as the Java example.

Actually you could build the component now and use it. However, there is one thing that has gone completely unnoticed until now—the type library for the component that contains the information about the property and the methods that need to be created for OLE components. And there is a good reason why it went unnoticed—`ClassWizard` took care of maintaining it.

Now you can build the component and register it using the regsvr32 utility. To test this yet-another `HelloWorld` example, use the ASP page presented in Listing 12.20.

LISTING 12.20 - USING THE MFC HELLOWORLD COMPONENT IN AN ASP PAGE

On the CD

```
01. <HTML>
02. <HEAD>
03. <TITLE>Chapter 12: MFC Hello World</TITLE>
04. </HEAD>
05. <BODY BGCOLOR=#ffffff>
06. <H1>Visual C++/MFC component</H1>
07. <%
08.    Set hworld = Server.CreateObject(
       ➥"Unlocking.MFCHelloWorld")
09.    hworld.Greeting = "Welcome to the universe of
       ➥components!"
10.    hworld.SayHello
11. %>
12.
13. </BODY>
14. </HTML>
```

Where to Go From Here

It would go beyond our scope to create extended components like the ones for Visual Basic or Java. The listings alone would take several pages. If you want to do more component programming with Visual C++ and MFC, here are some pointers to additional reference material:

◆ The Active Server Pages Roadmap contains a section named Programmer's reference where you can find extensive documentation about the ASP object's interfaces, with examples of how to invoke them.

◆ Navigate with your browser to http://www.microsoft.com/iis and go to the Samples and Components area. There are a lot of good examples not only for MFC, but also for Visual Basic, Java, and ATL.

And in case C++ and MFC still aren't powerful enough for you, see the next section about how to take advantage of the ActiveX Template Library.

Creating Components with Visual C++ 5.0 and ATL

If you want to create the most powerful, fastest, and smallest components, then there is no way around the ActiveX Template Library (ATL). However, there are still more advantages that come with the ATL. See the following list for the most compelling reasons for switching to the ATL to create your components.

◆ ATL helps produce small, fast, industrial-strength components.

◆ ATL supports all COM threading models (single, apartment, free).

◆ Creating dual interfaces is easy.

◆ ATL components support the OLE error mechanism.

◆ Method calls are very quick.

◆ You have a very fine control over COM features.

However, these compelling reasons don't come for free (at least for the moment). You are required to do more coding yourself than with, for example, Microsoft Foundation Classes. With Visual C++ 5.0 you also are now supported by a ClassWizard-like feature named "Visual COM Editing," which enables you to add properties and methods equally convenient to ATL objects as with ClassWizard to MFC objects.

Before you start creating the popular (in every respect) example Hello World, I have to point out that this section is not and cannot be a tutorial to the ATL (you can fill books on that topic). It is merely intended to show how to create a basic component so you can judge whether this is the development environment you want to use for your components.

Hello World

I promise you that this is the last time that I use Hello World as an example (in this chapter and the entire book). There are three major steps for this example:

1. Creating an ATL project

2. Adding a component

3. Adding properties and methods to the component

Finally, of course, you need an ASP page to test this newly created ATL component. Before you can do this, you have to start at step 1 of this outline—creating the ATL project.

Creating an ATL Project

The following steps outline the process for creating a new component project with the ATL COM AppWizard.

1. Open Visual C++ 5.0 and select File/New. Switch to the Project tab, select ATL COM AppWizard as project type, and enter **HelloWorldPrj** as the project name. Figure 12.16 shows how the New Project dialog box looks. Click OK to go on.

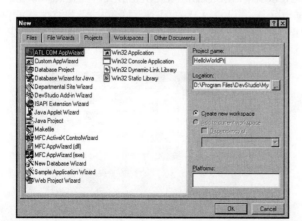

Figure 12.16

Selecting the ATL COM AppWizard for creating the new project.

2. The ATL COM AppWizard opens with its single step 1. You are presented with choices for the entire component project. For our Hello World project, leave all options untouched. To get a feeling of what you can do with the features, take a look at Figure 12.17.

Figure 12.17

Setting options for the component project.

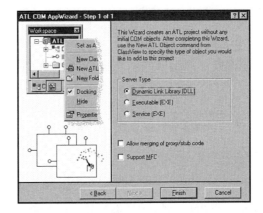

3. Click Finish in the wizard to create the ATL component project.

Now you have created the project, but there is still no component in it. The next section adds the Hello World component to this newly created project.

Adding a Component

The project by itself is only a container for multiple components that you have to provide. To help you create components, Visual C++ 5.0 has a new ATL Object Wizard that helps you get started with your components. The following steps show you how to create the component Hello World with this wizard:

1. Right-click on the **HelloWorldPrj** classes to open the context menu. Select New ATL object to open the ATL Object Wizard. Select ActiveX Server Component and click Next to go on. Figure 12.18 shows this first step in the ATL Object Wizard.

Figure 12.18

Choose to add an ActiveX Server Component in the ATL Object Wizard.

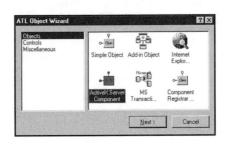

2. Now you're presented with the ATL Object Wizard Properties. Depending on the type of ATL object you are creating, you are presented with a different number of tabs in this dialog box. In the first tab you have to enter the name of the component you are creating (see Figure 12.19). Enter **HelloWorld** for this component.

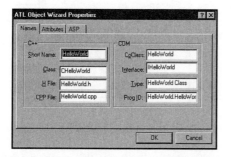

Figure 12.19

Setting the name for the new component.

3. Switch to the ASP tab. Here you can select to automatically create OnStartPage and OnEndPage methods. Also, you may select which objects to automatically extract from the ScriptingContext object and store in member variables. Select Response only and click **OK** to create the component. Figure 12.20 shows the finished ASP tab.

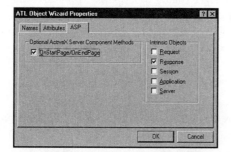

Figure 12.20

Selecting options for the component in the ASP tab.

Now you have a newly created component in your project with the OnStartPage and OnEndPage methods already implemented. You could compile this component now, but it would "do" nothing. See the next section for information about adding properties and methods to the Hello World component.

Adding Properties and Methods to the Component

All Hello World components created so far had a Greeting property and a SayHello method to demonstrate the creation and programming of properties and methods. This example implements both of these as well. The following outline shows how to add the stubs for the SayHello method as well as the Greeting property's put and get methods to your component using the new Visual COM Editing feature of Visual C++ 5.0.

1. Select the IHelloWorld interface in the ClassView pane of the current project. Right-click with the mouse on it to view the menu presented in Figure 12.21. Select Add Method.

Figure 12.21

Invoking Visual COM Editing for methods.

2. The Add Method to Interface dialog box opens. Specify **SayHello** as the method name. This method takes no parameters and the attributes don't need to be changed for this example. Click OK to generate this method, including the entries to the header, implementation, and IDL (interface description language) file.

3. To add the Greeting property to the IHelloWorld interface, right-click the interface and select Add property from the Visual COM Editing menu.

4. The Add property to interface dialog box opens. Enter **Greeting** as the property name and set its datatype to BSTR (see Figure 12.22 for a look at this dialog box). Click OK to let Visual C++ generate the get and put methods for the property.

Figure 12.22

Visual COM Editing for properties.

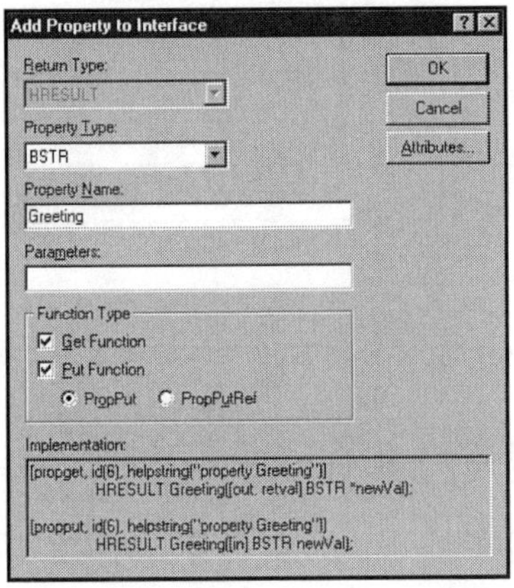

These steps performed for you by Visual COM Editing—inserting code in the header, implementation, and IDL file (which is used to generate the type library)—are the part you had to do by hand in ATL 1.1.

The now-finished declaration file for the component is presented in Listing 12.21.

LISTING 12.21 - THE DECLARATION FILE FOR THE ATL HELLO WORLD COMPONENT

On the
CD

```
01. // HelloWorld.h : Declaration of the CHelloWorld
02.
03. #ifndef __HELLOWORLD_H_
04. #define __HELLOWORLD_H_
05.
06. #include "resource.h" // main symbols
07. #include <asptlb.h> // Active Server Pages Definitions
08.
09. /////////////////////////////////////////////////////////
10. // CHelloWorld
11. class ATL_NO_VTABLE CHelloWorld :
12.         public CComObjectRootEx<CComSingleThreadModel>,
13.         public CComCoClass<CHelloWorld, &CLSID_HelloWorld>,
14.         public IDispatchImpl<IHelloWorld, &IID_IHelloWorld,
            ➡ &LIBID_HELLOWORLDPRJLib>
15. {
16. public:
17.         CHelloWorld():m_bstrGreeting(OLESTR("Hello World"))
18.         {
19.                 m_bOnStartPageCalled = FALSE;
20.         }
21.
22. public:
23.
24. DECLARE_REGISTRY_RESOURCEID(IDR_HELLOWORLD)
25.
26. BEGIN_COM_MAP(CHelloWorld)
27.         COM_INTERFACE_ENTRY(IHelloWorld)
28.         COM_INTERFACE_ENTRY(IDispatch)
29. END_COM_MAP()
30.
31. // IHelloWorld
32. public:
33.         STDMETHOD(get_Greeting)(/*[out, retval]*/
            ➡BSTR *pVal);
```

continues

```
34.        STDMETHOD(put_Greeting)(/*[in]*/ BSTR newVal);
35.        STDMETHOD(SayHello)();
36.        //Active Server Pages Methods
37.        STDMETHOD(OnStartPage)(IUnknown* IUnk);
38.        STDMETHOD(OnEndPage)();
39.
40. private:
41.        CComBSTR m_bstrGreeting;
42.        CComPtr<IResponse> m_piResponse; //Response Object
43.        BOOL m_bOnStartPageCalled;
       ➥//OnStartPage successful?
44. };
45.
46. #endif //__HELLOWORLD_H_
```

The method declarations for accessing the Greeting property and the method
SayHello start on line 33. The variable that is needed to store the greeting message is
declared on line 41 and is the only modification you have to make after all wizards
have finished. Notice the use of template classes through this listing—they provide all
the functionality of COM for you.

The implementation of the component doesn't differ too much from the component
written with MFC—in terms of lines of code. However, when dealing with the ATL,
you have only a very shallow wrapper between yourself and COM. This results in faster
and smaller components, but this is only possible if you have a thorough knowledge
about the inner workings of COM. See Listing 12.22 for the implementation of the
Hello World functionality in ATL.

**On the
CD**

**LISTING 12.22 - IMPLEMENTATION OF THE ATL HELLO WORLD
COMPONENT**

```
01. // HelloWorld.cpp : Implementation of CHelloWorld
02. #include "stdafx.h"
03. #include "HelloWorldPrj.h"
04. #include "HelloWorld.h"
05.
06. /////////////////////////////////////////////////////////////
07. // CHelloWorld
08.
09. STDMETHODIMP CHelloWorld::OnStartPage (IUnknown* pUnk)
10. {
```

```
11.        if(!pUnk)
12.            return E_POINTER;
13.
14.        CComPtr<IScriptingContext> spContext;
15.        HRESULT hr;
16.
17.        // Get the IScriptingContext Interface
18.        hr = pUnk->QueryInterface(IID_IScriptingContext,
    ➥(void **)&spContext);
19.        if(FAILED(hr))
20.            return hr;
21.
22.        // Get Response Object Pointer
23.        hr = spContext->get_Response(&m_piResponse);
24.        if(FAILED(hr))
25.        {
26.            return hr;
27.        }
28.
29.
30.        m_bOnStartPageCalled = TRUE;
31.        return S_OK;
32. }
33.
34. STDMETHODIMP CHelloWorld::OnEndPage ()
35. {
36.        m_bOnStartPageCalled = FALSE;
37.        // Release all interfaces
38.        m_piResponse.Release();
39.
40.        return S_OK;
41. }
42.
43.
44. STDMETHODIMP CHelloWorld::SayHello()
45. {
46.        if (m_bOnStartPageCalled)
47.            m_piResponse->Write(
               ➥CComVariant(m_bstrGreeting));
48.
49.        return S_OK;
50. }
```

continues

Listing 12.22, Continued

```
51.
52. STDMETHODIMP CHelloWorld::get_Greeting(BSTR * pVal)
53. {
54.     if (pVal == NULL)
55.         return E_POINTER;
56.
57.     *pVal = m_bstrGreeting.Copy();
58.
59.     return S_OK;
60. }
61.
62. STDMETHODIMP CHelloWorld::put_Greeting(BSTR newVal)
63. {
64.     if (newVal == NULL)
65.         return E_POINTER;
66.
67.     m_bstrGreeting = newVal;
68.
69.     return S_OK;
70. }
```

The OnStartPage (see lines 9 to 32) and OnEndPage methods (implemented on lines 34 to 41) were created entirely by the ATL Object Wizard. Because of choosing to use only the Response object in this component, only the IResponse interface is retrieved from the IScriptingContext interface (see line 23). When this retrieval succeeded, the member variable m_bOnStartPageCalled is set to TRUE. This member variable is used later to determine whether the Response interface member variable was initialized before trying to write any content back to the user (see the SayHello method, lines 46 and 47).

When you take a look at the get_Greeting and put_Greeting methods (starting on lines 52 and 62), you will notice that you have to deal everywhere with BSTRs and Variants. This isn't that bad, because with CComBSTR and CComVariant you get two powerful and easy-to-use wrapper classes for both. And that is what ATL is about; providing powerful and yet lightweight wrappers around basic OLE types. Do you see how powerful the ATL is?

The only thing that is left to do is create the ASP page that invokes the component (don't forget to build the component first!).

Using the ATL Hello World Component

The page used to create and work with the component is basically the same page as the one used for the MFC example (see the section earlier in this chapter, "Creating Components with Visual C++ 5.0 and MFC"), except that the type id had to be changed to resemble the one created for the ATL component.

LISTING 12.23 - USING THE ATL HELLO WORLD COMPONENT ON AN ASP PAGE

On the CD

```
01.  <HTML>
02.  <HEAD>
03.  <TITLE>Chapter 12: ATL Hello World</TITLE>
04.  </HEAD>
05.  <BODY BGCOLOR=#ffffff>
06.  <H1>Visual C++/ATL component</H1>
07.  <%
08.     Set hworld = Server.CreateObject(
         ➡"HelloWorld.HelloWorld.1")
09.     hworld.Greeting = "Welcome to the universe of
         ➡components!"
10.     hworld.SayHello
11.  %>
12.
13.  </BODY>
14.  </HTML>
```

When you open the page, you should notice that it opens much faster than any other pages containing Hello World examples programmed with other languages. This is because of its low-level access to COM. And this is why all industry-strength components should be written with ATL.

Where to Go From Here

Microsoft has provided excellent information about the ATL in Visual C++ 5.0. This should be your starting point for developing with the ATL.

When you are firm with the ATL, there are again the two references I mentioned in the section "Where to Go From Here" for component programming with MFC, p.330.

Cross Reference

Summary

This chapter presented four ways (with three programming languages) to create components for use with Active Server Pages. Which way you choose depends on the type of component you need to create. If you need the fastest, smallest, and most flexible components, there is no way around using the ActiveX Template Library. In case you need to bring legacy MFC code to your ASP applications, creating components with MFC is a good choice for both speed and easy approachability. If computational speed isn't your primary concern but speedy programming is, then your choice is surely Visual Basic 5.0 (with its native compiler, the speed penalty is no longer the big issue it used to be in older versions). Java, to come to the last choice, is a convenient way to create components when your knowledge is primarily based in the development with Java. And with the advent of native code compilers, Java also can be a very speedy choice.

CHAPTER 13

Creating a Guest Book

This chapter presents a hypothetical situation. Let's say that the clients for whom you're creating a site wants you to implement a guest book on their site. They not only want to collect information about the user, they want to know from the user what he or she thinks about the quality of the company's products, their technical support, and maybe the quality of the Internet presence (your work).

The guest book scenario is compelling enough to justify an entire chapter of its own, because it revisits some of the major topics that were covered in this book. The guest book implementation uses the following techniques that were already presented:

◆ Using the Voting component of the Microsoft Personalization System (presented in Chapter 9, "The Microsoft Personalization System").

◆ Working with the Connection Pooling feature found in ODBC 3.0 (for details, see Chapter 7, "Database Access with ActiveX Data Objects").

◆ Paging through a result set (presented in Chapter 7).

◆ Retrieving and inserting data with the ActiveX Data Objects (covered in Chapter 7).

Designing the Guest Book

Two major parts comprise an electronic guest book: enabling the user to add an entry to the guest book, and presenting the entries that are already in the database to the users. Both are implemented in the example in this chapter.

A schematic overview of a guest book implementation is presented in Figure 13.1.

Figure 13.1

An overview of how a guest book could be implemented.

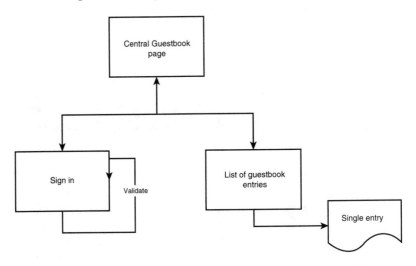

The central page of the guest book implementation presented in Figure 13.1 contains links to a sign-in form and page that lists all guest book entries. The sign-in form enables users to sign in to the guest book. It contains all the logic needed to insert the user's entry to the guest book. Viewing of all entries in the guest book is implemented in the list of entries page. This page uses the paging feature to present only a specific amount of entries at a time and views only a minimum of information per entry. From the list of entries you can zoom in on a specific entry to view all the information that was provided by the user.

The guest book information you want to gather includes more than the usual guest book information—information about products, support, and so on. Generally, people don't like to return questionnaires with their names on them. This is why it would be a great idea to separate the usual guest book entries like name, e-mail address, and so on from the questions about product quality and site design (or anything like this). Tell the user that information is processed separately; they will like that.

Implementing the Guest Book

When you're separating the standard guest book information from the questionnaire, the solution of implementing this type of guest book is very straightforward. You can use a database of your choice (I would still recommend SQL Server) to store the standard guest book information and use the Voting component part of the Microsoft Personalization System to manage the questionnaire.

The following list contains the information that is considered standard guest book information and is therefore stored in a separate table in the database:

◆ The guest's name.

◆ Optionally the e-mail address of the guest.

◆ Brief address information in the form "City, State/Country."

◆ An opinion the guest can supply at his or her discretion.

◆ Internally, the date of the entry creation is stored in addition to the hostname of the guest's computer (for later statistical analysis to help identify which domains are most active on your site).

Of course you can add more information if you would like. The questionnaire that is stored using the Voting component in this implementation contains only two questions that are presented to the user:

1. What do you think about the quality of the information presented on this site?

2. What do you think about the quality of the layout and graphical presentation on this site?

Again, you can add any number of questions you need for your site, however, these two are the standard questions that are asked on most sites.

Preparing the Database

The guest book example reuses the SQL Server database that was already used in Chapter 4, "Working with Visual InterDev," Chapter 7, "Database Access with ADO" and Chapter 9, "The Microsoft Personalization System": the *unlocking* database. However, in this example there are no SQL Server specific techniques included, so you can use any database management system you want.

You have to add only one table to the database that will hold the guest book information. The table's name is tGuests and it contains the columns depicted in Table 13.1.

TABLE 13.1
Table Definition for the tGuests Table

Column name	Datatype	Description
GuestId	int	Primary key index.
Guestname	varchar(255)	The guest's name.
EMail	varchar(255)	E-mail address of the guest (optional).
Addressinfo	varchar(255)	Address information about the guest. The information requested is brief—only town and state or country are requested. This field is entirely optional.
Signindate	datetime	The date the entry was created. Fills in the script that enters the guest's entry into the database.
HOST_NAME	varchar(255)	The name or IP address of the computer the guest was entering the guest book information from.
Opinion	text	A memo field containing any additional information the guest entered in the form.

If you're creating the table in Microsoft SQL Server, you can use the script in Listing 13.1 to create the table. Otherwise, you have to create the table definition using the tools your database management system offers.

LISTING 13.1 - THE SQL SCRIPT FOR CREATING THE tGuests TABLE

```
01. /****** Object: Table dbo.tGuests Script Date: 11.03.97 16:46:02 ******/
02. CREATE TABLE dbo.tGuests (
03.     GuestId int IDENTITY (1, 1) NOT NULL ,
04.     Guestname varchar (255) NULL ,
05.     Email varchar (255) NULL ,
06.     Addressinfo varchar (255) NULL ,
07.     Signindate datetime NOT NULL ,
08.     HOST_NAME varchar (255) NULL ,
```

```
09.        Opinion text NULL ,
10.        CONSTRAINT PK_tGuests PRIMARY KEY NONCLUSTERED
11.        (
12.            GuestId
13.        )
14. )
15. GO
```

With the exception of the `Signindate` and `GuestId` columns, all others are optional. If your design requires more columns to be non-optional, you can easily change it by inserting the `NOT` keyword in front of `NULL` for the column for which you require input.

You need to have the Voting tables in this database also. However, please refer to Chapter 9, "The Microsoft Personalization System," to follow the steps to set up these tables correctly, if you haven't already done so.

Another prerequisite is the ODBC system data source named unlocking. If you have created any database example presented in this book, you will already have set it up. If not, please refer to Chapter 7, "Database Access with ActiveX Data Objects," for information about how to set up a data source for either Microsoft Access or SQL Server.

Creating the ASP Pages

In the outline of this chapter I stated that this chapter's ASP pages use the ODBC 3.0 Connection Pooling feature. To refresh your memory on this feature, the three steps that are needed to take advantage of it follow:

1. Create a session variable to store the connection string. Remember, this isn't a must, merely a convenience to have a centralized location where a change to the connection string automatically promotes to all pages. For this example, the session variable is assigned in global.asa the following way:

   ```
   Session("GuestbookDSN") = "dsn=unlocking;uid=sa;pwd="
   ```

2. Every page that accesses the database creates a `Connection` object and uses the following syntax to retrieve a connection object out of the pool:

   ```
   Conn.Open Session("GuestbookDSN")
   ```

3. When you're finished using the connection, close it before you exit the page (or when you're finished with the database work on your page):

   ```
   Conn.Close
   ```

There's only one thing to mention: You must have enabled the connection pooling feature, which is disabled by default (means installation).

See Chapter 7, "Database access with ActiveX Data Objects," section "Optimizing Performance" p.201 for information about how to enable it.

**Cross
Reference**

This is the only thing that I had to mention before we can start coding the guest book.

Creating the Main Page for the Guest Book

The main page usually contains the links to the sign-in form and the guest list. For the most part, the guest books that I have seen are surrounded by nice graphics and embedded in a cool layout.

This is not what our main page is offering! We add more features to it to create the coolest guest book experience ever:

◆ The ten most recently entered entries in the guest book are presented in a scrolling marquee (this is a client-side ActiveX control).

◆ The results of the questionnaire are presented on the first page so that the guest can see how the other guests have already rated this site.

◆ Finally, of course, it contains links to the sign-in form and the guest list.

Before I start presenting the source code for the main page, please take a look at Figure 13.2 to get a feeling for what features this page sports. Notice the vertical image on the left side. It is used in the subsequent pages as a back link to this page.

The marquee isn't very easy to spot, however, you get the idea. Following the marquee are the links for the sign-in form and the guest list, and right below these is the analysis table the Voting component has created for the questionnaire that also is contained in the sign-in form. The source code for the main page itself is very easy and doesn't contain too much server-side code (Listing 13.2).

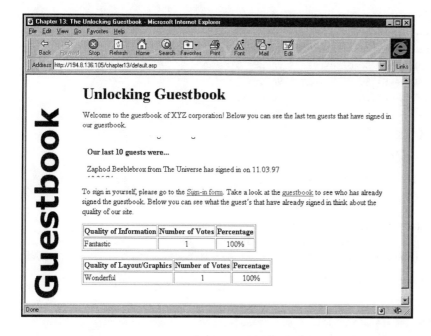

Figure 13.2

*The finalized
main page.*

LISTING 13.2 - THE PAGE DEFAULT.ASP FOR THE GUEST BOOK

**On the
CD**

```
01. <HTML>
02. <HEAD>
03. <TITLE>Chapter 13: The Unlocking Guest Book</TITLE>
04. </HEAD>
05. <BODY BGCOLOR=#ffffff>
06. <TABLE>
07. <TR>
08. <TD VALIGN=TOP WIDTH=100>
09. <IMG SRC="guestbook.gif" WIDTH=72 HEIGHT=435 ALT="Guest Book">
10. </TD>
11. <TD VALIGN=TOP>
12. <H1>Unlocking Guestbook</H1>
13.
14. Welcome to the guestbook of XYZ corporation! Below you can see the last
    ➥ten guests
15. that have signed in our guestbook.<P>
16.
17. <OBJECT ID="marqueeLast10" CLASSID="CLSID:1A4DA620-6217-11CF-BE62-
    ➥0080C72EDD2D"
18.        TYPE="application/x-oleobject" WIDTH=460 HEIGHT=80>
```

continues

LISTING 13.2, CONTINUED

```
19.    <PARAM NAME="szURL" VALUE="last10.asp">
20.    <PARAM NAME="ScrollPixelsX" VALUE="0">
21.    <PARAM NAME="ScrollPixelsY" VALUE="-2">
22.    <PARAM NAME="ScrollDelay" VALUE="50">
23.    <PARAM NAME="Whitespace" VALUE="0">
24.    <PARAM NAME="WidthofPage" VALUE="460">
25. </OBJECT>
26.
27.  <P>To sign in yourself, please go to the
     ➥<A HREF="signin.asp">Sign-in form</A>.
28. Take a look at the <A HREF="listguests.asp">guestbook
     ➥</A> to see who has already signed the guestbook.
29. Below you can see what the guests that have already
     ➥signed in think about the quality of our site.<P>
30.
31. <%
32.    Set vtc = Server.CreateObject("MPS.Vote")
33.    If True = vtc.Open("unlocking","sa","") Then
34.     retCode = vtc.SetBallotName("Guests' Opinions")
35.     Response.Write vtc.GetVote()
36.    End If
37. %>
38.
39. </TD></TR>
40. </TABLE>
41. </BODY>
42. </HTML>
```

There are only five lines of scripting code on this page. Beginning with line 32, they create the output of the questionnaire using the GetVote method of the Voting component to automatically generate the HTML table. If you want to customize the results table, then you have to replace these lines of code with your custom solution.

The marquee control that is inserted on line 17 can be added with either Visual InterDev, Control Pad, or by hand—however, I wouldn't recommend inserting it manually. By setting the szURL parameter on line 19 to last10.asp, you are inserting the file that contains the code for retrieving the last ten guest entries from the database. Listing 13.3 contains the source code for this page.

LISTING **13.3** - THE PAGE (LAST**10.**ASP) THAT IS
DISPLAYED IN THE MARQUEE

```
01. <%  Response.Expires = 0 %>
02. <!--#include file="adovbs.inc"-->
03. <HTML>
04. <HEAD>
05. <TITLE>Chapter 13: Creating a Guest Book</TITLE>
06. </HEAD>
07. <BODY BGCOLOR=#ffffff>
08. <H4>Our last 10 guests were...</H4>
09.
10. <%
11. ' On Error Resume Next
12.    Set Conn = Server.CreateObject("ADODB.Connection")
13.    Conn.Open Session("GuestbookDSN")
14.
15.    Set rsLast10Guests = Server.CreateObject("ADODB.Recordset")
16.    strSQL = "SELECT GuestId, Guestname, Addressinfo,
       ➥Signindate FROM tGuests ORDER BY GuestId DESC"
17.    rsLast10Guests.Open strSQL, Conn, adOpenKeyset, adLockReadOnly
18.
19.    If rsLast10Guests.EOF Then
20.     Response.Write "No guest has signed in so far!"
21.    Else
22.     rsLast10Guests.PageSize = 10
23.     rsLast10Guests.AbsolutePage = 1
24.    End If
25.
26.    While Not rsLast10Guests.EOF
27.     Response.Write rsLast10Guests("Guestname") & " from " &
       ➥rsLast10Guests("Addressinfo")
28.     Response.Write " has signed in on " &
       ➥rsLast10Guests("Signindate") & "<P>"
29.     rsLast10Guests.MoveNext
30.    Wend
31.
32.    rsLast10Guests.Close
33.    Conn.Close
34. %>
35.
36. </BODY>
37. </HTML>
```

Notice the first line: this file probably changes very often, so I have set the expiration period of this page to zero, which means that the browser has to fetch a new copy every time it needs to access the main page where it is contained. This ensures that the user always receives the most up-to-date information about the latest ten guest book entries.

The connection to the database is established on line 13 and closed on line 33. This is how to take advantage of connection pooling. The remainder of the code is dedicated to retrieving the ten most recent entries in the tGuests table. To achieve this, you need to issue a query that sorts records descending for the identity column GuestId and then retrieves only the first ten records of the resultset. If you're used to programming with Access, you also could issue a topvalue query to return only ten rows, however, SQL Server doesn't support the TOP keyword, so I chose to use this approach. The advantage is that you can use this code for all database management systems.

Now that you have set up your main page, you need to provide the sign-in form so your guests can contribute to this guest book.

Adding Entries to the Guest Book

The sign-in form that is used for adding entries to the guest book needs to contain the following fields, based on the design decision for this guest book:

◆ Guest's name.

◆ Guest's e-mail address.

◆ Brief address information.

◆ An opinion field.

In the previous chapters I merged the input form code with the data verification and insertion code on a single ASP page. This time, the script code would get too cluttered, therefore the input form is contained on a different page from the data verification and insertion code.

In Figure 13.3 you can see an image of this page that includes both the fields for the guest book and the questionnaire. I have only included a very weak statement about the fact that the questionnaire isn't associated with the guest's other information because I would otherwise have run out of space on the page.

Figure 13.3

The sign-in form with some information already entered.

The vertical image is now a hyperlink that points to the default.asp page, which is the main page. Just to remind you, if the user clicks this hyperlink, the list of the latest ten guests is updated.

Notice too, that the database columns HOST_NAME and Signindate don't have any fields associated in this form. The reason for this is that both are filled out by code that performs the database insert. The code for the sign-in form from Figure 13.3 is contained in Listing 13.4. However, there is only one piece of ASP code in it.

LISTING 13.4 - THE SIGNIN.ASP PAGE THAT IS USED

TO COLLECT INFORMATION FROM THE USER

On the CD

```
01. <HTML>
02. <HEAD>
03. <TITLE>Chapter 13: Creating a Guest Book</TITLE>
04. </HEAD>
05. <BODY BGCOLOR=#ffffff>
06. <TABLE>
07. <TR>
08. <TD VALIGN=TOP WIDTH=100>
09. <A HREF="default.asp"><IMG SRC="guestbook.gif"
    ➥WIDTH=72 HEIGHT=435 ALT="Go to the Guestbook" BORDER=0></A>
```

continues

LISTING 13.4, CONTINUED

```
10. </TD>
11. <TD VALIGN=TOP>
12.
13. <H1>Sign in!</H1>
14. <FORM ACTION="signinhandle.asp" METHOD=POST>
15. <INPUT TYPE=HIDDEN NAME="GoBackForm" VALUE=
    ➥"<%=Request.ServerVariables("SCRIPT_NAME")%>">
16. <TABLE BORDER=0>
17. <tr>
18. <td>Your name</td>
19. <td><INPUT TYPE=TEXT NAME="uname" SIZE=45></td></tr>
20. <tr>
21. <td>Your e-mail address (optional)</td>
22. <td><INPUT TYPE=TEXT NAME="uemail" VALUE=
    ➥"noemail@noemail.com" SIZE=45></td></tr>
23. <tr>
24. <td>Your address (optional)</td>
25. <td><INPUT TYPE=TEXT NAME="uaddress" SIZE=45 VALUE=
    ➥"SomeCity, SomeState/Country"></td></tr>
26. <tr>
27. <td valign=top>Your opinion about this site <BR>(optional)</td>
28. <td><TEXTAREA NAME="uopinion" COLS=60 ROWS=8></TEXTAREA></td></tr>
29. <tr><td colspan=2><hr>
30. <I>The information you provide below is only used for
    ➥statistics.</I ></td></tr>
31. <tr>
32. <td>The information presented is</td>
33. <td><select name="IMark">
34. <option>Fantastic<option>Wonderful<option>Interesting
    ➥<option>Boring<option>Don t know</select></td></tr>
35. <tr>
36. <td>The graphical layout/design is</td>
37. <td><select name="GMark" width=35>
38. <option>Wonderful<option>Nice<option>Fair<option>Ugly
    ➥<option>Don t know</select></td></tr>
39. <tr>
40. <td></TD><TD><INPUT TYPE=SUBMIT VALUE= "Submit guestbook entry"></td></tr>
41. </TABLE>
42. </FORM>
43.
44. </TD></TR>
```

```
45. </TABLE>
46. </BODY>
47. </HTML>
```

Only line 15 contains a short piece of ASP code: it inserts the current script name into a hidden field of the form. This field is used to provide the feature of linking back to this form from the data verification and insertion form even when the name of the sign-in form changes.

When the user has entered all information in this form and clicked the Submit button, the form data is passed to the verification and insertion page. The information the user has entered in the form is presented again to enable the user to verify the entries before finally submitting the guest book entry. Figure 13.4 shows the "Are you sure page" for the information that was entered in the form presented in Figure 13.3.

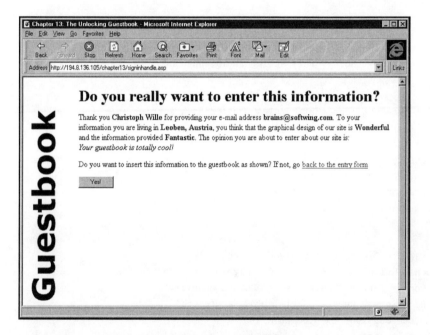

Figure 13.4

The user is asked to verify the information before it is inserted into the database.

When the user decides that the information is okay, the form data is resubmitted to the same page, with the exception that it is now inserted into the database. The code for the verification of the data and its insertion into the database is presented in Listing 13.5.

On the
CD

LISTING 13.5 - THE CODE FOR DATA VERIFICATION AND DATABASE INSERTION CONTAINED IN THE PAGE SIGNINHANDLE.ASP

```
01. <!--#include file="adovbs.inc"-->
02. <HTML>
03. <HEAD>
04. <TITLE>Chapter 13: Creating a Guest Book</TITLE>
05. </HEAD>
06. <BODY BGCOLOR=#ffffff>
07. <TABLE>
08. <TR>
09. <TD VALIGN=TOP WIDTH=100>
10. <A HREF="default.asp"><IMG SRC="guestbook.gif"
    ➥WIDTH=72 HEIGHT=435 ALT="Go to the Guestbook" BORDER=0></A>11. </TD>
12. <TD VALIGN=TOP>
13.
14. <%
15. If Not Request.ServerVariables("Content_Length")>0 Then
16.   strErrorMsgs = "Sorry, this script is intended only for valid data!<BR>"
17. End If
18.
19. ' insert here the code that handles invalid data entries
20.
21. If "" <> strErrorMsgs Then
22.   Response.Write "<H1>Error occured processing your entry!</H1>"
23.   Response.Write strErrorMsgs
24.   Response.Write "</BODY></HTML>"
25.   Response.End
26. End If
27.
28. If "Insert" = Request("ActionType") Then
29.   Response.Write "<H1>Thank you for signing in</H1>" & vbCRLF
30.   Set Conn = Server.CreateObject("ADODB.Connection")
31.   Set RS = Server.CreateObject("ADODB.RecordSet")
32.   Conn.Open Session("GuestbookDSN")
33.   RS.Open "tGuests", Conn , adOpenKeyset, adLockOptimistic
34.
35.   Conn.BeginTrans
36.   RS.AddNew
37.   RS("Guestname") = Request("uname")
38.   RS("EMail") = Request("uemail")
39.   RS("Addressinfo") = Request("uaddress")
40.   RS("Signindate") = Now()
```

```
41.   RS("HOST_NAME") = CStr(Request.ServerVariables("REMOTE_HOST"))
42.   If Len(Request("uopinion"))>0 Then
43.    RS("Opinion") = CStr(Request("uopinion"))
44.   End If
45.   RS.Update
46.   Conn.CommitTrans
47.
48.   Set vtc = Server.CreateObject("MPS.Vote")
49.   If True = vtc.Open("unlocking","sa","") Then
50.    retCode = vtc.SetBallotName("Guests' Opinions")
51.    retCode = vtc.Submit("Quality of Information", Request("IMark"))
52.    retCode = vtc.Submit("Quality of Layout/Graphics", Request("GMark"))
53.   End If
54.   Set vtc = Nothing
55.
56.   Response.Write "Your entry to the guestbook has been accepted.
      ➥Thank you for taking the time."
57.   RS.Close
58.   Conn.Close
59. Else
60. %>
61. <H1>Do you really want to enter this information?</H1>
62.
63. Thank you <B><%=Request("uname")%></B> for providing
    ➥your e-mail address <B><%=Request("uemail")%></B>.
64. To your information you are living in
    ➥<B><%=Request("uaddress")%></B>,
65. you think that the graphical design of our site is
    ➥<B><%=Request("GMark")%></B> and the
66. information provided <B><%=Request("IMark")%></B>.
    ➥The opinion you are about to enter about our site is:<BR>
67. <I><%=Request("uopinion")%></I><P>
68. Do you want to insert this information to the guestbook as shown?
69. If not, go <A HREF="<%=Request("GoBackForm")%>"> back to the entry form</A>
70.
71. <FORM METHOD=POST ACTION="<%=Request.ServerVariables("SCRIPT_NAME")%>">
72. <INPUT TYPE=HIDDEN NAME="uname" VALUE="<%=Request("uname")%>">
73. <INPUT TYPE=HIDDEN NAME="uemail" VALUE="<%=Request("uemail")%>">
74. <INPUT TYPE=HIDDEN NAME="uaddress" VALUE="<%=Request("uaddress")%>">
75. <INPUT TYPE=HIDDEN NAME="uopinion" VALUE="<%=Request("uopinion")%>">
76. <INPUT TYPE=HIDDEN NAME="IMark" VALUE="<%=Request("IMark")%>">
77. <INPUT TYPE=HIDDEN NAME="GMark" VALUE="<%=Request("GMark")%>">
```

continues

LISTING 13.5, CONTINUED

```
78. <INPUT TYPE=HIDDEN NAME="ActionType" VALUE="Insert">
79. <INPUT TYPE=SUBMIT VALUE="Yes!">
80. </FORM>
81. <%
82. End If
83. %>
84.
85. </TD></TR>
86. </TABLE>
87. </BODY>
88. </HTML>
```

This page contains a kind of error handling that you can easily extend to fit your needs. The strErrorMsgs variable is used to store the error information that sums up the process of parameter validation. Actually, the only check that is performed in this script is the one that checks for form data. Beginning with line 21, given that errors have occurred, the error information is written to the user and script processing is terminated.

The code that generated the verification page shown in Figure 13.4 starts on line 61. It simply uses the form fields to generate a text describing the information the user has entered and creates a form that is used to finally submit the verified information. The field that was created hidden in the sign-in form is now used to create the back link to this form (line 69), which the user can follow to change any of the provided information.

Inserting the guest information into the database is implemented so that it can be used with any database supporting transactions. The transaction isn't needed here, however, it encapsulates the insertion procedure. Even the code for storing the questionnaire is short, requiring only seven lines, starting on line 48.

Warning The code on line 42, which checks for zero length of the Opinion field, is inserted because of the behavior of text fields in SQL Server. If you supply zero length strings as a value to this field, you will receive an error message for line 45. However, this error message doesn't point directly to the problem of trying to insert a zero length string into the database with the statement in line 43. Always treat text fields with extra caution!

When all the information is saved successfully into the database, the user receives a thank you message and can go back to the main page to see himself in the list of the ten most recent guest entries. From the main page the user also can choose to page through the entire guest book. The next section deals with implementing this page.

Paging through the Guest Book

When you take a look at this design, only the implementation of the guest list is missing. The finished design will provide the ability to page through the guest book with ten entries per page and enable the user to zoom in on a specific entry. The guest list contains only a subset of all table columns. Only these three are presented in the list:

◆ Guest's name

◆ Brief address information

◆ The date the guest entry was created

The guest's name contains a hyperlink to more information like the opinion text. The list, when invoked for the first time, looks like Figure 13.5. The entries are ordered descending, meaning that the latest entries go first.

Figure 13.5

Paging through the list of guest entries.

When a user clicks a hyperlink, the same script page is opened to display the selected record. Figure 13.6 shows how it looks for a sample entry.

Figure 13.6

Viewing a single guest book entry.

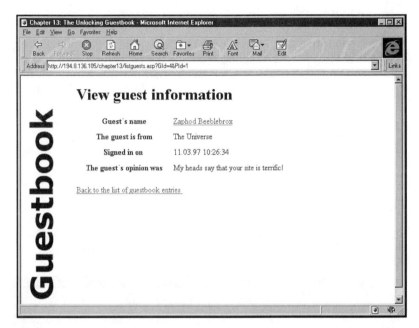

The paging mechanism and single-entry viewing mechanism are handled on the same page. The paging code is very similar to the one presented in Chapter 7 and the code for viewing a single entry is straightforward. See Listing 13.6 for the source code of this page.

On the CD

LISTING 13.6 - VIEWING THE GUEST LIST AND SINGLE ENTRIES, HANDLED IN THE FILE LISTGUESTS.ASP

```
01. <!--#include file="adovbs.inc"-->
02. <HTML>
03. <HEAD>
04. <TITLE>Chapter 13: Creating a Guest Book</TITLE>
05. </HEAD>
06. <BODY BGCOLOR=#ffffff>
07. <TABLE>
08. <TR>
09. <TD VALIGN=TOP WIDTH=100>
10. <A HREF="default.asp"><IMG SRC="guestbook.gif"
    ➥WIDTH=72 HEIGHT=435 ALT="Go to the Guestbook" BORDER=0></A>
11. </TD>
12. <TD VALIGN=TOP>
13.
14. <%
```

```
15.    Set Conn = Server.CreateObject("ADODB.Connection")
16.    Set RS = Server.CreateObject("ADODB.RecordSet")
17.    Conn.Open Session("GuestbookDSN")
18.
19.    If Len(Request("GId"))>0 Then
20.     Response.Write "<H1>View guest information</H1>"
21.     strSQL = "SELECT GuestId, Guestname, EMail, Addressinfo, Signindate,
        ➥Opinion "
22.     strSQL = strSQL + "FROM tGuests WHERE GuestId=" & Request("GId")
23.     RS.Open strSQL, Conn, adOpenKeyset,adLockReadOnly
24.     If RS.EOF Then
25.       Response.Write "Sorry, the guest s entry could not be located!"
26.     Else
27. %>
28. <TABLE BORDER=0 CELLSPACING=10>
29. <TR><TH WIDTH=180>Guest s name</TH><TD><A HREF="mailto:
    ➥<%=RS("EMail")%>"><%=RS("Guestname")%></A></TD></TR>
30. <TR><TH>The guest is from</TH>
    ➥<TD><%=RS("Addressinfo")%></TD></TR>
31. <TR><TH>Signed in on </TH><TD><%=RS("Signindate")%></TD></TR>
32. <%   If "" <> RS("Opinion") Then %>
33. <TR><TH>The guest s opinion was</TH><TD><%=RS("Opinion")%></TD></TR>
34. <%
35.     End If
36. %>
37. </TABLE>
38. <P><A HREF="<%=Request.ServerVariables("SCRIPT_NAME")
    ➥%>?PageTo=<%=Request("PId")%>">
39. Back to the list of guestbook entries
40. </A>
41. <%End If
42.   Else
43. %>
44.
45. <H1>List of guests that have signed in</H1>
46.
47. <%
48.   strSQL = "select GuestId, Guestname, Addressinfo,
      ➥Signindate from tGuests order by GuestId desc"
49.   RS.Open strSQL, Conn, adOpenKeyset,adLockReadOnly
50.
51.   strPageTo = Request("PageTo")
```

continues

Listing 13.6, Continued

```
52.    If strPageTo <> "" Then
53.      nPageTo = CLng(strPageTo)
54.      If nPageTo <  1 Then nPageTo = 1
55.    Else
56.        nPageTo = 1
57.    End If
58.
59.    RS.PageSize = 10
60.    RS.AbsolutePage = nPageTo
61. %>
62.
63. <H4>Page <%=nPageTo%></H4>
64. <P>
65. <TABLE BORDER=0 cellspacing=10>
66. <TR><TH>Guests name</TH><TH>From</TH><TH>Date</TH></TR>
67. <%
68.    nRowCount = RS.PageSize
69.    While Not RS.EOF and nRowCount > 0
70.      Response.Write "<TR><TD><A HREF=""" &
        ➥Request("SCRIPT_NAME") & "?GId=" & RS("GuestId")
71.      Response.Write "&PId=" & nPageTo & """>"
72.      Response.Write RS("Guestname") & "</A></TD><TD>"
73.      Response.Write RS("Addressinfo") & "</TD><TD>" &
        ➥RS("Signindate") & "</TD></TR>" & vbCRLF
74.      nRowCount = nRowCount -1
75.      RS.MoveNext
76.    Wend
77.    RS.Close
78.    Conn.Close
79. %>
80. </TABLE>
81.
82. <TABLE><TR>
83. <%
84. If nPageTo > 1 Then
85. %>
86.    <TD><FORM METHOD=POST ACTION="<%=Request.ServerVariables
        ➥("SCRIPT_NAME")%>">
87.    <INPUT TYPE=HIDDEN NAME="PageTo" VALUE=<%=nPageTo-1%>>
88.    <INPUT TYPE=SUBMIT VALUE="<<">
89.    </FORM></TD>
```

```
90. <%
91. End If
92. If nRowCount = 0 Then
93. %>
94.     <TD><FORM METHOD=POST ACTION= "<%=Request.ServerVariables
        ➥("SCRIPT_NAME")%>">
95.     <INPUT TYPE=HIDDEN NAME="PageTo" VALUE=<%=nPageTo+1%>>
96.     <INPUT TYPE=SUBMIT VALUE=">>">
97.     </FORM></TD>
98. <%
99. End If
100. %>
101. </TABLE>
102.
103. <%  End If%>
104.
105. </BODY>
106. </HTML>
```

The code for handling paging requests is located between lines 44 and the end of the listing. It is similar to the code introduced for paging in Chapter 7, so I won't repeat the explanations here. However, there are two interesting lines of code, 70 and 71, that are responsible for creating the hyperlink for the single entry viewing—to be able to preview the entry you need, of course, to pass the GuestId, however, to be able to go back to the same page of the guest book the user is currently viewing, you need to pass the current page number as well.

See "Paging Through the Results" to take a closer look on how to implement paging through a resultset. (Chapter 7), p.163.

Cross Reference

> **Warning** It might very well happen that the user doesn't receive exactly the same guest book page again when returning from viewing a single entry. This could happen because the query is executed every time the user accesses the guest book page, and while viewing the entry, new entries have been added to the database, changing the order of entries on the guest book pages.

Viewing a single guest book entry is handled in this page as well. The code for it is located between lines 19 and 42 and contains code for backlinking to the guest book page the user came from. This code also helps you perform a sanity check to see whether the requested record really exists (line 24). The Opinion field is only displayed when it contains data, and is otherwise omitted (line 32).

Warning The Opinion field also can be a trap when you're retrieving data from SQL Server. You will run into serious trouble—hard-to-spot errors—when text fields aren't the last ones that are returned from queries.

To avoid these errors, don't use a SELECT * statement. Instead, reference all fields explicitly and place text fields at the end.

Summary

In this chapter you have created a fully functional guest book using the most powerful techniques Active Server Pages offers to you, the developer. You have used the Connection Pooling feature of ODBC 3.0, used client-side ActiveX controls, created a sign-in form that inserts data into a table, and learned how to use MPS to manage the questionnaire that is included with this guest book.

Of course you can extend this guest book. You might want to include user guidance with the Microsoft Genie (a client-based extension) or a multi-page questionnaire that is added to the existing one. I suppose you can come up with even more compelling additions to this basic guest book.

CHAPTER 14

Creating a Shopping Bag

It is more and more common today for companies to create online stores in addition to their traditional stores. You—the programmer—have to provide all the functionality for this online store or shopping mall. This chapter deals with a very specific part of such an online store—the shopping bag—and covers the following topics:

- ◆ Design Issues for Shopping Bags

- ◆ Market Shopping Bag Solution

- ◆ Ticket Store Shopping Bag Solution

Design Issues for Shopping Bags

When setting up an online business, many people also set up an online store. Stores created on the Internet often very closely resemble a traditional store. This means that customers can browse the shelves and add items to the shopping bag, basket, or cart, and when done selecting the products they need or want, can proceed to the checkout. Having said this, you now know the handicaps that need to be solved:

◆ Creating a store where the customers can look at all the products the company is offering. You can achieve this by creating the contents of pages dynamically, and storing information in your existing company database or a specially created one for this task (the online store).

◆ Implementing a digital equivalent to the physical shopping bags that are found in traditional stores for managing the products the customers want to buy.

◆ Providing a checkout where the customers arrange for their method of payment and provide an address to where the products will be shipped.

The last point mentioned, providing the checkout, is the one that receives the most attention because of the problems with secure connections—for example, the transfer of credit card information—and the method of processing and storing information provided by the customer. Systems for validity checking of credit cards are evolving at the moment, just as are full-featured store solutions like the Microsoft Merchant Server. For a simple checkout solution, you can refer to the AdventureWorks example that comes with Active Server Pages.

The store solution itself—whether you want to organize your products by categories or just like a real store with shelves—depends upon your business needs. Again, the AdventureWorks example can be an invaluable starting point for your store solution.

By now I have mentioned the AdventureWorks example twice, so you might suspect that it implements a shopping bag solution, in addition to the preceding. And yes, it does. So why a discussion for this specific topic of online stores when there is an example for it? Because AdventureWorks falls short in some scenarios I have encountered.

The requirements for digital shopping bag solutions can be taken easily from their physical counterparts. So what are these requirements, or, to put it another way, what are you doing when you're shopping, say, in a supermarket? You're adding products—one or more—or you're removing products from the bag, maybe because you have decided that another product is better than the one you already have in your bag. When you're done with shopping, you proceed to the checkout, pay, and go home with the products you just bought. Figure 14.1 shows a flow diagram of how the solution works for the digital shopping bag.

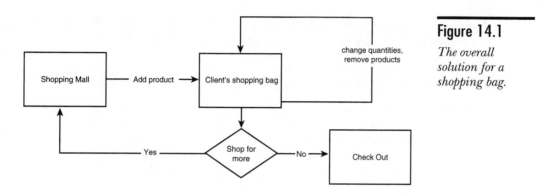

Figure 14.1

The overall solution for a shopping bag.

Notice that the changing of quantities is handled within the shopping bag, not by taking another product from the shelves as you would do in a traditional store.

Types of Shopping Bags

When designing shopping sites you can have two different problem cases that you need to solve:

1. Unlimited supply of products

2. Limited number of products available

The next two sections are dedicated to showing scenarios for both cases, and discuss the design issues that crop up with either case.

Unlimited Supply of Products

With unlimited supply I mean that products may be in stock for a limited quantity, however, the reseller (the online store) can order more from the manufacturer of the product.

The implication for your shopping bag solution is that you don't need to care within your shopping bag solution about the quantity a single customer orders and the number of items of this product in stock. This case is implemented in the section "Market Shopping Bag Solution" later in this chapter.

Limited Number of Products Available

If you are, for example, selling tickets for the Superbowl, you are surely limited by the quantity of tickets available. Other examples of limited supply include room reservations, special offers of products with a limited quantity, and more.

This time you need to take care of the quantity that's available for resale. The following list examines the steps involved from checking for availability of hypothetical Superbowl tickets to going to the checkout:

1. The customer decides to add two Superbowl tickets to the shopping bag.

2. Before the two tickets are added to the customer's shopping bag, you need to check to see whether there are still two tickets available. If so, add two tickets to the customer's shopping bag.

3. When the customer proceeds to the checkout, decrease the count of the available tickets by two.

I have introduced a subtle bug in the steps outlined here. The bug shows up when, for example, only two tickets are left and customers A and B shop for two tickets. Both are told that two are left and that they are added to their respective shopping bags, however, only the first one that finishes the checkout will receive tickets. The other one will be told that the tickets are no longer available. This is, at the least, not good business practice.

To circumvent this problem, you need to decrease the count of available tickets when a customer adds tickets to the shopping bag, to be sure that these reserved tickets are available at the checkout for this customer. Another problem to be solved is how to regain reserved but not bought tickets (i.e., a customer has left the site forever after adding 100 tickets to the shopping bag). All these issues are addressed in this chapter's section "Ticket Store Shopping Bag Solution."

Shopping Bag Considerations

Theoretically a customer could add as many items to the shopping bag as he or she wanted, however, depending on your solution, this may or may not be practical. For most cases, you probably want to implement an unlimited number of items in the shopping bag, because telling the user "Sorry, you already have ten items in the shopping bag. Check out and come back to buy more!" isn't very user-friendly. This is one of the shortcomings of the AdventureWorks example shopping bag solution—it limits the number of products that can be placed in the shopping bag.

There is an implementation issue concerning the management of the shopping bag. You are presented with two distinct solutions and a mix of both:

◆ **Session variables solution:** Store all information about the products and their selected quantities in an array that itself is stored as a session variable for the customer. This is a very time-efficient solution because you need no database lookups for product information when displaying the entire shopping bag. This solution might be memory inefficient with large shopping bags.

◆ **Database solution:** Store all information about products and their quantities to a table in the database and link it to the `SessionID`, which is a unique long value identifying the customer. Displaying the shopping bag is time-consuming because of database lookups.

◆ **Mixed solution:** A mixed solution is used when you're dealing with limited quantities in your database. The items in the shopping bag are stored in a session variable, and the reservation for products is stored in the database and linked to the customer's session. This solution enables these reservations to be deleted when either the checkout is performed by the customer or the session is abandoned due to a non-returning customer.

If you're designing for unlimited supply, the session variables solution is the best one. When dealing with the other, limited supply, the last option—the mixed solution—is best. However, the database solution can be useful too: it enables you to gather interesting statistical data, such as the following.

◆ How many times a customer changes items in a shopping bag

◆ How many shopping bags are created overall compared to the number of sales

In most cases, you will probably choose either the mixed solution or the session variables solution. An entire section with a full-featured sample implementation is dedicated to both. The mixed solution is presented in the section "Ticket Store Shopping Bag Solution" later in this chapter. Implementing the session variables solution is presented in the next section.

Market Shopping Bag Solution

This solution is based on the assumption of limitless supply and the concept that the user can put an indefinite amount of items in the shopping bag. For the purposes of keeping the example small and focused on the shopping bag implementation, I have provided only a simple product selection screen and no checkout possibility.

To create the selection screen with the products and pricing information, you need a small table that contains all information about the products the Small Online Store (SOS) is selling. Table 14.1 contains the definition for the database table.

TABLE 14.1
Table Definition for the tCompanyProducts Table

Column name	Datatype	Description
ProductID	int	Primary key index
ProductName	varchar(128)	Name of the product
Description	varchar(255)	Descriptive text for the product
PricePerUnit	float	Price per unit for this product

This is really a scaled-down sales store. In a real world scenario there would be additional fields for links to images, more descriptive text, an additional product code, rebate information, and more. Although this example doesn't necessarily depend on SQL Server, as a convenience, Listing 14.1 contains the SQL script code to generate this table.

LISTING 14.1 - SQL SCRIPT CODE TO GENERATE THE tCompanyProducts TABLE

```
01. CREATE TABLE dbo.tCompanyProducts (
02.     ProductID int IDENTITY (1, 1) NOT NULL ,
03.     ProductName varchar (128) NOT NULL ,
04.     Description varchar (255) NOT NULL ,
05.     PricePerUnit float NOT NULL ,
06.     CONSTRAINT PK_CompanyProductsTableKey PRIMARY KEY
        ➥NONCLUSTERED
07.     (
08.         ProductID
09.     )
10. )
```

The example of global.asa in Listing 14.2 assumes that you have created this table in a database that is accessed with the unlocking datasource. In my configuration, this is a Microsoft SQL Server database named unlocking.

LISTING 14.2 - THE GLOBAL.ASA THAT CONTAINS THE DSN

```
01. <SCRIPT  LANGUAGE=VBScript RUNAT=Server>
02. Sub Application_OnStart
03. End Sub
```

```
04.
05. Sub Application_OnEnd
06. End Sub
07.
08. Sub Session_OnStart
09.    Session("StoreDSN") = "dsn=unlocking;uid=sa;pwd="
10. End Sub
11.
12. Sub Session_OnEnd
13. End Sub
14. </SCRIPT>
tested - OK (mjg)
```

Note that there is no shopping bag code included so far in global.asa. Only code that sets the StoreDSN Session variable to the database that contains the table tCompanyProducts is contained in global.asa. This is done to take advantage of connection pooling.

Before a customer can select products and add them to the shopping bag, you must enable the customer to browse your products. The owner of the Small Online Store decided to view all the products in a single page, as shown in Figure 14.2.

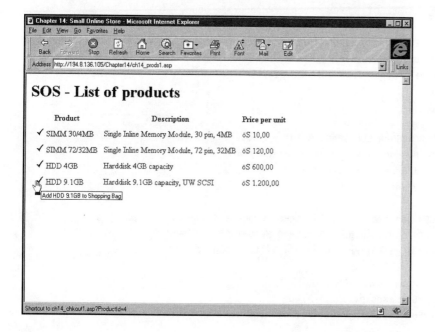

Figure 14.2

The list of products SOS has to offer the customer.

The source code for this page is contained in Listing 14.3. It opens a connection to the database, retrieves all results, and formats the results into a table. Each item has a link to the shopping bag (bag.asp) so the item can be added to it.

LISTING 14.3 - THE LIST OF PRODUCTS THE SMALL ONLINE STORE HAS TO OFFER

```
01. <!--#include file="adovbs.inc"-->
02. <HTML>
03. <HEAD>
04. <TITLE>Chapter 14: Small Online Store</TITLE>
05. </HEAD>
06. <BODY BGCOLOR=#ffffff>
07. <H1>SOS - List of products</H1>
08.
09. <%
10.    Set Conn = Server.CreateObject("ADODB.Connection")
11.    Set RS = Server.CreateObject("ADODB.RecordSet")
12.    Conn.Open Session("StoreDSN")
13.
14.    RS.Open "SELECT * FROM tCompanyProducts", Conn,
       ➥adOpenKeyset,adLockReadOnly
15.    If RS.EOF Then
16.      Response.Write "Sorry, there are no products that can
         ➥ be ordered from this company!"
17.    Else
18. %>
19.
20. <TABLE BORDER=0 CELLSPACING=10>
21. <TR><TH>Product</TH><TH>Description</TH>
    ➥<TH>Price per unit</TH></TR>
22. <% While Not RS.EOF %>
23. <TR><TD>
24. <A HREF="bag.asp?ProductId=<%=RS("ProductID")%>">
25. <IMG SRC="addtobag.gif" BORDER=0 HEIGHT=16 WIDTH=16
    ➥ALT="Add <%=RS("ProductName")%>  to Shopping Bag">
26. </A>
27. <%=RS("ProductName")%></TD>
28. <TD><%=RS("Description")%></TD>
29. <TD><%=FormatCurrency(RS("PricePerUnit"))%></TD>
30. </TR>
31. <%
```

```
32.        RS.MoveNext
33.      Wend
34. %>
35. </TABLE>
36.
37. <%
38.    End If
39.    RS.Close
40.    Conn.Close
41. %>
42.
43. </BODY>
44. </HTML>
```

The link to the shopping bag is generated on lines 24 through 26. The product is added with a clickable image that has an alternate text that displays the product to be added to the shopping bag as its ToolTip text. (See Figure 14.2 for an example ToolTip text.)

FormatCurrency is an interesting VBScript function. You can use it to format any number to different currency formats. If you call it with no parameters except the number to be converted, the standard preferences set on the server computer are used. It always includes the currency symbol set in the system control panel.

Warning In Figure 14.2, the prices are displayed as Austrian shillings, however, I tried to approximate US$ estimates for the products. So if you want to rely on the FormatCurrency function, ensure that the appropriate currency is set on the server computer on which you are running your site!

Until now there is nothing to see about the shopping bag except the reference to bag.asp. Now it's time to add the shopping bag code to this example.

The decision was to create an unlimited shopping bag that stores all information about products and quantities in a session variable. You're probably wondering what information has to be stored—see the following list:

◆ ID of the product

◆ Name of the product

◆ Description for the product

◆ Price per unit

◆ Quantity of products to be bought

If you're used to programming with Visual Basic and its cousin Visual Basic for Applications, your first idea would probably be to create a user-defined type for these five characteristics describing an item in the shopping bag. This is bad luck—VBScript only supports one type, Variant, and you cannot define your own types. What should you do now?

The solution is to create a two-dimensional array that stores these five characteristics for each item in the shopping bag. To help with the implementation of the shopping bag, I have created an include file (Listing 14.4) that contains constants to at least allow some sort of typified access to the information.

On the CD

LISTING 14.4 - THE INCLUDE FILE BAG.INC

```
01. <SCRIPT  LANGUAGE=VBScript RUNAT=Server>
02. const StartupBagMaxItems = 5
03. const AttributesPerProduct = 5
04.
05. Const bagProductID = 1
06. Const bagProductName = 2
07. Const bagDescription = 3
08. Const bagPricePerUnit = 4
09. Const bagItemQuantity = 5
10. </SCRIPT>
```

Line 2 declares the amount of items that can be placed in the bag. The default is five. When the customer adds more items, the array for the item information (shopping bag) is expanded. You can set this value to any initial size you want the bag to be. Line 3's declaration is only a helper for the creation of the array. Now take a look at how global.asa has changed in Listing 14.5.

On the CD

LISTING 14.5 - GLOBAL.ASA NOW CONTAINS ALL SHOPPING BAG INFORMATION

```
01. <!--#include virtual="/Chapter14/bag.inc"-->
02. <SCRIPT  LANGUAGE=VBScript RUNAT=Server>
03. Sub Application_OnStart
04. End Sub
05.
06. Sub Application_OnEnd
07. End Sub
08.
09. Sub Session_OnStart
10.     Session("StoreDSN") = "dsn=unlocking;uid=sa;pwd="
```

```
11.        ReDim abiCustomerBag(AttributesPerProduct,
           ➥StartupBagMaxItems)
12.        Session("Bag") = abiCustomerBag
13.        Session("MaxItems") = StartupBagMaxItems
14.        Session("ItemCount") = 0
15. End Sub
16.
17. Sub Session_OnEnd
18. End Sub
19. </SCRIPT>
```

For those of you used to programming, line 11 might look very suspicious, because the first dimension is usually the items, the second the attributes for these items. Why is it reversed here? Because of the handicap of resizing the array. You can only resize the last dimension of a VB array without losing its contents—and this is what you need to create a variable-size shopping bag.

Now that global.asa contains all the code you need to implement in the shopping bag, it's time to create bag.asp, the actual implementation of the shopping bag. Its first version, shown in Listing 14.6, only contains the necessary actions to add a product to the bag.

LISTING 14.6 - THE FIRST, MINIMAL VERSION OF THE SHOPPING BAG

```
01. <!—#include file="bag.inc"—>
02. <%
03. iCount = Session("ItemCount")
04. abiBag = Session("Bag")
05. Set Conn = Server.CreateObject("ADODB.Connection")
06.
07. If Request.QueryString("ProductId") <> "" Then
08.        If iCount = Session("MaxItems") Then
09.            ReDim Preserve abiBag(AttributesPerProduct,
               ➥iCount + 2)
10.            Session("MaxItems") = iCount + 2
11.        End if
12.        Conn.Open Session("StoreDSN")
13.        strSQL = "SELECT * FROM tCompanyProducts WHERE
           ➥ProductID=" & CLng(Request.QueryString("ProductId"))
14.        Set RS = Conn.Execute(strSQL)
15.        If Not RS.EOF Then
16.            iCount = iCount + 1
```

continues

LISTING 14.6, CONTINUED

```
17.          Session("ItemCount") = iCount
18.          abiBag(bagProductID,iCount) = RS("ProductID")
19.          abiBag(bagProductName,iCount) =
             ➥RS("ProductName")
20.          abiBag(bagDescription,iCount) =
             ➥RS("Description")
21.          abiBag(bagPricePerUnit,iCount) =
             ➥RS("PricePerUnit")
22.          abiBag(bagItemQuantity,iCount) = 1
23.          Session("Bag") = abiBag
24.          RS.Close
25.          Conn.Close
26.      End If
27. End If
28. %>
29.
30. <HTML>
31. <HEAD>
32. <TITLE>Chapter 14: SOS - Shopping Bag</TITLE>
33. </HEAD>
34. <BODY BGCOLOR=#ffffff>
35. <H1>SOS - Your Shopping bag</H1>
36.
37. <TABLE CELLSPACING=5><TR>
38. <TH>Confirm</TH><TH>Product Name</TH><TH>Description</TH>
    ➥<TH>Quantity</TH>
39. <TH>Unit Price</TH><TH>Unit Total</TH>
40. </TR>
41.
42. <%
43. nSumSubtotals = 0
44. For i = 1 To iCount
45. %>
46.   <TR>
47.   <TD><INPUT TYPE="CHECKBOX" NAME="Confirm<%=CStr(i)%>"
      ➥ VALUE="Confirmed" CHECKED>
48.   </TD>
49.   <TD><%=abiBag(bagProductName,i)%></TD>
50.   <TD WIDTH=150><%=abiBag(bagDescription,i)%></TD>
51.   <TD ALIGN=CENTER>
```

```
52.    <INPUT TYPE=TEXT NAME="Quantity<%=CStr(i)%>" VALUE=
       ➡"<%=abiBag(bagItemQuantity,i)%>" SIZE=2 MAXLENGTH=5>
53.    </TD>
54.    <TD ALIGN=RIGHT><%=FormatCurrency
       ➡(abiBag(bagPricePerUnit,i))%></TD>
55.    <TD ALIGN=RIGHT><%=FormatCurrency(abiBag
       ➡(bagPricePerUnit,i) * abiBag(bagItemQuantity,i))%></TD>
56.    </TR>
57. <%
58.    If (abiBag(bagPricePerUnit,i)) <> "" Then
59.       nSumSubtotals = nSumSubtotals + (abiBag
          ➡(bagPricePerUnit,i) * abiBag(bagItemQuantity,i))
60.    End If
61. Next
62. %>
63.
64. <TR>
65. <TD COLSPAN=4></TD>
66. <TD>Subtotal:</TD>
67. <TD ALIGN=RIGHT><%=FormatCurrency(nSumSubtotals)%></TD>
68. </TR>
69. </TABLE>
70.
71. </BODY>
72. </HTML>
```

I said that this script page can only add items to the bag, and so 72 lines are not very short for this purpose alone. Actually, it already contains code pieces for the next steps, changing the quantities of items and removing items from the shopping bag. Before I do the code walk-through, take a look at Figure 14.3 to see the output of this page.

The page is called from the list of products page with the ProductID of the product to be added to the shopping bag as its parameter. If this parameter is present, the execution of the code block between lines 7 and 27 begins. First, it is ensured that there is enough space in the shopping bag for this new item, and if not, more space is created (lines 8 to 11). You can use other allocation methods if you want. Next, the information for this product is retrieved from the table. If this product exists, its information is added to the bag array between lines 18 and 22, then the array is stored back into the session variable. Be sure to adjust the number of items in the shopping bag before you do store the array; lines 16 and 17 handle this.

Figure 14.3

An item added to the shopping bag.

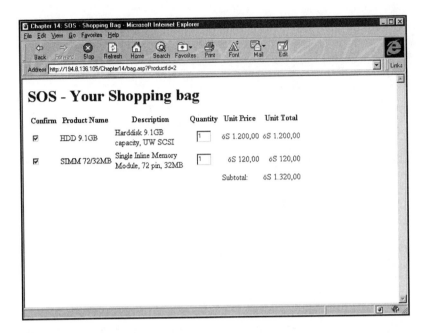

All the update work has been done now, however, the user still wants to see what's in his shopping bag. The HTML table that contains the items begins on line 37. The loop that is used to output the items starts on line 44 and ends on line 61. It already contains a checkbox for removing items (line 47) and an edit box for changing the quantity of this item (line 52). What's missing from both is the handling code in this page as well as a possibility of invoking this functionality. This is added in the next step.

This so-called next step adds the following functionality:

◆ **Shop for more:** Updates the information of the shopping bag (recalculating based on the customer's input, and removing items selected for removal). Then it redirects the user to the list of products.

◆ **Click to pay:** Same as the preceding in the updating of information to the shopping bag, however proceeds to the checkout. Remember, the checkout is not implemented!

◆ **Recalculate:** This only recalculates prices and removes items from the shopping bag. It shows the bag again after completed computations.

◆ **Cancel order:** Simply sets the item count of the shopping bag to zero and returns to the list of products of Small Online Store.

Listing 14.7 shows the finished shopping bag page. The new code blocks are lines 29 to 46, and 106 to132 (processing of the preceding actions), as well as 80 to 99, which insert command buttons to trigger these actions. Please notice too, that the HTML table is now enclosed by a <FORM> statement.

LISTING 14.7 - FINAL VERSION OF THE SHOPPING BAG

```
01. <!--#include file="bag.inc"-->
02. <%
03. iCount = Session("ItemCount")
04. abiBag = Session("Bag")
05. Set Conn = Server.CreateObject("ADODB.Connection")
06.
07. If Request.QueryString("ProductId") <> "" Then
08.       If iCount = Session("MaxItems") Then
09.             ReDim Preserve abiBag(AttributesPerProduct,
             ➥iCount + 2)
10.             Session("MaxItems") = iCount + 2
11.       End if
12.       Conn.Open Session("StoreDSN")
13.       strSQL = "SELECT * FROM tCompanyProducts WHERE
          ➥ProductID=" & CLng(Request.QueryString("ProductId"))
14.       Set RS = Conn.Execute(strSQL)
15.       If Not RS.EOF Then
16.             iCount = iCount + 1
17.             Session("ItemCount") = iCount
18.             abiBag(bagProductID,iCount) = RS("ProductID")
19.             abiBag(bagProductName,iCount) =
             ➥RS("ProductName")
20.             abiBag(bagDescription,iCount) =
             ➥RS("Description")
21.             abiBag(bagPricePerUnit,iCount) =
             ➥RS("PricePerUnit")
22.             abiBag(bagItemQuantity,iCount) = 1
23.             Session("Bag") = abiBag
24.             RS.Close
25.             Conn.Close
26.       End If
27. End If
28.
29. Select Case Request("Action")
```

continues

LISTING 14.7, CONTINUED

```
30. Case "Shop for More"
31.       RecalcBag abiBag, iCount
32.       Response.Redirect "ch14_prods1.asp"
33.
34. Case "Recalculate"
35.       RecalcBag abiBag, iCount
36.
37. Case "Cancel Order"
38.       iCount = 0
39.       Session("ItemCount") = iCount
40.       Response.Redirect "ch14_prods1.asp"
41.
42. Case "Click to Pay"
43.       RecalcBag abiBag, iCount
44.       Response.Redirect "checkout.asp"
          ➥' you have to provide this!!!
45.
46. End Select
47. %>
48.
49. <HTML>
50. <HEAD>
51. <TITLE>Chapter 14: SOS - Shopping Bag</TITLE>
52. </HEAD>
53. <BODY BGCOLOR=#ffffff>
54. <H1>SOS - Your Shopping bag</H1>
55.
56. <FORM METHOD=POST ACTION="<%=Request.ServerVariables
       ➥("SCRIPT_NAME")%>">
57. <TABLE CELLSPACING=5><TR>
58. <TH>Confirm</TH><TH>Product Name</TH><TH>Description</TH>
       ➥<TH>Quantity</TH>
59. <TH>Unit Price</TH><TH>Unit Total</TH>
60. </TR>
61.
62. <%
63. nSumSubtotals = 0
64. For i = 1 To iCount
65. %>
66.   <TR>
```

```
67.   <TD><INPUT TYPE="CHECKBOX" NAME="Confirm<%=CStr(i)%>"
      ➥ VALUE="Confirmed" CHECKED>
68.   </TD>
69.   <TD><%=abiBag(bagProductName,i)%></TD>
70.   <TD WIDTH=150><%=abiBag(bagDescription,i)%></TD>
71.   <TD ALIGN=CENTER>
72.   <INPUT TYPE=TEXT NAME="Quantity<%=CStr(i)%>" VALUE=
      ➥"<%=abiBag(bagItemQuantity,i)%>" SIZE=2 MAXLENGTH=5>
73.   </TD>
74.   <TD ALIGN=RIGHT><%=FormatCurrency(abiBag(
      ➥bagPricePerUnit,i))%></TD>
75.   <TD ALIGN=RIGHT><%=FormatCurrency(abiBag(
      ➥bagPricePerUnit,i) * abiBag(bagItemQuantity,i))%></TD>
76.   </TR>
77. <%
78.   If (abiBag(bagPricePerUnit,i)) <> "" Then
79.     nSumSubtotals = nSumSubtotals +
        ➥ (abiBag(bagPricePerUnit,i) * abiBag(bagItemQuantity,i))
80.   End If
81. Next
82. %>
83.
84. <TR>
85. <TD COLSPAN=4></TD>
86. <TD>Subtotal:</TD>
87. <TD ALIGN=RIGHT><%=FormatCurrency(nSumSubtotals)%></TD>
88. </TR>
89. <TR>
90. <TD ALIGN=RIGHT COLSPAN=3></TD>
91. <TD COLSPAN=3 ALIGN=RIGHT>
92.     <INPUT TYPE=SUBMIT NAME="Action" VALUE=
        ➥"Shop for More">
93. <%  If iCount > 0 Then %>
94.     <INPUT TYPE=SUBMIT NAME="Action" VALUE=
        ➥"Click to Pay">
95.     <INPUT TYPE=SUBMIT NAME="Action" VALUE="Recalculate">
96. <%  End If %>
97. <INPUT TYPE=SUBMIT NAME="Action" VALUE="Cancel Order">
98. </TD>
99. </TR>
100. </TABLE>
```

continues

```
101. </FORM>
102.
103. </BODY>
104. </HTML>
105.
106. <SCRIPT  LANGUAGE=VBSCRIPT RUNAT=SERVER>
107. Sub RecalcBag(abiBag, iCount)
108.      For i = 1 to iCount
109.           Quantity = Request("Quantity" & CStr(i))
110.           If IsNumeric(Quantity) And Quantity > 0 Then
111.                abiBag(bagItemQuantity,i) =
                    ➥Abs(CLng(Quantity))
112.           Else
113.                abiBag(bagItemQuantity,i) = 1
114.           End If
115.      Next
116.      ' remove items that are marked to be removed
117.      For i = 1 to iCount
118.           If Request("Confirm" & CStr(i)) = "" Then
119.                iCount = iCount - 1
120.                nCurItem = i
121.                While nCurItem <  Session("MaxItems")
122.                     For theAttributes = 1 to
                         ➥AttributesPerProduct
123.                          abiBag(theAttributes,nCurItem)
                             ➥ = abiBag(theAttributes, nCurItem + 1)
124.                     Next
125.                     nCurItem = nCurItem + 1
126.                Wend
127.           End If
128.      Next
129.      Session("Bag") = abiBag
130.      Session("ItemCount") = iCount
131. End Sub
132. </SCRIPT>
```

The simpler part of the new code is between lines 89 and 99. A maximum of four buttons are inserted into the form to allow for the actions that were outlined (Shop for More, Click to Pay, Recalculate, and Cancel Order). However, Click to Pay and Recalculate only make sense when there are items in the shopping bag, so they are only visible when at least one item is in it.

These buttons trigger actions in this page, which are implemented between lines 29 and 46. The `Select Case` statement looks similar to the one found in the AdventureWorks example, however, the actions are now performed in separate procedures to provide a better modularization.

There are four `Case` statements, of which three contain calls to the procedure `RecalcBag`, which is implemented between lines 106 and 132. This procedure adjusts the amount of items to ship per product and cuts out items that the user selected to remove. The removal code (lines 121 to 126) shifts up the remaining items in the array by one. This is done for every item to be removed.

The Cancel Order action sets the amount of items to zero and returns the customer to the list of products. The Recalculate action simply calls the `RecalcBag` procedure and shows the adjusted shopping bag, Shop for More recalculates and then redirects to the list of products, and finally, Click to Pay recalculates and then redirects to the checkout, which you have to implement on your own. Figure 14.4 shows the finished shopping bag page.

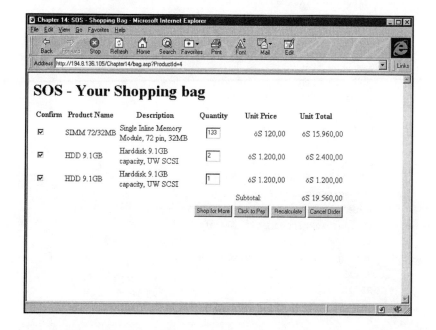

Figure 14.4

The finished shopping bag with some interesting items in it.

When you take a closer look at this screenshot, you will notice that the 9.1 GB harddisk item appears twice, with two different quantities. This has happened because I first selected the harddisk, changed its quantity, and after going back to the list of products, re-selected it. This is definitely not the behavior one wants, so a slight change has to be introduced (Listing 14.8).

LISTING 14.8 - REPLACEMENT CODE FOR LINES 7 TO 27 OF LISTING 14.7

```
01. If Request.QueryString("ProductId") <> "" Then
02.         If iCount = Session("MaxItems") Then
03.             ReDim Preserve abiBag(AttributesPerProduct,
                ➥iCount + 2)
04.             Session("MaxItems") = iCount + 2
05.         End if
06.         fAddProductNeeded = True
07.         For i = 1 to iCount
08.             If (abiBag(bagProductID,i) =
                ➥CLng(Request.QueryString("ProductId"))) Then
09.                 fAddProductNeeded = False
10.             End If
11.         Next
12.         If (True = fAddProductNeeded) Then
13.             Conn.Open Session("StoreDSN")
14.             strSQL = "SELECT * FROM tCompanyProducts WHERE
                ➥ProductID=" & CLng(Request.QueryString("ProductId"))
15.             Set RS = Conn.Execute(strSQL)
16.             If Not RS.EOF Then
17.                 iCount = iCount + 1
18.                 Session("ItemCount") = iCount
19.                 abiBag(bagProductID,iCount) =
                    ➥RS("ProductID")
20.                 abiBag(bagProductName,iCount) =
                    ➥RS("ProductName")
21.                 abiBag(bagDescription,iCount) =
                    ➥RS("Description")
22.                 abiBag(bagPricePerUnit,iCount) =
                    ➥RS("PricePerUnit")
23.                 abiBag(bagItemQuantity,iCount) = 1
24.                 Session("Bag") = abiBag
25.                 RS.Close
26.                 Conn.Close
27.             End If
28.         End If
29. End If
```

Now, if a product that has already been added to the shopping bag is to be added again, this request is simply ignored. This time, the scenario is really completed and ready for use in real world scenarios!

This section covered scenarios where you don't need to care about the number of products in stock. You could allow the user to put as many products into the bag as he or she wanted. The next section's scenario, however, is entirely different: you now need to take care of how many products you can sell because of a limited supply.

Ticket Store Shopping Bag Solution

If you're going to buy tickets for the Superbowl, you can expect that they are in limited supply. For example, you cannot order 20 tickets for the Superbowl when there are only 12 left. Seats won't be added just because you need 8 more places.

This is the difference between this example and the previous example: you have to take care of the amount of goods (in this case, the tickets) a single person places in his or her shopping bag because you cannot sell more than you have in stock. You have to adjust the amount of tickets available right after the customer added them to the shopping bag. Why not when the customer proceeds to the checkout? The reason is that when a customer puts the tickets in the shopping bag, he or she expects them to be reserved and available at the checkout. However, when the customer doesn't buy the tickets, you have to take care of releasing these "reservations" and add the tickets to the stock again.

Therefore, you have to take care of managing the amount of tickets that are still available and the per-customer tickets that are in their respective shopping bags. There are two possible solutions to tracking the amount of tickets currently reserved in the shopping bags of the customers and those that are still available:

- ◆ The amount of tickets that are reserved is subtracted from the total amount available at the time the customer adds the tickets to the shopping bag. Also, the tickets are tracked on a per customer basis in a table and in a session variable. The advantage is that when checkout is performed, you don't need to adjust the total amount and you have one central location to check for ticket availability. The drawback is that you are working with the total amount before any real change has been performed.

- ◆ The second approach is somewhat different. The total amount of tickets isn't touched until checkout, but tickets are still tracked on a per customer basis. The advantage is that you can't inadvertently muck with the total amount, and the (minor) drawback is that you first have to sum up the reserved ticket amount per event and subtract it from the total before you know the number of tickets that are left for a specific event.

To show the differences between the two approaches—and in fact how much safer and easier the second solution is—both are implemented in the sections to follow. There is one thing that both solutions have in common, however; the database design.

Creating the Database for the Ticket System

Again, as with the online store, the tables needed do contain only the minimum that's required for creating a running solution. One table is needed for the storage and retrieval of events and ticket information (availability and pricing) and a second one is needed for storing the amount of tickets reserved by each customer.

First of all, you need a table where all the events are listed, with the amount of tickets available, the price for the single ticket, and the name and a description for the event. Notice that other information like date and location of the event are omitted and that all tickets have the same price; no categories are available.

TABLE 14.2
Table Definition for the *tTicketsForEvents* Table

Column name	Datatype	Description
EventID	int	Primary key index
EventName	varchar(128)	Name of the event
Description	varchar(255)	Description of this event
TicketPrice	float	Price for the ticket. To simplify, there is one price for all tickets
NumOfTicketsAvail	int	Amount of tickets that are available for this event

For simplicity, the EventID column is an identity column (for Access users: this is equal to the AutoNumber datatype) to provide a simple primary key for the purpose of this store. As mentioned earlier, this table only contains a minimum of the information that you would present to a customer.

To enable tracking of the reservation of tickets for both solutions outlined in the previous section, a second table is needed to store the amount of tickets reserved by a customer for a specific event. In order for either of the two solutions to be presented, the data in the reservations table is used as a supplement to the information that's stored as a session variable. If the server isn't shut down properly, this information—tracked ticket reservations—is used to recreate a healthy state of the site.

TABLE 14.3
Table definition for the *tTicketsForEvents* table

Column name	Datatype	Description
FK_EventID	int	Foreign Key linked to the EventID column of the tTicketsForEvents table
SessionID	int	ID of the Session the customer has been assigned to
NumOfCards	int	Amount of tickets the customer has in his shopping bag

The first two columns are used to create a unique index to allow only one row per customer and event (remember the online store example). The only additional column is for tracking the amount of tickets this customer has added to the shopping bag.

Now that I have introduced the table design, there is one thing to do—create them in a database. The examples don't rely on Microsoft SQL Server, however, I recommend that you use it. To provide a convenience for SQL users again, Listing 14.9 contains the SQL script code to generate both tables, the relationship, and the index.

LISTING 14.9 - SQL SCRIPT CODE TO GENERATE THE TABLES, INDICES, AND RELATIONSHIP

```
01. CREATE TABLE dbo.tTicketsForEvents (
02.      EventID int IDENTITY (1, 1) NOT NULL ,
03.      EventName varchar (128) NOT NULL ,
04.      Description varchar (255) NULL ,
05.      TicketPrice float NOT NULL ,
06.      NumOfTicketsAvail int NOT NULL ,
07.      CONSTRAINT PK_TicketsForEventsTable PRIMARY KEY
         ➥NONCLUSTERED
08.      (
09.          EventID
10.      )
11. )
12. GO
13.
14. CREATE TABLE dbo.tTicketReservations (
15.      FK_EventID int NOT NULL ,
16.      SessionID int NOT NULL ,
```

continues

```
17.        NumOfCards int NOT NULL ,
18.        CONSTRAINT FK_tTicketRese_tTicketsFor FOREIGN KEY
19.        (
20.            FK_EventID
21.        ) REFERENCES dbo.tTicketsForEvents (
22.            EventID
23.        )
24. )
25. GO
26.
27. CREATE UNIQUE INDEX IX_tTicketReservations ON
28.     dbo.tTicketReservations(FK_EventID, SessionID)
        ➥WITH IGNORE_DUP_KEY
29. GO
```

The code in both implementations assumes the datasource name to be unlocking. However, because of the use of connection pooling and storing the DSN as a Session variable, you can easily use another database by changing this variable.

Tracking Amount in Both Tables

This is the solution where the amount of tickets available that is stored in the tTicketsForEvents table is automatically adjusted when customers add or remove tickets from the shopping bags. If, for example, there are 12 tickets left and a customer puts three in the shopping bag, the amount of tickets that are stored in the tTicketsForEvents table is reduced by three and a row is added to the table tTicketReservations with the amount of reserved tickets set to three for this event. You could easily store the last information in the same way as in the online store example, however, because the total amount has been changed, you need to be able to revert to the original value when disaster strikes (uncontrolled shutdown of the server). Every time the user changes the amount of tickets, both tables are updated.

Now you can already see the problems that are involved with this approach: you have to guard yourself against inconsistencies with the total amount of tickets for events, and every time you have to modify two tables to readjust this amount.

I have started creating this example with the source code of the previous online store example, so there is a page with the list of events where the customer can select the event and a page that handles the shopping bag logic. Additionally, the two invisible pieces of code are the global.asa file and the include file containing the definitions for the items in the shopping bag (see Listing 14.10).

LISTING 14.10 - THE INCLUDE FILE TICKETBAG.INC

```
01. <SCRIPT  LANGUAGE=VBScript RUNAT=Server>
02. const StartupBagMaxItems = 2
03. const AttributesPerEvent = 5
04.
05. Const bagEventID = 1
06. Const bagEventName = 2
07. Const bagDescription = 3
08. Const bagPricePerTicket = 4
09. Const bagTicketQuantity = 5
10. </SCRIPT>
tested OK - (mjg)
```

The code in this listing is mainly the same as that for the include file bag.inc of the online store, except that I have reduced the initial size of the shopping bag.

The List Of Events

The first page that uses this include file is the list of events (note that the first script that uses it is global.asa, however, the code is exactly like the one shown in Listing 14.5, so I add it later). The page is modified to additionally display the amount of tickets available for the event and, as an extra, no longer displays events for which no tickets are available (see Listing 14.11).

LISTING 14.11 - THE PAGE THAT GENERATES THE LIST OF EVENTS

```
01. <!--#include file="adovbs.inc"-->
02. <HTML>
03. <HEAD>
04. <TITLE>Chapter 14: Small Ticket Store</TITLE>
05. </HEAD>
06. <BODY BGCOLOR=#ffffff>
07. <H1>STS - List of events where tickets are still
    ➥available</H1>
08.
09. <%
10.    Set Conn = Server.CreateObject("ADODB.Connection")
11.    Set RS = Server.CreateObject("ADODB.RecordSet")
12.    Conn.Open Session("StoreDSN")
13.    strSQL = "SELECT * FROM tTicketsForEvents WHERE
       ➥NumOfTicketsAvail>0"
14.    RS.Open strSQL, Conn, adOpenKeyset,adLockReadOnly
```

continues

LISTING 14.11, CONTINUED

```
15.    If RS.EOF Then
16.      Response.Write "Sorry, there are no events that have
         ➡tickets left!"
17.    Else
18. %>
19.
20. <TABLE BORDER=0 CELLSPACING=10>
21. <TR><TH>Event</TH><TH>Description</TH><TH>Price per unit
    ➡</TH><TH>Tickets left</TH></TR>
22. <%  While Not RS.EOF %>
23. <TR><TD>
24. <A HREF="ticketbag.asp?EventId=<%=RS("EventID")%>">
25. <IMG SRC="addtobag.gif" BORDER=0 HEIGHT=16 WIDTH=16
    ➡ALT="Add <%=RS("EventName")%>  to Shopping Bag">
26. </A>
27. <%=RS("EventName")%></TD>
28. <TD WIDTH=250><%=RS("Description")%></TD>
29. <TD><%=FormatCurrency(RS("TicketPrice"))%></TD>
30. <TD><%=RS("NumOfTicketsAvail")%></TD>
31. </TR>
32. <%
33.        RS.MoveNext
34.      Wend
35. %>
36. </TABLE>
37.
38. <%
39.    End If
40.    RS.Close
41.    Conn.Close
42. %>
43.
44. </BODY>
45. </HTML>
```

The SQL statement that returns only events with tickets left to sell is generated on line 13. The SQL statement is very easy to create because the most current amount is always available in the tTicketsForEvents table. As an orientation aid for the customers, the number of available tickets also is presented. These are the only differences between this listing and the list of products page that was presented in the online store example (see Listing 14.3, section "Market Shopping Bag Solution").

The Shopping Bag

The shopping bag implementation is very different. Now, on every change to the amount of tickets not only the amount stored as a session variable needs to be adjusted, but the database has to be updated as well. And the database takes precedence over the session variable because of the limitation of the amount.

Because the listing of this page would be too long, I have split it into two parts and omitted the code that is responsible for creating the table of items with the buttons and subtotal. Actually, it is identical to the online store bag, and the entire code for this page can be found on the CD accompanying the book.

Listing 14.12 shows code from the beginning of the page and handles all the requests for adding tickets, changing amounts, going to the checkout, and shopping for more.

LISTING **14.12** - THE FIRST PART OF THE SHOPPING BAG PAGE (TICKETBAG.ASP) THAT CONTAINS THE PROGRAM LOGIC

On the CD

```
01. <!--#include file="adovbs.inc"-->
02. <!--#include file="ticketbag.inc"-->
03. <%
04. iCount = Session("ItemCount")
05. abiBag = Session("Bag")
06. Set Conn = Server.CreateObject("ADODB.Connection")
07.
08. If Request.QueryString("EventId") <> "" Then
09.     If iCount = Session("MaxItems") Then
10.         ReDim Preserve abiBag(AttributesPerEvent,
            ➥iCount + 2)
11.         Session("MaxItems") = iCount + 2
12.     End if
13.     fAddProductNeeded = True
14.     For i = 1 to iCount
15.         If (abiBag(bagEventID,i) =
            ➥CLng(Request.QueryString("EventId"))) Then
16.             fAddProductNeeded = False
17.         End If
18.     Next
19.     If (True = fAddProductNeeded) Then
20.         Conn.Open Session("StoreDSN")
21.         strSQL = "SELECT * FROM tTicketsForEvents
            ➥WHERE EventID=" & CLng(Request.QueryString("EventId"))
22.         Set RS = Conn.Execute(strSQL)
```

continues

LISTING 14.12, CONTINUED

```
23.            If Not RS.EOF Then
24.                iCount = iCount + 1
25.                Session("ItemCount") = iCount
26.                abiBag(bagEventID,iCount) = RS("EventID")
27.                abiBag(bagEventName,iCount) =
                   ➥RS("EventName")
28.                abiBag(bagDescription,iCount) =
                   ➥RS("Description")
29.                abiBag(bagPricePerTicket,iCount) =
                   ➥RS("TicketPrice")
30.                abiBag(bagTicketQuantity,iCount) = 1
31.                RS.Close
32.                If Not AddQuantity(abiBag,iCount,1) Then
33.                    iCount = iCount - 1
34.                    Session("ItemCount") = iCount
35.                Else
36.                    Session("Bag") = abiBag
37.                End If
38.            End If
39.            Conn.Close
40.        End If
41. End If
42.
43. Select Case Request("Action")
44. Case "Shop for More"
45.        RecalcBag
46.        Response.Redirect "ticketsales.asp"
47.
48. Case "Recalculate"
49.        RecalcBag
50.
51.
52. Case "Cancel Order"
53.        For i = 1 to iCount
54.            DeleteItem abiBag, i
55.        Next
56.        iCount = 0
57.        Session("ItemCount") = iCount
58.        Response.Redirect "ticketsales.asp"
59.
60. Case "Click to Pay"
```

```
61.        RecalcBag
62.        Response.Redirect "checkout.asp"
       ➡' you have to provide this!!!
63.
64. End Select
65. %>
```

The first time that the code differs from the previous bag solution is between lines 32 and 37. Here the function AddQuantity is called to perform the database update with the amount of tickets to be reserved. When the addition is successful, the processing is again identical to the first bag solution. However, if the amount of tickets could not be reserved (too few tickets are available), the ticket item line is again removed from the session array.

The Select statement from lines 43 to 64 differs only for Cancel Order, because the code changes for the ticket store shopping bag have been made in the RecalcBag procedure for the other cases—thanks to the modularization, the changes need to be made only in a single place. For the case of Cancel Order, all items that were put in the shopping bag are removed with the DeleteItem procedure, which ensures that both the total amount is adjusted and the row for this ticket reservation is deleted from the tTicketReservations table.

Now there are three procedures or functions that were referenced in the code listing; AddQuantity, RecalcBag, and DeleteItem. These comprise the second part of the page, which is shown in Listing 14.13.

**LISTING 14.13 - THE SECOND PART OF THE SHOPPING BAG PAGE
CONTAINING THE HELPER FUNCTIONS**

On the
CD

```
124. <SCRIPT  LANGUAGE=VBSCRIPT RUNAT=SERVER>
125. Sub RecalcBag()
126.     For i = 1 To iCount
127.         Quantity = Request("Quantity" & CStr(i))
128.         If IsNumeric(Quantity) And Quantity > 0 Then
129.             nNewQuantity = Abs(CLng(Quantity))
130.         Else
131.             nNewQuantity = 1
132.         End If
133.         If abiBag(bagTicketQuantity,i) <>
             ➡nNewQuantity Then
134.             ChangeQuantity i, nNewQuantity
135.         End If
136.     Next
```

continues

```
137.        ' remove items that are marked to be removed
138.        For i = 1 to iCount
139.            If Request("Confirm" & CStr(i)) = "" Then
140.                iCount = iCount - 1
141.                nCurItem = i
142.                DeleteItem abiBag, i ' remove from database
143.                While nCurItem <  Session("MaxItems")
144.                    For theAttributes = 1 to
                        ➥AttributesPerEvent
145.                        abiBag(theAttributes,nCurItem)
                            ➥ = abiBag(theAttributes, nCurItem + 1)
146.                    Next
147.                    nCurItem = nCurItem + 1
148.                Wend
149.            End If
150.        Next
151.        Session("Bag") = abiBag
152.        Session("ItemCount") = iCount
153. End Sub
154.
155. Sub ChangeQuantity(nBagItem, nChangeTo)
156.        Conn.Open Session("StoreDSN")
157.        Set RSEval = Server.CreateObject(
            ➥"ADODB.RecordSet")
158.        Conn.BeginTrans
159.            nNewTicketCount = abiBag(bagTicketQuantity,
                ➥nBagItem) - nChangeTo
160.            strSQL = "SELECT NumOfTicketsAvail FROM
                ➥tTicketsForEvents WHERE EventID="
161.            strSQL = strSQL & abiBag(bagEventID,nBagItem)
162.            RSEval.Open strSQL, Conn, adOpenKeyset,
                ➥adLockPessimistic
163.            If Not RSEval.EOF And
                ➥(RSEval("NumOfTicketsAvail") + nNewTicketCount) >= 0 Then
164.                RSEval("NumOfTicketsAvail") =
                    ➥RSEval("NumOfTicketsAvail") + nNewTicketCount
165.                RSEval.Update
166.                RSEval.Close
167.                strSQL = "UPDATE tTicketReservations SET
                    ➥NumOfCards=" & CLng(nChangeTo)
```

```
168.                  strSQL = strSQL & " WHERE FK_EventID="
                      ➥ & CLng(abiBag(bagEventID,nBagItem))
169.                  strSQL = strSQL & " AND SessionID=" &
                      ➥Session.SessionId
170.                  Conn.Execute strSQL
171.                  abiBag(bagTicketQuantity,nBagItem) =
                      ➥nChangeTo
172.             End If
173.         Conn.CommitTrans
174.         Conn.Close
175. End Sub
176.
177. Function AddQuantity(abiBag, iCount, nAddAmount)
178.         AddQuantity = False
179.         ' Conn.Open Session("StoreDSN")
180.         Set RSEval = Server.CreateObject(
             ➥"ADODB.RecordSet")
181.         Conn.BeginTrans
182.             nNewTicketCount = abiBag(bagTicketQuantity,
                 ➥iCount) - nChangeTo
183.             strSQL = "SELECT NumOfTicketsAvail FROM
                 ➥tTicketsForEvents WHERE EventID="
184.             strSQL = strSQL & abiBag(bagEventID,iCount)
185.             RSEval.Open strSQL, Conn, adOpenKeyset,
                 ➥adLockPessimistic
186.             If Not RSEval.EOF And
                 ➥RSEval("NumOfTicketsAvail") >= nAddAmount Then
187.                 RSEval("NumOfTicketsAvail") =
                     ➥RSEval("NumOfTicketsAvail") - nAddAmount
188.                 RSEval.Update
189.                 RSEval.Close
190.                 strSQL = "INSERT tTicketReservations(
                     ➥FK_EventID,SessionID,NumOfCards) VALUES("
191.                 strSQL = strSQL &
                     ➥CLng(abiBag(bagEventID,iCount)) & ","
192.                 strSQL = strSQL & Session.SessionId &
                     ➥"," & nAddAmount & ")"
193.                 Conn.Execute strSQL
194.                 AddQuantity = True
195.             End If
196.             abiBag(bagTicketCount,iCount) = nAddAmount
197.         Conn.CommitTrans
```

continues

```
198.        ' Conn.Close
199. End Function
200.
201. Sub DeleteItem(abiBag, nBagItem)
202.        Conn.Open Session("StoreDSN")
203.        Conn.BeginTrans
204.            strSQL = "UPDATE tTicketsForEvents SET
                ➥NumOfTicketsAvail=NumOfTicketsAvail+"
205.            strSQL = strSQL &
                ➥CLng(abiBag(bagTicketQuantity,nBagItem))
206.            Conn.Execute strSQL
207.            strSQL = "DELETE FROM tTicketReservations"
208.            strSQL = strSQL & " WHERE FK_EventID=" &
                ➥abiBag(bagEventID,nBagItem)
209.            strSQL = strSQL & " AND SessionID=" &
                ➥Session.SessionId
210.            Conn.Execute strSQL
211.        Conn.CommitTrans
212.        Conn.Close
213. End Sub
214. </SCRIPT>
```

Notice that all code that needs to modify both tables at the same time is guarded with a transaction. The transactions are needed to guarantee database consistency. Because there is no On Error Resume Next statement, I can safely omit error detection and therefore omit calls to RollbackTrans because when the script terminates with an error, the transaction is rolled back automatically.

The easiest procedure to start with is DeleteItem on line 201. It simply adds the amount of tickets that were reserved by this item line in the shopping bag to the total amount and then deletes the row in the table tTicketReservations. Because both operations must complete successfully, they are guarded in a transaction.

The next function is AddQuantity on line 177. It checks to see whether there are enough tickets available for this request, and if this evaluates to true, decreases the total amount of tickets and adds a row with the information about the customer and ticket reservation. The result returned by this function is used to determine if the item line can be added successfully to the shopping bag.

There is one additional helper procedure in this listing, ChangeQuantity (line 155), that I didn't mention before I introduced the listing. This procedure is used to adjust quantities of tickets for events the customer already has tickets in the shopping bag for. Again, enough tickets must be available and changes in both tables must be successful.

The last procedure that needs to be presented is `RecalcBag` (top of the listing), which has changed just a little bit from its counterpart presented for the online store. The changes are that adjustments to the quantities are only made when they differ from the previous values (line 133) and an additional call to perform the cleanup in the database for a deleted item on line 142.

Global.asa For Cleanup

There are two more cases when the database needs to be adjusted—when the user leaves the site with items in the shopping bag and, secondly, when the server isn't shut down cleanly. The first case is handled in the `Session_OnEnd` event handler, and the second is handled when the server recovers from the shutdown, that is, when the `Application_OnStart` event handler is called. Listing 14.14 shows the code for global.asa.

Listing 14.14 - Global.asa

```
01. <!--#include virtual="/Chapter14/ticketbag.inc"-->
02. <SCRIPT  LANGUAGE=VBScript RUNAT=Server>
03. Sub Application_OnStart
04.       Set Conn = Server.CreateObject("ADODB.Connection")
05.       Set RSToDelete =
          ➥Server.CreateObject("ADODB.RecordSet")
06.       Conn.Open "dsn=unlocking;uid=sa;pwd="
07.       Conn.BeginTrans
08.
09.           strSQL = "SELECT SUM(NumOfCards) RegainCards,
              ➥FK_EventID FROM tTicketReservations"
10.           strSQL = strSQL & " GROUP BY FK_EventID"
11.           RSToDelete.Open strSQL, Conn, 1, 2
12.           While Not RSToDelete.EOF
13.               strSQL = "UPDATE tTicketsForEvents SET
                  ➥NumOfTicketsAvail=NumOfTicketsAvail+"
14.               strSQL = strSQL &
                  ➥RSToDelete("RegainCards")
15.               strSQL = strSQL + " WHERE EventID=" &
                  ➥RSToDelete("FK_EventID")
16.               Conn.Execute strSQL
17.               RSToDelete.MoveNext
18.           Wend
19.           RSToDelete.Close
20.           Conn.Execute "DELETE FROM tTicketReservations"
21.       Conn.CommitTrans
```

continues

LISTING 14.14, CONTINUED

```
22.        Conn.Close
23. End Sub
24.
25. Sub Application_OnEnd
26. End Sub
27.
28. Sub Session_OnStart
29.     Session("StoreDSN") = "dsn=unlocking;uid=sa;pwd="
30.     ReDim abiCustomerBag(AttributesPerEvent,
        ➥StartupBagMaxItems)
31.     Session("Bag") = abiCustomerBag
32.     Session("MaxItems") = StartupBagMaxItems
33.     Session("ItemCount") = 0
34. End Sub
35.
36. Sub Session_OnEnd
37.        Set Conn = Server.CreateObject("ADODB.Connection")
38.        Set RSToDelete =
           ➥Server.CreateObject("ADODB.RecordSet")
39.        Conn.Open "dsn=unlocking;uid=sa;pwd="
40.        Conn.BeginTrans
41.            strSQL = "SELECT NumOfCards,FK_EventID FROM
               ➥tTicketReservations WHERE SessionID="
42.            strSQL = strSQL & Session.SessionID
43.            RSToDelete.Open strSQL, Conn, 1, 2
44.            While Not RSToDelete.EOF
45.                strSQL = "UPDATE tTicketsForEvents SET
                   ➥NumOfTicketsAvail=NumOfTicketsAvail+"
46.                strSQL = strSQL &
                   ➥RSToDelete("NumOfCards")
47.                strSQL = strSQL & " WHERE EventID=" &
                   ➥RSToDelete("FK_EventID")
48.                Conn.Execute strSQL
49.                RSToDelete.MoveNext
50.            Wend
51.            RSToDelete.Close
52.            Conn.Execute "DELETE FROM tTicketReservations
               ➥ WHERE SessionID=" & Session.SessionID
53.        Conn.CommitTrans
54.        Conn.Close
55. End Sub
56. </SCRIPT>
```

When the `Session` object for the customer is destroyed, the `Session_OnEnd` event method is executed. It contains a loop over all rows that were created in the `tTicketReservations` table for the customer and adjusts the total amount of tickets accordingly. Finally, these rows are deleted.

The recovery code that is included in the `Application_OnStart` event handler is merely the same as in `Session_OnEnd`, with the exception that all item lines for all previous customers are merged back to the `tTicketsForEvents` table.

From This Point On

I hope to have proved that this implementation of the ticket sales system is clumsy, complicated, and error prone. I presented this solution to show you how to use transactions to ensure that both dependent operations finish successfully or both fail. I also wanted to point out the different circumstances in which you have to take care of recovery for the database.

To show you the other approach—storing quantity information only for customers, not overall—I have created another example application that is presented in the next section.

Tracking Reservations Only

The implementation in the previous section had to perform actions in two tables. In this section, I have changed the application to track the shopping bag items and manage quantity calculations with the `tTicketReservations` table only.

The starting point for this new application was the scripts from the previous section. The only one left untouched is the include file with the bag definitions (ticketbag.inc file). See Listing 14.10.

The List Of Events

I am a lazy programmer and try to minimize changes to existing source code wherever possible. So I searched for a way to leave the script page almost untouched and to do all the quantity calculations now necessary within the database.

What calculations are involved? The total amount of tickets available isn't touched this time until checkout, however, to be able to present the user with the number of tickets that aren't in someone else's shopping bag, these numbers have to be summed and subtracted from the total amount of tickets. The solution presented here uses Microsoft SQL Server, however, the views in Listing 14.15 are easily converted to, for example, Microsoft Access queries.

LISTING 14.15 - SQL SCRIPT FOR THE VIEWS THAT ARE NEEDED TO MAKE THE TRANSITION TO THE NEW APPLICATION VERY EASY

```
01. CREATE VIEW view_reservations AS
02. SELECT SUM(NumOfCards) TicketsReserved, FK_EventID FROM
    ➥tTicketReservations
03.     GROUP BY FK_EventID
04. GO
05.
06. CREATE VIEW view_listpage AS
07. SELECT EventID, EventName, Description, TicketPrice,
08.     TicketsNotReserved = NumOfTicketsAvail -
    ➥COALESCE(TicketsReserved,0)
09.     FROM tTicketsForEvents, view_reservations
10.     WHERE tTicketsForEvents.EventID *=
    ➥view_reservations.FK_EventID
11. GO
```

These two views need some further explanations. Because I have to compute the number of tickets still available for each event by subtracting all reservations from the total available amount, I first need to sum up the reservations for each event. This is performed by the view view_reservations, which begins on line 1. Next, I have to subtract the sums I created from the totals. However, there may be some events for which there are currently no reservations (=items in someone's shopping bag), therefore I have to make an outer join (line 10) and return 0 for sums (line 8) where the join yields to no match. The COALESCE keyword is part of Transact-SQL from SQL Server. When you are using Microsoft Access, replace it with the IIF construct.

With these two views, the code changes to the list page are reduced to only two lines of code. The first one is of course the SQL statement:

```
13.    strSQL = "select * from view_listpage where TicketsNotReserved>0"
```

The table has been replaced by the view and the name of the column has changed from the total amount to the computed amount from the view. The second line to be changed is even simpler:

```
30. <TD><%=RS("TicketsNotReserved")%></TD>
```

That is actually all you have to do for the list of events page!

The Shopping Bag

Even the shopping bag page is getting easier. The changes—thanks to the modularization—need to be done only in three procedures (functions). RecalcBag itself doesn't even need to be touched. Listing 14.16 contains the code for the changes, and the entire file can be found on the accompanying CD for this book. Note that the listing is now shorter in comparison to the previous section's shopping bag implementation.

LISTING **14.16** - CHANGES NEEDED FOR THE SHOPPING BAG PAGE

On the CD

```
155. Sub ChangeQuantity(nBagItem, nChangeTo)
156.      Conn.Open Session("StoreDSN")
157.      Set RSEval = Server.CreateObject(
         ➥"ADODB.RecordSet")
158.      Conn.BeginTrans
159.          nNewTicketCount =
             ➥abiBag(bagTicketQuantity,nBagItem) - nChangeTo
160.          strSQL = "SELECT TicketsNotReserved FROM
             ➥view_listpage WHERE EventID="
161.          strSQL = strSQL & abiBag(bagEventID,nBagItem)
162.          RSEval.Open strSQL, Conn, adOpenKeyset,
             ➥adLockPessimistic
163.          If Not RSEval.EOF And
             ➥(RSEval("TicketsNotReserved") + nNewTicketCount) >= 0 Then
164.              RSEval.Close
165.              strSQL = "UPDATE tTicketReservations SET
                 ➥ NumOfCards=" & CLng(nChangeTo)
166.              strSQL = strSQL & " WHERE FK_EventID=" &
                 ➥ CLng(abiBag(bagEventID,nBagItem))
167.              strSQL = strSQL & " AND SessionID=" &
                 ➥Session.SessionId
168.              Conn.Execute strSQL
169.              abiBag(bagTicketQuantity,nBagItem) =
                 ➥nChangeTo
170.          End If
171.      Conn.CommitTrans
172.      Conn.Close
173. End Sub
174.
175. Function AddQuantity(abiBag, iCount, nAddAmount)
176.      AddQuantity = False
177.      Set RSEval = Server.CreateObject(
         ➥"ADODB.RecordSet")
178.      nNewTicketCount = abiBag(bagTicketQuantity,iCount)
         ➥ - nChangeTo
```

continues

LISTING 14.16, CONTINUED

```
179.      strSQL = "SELECT TicketsNotReserved FROM
          ➥view_listpage WHERE EventID="
180.      strSQL = strSQL & abiBag(bagEventID,iCount)
181.      RSEval.Open strSQL, Conn, adOpenKeyset,
          ➥adLockPessimistic
182.      If Not RSEval.EOF And
          ➥RSEval("TicketsNotReserved") >= nAddAmount Then
183.          strSQL = "INSERT tTicketReservations
              ➥ (FK_EventID,SessionID,NumOfCards) VALUES("
184.          strSQL = strSQL & CLng(abiBag(bagEventID,
              ➥iCount)) & ","
185.          strSQL = strSQL & Session.SessionId & ","
              ➥& nAddAmount & ")"
186.          Conn.Execute strSQL
187.          AddQuantity = True
188.          RSEval.Close
189.      End If
190.      abiBag(bagTicketCount,iCount) = nAddAmount
191. End Function
192.
193. Sub DeleteItem(abiBag, nBagItem)
194.      Conn.Open Session("StoreDSN")
195.      strSQL = "DELETE FROM tTicketReservations"
196.      strSQL = strSQL & " WHERE FK_EventID=" &
          ➥abiBag(bagEventID,nBagItem)
197.      strSQL = strSQL & " AND SessionID=" &
          ➥Session.SessionId
198.      Conn.Execute strSQL
199.      Conn.Close
200. End Sub
201. </SCRIPT>
```

All the transaction statements are no longer needed, the code for updating the tTicketsForEvents table is gone, and the references to this table have been exchanged for view_listpage to retrieve the amount of tickets available. You see, it got shorter and simpler.

Global.asa For Cleanup

The cleanup issues are still the same—uncontrolled server shutdown and customers leaving the site without buying the tickets in the shopping bag. However, due to the new design, the code that is necessary only contains simple DELETE statements to remove the rows from the tTicketReservations table. Listing 14.17 shows the code for the global.asa file that's needed to perform the cleanup.

LISTING 14.17 - GLOBAL.ASA

On the
CD

```
01. <!--#include virtual="/Chapter14/ticketbag.inc"-->
02. <SCRIPT  LANGUAGE=VBScript RUNAT=Server>
03. Sub Application_OnStart
04.     Set Conn = Server.CreateObject("ADODB.Connection")
05.     Conn.Open "dsn=unlocking;uid=sa;pwd="
06.     Conn.Execute "DELETE FROM tTicketReservations"
07.     Conn.Close
08. End Sub
09.
10. Sub Application_OnEnd
11. End Sub
12.
13. Sub Session_OnStart
14.     Session("StoreDSN") = "dsn=unlocking;uid=sa;pwd="
15.     ReDim abiCustomerBag(AttributesPerEvent,
        ⮕StartupBagMaxItems)
16.     Session("Bag") = abiCustomerBag
17.     Session("MaxItems") = StartupBagMaxItems
18.     Session("ItemCount") = 0
19. End Sub
20.
21. Sub Session_OnEnd
22.     Set Conn = Server.CreateObject("ADODB.Connection")
23.     Conn.Open "dsn=unlocking;uid=sa;pwd="
24.     Conn.Execute "DELETE FROM tTicketReservations WHERE
        ⮕SessionID=" & Session.SessionID
25.     Conn.Close
26. End Sub
27. </SCRIPT>
```

As I have stated before the listing, lines 6 and 24 only contain DELETE statements to remove the rows for all and for a single customer.

Real World Scenarios

With this approach, you now have the solution at hand to create a shopping site for any kind of limited supply, be it tickets, hotel rooms, or anything else. For real world scenarios you might add some additional guidance for users when the requested amount of items aren't available, which the current solution handles by simply leaving the old amount in place.

Still, you need to implement the checkout, where you need to update the total amount of tickets available. You can take the source code for it from the previous section's implementation of AddQuantity.

Summary

This chapter presented two different types of shopping bag systems to you. The two scenarios you encounter in the real world are most commonly where the amount of products in stock isn't a constraint for the quantity a customer can order. Not quite as commonly, the quantity in stock is sometimes a constraint and you have to restrict the customer during shopping to the amount of items in stock.

The solutions presented in this chapter deal only with the shopping bag itself, not the entire shopping experience for a customer. The parts that were omitted are the shelves to present the products and the checkout. For the latter there are many solutions available today, but the former depends on your choice. A good starting point for both might be the AdventureWorks example that comes with Active Server Pages.

CHAPTER 15

Implementing a Search Wizard

S earching for information on the Internet can take a lot of time because you have to check multiple search engines to be sure you find all the information you need. All these search engines provide some kind of index of web sites on the Internet. You can enhance the search experience for the people who use your server by including a small search engine solely for your server. An advantage to using Internet Information Server is that you don't have to create one—you can use an existing, free one, the Microsoft Index Server.

A feature you can provide that also enhances searches is a single page where users not only can search the local server, but also can search the most common Internet search engines. Microsoft's Internet site includes such a search wizard.

This chapter shows you how to:

◆ Use Microsoft Index Server

◆ Create a search wizard like the one on Microsoft's Internet site

Microsoft Index Server

If you're running either Internet Information Server (IIS) or any Peer Web Services (PWS) implementation (Windows 95 or NT Workstation), you can use this free add-on module. The Microsoft Index Server is a content-indexing and searching solution designed to index full text and document properties for files located on an IIS or PWS-based server. Files that can be indexed directly by Index Server include HTML and text files, as well as Microsoft Word, Excel, and PowerPoint files. To be extensible for indexing of other file types, Index Server can be extended with content filters for any kind of file types.

 Note You can download Index Server for free from the Internet Information Server site. Point your browser to http://www.microsoft.com/iis. You also can learn how to install the Index Server from the Microsoft site http://www.microsoft.com/ntserver/search/docs/install.htm or from the documentation that comes with Index Server.

Queries that are submitted to Index Server can range from simple to complex, depending on the needs of your users. Index Server itself comes with sample forms that are used to submit queries to the search engine. The simplest search form provided is shown in Figure 15.1.

Figure 15.1

The example query form that comes with Index Server.

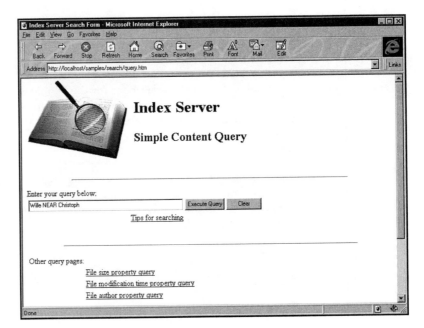

In this very simple search form, you can't restrict the number of results returned per page, or specify any document properties. However, the search string, with its powerful query language, is available. When you click Execute Query, Index Server looks up the files that match the criteria in the search string. The query results are returned to the user based on the visual layout of a template file that's used to merge the results. Figure 15.2 shows the results returned for the query presented in Figure 15.1.

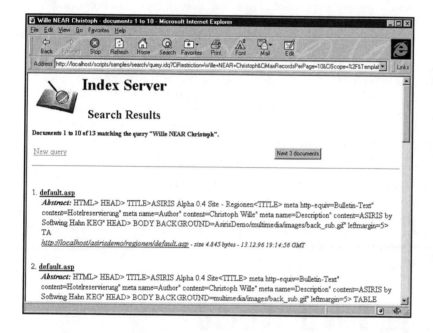

Figure 15.2

Results returned from the query issued from the form in Figure 15.1.

The output shown in Figure 15.2 is created based on inputs from two files—the query file and the template file. This chapter doesn't tell you how to create Index Server query and template files, so if you're interested in how these are used and want to create more sophisticated ones, please refer to the Index Server documentation that's installed with the product.

The basic querying features described in the following list illustrate the power of Index Server:

◆ **Scope:** Describes the set of documents of your site that will be searched. Scopes are typically defined by a directory path.

◆ **Restriction:** Equals the search string. Only documents that meet the restrictions are returned in the result set. You can search for multiple words using a sophisticated query language. You can apply Boolean operators such as AND, OR, and NOT, and also can use NEAR to search for words or phrases near other words and phrases. Index Server also enables you to issue free-text queries.

◆ **Result set:** The results that are returned from a query are assembled into result sets. All security restrictions that apply to the files searched apply to the result set—a user can see documents only when that document's access control list allows it to be read by that user (only for NTFS volumes).

In addition to these basic features, you can control ranking of hits, return specified property data, and search with wild cards. For a complete reference of Index Server features, please refer to its documentation.

A feature that is part of restricting result sets is the support of fuzzy queries that support linguistic stemming to match inflected and base forms of query words. An example of this is to search for "go**," which is expanded by Index Server to "goes," "going," "went," "gone," and so on. This feature is supported for multiple languages, such as English, German, and French. Multiple languages in a single document also are supported. I have provided a quick overview of Index Server and its usefulness. Index Server provides powerful search capabilities and enables you to customize result sets.

With the Microsoft Index Server, users can search your server. However, when they need information that's not located on your server, they still need to go to different search servers, which all have different user interfaces. They also need to remember the URLs of the search engines on the Internet they use most often. The next section shows you how you can create a single search form for different Internet search engines, including your local Index Server.

Creating a Search Wizard

This section describes how to create a single interface for all—or at least the most common—Internet search engines, including your own Index Server. It also shows you how to make this interface work like the Microsoft Search Wizard (see Figure 15.3).

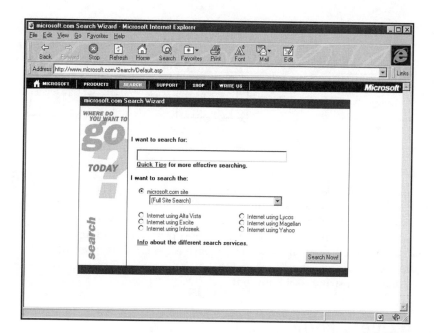

Figure 15.3

Recreating Microsoft's Search Wizard is our goal.

You have to enter the search expression and then choose the search engine upon which you want to execute the search. Given this single page, you can search with seven different search engines, including the local server. The goal of this section is to recreate this Search Wizard. With the power of Active Server Pages, it's fairly easy to implement the features provided by this Search Wizard.

I have decided to implement the following Internet search engines for this wizard (you can choose to implement others as well):

◆ AltaVista – `http://altavista.digital.com`

◆ Excite – `http://www.excite.com`

◆ HotBot – `http://www.hotbot.com`

◆ Infoseek – `http://www.infoseek.com`

◆ Lycos – `http://www.lycos.com`

◆ Yahoo – `http://www.yahoo.com`

Each of these servers provides a form for the user to input the query information. This information is posted to a page responsible for querying the data store of the search engine. It also returns the results to the user. See Figure 15.4 for details.

Figure 15.4

Pages for submitting queries and paging in the result set.

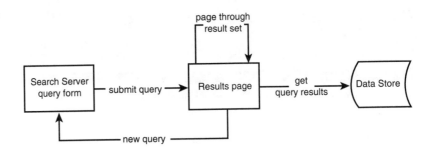

Our search wizard solution takes over the part of the query form in this figure for all the different search engines you want to implement. Therefore, the wizard has to take care of submitting the right number of arguments to each respective search engine. This is described in the section "Redirecting to the Appropriate Search Engine" later in this chapter. The first task in creating a search wizard is to create the user interface for gathering information about the search server to use (the query form). The next task is to create the search string to submit to it.

Creating a Query Form

I presented a screenshot of the Microsoft Search Wizard in Figure 15.3. When I examined this Search Wizard's source code to figure out how Microsoft had implemented the search capabilities, I decided to change the source code by adding the search servers I use most often and by adding search scope restrictions for the local server I administer. Listing 15.1 contains the resulting code.

On the CD

LISTING 15.1 - SOURCE CODE FOR THE QUERY FORM (SEARCH.ASP)

```
01.  <HTML>
02.  <HEAD>
03.  <TITLE>softwing.com Search Wizard</TITLE>
04.  </HEAD>
05.
06.  <BODY BGCOLOR="#FFFFFF">
07.
08.  <FORM ACTION="redir.asp" METHOD="GET">
09.  <CENTER>
10.  <TABLE BORDER=0 BORDERCOLOR="#000000" CELLPADDING=0
     ➥CELLSPACING=0 HEIGHT=318 WIDTH="555">
11.  <TR>
12.  <TD WIDTH="555" VALIGN=TOP HEIGHT=18 COLSPAN=7
     ➥BGCOLOR="#000084">
```

```
13. <INPUT TYPE="HIDDEN" NAME="TemplateName" VALUE="query">
14. <INPUT TYPE="HIDDEN" NAME="CiMaxRecordsPerPage"
    ➥VALUE="10">
15. <INPUT TYPE="HIDDEN" NAME="CiSort" VALUE="rank[d]">
16. <INPUT TYPE="HIDDEN" NAME="HTMLQueryForm" VALUE="
    ➥<%= Request.ServerVariables("PATH_INFO")%>">
17. <INPUT TYPE="HIDDEN" NAME="IDQFile"
    ➥VALUE="/scripts/samples/search/query.idq">
18.
19. <FONT SIZE="1" COLOR="#FFFFFF" FACE="MS Sans Serif,
    ➥Arial, Helv">
20. <B>
21. softwing.com Search Wizard
22. </B></FONT>
23. </TD>
24. </TR>
25.
26. <TR>
27. <TD WIDTH=1 ROWSPAN=7 HEIGHT=318 VALIGN=TOP>
28. <IMG SRC="BLACK.gif" HEIGHT="318" WIDTH="1" BORDER=0>
29. </TD>
30. <TD WIDTH=95 ROWSPAN=7 HEIGHT=318 VALIGN=TOP>
31. <IMG SRC="searchbar.gif" HEIGHT="318" WIDTH="95"
    ➥BORDER=0>
32. </TD>
33. <TD></TD>
34. <TD></TD>
35. <TD WIDTH=1 ROWSPAN=7 HEIGHT=318 VALIGN=TOP ALIGN=RIGHT>
36. <IMG SRC="BLACK.gif" HEIGHT="318" WIDTH="1" BORDER=0>
37. </TD>
38. </TR>
39.
40. <TR>
41. <TD WIDTH="450" VALIGN=TOP COLSPAN="2">
42. <FONT FACE="MS Sans Serif, Arial, Helv" SIZE="1">
43. <BR>
44.   <STRONG>I want to search for:</STRONG><P>
45.       <INPUT NAME="SearchString" VALUE="" TYPE="TEXT"
          ➥SIZE="58">
46. <BR>
47.       <B><A HREF="Link2Desert.htm">Quick Tips</A>
          ➥for more effective searching.</B>
```

continues

LISTING **15.1,** CONTINUED

```
48. </FONT>
49. </TD>
50. </TR>
51.
52. <TR>
53. <TD WIDTH="450" COLSPAN="2">
54.
55. <FONT FACE="MS Sans Serif, Arial, Helv" SIZE="1">
56. <BR>  <STRONG>I want to search the:</STRONG>
57. </FONT>
58. </TD>
59. </TR>
60.
61. <TR>
62. <TD COLSPAN="2" WIDTH="450">
63. <FONT FACE="MS Sans Serif, Arial, Helv" SIZE="1">
64. <BR>
65. ' start the local (Index Server) search engine part
66. <INPUT NAME="SearchType" TYPE="RADIO" CHECKED
       ➥VALUE="local">softwing.com site<BR>
67.
68. ' The <SELECT> statement is used to limit the scope
69. ' of the query submitted by the user. A slash searches
70. ' the entire site, the other values restrict to
       ➥distinct sub-branches
71.
72. <SELECT NAME="SearchArea">
73. <OPTION VALUE="/">(Full Site Search)
74. <OPTION VALUE="/AsirisDemo/">ASIRIS Demo
75. <OPTION VALUE="/EventCalender/">EventCalender
76. <OPTION VALUE="/~brains/">Christoph Wille´s homepage
77. </SELECT>
78. <BR>
79. </FONT>
80. </TD>
81. </TR>
82.
83.
84. <TR>
85. <TD WIDTH="225" COLSPAN="1">
86. <FONT FACE="MS Sans Serif, Arial, Helv" SIZE="1">
```

```
87.  <BR>
88.
89.  <INPUT NAME="SearchType" TYPE="RADIO" VALUE="altavista">
     ➥Internet using Alta Vista<BR>
90.
91.  <INPUT NAME="SearchType" TYPE="RADIO" VALUE="excite">
     ➥Internet using Excite<BR>
92.
93.  <INPUT NAME="SearchType" TYPE="RADIO" VALUE="infoseek">
     ➥Internet using Infoseek<BR>
94.  </FONT>
95.  </TD>
96.
97.  <TD WIDTH="225" COLSPAN="1">
98.  <FONT FACE="MS Sans Serif, Arial, Helv" SIZE="1">
99.  <BR>
100. <INPUT NAME="SearchType" TYPE="RADIO" VALUE="lycos">
     ➥Internet using Lycos<BR>
101. <INPUT NAME="SearchType" TYPE="RADIO" VALUE="hotbot">
     ➥Internet using HotBot<BR>
102. <INPUT NAME="SearchType" TYPE="RADIO" VALUE="yahoo">
     ➥Internet using Yahoo<BR>
103. </FONT>
104. </TD>
105. </TR>
106.
107. <TR>
108. <TD WIDTH="450" COLSPAN="2">
109. <FONT FACE="MS Sans Serif, Arial, Helv" SIZE="1">
110. <BR>
111.        <B><A HREF="Link2Desert.htm">Info</A> about the
            ➥different search services.</B>
112. </FONT>
113. </TD>
114. </TR>
115.
116. <TR>
117. <TD WIDTH="450" HEIGHT=40 ALIGN=RIGHT COLSPAN="2">
118. <FONT FACE="MS Sans Serif, Arial, Helv" SIZE="1">
119.
120. <INPUT TYPE="SUBMIT" NAME="Finish" VALUE="Search Now!">
121.
```

continues

Listing 15.1, Continued

```
122. <br>
123. </FONT>
124. </TD>
125. </TR>
126. <TR>
127. <TD WIDTH="555" VALIGN=TOP HEIGHT=18 COLSPAN=7
     ➥BGCOLOR="#000084">
128. <BR>
129. </TD>
130. </TR>
131. </TABLE>
132. </CENTER>
133. </FORM>
134. </BODY>
135. </HTML>
```

The form including all input fields is enclosed by the <FORM…> and </FORM> statements on lines 8 and 133. The first block of these fields is between lines 13 and 17, which are defined as hidden and used as parameters for local Index Server queries. Line 16 uses the only ASP code in the entire page to insert path information about the current script. This information is then used by Index Server to provide a link back to the query form. Line 17 points to the query file that contains information about the query and merges the result sets with the template. In line 17, a sample query file that comes with Index Server is used—the path to this file should be correct for your server as well.

If you're interested in good HTML code, the next lines are interesting because they create the side bars for the wizard. In terms of interesting code for the search wizard implementation, line 45 is again important, because it creates the input field for the search string.

The selection of the seven different search engines is handled with a group of radio buttons. The first search server defined is the local Index Server (line 66). The <SELECT> statement that follows this first radio button creates a combobox to enable the user to restrict the scope of the query. I have added four different search areas (scopes), starting with line 73 for the local server. You can add as many different search areas as there are directories on your server.

The remaining six nonlocal search engines follow on lines 89 to 102. Please note that the value that is specified for each radio button is submitted to the page that handles all requests, which is redir.asp (part of the <FORM> statement on line 8).

Now that you have seen all parameters, Table 15.1 reviews all parameters that are sent to redir.asp. With the exception of the first two parameters, all others are specific to Index Server. These are needed for the Index Server search template used in this example (query.idq) as input parameters. You could have hard-coded all of these in the redirection file too, however, you are more flexible in changing values when supplying these via a web-based form every time.

TABLE 15.1
Parameters submitted to redir.asp

Parameter	Description
SearchString	Contains the search string submitted by the user.
SearchType	Specifies the search engine the search string will be submitted to.
SearchArea	Defines the scope for the search.
CiMaxRecordsPerPage	Specifies the maximum number of records returned per page.
TemplateName	Template to be used for displaying the results.
CiSort	Sets the result set sorting to descending rank.
IDQFile	The query file that the search string and other parameters are submitted to.
HTMLQueryForm	The form used to submit the query to Index Server. Used to provide a backlink to this form from the results page.

With this information on parameters that is passed to the form-handling file redir.asp, the discussion of the user interface part of the search wizard is complete. The next section presents the scripting code that handles the actual redirection to the appropriate search engines.

Redirecting to the Appropriate Search Engine

This section is dedicated to the "magic" that's behind the search wizard: sending the search string with the appropriate parameters to the different search engines. The main problem is that every search engine expects different parameters for the search pages. Figuring out what these parameters are and what they mean can be time-consuming. When you have this information, there's no magic to creating the redirection file.

This section covers:

◆ Search engines parameters

◆ The redirection page

◆ Making the redirection page frame-aware

Search Engines Parameters

The next seven sections explain the parameters submitted to the most common query pages of the respective search engines implemented in this search wizard. Of these seven search engines one is the local Index Server, so there are only six search engines from the Internet implemented. If you want to add more search engines to your search wizard, you first have to figure out the parameters that need to be submitted to the search engine's query page. Follow these steps to figure out the parameters:

1. Navigate with your browser to the search engine's query form you want to add to the wizard.

2. Enter a sample query into this form and submit it to the search engine.

3. The URL you're receiving now includes all the parameters that need to be submitted to the search page of this search engine. The only information you really need to figure out is which parameter the search string is assigned to. Note the values of the other parameters too, so that you can re-create the URL for the query page entirely.

I followed this method exactly to obtain parameter information for the search engines. The information I found is presented in the next several sections.

Index Server

Most parameters for this search engine are already passed to redir.asp from the query form. Even the query file is passed, which is the example located under `/scripts/samples/search/query.idq` for this implementation. The other parameters that need to be passed to this file are listed in Table 15.2.

Table 15.2
Index Server Parameters

Parameter	Value	Description
CiRestriction	SearchString	Contains the search string submitted by the user.

Parameter	Value	Description
CiMaxRecordsPerPage	"10"	Specifies the maximum number of records returned per page.
CiScope	SearchArea	Restricts the search to a specific part of the web site.
TemplateName	"query"	Template to be used for displaying the results.
CiSort	"rank[d]"	Sets the result set sorting to descending rank.
HTMLQueryForm	HTMLQueryForm	The form used to submit the query to Index Server. Used to provide a backlink to this form from the results page.

AltaVista

For AltaVista searches I chose to use the capabilities provided by the standard form. The parameters that need to be passed to the query page http://altavista. digital.com/cgi-bin/query are described in Table 15.3. Notice that searches are limited to the Web. If you want to provide searching capabilities to Newsgroups, for example, you have to change the what parameter.

TABLE 15.3
AltaVista Parameters

Parameter	Value	Description
pg	"q"	Specifies type of query to be submitted.
what	"web"	Specifies which AltaVista index to search. Our search is limited to the web.
fmt	" "	Selects the format for output. An empty string indicates to use the default format.
q	SearchString	Contains the search string submitted by the user.

Yahoo

Searches are handled by a special search server of Yahoo. There's only one parameter that's submitted to the query page `http://search.yahoo.com/bin/search` (see Table 15.4).

TABLE 15.4
Yahoo Parameters

Parameter	Value	Description
p	SearchString	Contains the search string submitted by the user.

Lycos

The Lycos search engine located under `http://www.lycos.com/cgi-bin/pursuit` takes two parameters for querying its data store. See Table 15.5 for a description of these.

TABLE 15.5
Lycos Parameters

Parameter	Value	Description
cat	"lycos"	Specifies the category to search.
query	SearchString	Contains the search string submitted by the user.

Infoseek

Infoseek's search page is located at `http://www.infoseek.com/Titles` and takes five parameters (described in Table 15.6). Only one parameter, the one that takes the search string, is of interest for our search wizard.

TABLE 15.6
Infoseek Parameters

Parameter	Value	Description
col	"WW"	Category to search.
qt	SearchString	Contains the search string submitted by the user.

Parameter	Value	Description
sv	"IS"	Infoseek parameter.
lk	"noframes"	Infoseek parameter.
nh	"10"	Infoseek parameter.

Excite

Excite is another interesting search engine. It enables the user, as does AltaVista, to search different areas of the Internet. Because our search wizard is targeted at finding information located on web servers, the collection parameter is set to web (see Table 15.7). For a complete reference of parameters for the Excite search page at http://www.excite.com/search.gw.

TABLE 15.7
Excite Parameters

Parameter	Value	Description
trace	"a"	Excite parameter.
search	SearchString	Contains the search string submitted by the user.
collection	"web"	Specifies to search the web index.

HotBot

HotBot, one of the newer and faster search engines, is finding new friends daily. Because it provides great flexibility, the search page http://www.hotbot.com/ I am using is set to accept Boolean expressions in the search string. See Table 15.8 for more details.

TABLE 15.8
HotBot Parameters

Parameter	Value	Description
SW	"the Web"	Specifies to search the web index.

continues

TABLE 15.8, CONTINUED
HotBot Parameters

Parameter	Value	Description
SM	"B"	Specifies to evaluate the submitted search string as a Boolean expression.
MT	SearchString	Contains the search string submitted by the user.
DC	"10"	Returns 10 results per page.
DE	"2"	Enables full descriptions.
RG	"NA"	HotBot parameter.
_V	"2"	HotBot parameter.

The Redirection Page

So far, this chapter has discussed the creation of the search wizard query form page and introduced all the parameters that need to be submitted to each search engine. The actual work of sending the parameters to the search pages is handled in the file redir.asp (see Listing 15.2). This script page consists mainly of one large Select Case statement that creates the redirection URL with the appropriate parameters for every search server and then redirects to the URL it generated.

On the CD

LISTING 15.2 - THE REDIRECTION FILE (REDIR.ASP)

```
01. <%@ LANGUAGE="VBSCRIPT"%>
02.
03. <%
04. ' when we do it this way, we can handle POST and GET
    ➥with one piece of code
05. SearchType = Trim(Request("SearchType"))
06. URLRedirTo = ""
07. strSearchString = Server.URLEncode(
    ➥Trim(Request("SearchString")))
08.
09. Select Case SearchType
10.     Case "local"
11.         'first assumed is our server to be searched for
12.         URLRedirTo = Trim(Request("IDQFile")) &
            ➥"?CiRestriction=" & strSearchString
```

```
13.          URLRedirTo = URLRedirTo &
             ➥"&CiMaxRecordsPerPage=" & Server.URLEncode(Trim(
             ➥Request("CiMaxRecordsPerPage")))
14.          URLRedirTo = URLRedirTo & "&CiScope=" &
             ➥Server.URLEncode(Trim(Request("SearchArea")))
15.          URLRedirTo = URLRedirTo & "&TemplateName=" &
             ➥Server.URLEncode(Trim(Request("TemplateName")))
16.          URLRedirTo = URLRedirTo & "&CiSort=" &
             ➥Server.URLEncode(Trim(Request("CiSort")))
17.          URLRedirTo = URLRedirTo & "&HTMLQueryForm=" &
             ➥Server.URLEncode(Trim(Request("HTMLQueryForm")))
18.
19.      Case "altavista"
20.          URLRedirTo =
             ➥"http://altavista.digital.com/cgi-bin/query" & "?pg=q"
21.          URLRedirTo = URLRedirTo & "&what=web&fmt="
22.          URLRedirTo = URLRedirTo & "&q=" &
             ➥strSearchString
23.
24.      Case "excite"
25.          URLRedirTo = "http://www.excite.com/search.gw"
26.          URLRedirTo = URLRedirTo & "?trace=a&search="
             ➥& strSearchString & "&collection=web"
27.
28.      Case "infoseek"
29.          URLRedirTo = "http://www.infoseek.com/Titles"
30.          URLRedirTo = URLRedirTo & "?col=WW&qt=" &
             ➥strSearchString & "&sv=IS&lk=noframes&nh=10"
31.
32.      Case "lycos"
33.          URLRedirTo =
             ➥"http://www.lycos.com/cgi-bin/pursuit"
34.          URLRedirTo = URLRedirTo & "?cat=lycos&query="
             ➥& strSearchString
35.
36.      Case "hotbot"
37.          URLRedirTo = "http://www.hotbot.com/"
38.          URLRedirTo = URLRedirTo &
             ➥"?SW=the+Web&SM=B&MT=" & strSearchString
39.          URLRedirTo = URLRedirTo &
             ➥"&DC=10&DE=2&RG=NA&_v=2"
40.
```

continues

LISTING **15.2,** CONTINUED

```
41.        Case "yahoo"
42.            URLRedirTo =
               ➥"http://search.yahoo.com/bin/search"
43.            URLRedirTo = URLRedirTo & "?p=" &
               ➥strSearchString
44.
45.        Case Else
46.            ' no search machine we've implemented
47. End Select
48.
49. if ("" <> URLRedirTo) then
50.        Response.Redirect(URLRedirTo)
51. else
52. %>
53.
54. <HTML>
55. <HEAD>
56. <META NAME="GENERATOR" Content=
    ➥"Microsoft Visual InterDev 1.0">
57. <META HTTP-EQUIV="Content-Type" content="text/html;
    ➥charset=ISO-8859-1">
58. <TITLE>No Search Engine specified</TITLE>
59. </HEAD>
60. <BODY bgcolor=#ffffff>
61. <FONT face=Verdana>
62. <center>
63. Sorry, you didn't specify a search engine!
    ➥<A HREF="<%=Trim(Request("HTMLQueryForm"))%>">Back</A>
64. </center>
65. </BODY>
66. </HTML>
67.
68. <% end if %>
```

The Select Case statement spans the lines 9 to 47. In each Case statement the URL for the corresponding search engine is created. The biggest Case statement is the one for the local Index Server, because so many parameters have to be passed. If you need information about the parameters used, please refer to the previous sections.

Notice that the string parameters extracted from the Request are again URLEncoded: this is necessary because by retrieving variables from the Request object, they are automatically URL-decoded. Because an URL is being recreated, this encoding has to be reapplied.

The redirection is invoked on line 50; the surrounding `If` block is used to catch requests for search engines that aren't implemented. This feature comes in handy when you want to add new search engines to your wizard.

Now you're done with the wizard and can try it. You need only the two pages just built to create a great user experience and to provide users with a single starting point for their Internet searches. You can use this implementation right now. If you want to learn more about tricks of the trade, however, read the next section!

Making the Redirection Page Frame-Aware

Why does the redirection page need to be frame-aware? Many sites today are implemented using frames, which means that a user can't see whether the page presented in, for example, the lower-left pane is located on the current server or is from another server somewhere else on the Internet.

This can be a problem when you're running the search wizard inside a frame because all search engines are invoked in the pane where the search wizard is located. When the user selects a site from the result set returned from any of the search engines offered by the search wizard and the site they select also was created using frames, the browser window gets cluttered and the user may become confused.

It would be beneficial, therefore, to display the results returned by the different search engines at top level, outside the frame. You can achieve this by simply replacing line 8 of Listing 15.1 (search.asp) with

```
<FORM ACTION="redir.asp" METHOD="GET" TARGET="_top">
```

This solution, however, doesn't take into account the local Index Server. Because the Index Server resides on your site, the query results should be displayed inside the original frame. If you use the preceding solution, you can't specify targets depending on the choice of the search engine on the client side—only one target is allowed and it has to be specified in the `<FORM>` tag. On the server side, in contrast, you know what target you want to display the results in for each search engine, but this knowledge is of no use to you (at least at the moment) because server-side scripting logic cannot redirect a page it is currently processing to a specific pane in a frame at the client side. This is because the web server doesn't know whether a page requested is part of a frame. It could just as easily be requested outside of a frame.

The only solution to this problem—opening the result sets of search engines at top level when demanded—is to mix server-side and client-side code. The search string is created on the server side and the redirection to the search engine using the search string is executed on the client side. This needs to be done, however, only when you want to leave the frame; no action needs to be performed on the client side when the redirection should be executed in the current frame pane. Listing 15.3 shows the client-side JavaScript code you can use to reload a specified URL in the browser at top level when the current page opens. This code is used later in the implementation of the search wizard redirection page.

LISTING 15.3 - CLIENT-SIDE CODE TO LOAD A SPECIFIC URL TOPMOST IN A BROWSER.

```
01. <SCRIPT  LANGUAGE="JavaScript" FOR="window"
    ➥EVENT="onLoad()">
02. <!--
03.    parent.location = "http://www.zauner.at";
04. //-->
05. </SCRIPT>
```

I decided to use JavaScript because it's supported in most of the modern browsers—at least in those that are most widely used today. You can use VBScript also, but it is not (by far) as widely implemented in browsers as JavaScript is.

Now that you have the client-side code, you need to be able to jump out of the frame. This code has to be added to the response generated by the redirection file because the client has to execute the redirection code. I have encapsulated the creation of the client code into a procedure. Listing 15.4 shows how I incorporated this new functionality into the existing redir.asp. Notice that only the scripting code is printed here; you can find the entire file on this book's accompanying CD.

**On the
CD**

LISTING 15.4 - THE FIRST PART OF REDIR_FRAMES.ASP

```
01. <%@ LANGUAGE="VBSCRIPT"%>
02.
03. <SCRIPT  LANGUAGE="VBSCRIPT" RUNAT="SERVER">
04. Sub JumpOutOfFrame(strTarget)
05.    Response.Write "<SCRI"
06.    Response.Write "PT LANGUAGE=""JavaScript""
       ➥FOR=""window"" EVENT=""onLoad()"">" & vbCRLF
07.    Response.Write "<!"
08.    Response.Write "--" & vbCRLF
09.    Response.Write "parent.location = """ & strTarget &
       ➥""";" & vbCRLF
10.    Response.Write "//-->" & vbCRLF
11.    Response.Write "</SC"
12.    Response.Write "RIPT>" & vbCRLF
13. End Sub
14. </SCRIPT>
15.
```

```
16. <%
17. ' when we do it this way, we can handle POST and GET
    ➥with one piece of code
18. SearchType = Trim(Request("SearchType"))
19. URLRedirTo = ""
20. strSearchString = Server.URLEncode(
    ➥Trim(Request("SearchString")))
21. bJumpOutOfFrame = True
22.
23. Select Case SearchType
24.     Case "local"
25.             ' first assumed is our server to be searched
26.             URLRedirTo = Trim(Request("IDQFile")) &
                ➥"?CiRestriction=" & strSearchString
27.             URLRedirTo = URLRedirTo &
                ➥"&CiMaxRecordsPerPage=" & Server.URLEncode(Trim(Request
                ➥("CiMaxRecordsPerPage")))
28.             URLRedirTo = URLRedirTo & "&CiScope=" &
                ➥Server.URLEncode(Trim(Request("SearchArea")))
29.             URLRedirTo = URLRedirTo & "&TemplateName=" &
                ➥Server.URLEncode(Trim(Request("TemplateName")))
30.             URLRedirTo = URLRedirTo & "&CiSort=" &
                ➥Server.URLEncode(Trim(Request("CiSort")))
31.             URLRedirTo = URLRedirTo & "&HTMLQueryForm="
                ➥& Server.URLEncode(Trim(Request("HTMLQueryForm")))
32.             bJumpOutOfFrame = False
33.
34.     Case "altavista"
35.             URLRedirTo =
                ➥"http://altavista.digital.com/cgi-bin/query" & "?pg=q"
36.             URLRedirTo = URLRedirTo & "&what=web&fmt="
37.             URLRedirTo = URLRedirTo & "&q=" &
                ➥strSearchString
38.
39.     Case "excite"
40.             URLRedirTo = "http://www.excite.com/search.gw"
41.             URLRedirTo = URLRedirTo & "?trace=a&search="
                ➥& strSearchString & "&collection=web"
42.
43.     Case "infoseek"
44.             URLRedirTo = "http://www.infoseek.com/Titles"
```

continues

```
45.             URLRedirTo = URLRedirTo & "?col=WW&qt=" &
                ➡strSearchString & "&sv=IS&lk=noframes&nh=10"
46.
47.        Case "lycos"
48.             URLRedirTo =
                ➡"http://www.lycos.com/cgi-bin/pursuit"
49.             URLRedirTo = URLRedirTo & "?cat=lycos&query="
                ➡& strSearchString
50.
51.        Case "hotbot"
52.             URLRedirTo = "http://www.hotbot.com/"
53.             URLRedirTo = URLRedirTo &
                ➡"?SW=the+Web&SM=B&MT=" & strSearchString
54.             URLRedirTo = URLRedirTo &
                ➡"&DC=10&DE=2&RG=NA&_v=2"
55.
56.        Case "yahoo"
57.             URLRedirTo =
                ➡"http://search.yahoo.com/bin/search"
58.             URLRedirTo = URLRedirTo & "?p=" &
                ➡strSearchString
59.
60.        Case Else
61.             ' no search machine we've implemented
62. End Select
63.
64. If ("" <> URLRedirTo) Then
65.        If Not bJumpOutOfFrame Then
66.             Response.Redirect(URLRedirTo)
67.        Else
68.             JumpOutOfFrame URLRedirTo
69.        End If
70. Else
71. %>
```

You might wonder about the implementation of JumpOutOfFrame starting on line 4. There's a reason for splitting the client-side statements to different lines: ASP treats these as if they weren't enclosed in valid VBScript code. For example

```
Response.Write "<SCRIPT LANGUAGE=""JavaScript""
➥FOR=""window"" EVENT=""onLoad()"">" & vbCRLF
```

is equal to lines 5 and 6, generating the error in Listing 15.5.

LISTING 15.5 - AN ERROR RETURNED BY REWRITING LINES 5 AND 6 OF LISTING 15.4 TO THE SINGLE LINE VERSION.

```
Active Server Pages error 'ASP 0138'
Nested Script Block
/Chapter15/redir_frames.asp, line 3
A script block cannot be placed inside another script block.
```

The only solution is to split the statements—the error will never show up again. The same is true for the comment statements—simply split the statement and it will work fine.

Now it's time to get back to the newly added features of the redirection file. The only further change besides the new procedure is the variable bJumpOutOfFrame. This variable indicates whether to insert the client-side code (lines 65 to 69). The only search engine for which no client-side code is added to the response is Index Server. All other servers are opened outside the frame where the search wizard was located.

The solution presented here for leaving frames works for more than the search wizard scenario—you can reuse this procedure wherever you need to leave a frame using server-side logic.

Summary

This chapter presented the creation of a search wizard that works like the one found at Microsoft's Internet site. Besides using Internet search engines with it, you also can use the powerful Microsoft Index Server add-on for Internet Information Server and Peer Web Services. These enable users to index and search content located on the local web server. The code presented in this chapter enables you to add this search wizard functionality to your site immediately.

CHAPTER 16

Creating a Web Front-End for SQL Server

Microsoft delivers web-based administration tools not only for the Internet Information Server product and the Index Server, but also for administering Windows NT via a web browser. With these three tools, you can administer a web server remotely through any web browser. However, when you create great dynamic and interactive web sites, you need to use a large scale database, and in most cases, you will probably use Microsoft SQL Server—and this product has no web-based administration utility to offer. Therefore, you have to create one!

This chapter explains the following:

◆ How to design a web front-end for SQL Server

◆ The SQL distributed management objects

◆ The most common functions provided by SQL web applications

◆ How to log into a database

◆ How to print information about SQL objects

◆ How to use the SQL Query and Results page

Designing the Web Front-End

Ideally, the SQL web application should closely resemble the programs that come with Microsoft SQL Server. People often use an SQL Server tool called ISQL/w (Interactive SQL) for testing SQL commands, tracing the results, and monitoring their execution. Another popular tool is Enterprise Manager, which enables you to easily administer all aspects of SQL Server. Figure 16.1 shows this tool with the unlocking database selected.

Figure 16.1

SQL Enterprise opened with the unlocking database selected.

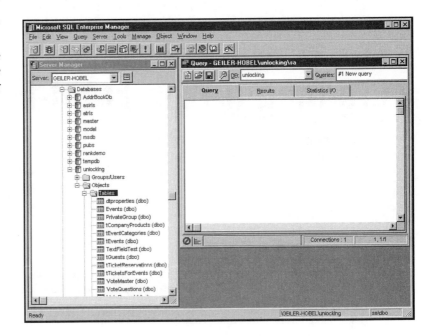

Notice the open query window in Figure 16.1; it's the same as the one used in ISQL/w. Therefore, the number of tools needed can be reduced to one: SQL Enterprise Manager. It enables you to view, create, or modify definitions for tables, views, stored procedures, rules, user-defined datatypes, and more. You can create databases, make backups or restore databases, configure task execution, or manage the logins for databases. And this is only an overview of what you can do with this powerful tool.

Parts of this functionality—if not all—would be beneficial if you could remotely access them with any web browser. How can you access all the SQL Server functionality? A simple ODBC connection won't do the trick. You can use the DB-Library for SQL Server, which is a C-based API for accessing SQL Server. It enables you to create Automation objects that wrap the functionality provided by the API functions. You can then call these in ASP pages. This process, however, is very time-consuming.

Fortunately you don't need to do this work because SQL Server already ships with an object library that wraps all the functionality that's included with SQL Server: the SQL Distributed Management Objects (SQL-DMO).

The SQL Distributed Management Objects

The SQL Distributed Management Objects (SQL-DMO) are installed automatically with the SQL Server management tools, because Enterprise Manager uses this object library to implement its functionality. So when you look at the Enterprise Manager, you know what functionality you can provide with the object library. The entire object model for the SQL-DMO is presented in Figure 16.2.

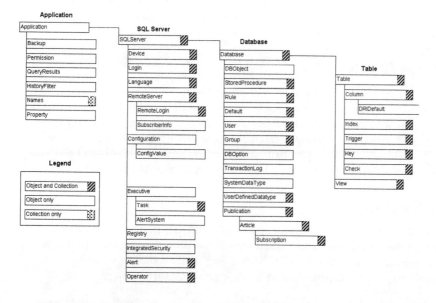

Figure 16.2

The Object Model of the SQL Database Management Objects.

With these objects, you can recreate the entire Enterprise Manager that ships with SQL Server. This object model is split in five sub-blocks grouped by functionality:

◆ Application scope objects

◆ SQL Server scope objects

◆ Service scope objects

◆ Database scope objects

◆ Table scope objects

Take a closer look at Enterprise Manager and you will see immediately where these groups are used.

Application Scope Objects

Objects that have Application scope are used to provide common functionality for all SQL Servers that are managed within this SQL-DMO application. This application contains a collection, SQLServers, where all the SQL Servers are listed that are currently registered with this application (this resembles the list of SQL Servers in Enterprise Manager). For example, backups are managed by the Backup object that has Application scope.

SQL Server Scope Objects

A single SQL Server's functionality is managed by the SQL Server scope objects. Using these objects, you can manage devices, logins, and the entire configuration for a particular server. You can create, delete, modify, and enumerate, for example, user logins or database devices, which are used to store databases.

Service Scope Objects

SQL Server enables the execution of tasks at pre-defined times or at recurring times within specified intervals. This functionality is provided by the SQL Executive, which is managed by the objects with Service scope. You can configure tasks not only to execute SQL statements (for example, database cleanup or word indexing), but also to launch applications (for example, issue restart commands for IIS, which I did with earlier versions of IIS when crashes could be expected at regular intervals).

Database Scope Objects

The SQL Server object contains a collection of all databases that are available for this server. Each of these Database objects itself contains objects that are used to manage stored procedures, rules, defaults, tables, views, user-defined data types, and more. Figure 16.3 shows how Enterprise Manager presents this information to the user.

This part of the SQL-DMO object model is most interesting for database developers because it consists of tables, views, and stored procedures, which are used most often for database applications. If you want to provide a web site that has active content via a database, the Database scope objects will be very useful to you.

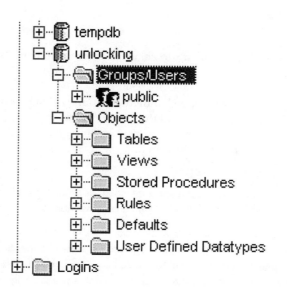

Figure 16.3

How Enterprise Manager provides Database scope objects with functionality for the user.

Table Scope Objects

Objects with table scope are the View and Table objects with the respective objects that define the properties in a table. All views and tables are represented with a collection in the Database object. However, they are grouped separately because of the additional objects that make up a table. You can reference columns, indexes, triggers, keys, and checks via objects in their respective collections for each table.

Deciding About Functionality

Of course, you could implement all the functionality that's found in the Enterprise Manager of SQL Server in a web-based administrator utility. However, some parts of the functionality are used more often than others and some can be recreated with SQL statements (for example, database creation).

So what are the most common scenarios when you're using Enterprise Manager? A list of common tasks that are performed when creating a web application that uses SQL Server follows:

◆ Creating tables with indexes, keys, referential integrity, and user-defined datatypes.

◆ Creating, modifying, and deleting views and stored procedures.

◆ Adding rows to the tables.

◆ Issuing quick SQL statements to check whether the data in the tables is as expected.

Notice that all of these tasks can be handled with standard SQL statements. This is the goal of the online administration tool the chapter shows you how to create—providing functionality that enables the user to view existing objects in the database as well as to create, modify, or delete objects in it.

 Note The tool created in this chapter is intended for production servers that you can't access directly from the Internet with Enterprise Manager.

This tool helps you make updates or additions to databases that reside on the production server. The usual process is to test these changes to the database on a development server first, where you can use sophisticated tools like Visual InterDev or any other database utility. These tools enable you to easily create the SQL statements that are then issued against the production server's SQL Server database using the web front-end created in this chapter.

Now that you know which functionality to implement, the only question left is how to organize the features of this web application.

In general, before anyone can administer any SQL Server, this person has to login to the server under an sa (system administrator) or equivalent privileges account. Therefore, a solution has to include a login page to the SQL Server of choice that a user must pass before going on to the administration pages. Figure 16.4 shows this approach for the application.

Figure 16.4

An application functionality model.

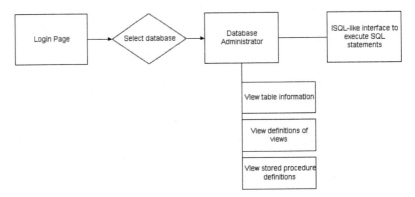

The Database Administrator main page in Figure 16.4 provides access to two different parts of the application:

◆ Viewing information about existing objects.

For this implementation, viewing of tables, views, and stored procedures is supported. Information displayed about the tables includes column, datatype, and index information. The information displayed about the stored procedures and views is the SQL statement used to create them. You can use this part of the application to find out what tables, views, and stored procedures look like.

◆ Submitting any SQL statements to the database, including CREATE TABLE, CREATE VIEW, and CREATE PROCEDURE statements.

You can choose the number of rows to return from any statement you submit. You can use this part of the application to issue any SQL command to the database, be it to test a statement or to create any database object.

Now that the functionality is specified, you can go about implementing the solution with Active Server Pages.

Implementing the Solution

Figure 16.5 shows what the solution looks like for the Database Administrator main page.

Notice that the page is created using frames. It contains three panes: the top-left pane is used for selecting the database, the pane below displays database objects and the third (the rightmost pane), is used to display definitions for tables, views, and stored procedures. In this screenshot, it opens up the ISQL-like interface to issue SQL commands.

The steps outlined in the following list walk you through the process of login to a SQL Server until you reach the point where I took the following screenshot:

1. In the login page, enter the name of the SQL Server and a valid sa (system administrator) or equivalent account and its password to login to this server.

2. You're presented with the Database Administrators page, which has information filled in about the available databases on this server in the upper-left pane. Select the appropriate database name and click the Show! button.

3. Now the pane below the database's selection is populated with a list of all tables, stored procedures, and views that are defined in this database. Also, a link to an ISQL like utility page is added. Follow this link.

4. The page you see now should resemble Figure 16.5. You can now issue any SQL command against the database or go back to the list on the left side and view a definition for any of the listed objects.

Figure 16.5

The Database Administrator page in action.

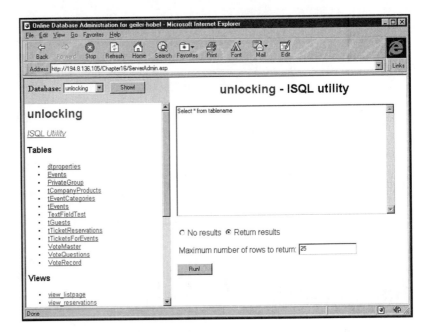

From this list, you should implement the following pages:

◆ A login page

◆ A page that implements the frame for the three panes presented earlier. These three panes are filled by three different pages. You need a page listing the databases for this SQL Server, one for listing tables, views, and stored procedures contained in a selected database, and a page for displaying definitions for these objects.

◆ A page for creating the SQL statement execution utility

The implementation of the entire application falls into three sections, which this chapter covers next:

◆ Logging into a database server

◆ Printing information about SQL objects

◆ The SQL Query and Results page

Because the login is a prerequisite to managing an SQL Server, this is the first thing that is covered.

Logging into a Database Server

When you're adding a new SQL Server to the list of servers in Enterprise Manager, you're asked to provide the server's name and the credentials (system administrator or equivalent) used to login to the server. If the connection was established and the credentials you supplied were sufficient, the server is added to the list of servers in Enterprise Manager. In contrast to this approach, the online administrator utility being discussed here enables access to a single server at a given time only.

To provide the login, you need to create a page asking for server name and credentials. Listing 16.1 contains the login page used for this application.

LISTING 16.1 - THE LOGIN PAGE FOR THE APPLICATION (DEFAULT.ASP) On the CD

```
01. <HTML>
02. <HEAD>
03. <TITLE>Online SQL Server Maintenance Utility</TITLE>
04. </HEAD>
05. <BODY BGCOLOR="#FFFFFF">
06. <FONT FACE="Verdana">
07.
08. <CENTER>
09. <H1><FONT COLOR="blue">Online SQL Server Maintenance Utility</FONT></H1>
10.  <P>
11.
12. <TABLE CELLPADDING=10 BORDER=2 BGCOLOR="Aqua" WIDTH=300><TR><TD>
13. <FORM ACTION="ServerAdmin.asp" METHOD="POST">
14. <TABLE BORDER=0>
15. <TR><TH ALIGN=RIGHT>Server name:</TH>
16. <TD>
17. <INPUT TYPE=TEXT SIZE=20 MAXLENGTH=256 NAME="ServerName" VALUE="<%=Request.
     ➥ServerVariables("SERVER_NAME")%>">
18. </TD>
19. </TR>
20. <TR><TH ALIGN=RIGHT>Login:</TH>
21. <TD>
22. <INPUT TYPE=TEXT SIZE=20 MAXLENGTH=256 NAME="Login" VALUE="<%=Request.
     ➥ServerVariables("LOGON_USER")%>">
23. </TD>
```

continues

LISTING 16.1, CONTINUED

```
24. </TR>
25. <TR><TH ALIGN=RIGHT>Password:</TH>
26. <TD><INPUT TYPE=PASSWORD SIZE="20" MAXLENGTH="256" NAME="Password"></TD>
27. </TR>
28. <TR><TD></TD><TD ALIGN=LEFT> <P><INPUT TYPE=SUBMIT VALUE="Login"></TD>
29. </TR></TABLE>
30. </FORM>
31. </TD></TR></TABLE>
32.
33. </CENTER>
34. </BODY>
35. </HTML>
```

There is no real Active Server Pages magic included in this page. Only lines 17 and 22 insert some code that might be helpful. Line 17 inserts the server name of the web server as a default value for the SQL server's name.

```
17. <INPUT TYPE=TEXT SIZE=20 MAXLENGTH=256 NAME="ServerName"VALUE="<%=Request.
     ➥ServerVariables("SERVER_NAME")%>">
```

This line is used just in case both servers run on the same machine, which is only true for very small sites.

Line 22 inserts the name of the user currently logged-on as a default.

```
22. <INPUT TYPE=TEXT SIZE=20 MAXLENGTH=256 NAME="Login"VALUE="<%=Request.
     ➥ServerVariables("LOGON_USER")%>">
```

This feature is only available for secured directories where the user was required to logon.

Warning It's strongly recommended that you secure the directory where this application is running. When a user can access these pages—given that you did not change the password of the sa account—he or she can access and modify all data on your server. Also, if you have an SSL-secured branch of your server, put the directory there so your traffic to and from the server is encoded.

Now the page for login is created. However, no login code has been added and it still needs to be implemented. I decided to place the logon code in the page that creates the frame, because this page can only be displayed when an SQL Server connection has been established (remember, this frame is the Database Administrator page). Listing 16.2 contains the code for both the logon and the frame.

Listing 16.2 - The Database Administrator page (ServerAdmin.asp)

On the
CD

```
01. <%@ LANGUAGE = VBScript %>
02.
03. <HTML>
04. <HEAD>
05. <TITLE>Online Database Administration for <%=Request.Form("Servername")%>
    ➥</TITLE>
06. </HEAD>
07.
08. <%
09. On Error Resume Next
10. Dim oSQLServer
11. Set oSQLServer = CreateObject ("SQLOLE.SQLServer")
12.
13. Set Session("SQLServer") = Nothing
14.
15. If Err.Number > 0 Then
16.      Response.Write("SQL DMO could not be initialized!<BR>" & Err.
         ➥Description)
17.      Err.Clear
18.      Response.End
19. End If
20.
21. strServer = Request.Form("ServerName")
22. strLogin = Request.Form("Login")
23. strPwd = Request.Form("Password")
24.
25.
26. oSQLServer.Connect strServer,strLogin,strPwd
27.
28. If Err.Number > 0 Then
29.      Response.Write("Failed to connect to SQL Server!<BR>" & Err.
         ➥Description)
30.      Err.Clear
31.      Response.End
32. End If
33.
34. Set Session("SQLServer") = Nothing
35. Set Session("SQLServer") = oSQLServer
36. Set oSQLServer = Nothing
37. %>
38.
```

continues

LISTING **16.2,** CONTINUED

```
39. <FRAMESET FRAMEBORDER="0" FRAMESPACING="0" COLS="300,*">
40.     <FRAMESET FRAMEBORDER="0" FRAMESPACING="0" ROWS="50,*">
41.         <FRAME MARGINWIDTH="2" MARGINHEIGHT="0"
            ➥SRC="Databases.asp" NAME="databases" NORESIZE SCROLLING="no">
42.         <FRAME MARGINWIDTH="2" MARGINHEIGHT="0" SRC="pane1.htm"
            ➥NAME="dbitems" NORESIZE SCROLLING="auto">
43.     </FRAMESET>
44.     <FRAME MARGINWIDTH="10" MARGINHEIGHT="5" SRC="emptypage.htm"
        ➥NAME="showpane">
45. </FRAMESET>
46.
47. <NOFRAMES>
48. <BODY BGCOLOR=#FFFFFF>
49. <FONT FACE=Verdana>
50. Frames required!
51. </NOFRAMES>
52.
53. </BODY>
54. </HTML>
```

Note The two pages emptypage.htm (line 44) and pane1.htm (line 42) are included for displaying usage information to the user before the user has selected a database. Both are contained on the accompanying CD, but there are no listings showing their contents in this chapter.

Notice that this page's scripting language is set to VBScript on line 1. As an aid for the administrator, the name of the SQL Server is added to the title of the page (line 5).

The main code for establishing a connection to the SQL Server is contained between lines 8 and 37 and is written to handle scripting errors inline. On line 11, a new SQLServer object is created. Notice that I don't need to create the application first because this is done automatically. By referencing the read-only property application of the SQLServer object, you can gain access to this object. Line 15 and following lines check for and report to the user when there's an error during object creation. Next, the information about server name, user, and password is extracted from the request and used on line 26 to establish the connection to the SQL Server to which the server name variable points.

Line 28 checks to see if this operation failed. If all went okay, the newly created SQLServer object is assigned as a session variable for this user so that further requests can be handled more quickly. Notice that this listing has many statements that set some object variables to Nothing. These are needed to free references for the objects.

Did you notice the flaw I introduced in this page? If you click refresh for the page, you will receive a "failed to connect" error message even if you connected success-fully. This is because there's no form data with logon information available. To resolve this problem, simply include the following statement right before line 8:

```
If (Request.ServerVariables("„CONTENT_LENGTH"))>0 Then
```

However, don't forget the closing End If after line 37!

Now that the user is logged in successfully to the server, you must provide a list of databases to the user that are available on the server to administer. This is done with the page databases.asp, presented in Listing 16.3.

LISTING 16.3 - PROVIDING THE LIST OF DATABASES FOR THE SQL SERVER (DATABASES.ASP)

On the
CD

```
01. <%@ LANGUAGE = VBScript %>
02. <HTML>
03. <HEAD>
04. <TITLE>Online Database</TITLE>
05. </HEAD>
06.
07. <HTML>
08. <BODY BGCOLOR="aqua" leftmargin=5 topmargin=5>
09.
10. <%
11. On Error Resume Next
12.
13. If Not IsObject(Session("SQLServer")) Then
14.    Response.Write("SQL Server connection object does not exist!")
15.    Response.End
16. End If
17.
18. Dim oSQLServer
19. Set oSQLServer = Session("SQLServer")
20. %>
21.
22. <FORM ACTION="DBItems.asp" METHOD="GET" TARGET="dbitems">
23. <TABLE><TR><TD><B>Database:</B></TD><TD>
24. <SELECT NAME="Database">
25. <%
26. For Each SQLDB In oSQLServer.Databases
27.    If Not SQLDB.SystemObject Then
```

continues

```
28.    Response.Write "<OPTION VALUE=""" & SQLDB.Name & """>" & SQLDB.Name
   ➥& " "
29.    End If
30. Next
31. Set oSQLServer = Nothing
32. %>
33. </SELECT>
34. </TD><TD><INPUT TYPE="submit" VALUE="Show!"></TD></TR></TABLE>
35. </FORM>
36.
37. </BODY>
38. </HTML>
```

Again, the default scripting language for this page is set to VBScript. Because this page can return only databases when the login to the server was successful, the check on line 13 is needed to end processing when this isn't the case. Notice that on line 19, the session variable is assigned to a local variable that is used for the processing between lines 25 and 32. This code outputs all databases in the Databases collection, except those that are marked as system objects. When the local variable for the database is no longer needed, it is released (see line 31).

Now the user is logged into the server and presented with the choice of databases. The next thing to do is to provide information about objects that are stored in the database. The user can then select an object to view information about.

Printing Information about SQL Objects

Before you can print information about tables, views, or stored procedures, seeing a list of these objects would be nice. This list is what is created when the form that is contained in databases.asp (Listing 16.3) is submitted. It opens a page that contains a list of all the elements in the collections of the previously mentioned three object types (tables, views, and stored procedures). The code for this page is contained in Listing 16.4.

On the CD

LISTING 16.4 - ALL ELEMENTS FOR TABLES, VIEWS, AND
STORED PROCEDURES (DBITEMS.ASP)

```
01. <%@ LANGUAGE = VBScript %>
02. <HTML>
03. <HEAD>
04. <TITLE>Online Database</TITLE>
05. </HEAD>
06. <BODY BGCOLOR=#ffffff leftmargin=5 topmargin=5>
```

```
07. <FONT FACE=Arial>
08.
09. <%
10. On Error Resume Next
11.
12. If Not IsObject(Session("SQLServer")) Then
13.     Response.Write("SQL Server connection object does not exist!")
14.     Response.End
15. End If
16.
17. Dim oSQLServer
18. Set oSQLServer = Session("SQLServer")
19.
20. ' now find the database we need
21. Set thisDb = oSQLServer.Databases(CStr(Request("Database")))
22. If Err.Number > 0 Or Not IsObject(thisDb) Then
23.     Response.Write("Database does not exist on SQL Server!
        ➥<BR>" & Err.Description)
24.     Response.End
25. End If
26.
27. Set Session("ActiveSQLdb") = Nothing
28. Set Session("ActiveSQLdb") = thisDb
29. %>
30. <H2><font color="blue"><%=thisDb.Name%></font></H2>
31. <A HREF="isql.asp" target="showpane"><I>ISQL Utility</I></A><P>
32.
33. <B>Tables</B>
34. <font size=-1>
35. <UL>
36. <%
37. For Each DBTable In thisDb.Tables
38.     If Not DBTable.SystemObject Then
39.         Response.Write "<LI>" & "<A TARGET=""showpane""
            ➥HREF=""DBMap.asp?DBOType=Table&DBObject="
40.         Response.Write DBTable.Name & """>" & DBTable.Name
            ➥& "</A>" & vbCRLF
41.     End If
42. Next
43. %>
44. </font>
45. </UL>
```

continues

LISTING **16.4,** CONTINUED

```
46.
47. <P>
48. <B>Views</B>
49. <font size=-1>
50. <UL>
51. <%
52. For Each DBView In thisDb.Views
53.    If Not DBView.SystemObject Then
54.       Response.Write "<LI>" & "<A TARGET=""showpane""
          ➥HREF=""DBMap.asp?DBOType=View&DBObject="
55.       Response.Write DBView.Name & """>" & DBView.Name
          ➥& "</A>" & vbCRLF
56.    End If
57. Next
58. %>
59. </font>
60. </UL>
61.
62. <P>
63. <B>Stored Procedures</B>
64. <font size=-1>
65. <UL>
66. <%
67. For Each DBsp In thisDb.StoredProcedures
68.    If Not DBsp.SystemObject Then
69.       Response.Write "<LI>" & "<A TARGET=""showpane""
          ➥HREF=""DBMap.asp?DBOType=SP&DBObject="
70.       Response.Write DBsp.Name & """>" & DBsp.Name &
          ➥"</A>" & vbCRLF
71.    End If
72. Next
73. %>
74. </font>
75. </UL>
76. <P>
77.
78. <%
79. Set oSQLServer = Nothing
80. %>
81.
82. </BODY>
83. </HTML>
```

This page—like databases.asp—contains a check to see whether a logon to an SQL Server was successful (performed on lines 12 to 15). Next, the database name that was submitted in the form is looked up in the Databases collection (line 21). Again, if this wasn't successful, an error is reported to the user. Upon successful connection to the database, it is assigned to a session variable like the SQLServer object. The reason is that for further requests like printing of table definitions or creation statements for views and stored procedures, as well as the execution of SQL statements, this object needs to be reused.

The code that's found between lines 36 and 43 for listing the tables is repeated only with changes for the collection names on lines 51 to 58 and 66 to 73 for views and stored procedures. All three code blocks iterate over the respective collections and create hyperlinks for all elements (given that they aren't system objects) so that their definitions can be viewed in the third pane.

One link is left to be mentioned: line 31 contains a link to the isql.asp page, which contains the code for issuing SQL commands against the database. The next section is dedicated to this page.

Before jumping into this topic, the page for viewing definitions for tables, views, and stored procedures, dbmap.asp, needs to be created. Its code is shown in Listing 16.5 and is designed so that you can extend it with, for example, viewing defaults, rules, and user-defined datatypes.

LISTING 16.5 - VIEWING DEFINITIONS FOR TABLES, VIEWS, AND STORED PROCEDURES (DBMAP.ASP)

On the CD

```
01. <%@ LANGUAGE = VBScript %>
02. <HTML>
03. <HEAD>
04. <TITLE>Online Database</TITLE>
05. </HEAD>
06. <BODY BGCOLOR=#ffffff leftmargin=5 topmargin=5>
07. <FONT FACE=Arial>
08.
09. <%
10. On Error Resume Next
11.
12. If Not IsObject(Session("ActiveSQLdb")) Then
13.     Response.Write("No connection to a database established!")
14.     Response.End
15. End If
16.
17. Dim thisDb
```

continues

Listing 16.5, Continued

```
18. Set thisDb = Session("ActiveSQLdb")
19.
20. Select Case Request("DBOType")
21.    Case "Table"
22.       Set theTable = thisDb.Tables(CStr(Request("DBObject")))
23.       If Err.Number > 0 Then
24.          Response.Write("Table does not exist in Database!
             ➥<BR>" & Err.Description)
25.          Response.End
26.       End If
27.       PrintTable theTable
28.       Set theTable = Nothing
29.
30.    Case "SP"
31.       Set theSP = thisDb.StoredProcedures(CStr(Request("DBObject")))
32.       If Err.Number > 0 Then
33.          Response.Write("SP does not exist in Database!
             ➥<BR>" & Err.Description)
34.          Response.End
35.       End If
36.       PrintSP theSP
37.       Set theSP = Nothing
38.
39.    Case "View"
40.       Set theView = thisDb.Views(CStr(Request("DBObject")))
41.       If Err.Number > 0 Then
42.          Response.Write("View does not exist in Database!
             ➥<BR>" & Err.Description)
43.          Response.End
44.       End If
45.       PrintView theView
46.       Set theView = Nothing
47.
48.    Case Else
49.       Response.Write("Not a valid action selected!")
50.        Response.End
51. End Select
52.
53. Set thisDb = Nothing
54. %>
55.
56.
```

```
57. <SCRIPT  RUNAT=SERVER LANGUAGE=VBScript>
58. Sub PrintView(thisView)
59. If Not thisView.SystemObject Then
60.     Response.Write "<CENTER><H3>" & thisView.Name &
        ➥ " view</H3><CENTER>"
61.     Response.Write "<TABLE BORDER=1 WIDTH=""80%""><tr><td>"
62.     Response.Write "<PRE>" & thisView.Text & "</PRE>"
63.     Response.Write "</td></tr></TABLE>"
64. End If
65. End Sub
66.
67. Sub PrintSP(thisSP)
68. If Not thisSP.SystemObject Then
69.     Response.Write "<CENTER><H3>" & thisSP.Name &
        ➥" stored procedure</H3><CENTER>"
70.     Response.Write "<TABLE BORDER=1 WIDTH=""80%""><tr><td>"
71.     Response.Write "<PRE>" & thisSP.Text & "</PRE>"
72.     Response.Write "</td></tr></TABLE>"
73. End If
74. End Sub
75.
76. Sub PrintTable(thisTable)
77. If Not thisTable.SystemObject Then
78.     HasDef = False
79.     Response.Write "<CENTER><H3>" & thisTable.Name &
        ➥" table</H3><CENTER>"
80.     Response.Write "<TABLE BORDER=1 WIDTH=""80%"">"
81.     Response.Write "<tr><th>Name</th><th>Datatype</th>
        ➥<th>Length</th><th>Indexinfo</th></tr>"
82.
83.     For Each tblColumn In thisTable.Columns
84.             Indexed = False
85.             Response.write "<TR><TH WIDTH=""35%"">"
86.             Response.write tblColumn.Name & "</TH><TD WIDTH=""15%"">"
87.             Response.write tblColumn.Datatype & "</TD><TD WIDTH=""15%"">"
88.             Response.write tblColumn.Length & "</TD><TD WIDTH=""15%"">"
89.
90.             If tblColumn.InPrimaryKey Then
91.                 bIsPrimaryKey = True
92.             Else
93.                 bIsPrimaryKey = False
94.             End If
95.
```

continues

LISTING 16.5, CONTINUED

```
96.          If tblColumn.AllowNulls Then
97.              bNullsAllowed = True
98.          Else
99.              bNullsAllowed = False
100.         End If
101.
102.     DefID = tblColumn.default
103.     DefID = Mid(DefID, 5, Len(DefID))
104.
105.     For Each DBDefault In thisDb.Defaults
106.         If DefID = DBDefault.Name Then
107.             DefArray(I, 0) = thisTable.Name
108.             DefArray(I, 1) = tblColumn.Name
109.             DefArray(I, 2) = DBDefault.Text
110.             I = I + 1
111.             HasDef = True
112.         End If
113.     Next
114.
115.     For Each DBIndex In thisTable.Indexes
116.         If DBIndex.Name = tblColumn.Name Then
117.             Indexed = True
118.             Exit For
119.         End If
120.     Next
121.     If bIsPrimaryKey Then
122.         Response.write "Key & Indexed "
123.     Else
124.         If Indexed Then
125.             Response.write "Indexed "
126.         End If
127.     End If
128.     If Not bNullsAllowed Then
129.         Response.write "Not Null"
130.     End If
131.     If HasDef Then
132.         Response.write "<EM>(" & I & ")</EM>"
133.         HasDef = False
134.     End If
```

```
135.          Response.write " </TD></TR>"
136.      Next
137.      Response.write "</TABLE><BR><BR>"
138. End If
139. End Sub
140. </SCRIPT>
141.
142. </BODY>
143. </HTML>
```

There are two major blocks of code in this page: the first one validates the form data that is received (lines 9 to 54), and the second (lines 57 to 140) consists of three procedures to print definition information for a specific table, view, or stored procedure. The PrintView and PrintSP procedures only print the SQL statement that was used to create this object and format it into a table using the <PRE> tags to conserve the original line break information.

The PrintTable procedure outputs more information about a table and its columns: you receive an HTML table that holds information about each column, its datatypes, the length of the type, and index information. All of this information is retrieved from the collections that are contained in the Table object that is currently examined.

If you're adding more object types to be printed, you simply have to add another Case statement to the preceding code—using a procedure is optional, but it makes the code more readable.

The SQL Query and Results Page

There's only one feature missing in this implementation of the Web- based SQL Server Administrator—the page for the ISQL-like query page. The main purpose of this utility is to issue any SQL command against the server's database and return the results of its execution. One feature however, that is implemented in the "real" ISQL/w application—the Statistics/IO pane—isn't available in this web-based solution. However, all other major features are included.

The page for this utility contains both the input form and the results page. When no form data is being posted to the page, the user is presented a form for submitting an SQL statement. The user can choose either to submit a statement that doesn't return rows (such as CREATE TABLE or other statements) or set the number of rows to return for the statement being submitted. Listing 16.6 contains the source code for this page.

LISTING 16.6 - THE SQL QUERY PAGE CONTAINING BOTH THE INPUT FORM AND THE RESULT PAGE (ISQL.ASP)

```
01. <%@ LANGUAGE = VBScript %>
02. <HTML>
03. <HEAD>
04. <TITLE>Online Database - ISQL</TITLE>
05. </HEAD>
06.
07. <BODY BGCOLOR=#ffffff leftmargin=10 topmargin=10>
08. <FONT FACE=Arial>
09.
10. <%
11. 'On Error Resume Next
12.
13. If Not IsObject(Session("ActiveSQLdb")) Then
14.     Response.Write("No connection to a database established!")
15.     Response.End
16. End If
17.
18. Dim thisDb
19. Set thisDb = Session("ActiveSQLdb")
20. %>
21. <center>
22. <H2><font color="blue"><%=thisDb.Name%></font> - ISQL utility</H2>
23.
24. <%
25. If Len(Request("isqlhtm"))>0 Then
26.     Select Case Request("isqltype")
27.        Case "nores"
28.        thisDb.ExecuteImmediate Request("isqlhtm"),SQLOLEExec_Default
29.        Case Else
30.        Set qryResults = thisDb.ExecuteWithResults(Request("isqlhtm"))
31.     End Select
32.
33.     nColNumbers = qryResults.Columns
34.     Response.Write "<TABLE BORDER=1><TR>"
35.     For i=1 To nColNumbers
36.       Response.Write "<TH>" & Server.HTMLEncode(qryResults.ColumnName(i))
                ➥& "</TH>"
37.     Next
38.     Response.Write "</TR>"
39.
40.     nRowsToReturn = qryResults.Rows
```

```
41.    If nRowsToReturn > CLng(Request("isqlrows")) Then
       ➥nRowsToReturn = CLng(Request("isqlrows"))
42.
43.    For i=1 to nRowsToReturn
44.      Response.Write "<TR>"
45.      For j=1 to nColNumbers
46.        Response.Write "<TD>" & Server.HTMLEncode(
           ➥qryResults.GetColumnString(i,j)) & "</TD>" & Chr(13)
47.      Next
48.        Response.Write "</TR>"
49.    Next
50.    Response.Write "</TABLE> <P>"
51.    Response.Write "Maximum of " & qryResults.Rows &
       ➥" records would be available!<BR>"
52.
53.    Set qryResults = Nothing
54.    Set thisDb = Nothing
55. %>
56.
57. <P>
58. Back to the <A HREF="<%=Request.ServerVariables(
    ➥"SCRIPT_NAME")%>">ISQL</A> main screen!
59.
60. <%  Else %>
61. <table border=0>
62. <tr><td>
63. <FORM ACTION="<%=Request.ServerVariables(
    ➥"SCRIPT_NAME")%>" method="post">
64. <TEXTAREA COLS=90 ROWS=15 NAME="isqlhtm">
    ➥Select * from tablename</TEXTAREA><BR>
65. </td></tr>
66. <tr><td> <BR>
67. <input type=radio name=isqltype value="nores">No results
68. <input type=radio CHECKED name=isqltype value="res">
    ➥Return results<P>
69. Maximum number of rows to return: <input type=text name=isqlrows
    ➥value="25"><P>
70. <input type=submit value="Run!">
71. </FORM>
72. </td></tr></table>
73. <%  End If %>
74.
```

continues

```
75. </center>
76.
77. </BODY>
78. </HTML>
```

The code for the form that contains the input field for the SQL statement to be submitted starts on line 60 and ends on line 72. This form also contains fields that enable the user to state the number of rows to return and to say whether this statement is expected to return rows.

Executing the submitted SQL statement is handled by the code following line 25. The code between lines 33 and 38 is already familiar because it looks like one for outputting result column names returned by ADO recordsets. The same is true for the code starting on line 43, which returns the specified number of records to the user. As a special feature, line 51 returns the number of rows that could be returned by this statement.

Given this page, you can do anything from executing small statements with the SQL Server to executing large scripts that you generated on some other server and want to move to this machine.

Summary

This chapter presented you with information about leveraging the existing SQL-DMO in a web-based application. The SQL Server management utility that was created to present the use of the SQL-DMO is intended as a starting point. You should customize it to fit your needs. With SQL-DMO, you aren't limited to building only a general purpose management tool; you can incorporate it into a management tool that you write specifically for your web site or application.

CHAPTER 17

Adding Personalization to Your Site

Static web sites are history today; dynamic sites are the standard now, and in the future, Internet sites will all be personalized. The top sites have always been at the forefront in their use of new technologies. Therefore, it's only logical to use the personalization features on your site to create personalized pages for your users.

This chapter shows you how to add personalization to a site and provides you with starter pages that you can add to your existing sites that don't use personalization features. All the examples in this chapter use the personalization features provided by the Microsoft Personalization System (MPS), which was already presented in Chapter 9, "The Microsoft Personalization System." Please refer to Chapter 9 for an in-depth presentation of the features of MPS.

This chapter covers the following topics:

♦ Designing a Site for Personalization

♦ Gathering the Personalization Information

♦ Creating the Personalized Content

Designing a Site for Personalization

Adding features at the design stage to a project is always easier than adding new technologies to the site after it has been deployed. The worst case is having to redesign the site many times during its development. This is especially painful when you decide to add personalization features to a site, because usually you have to personalize several pages. For example, if you want to enable the user to set up custom text colors, you have to change every single page of the site to reflect the preferred color for every user.

Every site that supports personalization should offer a set of pages that gives the user the capability to change his or her preferred colors, online offerings, event selection, and other options you decide the user should be able to personalize.

Nearly all sites offering personalization ask for some personal information about the user. In contrast, only a very few sites offer a summary of what the user has personalized and what choices he or she has made in the process. However, such a summary page gives very useful feedback to the user and is worthwhile to add.

So now your goal is to have two pages—one at the start of the personalization for gathering user-specific information and one at the end: the summary page. In between, you can add as many pages as you want for personalizing your site. In the example in this chapter, the page design of your site can be personalized by the user. Additionally, the user can choose favorite web picks that are displayed on the main page and select his or her favorite search servers to present in the search wizard. You can add personalization for events in favorite categories, or perhaps even favorite restaurants. Add personalization that is appropriate to your site. All these choices presented to the user may influence different pages in your site—or your entire site, as with text color, background color, and other page design options presented to the user.

To learn more about search servers and how to implement a search wizard, see Chapter 15, "Implementing a Search Wizard."

Cross Reference

The organization of the site presented in this chapter is shown in Figure 17.1. Only two pages are being personalized—the main page and the search wizard. The other pages provide the user interface and functionality for the user to personalize the site.

I chose to put more emphasis on dealing with gathering personalization information, because this is an interesting programming challenge. These pages can be reused more easily than personalized pages, which differ depending on your needs. The pages that I show you how to personalize—the main page and the search wizard—are sufficient for demonstrating how to personalize pages using the preferences stored for the current user.

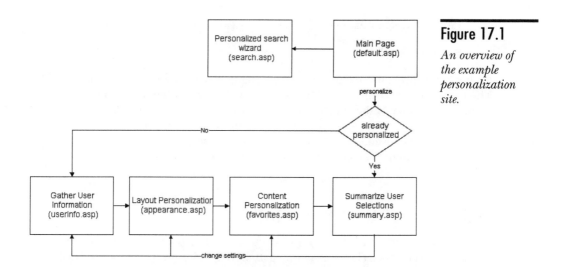

Figure 17.1

An overview of the example personalization site.

In the example that follows, personal information is first gathered from the user. The user then can decide about the layout of the site on the second page; the options include text and background colors. The decisions the user makes here affect all pages of the site. The third page of personalization is used to gather user preferences about special web picks and preferred search servers. The choices the user makes for special web picks personalize the main page. The user chooses specific search servers, personalizing the search wizard. The last page presents a summary of choices where the user can choose to go back and change the preferences.

All of this information is then used to personalize the two pages of this site: the main page and the search wizard. The techniques presented in these two pages are sufficient to create really sophisticated sites.

Gathering the Personalization Information

The personalization process is split into four parts. You can add as many parts in between as you need for your site's needs:

1. Gathering of user information

2. Personalization of the layout

3. Content personalization

4. Summarizing the choices

Each of these processes comprises a single page, as already presented in Figure 17.1. The pages contain both the HTML code for the forms and the script code for handling the entry of the choices in the User Property Database (UPD) of MPS. They are chained together; a user has to fill out all the pages before the summary is presented. As a convenience, the user may also choose to cancel the personalization process at any point. The choices made prior to cancellation are preserved in the UPD.

Gathering of User Information

Information about the users visiting your site are invaluable for e-mail lists and statistics of every type. The information gathered by this sample form includes the following:

◆ Name of the user

◆ E-mail address

◆ Address information

◆ A choice about whether the user wants to receive a personalized greeting for the main page or not.

One thing you could add is an offering of a newsletter that will be delivered twice a month (or any other period) to the user. Include everything that might offer extra value and the user will be more likely to enter all address information.

Before going on to the presentation of the source code for this page, study Figure 17.2 to see what the finalized page looks like. Notice that I used an image (two right-arrows) rather than a button for the user to submit the information and go to the next page.

This form is used for new and returning users; for returning users, it must present previous values for each field in this form; for new users, it must present empty fields. See Listing 17.1 to see how this is handled.

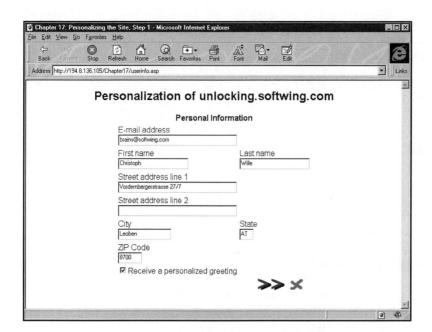

Figure 17.2

The input form for collecting information about the user.

LISTING 17.1 - COLLECTING INFORMATION ABOUT THE USER (USERINFO.ASP)

On the
CD

```
01. <%
02.    Set PROP = Server.CreateObject("MPS.PropertyDatabase")
03.    Response.Expires = 0
04.
05.    If (Request.ServerVariables("Content_Length") > 0) Then
06.        PROP("EmailAddress") = Request("EmailAddress")
07.        PROP("FirstName") = Request("FirstName")
08.        PROP("LastName") = Request("LastName")
09.        PROP("Address1") = Request("Address1")
10.        PROP("Address2") = Request("Address2")
11.        PROP("City") = Request("City")
12.        PROP("State") = Request("State")
13.        PROP("PostalCode") = Request("PostalCode")
14.        If ("" = Request("PersonalGreeting")) Then
15.            PROP("PersonalGreeting") = "off"
16.        Else
17.            PROP("PersonalGreeting") = "on"
18.        End if
19.        PROP("Personalized") = "True"
```

continues

Listing 17.1, Continued

```
20.      Response.Redirect "appearance.asp"
21.   End If
22. %>
23.
24. <HTML>
25. <HEAD>
26. <TITLE>Chapter 17: Personalizing the Site, Step 1</TITLE>
27. </HEAD>
28.
29. <BODY BGCOLOR=#FFFFFF TEXT=#000000 LINK=#336600
    ➥VLINK=#336600 ALINK=#FF0000>
30. <FONT FACE="Arial, Geneva" SIZE=2>
31. <CENTER>
32. <H2>Personalization of unlocking.softwing.com</H2>
33.
34. <FORM METHOD=POST ACTION="<%=Request("SCRIPT_NAME")%>">
35. <TABLE BORDER=0 CELLSPACING=5 CELLPADDING=0>
36. <TR><TH COLSPAN=2>Personal Information</TH></TR>
37. <TR><TD>E-mail address<BR>
38. <INPUT TYPE=Text NAME="EmailAddress" value="
    ➥<%=PROP("EmailAddress")%>" SIZE=45></TD><TD></TD></TR>
39. <TR><TD>First name<BR>
40. <INPUT TYPE=Text NAME="FirstName" value="
    ➥<%=PROP("FirstName")%>" SIZE=25></TD>
41. <TD>Last name<BR>
42. <INPUT TYPE=Text NAME="LastName" value="
    ➥<%=PROP("LastName")%>" SIZE=25></FONT></TD></TR>
43. <TR><TD>Street address line 1<BR>
44. <INPUT TYPE=Text NAME="Address1" value="
    ➥<%=PROP("Address1")%>" SIZE=45></TD><TD></TD></TR>
45. <TR><TD>Street address line 2<BR>
46. <INPUT TYPE=Text NAME="Address2" value="
    ➥<%=PROP("Address2")%>" SIZE=45></TD><TD></TD></TR>
47. <TR><TD>City<BR>
48. <INPUT TYPE=Text NAME="City" value="<%=PROP("City")%>"
    ➥ SIZE=18></TD>
49. <TD>State<BR>
50. <INPUT TYPE=Text NAME="State" value="<%=PROP("State")%>"
    ➥ SIZE=2></FONT></TD></TR>
51. <TR><TD>ZIP Code<BR>
52. <INPUT TYPE=Text NAME="PostalCode" value="
    ➥<%=PROP("PostalCode")%>" SIZE=6></TD><TD></TD></TR>
```

```
53. <TR><TD COLSPAN=2><INPUT TYPE=CHECKBOX NAME=
    ➥"PersonalGreeting" <%=UPDCheckBox("PersonalGreeting")%>>
54.   Receive a personalized greeting</TD></TR>
55. <TR><TD COLSPAN=2 ALIGN=RIGHT>
56. <INPUT TYPE=IMAGE SRC="next.gif" WIDTH=60 HEIGHT=25
    ➥BORDER=0 ALIGN=MIDDLE HSPACE=2 ALT="Next page">
57. <A HREF="default.asp"><IMG SRC="cancel.gif" BORDER=0
    ➥WIDTH=35 HEIGHT=24 ALT="Cancel"></A>
58. </TD></TR>
59. </FORM>
60.
61. </TABLE>
62. </CENTER>
63.
64. </BODY>
65. </HTML>
66.
67. <SCRIPT  LANGUAGE="VBScript" RUNAT=SERVER>
68. Function UPDCheckBox(strLook)
69.   If (PROP(strLook) = "on") Then UPDCheckBox = " CHECKED "
70. End Function
71. </SCRIPT>
```

The code of the page for gathering user information is located between lines 24 and 65. To provide returning users with their previous selections, these have to be retrieved from the UPD. To achieve this, first, a UPD object has to be instantiated (line 2) and the value for this property retrieved. An example of this is line 38 retrieving the value for the EmailAddress property. For new users, this statement returns an empty string, because the property's value isn't set yet.

Another interesting piece of code is located on line 53. It contains a call to the UPDCheckBox function defined between lines 68 and 70. The code found in this function is used to either add a check to the "Receive a personalized greeting" checkbox or not. Of course you could have added the code inline; however, this is a "cleaner" solution.

The task of inserting the form data, submitted by the user from this form into the UPD, is handled by the code between lines 5 and 21. With the exception of the PersonalizedGreeting property, all properties are assigned the values of the respective Request variables. The PersonalizedGreeting property needs special treatment, because when a checkbox is deselected, no parameter is sent with the form data. Therefore, an empty string for this variable indicates that the checkbox was deselected in the form and the user doesn't want to be greeted personally. When all information is entered into the UPD, the user is redirected to the next page for personalizing the layout of the site.

Personalization of the Layout

The choices made by the user in this page affect all pages of this site. For the sample site, these include the following:

◆ Background color

◆ Text color

◆ Viewed link color

◆ Unviewed link color

The entered information is used to provide a user-defined background color, text color, and viewed and unviewed link color for every page of the site. You can add a selection for the preferred font and font size as well as graphics resolution choices. Figure 17.3 shows what this form looks like (although the form was too big to present it in its entirety).

Figure 17.3

Personalizing the layout of the example site.

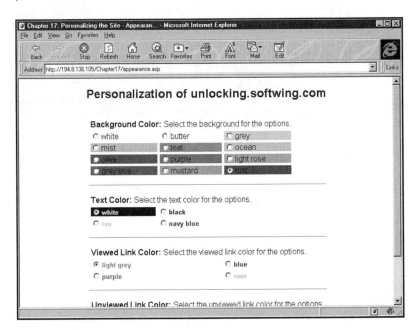

Because all four choices result in more or less the same code, I have omitted background, text, and viewed link color choices in Listing 17.2 to make it shorter. The entire source code is contained on the accompanying CD.

LISTING 17.2 - COLLECTING INFORMATION ABOUT THE APPEARANCE OF PAGES (APPEARANCE.ASP)

On the
CD

```
01. <%
02.    Set PROP = Server.CreateObject("MPS.PropertyDatabase")
03.    Response.Expires = 0
04.
05.    Dim aryInsert(4)
06.    aryInsert(0) = "BGC"
07.    aryInsert(1) = "TBGC"
08.    aryInsert(2) = "VBGC"
09.    aryInsert(3) = "UBGC"
10.
11.    If (Request.ServerVariables("Content_Length") > 0) Then
12.        For i = 0 To 3
13.            PROP(aryInsert(i)) = Request(aryInsert(i))
14.        Next
15.        PROP("Personalized") = "True"
16.        Response.Redirect "favorites.asp"
17.    End If
18. %>
19.
20. <HTML>
21. <HEAD>
22. <TITLE>Chapter 17: Personalizing the Site - Appearance,
    ➥Step 2</TITLE>
23. </HEAD>
24.
25. <BODY BGCOLOR=#FFFFFF TEXT=#000000 LINK=#336600
    ➥VLINK=#336600 ALINK=#FF0000>
26. <FONT FACE="Arial, Geneva" SIZE=2>
27. <CENTER>
28. <H2>Personalization of unlocking.softwing.com</H2>
29.
30. <FORM METHOD=POST ACTION="<%=Request("SCRIPT_NAME")%>">
31. <TABLE BORDER=0>
32.
```

continues

Listing 17.2, Continued

```
...
...
135.
136. <HR>
137.
138. <TABLE BORDER=0 CELLSPACING=5 CELLPADDING=0>
139. <TR>
140. <TD COLSPAN=2><B>Unviewed Link Color:</B>
     ➥Select the unviewed link color for the options.</TD>
141. </TR>
142. <TR>
143. <TD BGCOLOR="#FFFFFF">
144. <INPUT TYPE=RADIO NAME="UBGC" VALUE="336600"
     ➥<%=ChkB("UBGC", "336600")%>>
145. <FONT COLOR="336600" SIZE=2><B>green</B></FONT>
146. </TD>
147. <TD BGCOLOR="#FFFFFF">
148. <INPUT TYPE=RADIO NAME="UBGC" VALUE="0000FF"
     ➥<%=ChkB("UBGC", "0000FF")%>>
149. <FONT COLOR="0000FF" SIZE=2><B>blue</B></FONT>
150. </TD></TR>
151.
152. <TR>
153. <TD BGCOLOR="#FFFFFF">
154. <INPUT TYPE=RADIO NAME="UBGC" VALUE="FF9999"
     ➥<%=ChkB("UBGC", "FF9999")%>>
155. <FONT COLOR="FF9999" SIZE=2><B>rose</B></FONT>
156. </TD>
157. <TD BGCOLOR="#FFFFFF">
158. <INPUT TYPE=RADIO NAME="UBGC" VALUE="9999FF"
     ➥<%=ChkB("UBGC", "9999FF")%>>
159. <FONT COLOR="9999FF" SIZE=2><B>corn blue</B></FONT>
160. </TD></TR>
161. </TABLE>
162.
163.
164. <TR><TD ALIGN=RIGHT>
165. <INPUT TYPE=IMAGE SRC="next.gif" WIDTH=60 HEIGHT=25
     ➥BORDER=0 ALIGN=MIDDLE HSPACE=2 ALT="Next page">
166. <A HREF="default.asp"><IMG SRC="cancel.gif" BORDER=0
     ➥WIDTH=35 HEIGHT=24 ALT="Cancel"></A>
```

```
167. </TD></TR>
168. </TABLE>
169. </FORM>
170.
171. </CENTER>
172.
173. </BODY>
174. </HTML>
175.
176. <SCRIPT LANGUAGE="VBScript" RUNAT=SERVER>
177. Function ChkB(strLookup, strComp)
178.  If (PROP(strLookup) = strComp) Then ChkB = " CHECKED "
179. End Function
180. </SCRIPT>
```

The form page starts on line 20 and ends on line 174. Omitted are lines 33 to 134, which contain the code for background, text, and viewed color selections. These three are—with the exception of the property name—mainly identical to the selection of the unviewed link color, which is still included in this listing (lines 138 to 161). Because the user can choose only a single color (out of four choices), radio buttons are used. As with the checkbox in the previous section, the selection of the returning user has to be preserved. Therefore, I modified the function to check for specific property values and inserted the CHECKED tag only when the color value matches.

Also slightly modified is the code for inserting the properties into the UPD (lines 5 to 17). First an array of properties to be inserted is created, which is then used to insert all properties with a For loop (lines 12 to 14). After all properties have been inserted, the user is directed to the content choices page.

Content Personalization

Here, the provided example differs most from your implementations, because the kind of contents that can be personalized depend on the site. To present the different methods of achieving the personalization, I have implemented the following groups of content choices:

◆ Web picks

◆ Search servers to use for the search wizard

Both of these choice groups are presented to the user with a list of items that can be selected with checkboxes. These lists are generated dynamically. Figure 17.4 shows an example selection for web picks and search servers.

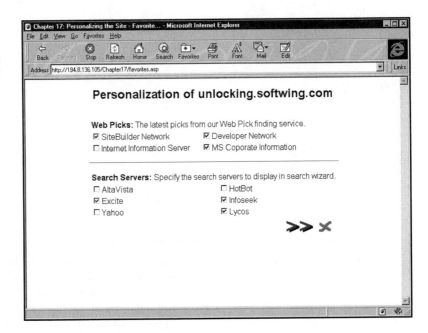

Figure 17.4

Personalizing the content of the example site.

You can use a database to provide the choices dynamically, for example, event categories or restaurant categories. In this example, however, a simple include file with an array of choices for both the web picks and the search servers is used. This is only to save the time involved in creating tables and inserting sample data. The data structures and sample data are contained in the file presented in Listing 17.3. The entire source code can be found on the accompanying CD.

On the CD

LISTING 17.3 - THE FAVORITES DEFINITIONS FILE (WEBLINKS.ASP)

```
01. <%
02.     Dim WebTitle(4)
03.     Dim WebLinks(4)
04.     Dim WebDescription(4)
05.
06.     WebTitle(0) = "SiteBuilder Network"
07.     WebLinks(0) = "<A HREF=""http://www.microsoft.com/
        ➥sitebuilder/""><B>sitebuilder</B></A>"
08.     WebDescription(0) = "Find everything for the
        ➥site-building computer professional"
...
...
22.     Dim SearchServers(6)
```

```
23.        SearchServers(0) = "AltaVista"
24.        SearchServers(1) = "HotBot"
25.        SearchServers(2) = "Excite"
26.        SearchServers(3) = "Infoseek"
27.        SearchServers(4) = "Yahoo"
28.        SearchServers(5) = "Lycos"
29. %>
```

Three arrays are used for the web picks: one for the title of the link, one for the link itself, and the third for a longer description. The search servers array only contains the names of the respective servers.

The content personalization page presented in Listing 17.4 includes the previously mentioned file to create the dynamic list of selections in both groups.

LISTING 17.4 - CONTENT PERSONALIZATION PAGE (FAVORITES.ASP)

On the
CD

```
01. <!--#include file="weblinks.asp"-->
02. <%
03.    Set PROP = Server.CreateObject("MPS.PropertyDatabase")
04.    Response.Expires = 0
05.
06.    If (Request.ServerVariables("Content_Length") > 0) Then
07.        For i = 1 To PROP("WebPicks").Count
08.            PROP("WebPicks").Remove(1)
09.        Next
10.        For i=1 To Request("WebPicks").Count
11.            PROP("WebPicks").Append(Request("WebPicks")(i))
12.        Next
13.        ' now insert the search server selections
14.        For i = 1 To PROP("SearchServers").Count
15.            PROP("SearchServers").Remove(1)
16.        Next
17.        For i=1 To Request("SearchServers").Count
18.            PROP("SearchServers").Append(
                   ➡Request("SearchServers")(i))
19.        Next
20.        PROP("Personalized") = "True"
21.        Response.Redirect "summary.asp"
22.    End If
23. %>
24.
```

continues

Listing 17.4, Continued

```
25.  <HTML>
26.  <HEAD>
27.  <TITLE>Chapter 17: Personalizing the Site - Favorites,
     ➥Step 3</TITLE>
28.  </HEAD>
29.
30.  <BODY BGCOLOR=#FFFFFF TEXT=#000000 LINK=#336600
     ➥VLINK=#336600 ALINK=#FF0000>
31.  <FONT FACE="Arial, Geneva" SIZE=2>
32.  <CENTER>
33.  <H2>Personalization of unlocking.softwing.com</H2>
34.
35.  <FORM METHOD=POST ACTION="<%=Request("SCRIPT_NAME")%>">
36.  <TABLE BORDER=0>
37.
38.  <TABLE BORDER=0 CELLSPACING=5 CELLPADDING=0>
39.  <INPUT TYPE=HIDDEN NAME="WebPicks" Value="none">
40.  <TR><TD COLSPAN=3><B>Web Picks:</B> The latest picks from
     ➥our Web Pick finding service.</TD></TR>
41.  <% For nWebPick = 0 to (UBound (WebTitle) - 1) Step 2 %>
42.   <TR>
43.    <TD><INPUT TYPE=CHECKBOX NAME="WebPicks" Value="
       ➥<%=nWebPick%>" <%=PickCheckBox("WebPicks", nWebPick)%>>
44.    <%=WebTitle(nWebPick) %></TD>
45.    <% If (nWebPick+1) < UBound(WebTitle) Then %>
46.     <TD><INPUT TYPE=CHECKBOX NAME="WebPicks" Value="
        ➥<%=nWebPick+1%>" <%=PickCheckBox("WebPicks",nWebPick+1)%>>
47.     <%=WebTitle(nWebPick+1) %></TD>
48.    <% End If %>
49.  </TR>
50.  <% Next %>
51.  </TABLE>
52.
53.  <HR>
54.  <TABLE BORDER=0 CELLSPACING=5 CELLPADDING=0>
55.  <INPUT TYPE=HIDDEN NAME="SearchServers" Value="none">
56.  <TR><TD COLSPAN=3><B>Search Servers:</B> Specify the
     ➥search servers to display in search wizard.</TD></TR>
57.  <% For nSSServer=0 to (UBound(SearchServers)-1) Step 2 %>
58.   <TR>
```

```
59.  <TD><INPUT TYPE=CHECKBOX NAME="SearchServers" Value="
     ➥<%=nSServer%>" <%=PickCheckBox("SearchServers", nSServer)%>>
60.  <%=SearchServers(nSServer) %></TD>
61.  <% If (nSServer+1) < UBound(SearchServers) Then %>
62.    <TD><INPUT TYPE=CHECKBOX NAME="SearchServers" Value="
       ➥<%=nSServer+1%>" <%=PickCheckBox(
       ➥"SearchServers", nSServer+1)%>>
63.    <%=SearchServers(nSServer+1) %></TD>
64.  <% End If %>
65. </TR>
66. <% Next %>
67. </TABLE>
68.
69. <TR><TD ALIGN=RIGHT>
70. <INPUT TYPE=IMAGE SRC="next.gif" WIDTH=60 HEIGHT=25
    ➥BORDER=0 ALIGN=MIDDLE HSPACE=2 ALT="Next page">
71. <A HREF="default.asp"><IMG SRC="cancel.gif" BORDER=0
    ➥WIDTH=35 HEIGHT=24 ALT="Cancel"></A>
72. </TD></TR>
73. </TABLE>
74. </FORM>
75.
76. </CENTER>
77.
78. </BODY>
79. </HTML>
80.
81. <SCRIPT LANGUAGE="VBScript" RUNAT=SERVER>
82. Function PickCheckBox(strLookup, strCompare)
83.      If (InStr(PROP(strLookup), strCompare) > 0)
            ➥Then PickCheckBox = " CHECKED "
84. End Function
85. </SCRIPT>
```

The web picks group is inserted between lines 38 and 51, and the selection of search servers is generated by the code from lines 54 to 67. Again, a helper function is used to generate the checked state for the checkboxes. The only reason why the source code looks beastly is that the choices are split into two columns, which makes some additional checking necessary.

The choices made for both groups are stored in the UPD as multiple value properties. To minimize the storage, only the index to the choice in the array is stored (when using tables, store the value of the primary key). Because deselected choices aren't sent with the Request, the existing values in the property need special attention. One solution could be to check which items need to be removed and which need to be added to the property. The simpler method is to remove all previous selections first, as used in this example (lines 7 to 9 and 14 to 16). After the removal, the new selections are inserted into the property store.

This was the last page for gathering personalization in this example. You could line up more pages after this one to present the user with more interesting choices for customizing the site. Because this is the last page in this sample site, however, the user is now presented with the summary of choices.

Summarizing the Choices

Providing users with a central location for reviewing their choices is useful for returning users who want to change only specific items of the personalization. For users who have filled in the personalization pages for the first time, it's a review for their choices. Figure 17.5 shows what a summary page for a user visiting the sample site might look like.

Figure 17.5

A summary about the selections a user has made.

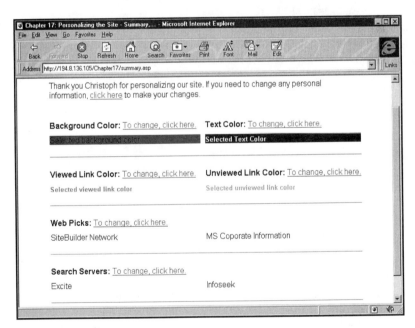

The source code presented in Listing 17.5 creates the page shown in Figure 17.5. Links to change the choices are presented for every choice category. Color selections are presented with examples.

LISTING 17.5 - SUMMARIZING THE PERSONALIZATION FOR THE USER (SUMMARY.ASP)

On the
CD

```
01. <!--#include file="weblinks.asp"-->
02. <%
03.    Set PROP = Server.CreateObject("MPS.PropertyDatabase")
04.    Response.Expires = 0
05.    If "" = PROP("Personalized") Then
       ➥Response.Redirect("userinfo.asp")
06. %>
07.
08. <HTML>
09. <HEAD>
10. <TITLE>Chapter 17: Personalizing the Site - Summary,
    ➥Final Step</TITLE>
11. </HEAD>
12.
13. <BODY BGCOLOR=#FFFFFF TEXT=#000000 LINK=#336600
    ➥VLINK=#336600 ALINK=#FF0000>
14. <FONT FACE="Arial, Geneva" SIZE=2>
15.
16. <CENTER>
17. <H2>Personalization of unlocking.softwing.com</H2>
18.
19. <TABLE BORDER=0 CELLSPACING=10 CELLPADDING=0 WIDTH=650>
20. <TR><TD COLSPAN=2>
21. Thank you <%=PROP("FirstName")%> for personalizing
    ➥our site.
22. If you need to change any personal information,
    ➥<A HREF="userinfo.asp">
23. click here</A> to make your changes.<P> <P>
24. </TD></TR>
25. <TR><TD><B>Background Color:</B>
26. <A HREF="appearance.asp">To change, click here.</A></TD>
27. <TD><B>Text Color:</B>
28. <A HREF="appearance.asp">To change, click here.</A></TD>
29. </TR><TR>
30. <TD BGCOLOR="#<%=PROP("BGC")%>">Selected background color
    ➥</TD>
31. <%
32.    nBgColor = "FFFFFF"
33.    If "FFFFFF" = PROP("TBGC") Then nBgColor = "000000"
```

continues

LISTING 17.5, CONTINUED

```
34. %>
35. <TD BGCOLOR="#<%=nBgColor%>">
36. <FONT COLOR="<%=PROP("TBGC")%>" SIZE=2><B>Selected Text
    ➥Color</B></FONT>
37. </TD>
38. </TR>
39.
40. <TR><TD COLSPAN=2><HR></TD></TR>
41.
42. <TR><TD><B>Viewed Link Color:</B>
43. <A HREF="appearance.asp">To change, click here.</A></TD>
44. <TD><B>Unviewed Link Color:</B>
45. <A HREF="appearance.asp">To change, click here.</A></TD>
46. </TR>
47. <TR><TD BGCOLOR="#FFFFFF">
48. <FONT COLOR="<%=PROP("VBGC")%>" SIZE=2><B>Selected viewed
    ➥link color</B></FONT>
49. </TD><TD BGCOLOR="#FFFFFF">
50. <FONT COLOR="<%=PROP("UBGC")%>" SIZE=2><B>Selected
    ➥unviewed link color</B></FONT>
51. </TD></TR>
52.
53. <TR><TD COLSPAN=2><HR></TD></TR>
54.
55. <TR><TD COLSPAN=2><B>Web Picks:</B>
56. <A HREF="favorites.asp">To change, click here.</A>
    ➥</TD></TR>
57. <%
58. bRowEnd = True
59. For nWebPick = 1 to PROP("WebPicks").Count
60.     If (PROP("WebPicks")(nWebPick) <> "none") Then
61.         If bRowEnd Then
62.             Response.Write "<TR><TD>"
63.             Response.Write WebTitle(
                ➥CLng(PROP("WebPicks")(nWebPick))) & "</TD>"
64.             bRowEnd = False
65.         Else
66.             Response. Write "<TD>" & WebTitle(
                ➥CLng(PROP("WebPicks")(nWebPick))) & "</TD></TR>" &vbCRLF
67.             bRowEnd = True
68.         End If
```

```
69.    End If
70. Next
71. %>
72.
73. <TR><TD COLSPAN=2><HR></TD></TR>
74.
75. <TR><TD COLSPAN=2><B>Search Servers:</B>
76. <A HREF="favorites.asp">To change, click here.</A>
    ➥</TD></TR>
77. <%
78. bRowEnd = True
79. For nSServers = 1 to PROP("SearchServers").Count
80.     If (PROP("SearchServers")(nSServers) <> "none") Then
81.         If bRowEnd Then
82.             Response.Write "<TR><TD>"
83.             Response.Write SearchServers(
                ➥CLng(PROP("SearchServers")(nSServers))) & "</TD>"
84.             bRowEnd = False
85.         Else
86.             Response. Write "<TD>" & SearchServers(CLng
                ➥(PROP("SearchServers")(nSServers))) & "</TD></TR>" &vbCRLF
87.             bRowEnd = True
88.         End If
89.     End If
90. Next
91. %>
92.
93. <TR><TD COLSPAN=2><HR></TD></TR>
94. </TABLE>
95.
96. <CENTER>
97. <A HREF="default.asp">Visit the now personalized
    ➥home page</A>
98. </CENTER>
99.
100. </BODY>
101. </HTML>
```

A property used in this page that I haven't mentioned until now is the Personalized property. To disallow viewing of the summary page for users that haven't personalized anything yet, I have introduced it to automatically redirect them to the first page, which is userinfo.asp. A check to see if the PropertyString property of the UPD is empty wouldn't be appropriate for this purpose, because the ID of the user is always stored there and the string is therefore never empty. The `Personalized` property is set the first time any personalization page adds properties to the UPD store (see Listings 17.1, 17.2, and 17.4).

When taking a look at the code used for summarizing the choices, you should notice that for the presentation of the color selections the code from the layout personalization page is used to show an example of what the user's choice will look like. The code for presenting the chosen web picks and search servers uses the UPD object to query values for the property, which are then used to retrieve the selection out of the arrays via their index.

All personalization has now taken place. You can follow the hyperlink to the main page to see how it has changed with the choices made during the personalization process. An additional link to the search wizard is incorporated in the main page as well, so you can visit the personalized version of it.

Creating the Personalized Content

Personalizing a site is, of course, not limited to only two files as presented in this example. Nevertheless, I have incorporated the most common scenarios into both.

◆ **Main page:** Shows how to add choices to pages and deal with users that haven't incorporated the personalization yet.

◆ **Search wizard:** Illustrates how to incorporate personalization in existing source code.

Personalizing the Main Page

What is personalized in the main page? All of the color selections made by the user, possibly a personal greeting, and the selected web picks. I'm sorry that I can't show a very extravagant color scheme for the main page—I had to stick with white background and black text—because in print it wouldn't have looked good otherwise. So the main page presented in Figure 17.6 shows only the personal greeting and the web picks.

The color selections are, of course, implemented in the script code for this page. The web picks are inserted with title, link, and description. A link to the personalized search wizard also is presented. See Listing 17.6 for the source code of the main page of the sample site.

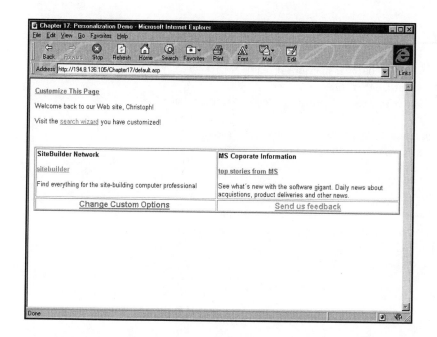

Figure 17.6

The main page now being personalized.

LISTING 17.6 - A SIMPLE MAIN PAGE (DEFAULT.ASP)

On the CD

```
01. <!--#INCLUDE FILE="weblinks.asp"-->
02. <%
03.    Set PROP = Server.CreateObject("MPS.PropertyDatabase")
04.    Response.Expires = 10
05.    PROP.Defaults = "BGC=FFFFFF&TBGC=000000&VBGC=808080
       ➥&UBGC=336600"
06. %>
07.
08. <HTML>
09. <HEAD>
10. <TITLE>Chapter 17: Personalization Demo</TITLE>
11. </HEAD>
12.
13. <BODY BGCOLOR=#<%=PROP("BGC")%>  LINK=#<%=PROP("UBGC")%>
       ➥VLINK=#<%=PROP("VBGC")%>>
14. <FONT FACE="Arial, Geneva" SIZE=2 COLOR="
       ➥<%=PROP("TBGC")%>">
15.
16. <P><A HREF="summary.asp"><B>Customize This Page</B></A>
```

continues

LISTING 17.6, CONTINUED

```
17.  <P>
18.  <% If ("on" = PROP("PersonalGreeting") And "" <>
     ➡PROP("FirstName")) Then %>
19.     Welcome back to our Web site, <%=PROP("FirstName")%>!
20.  <% Else %>
21.        Welcome to this Web site on <%=Day(Now) & ". "
           ➡& MonthName(Month(Now)) & " " & Year(Now)%>!
22.  <% End If %>
23.
24.  <P>
25.  <% If PROP("SearchServers").Count > 0 Then %>
26.  Visit the <A HREF="search.asp">search wizard</A>
     ➡you have customized!
27.  <% End If%>
28.
29.  <P> <P>
30.  <CENTER>
31.
32.  <TABLE BORDER=2>
33.  <%
34.  If PROP("WebPicks").Count > 0 Then
35.    bRowEnd = True
36.    For nWebPick = 1 to PROP("WebPicks").Count
37.      If (PROP("WebPicks")(nWebPick) <> "none") Then
38.        nCurPickIndex = CLng(PROP("WebPicks")(nWebPick))
39.        If bRowEnd Then Response.Write "<TR>"
40.
41.        Response.Write "<TD WIDTH=400 VALIGN=TOP>
           ➡<FONT SIZE=2 COLOR=#" & PROP("TBGC") & "><B>"
42.        Response.Write WebTitle(nCurPickIndex) & "</B><P>"
43.        Response.Write WebLinks(nCurPickIndex) & "<P>"
44.        Response.Write WebDescription(nCurPickIndex)
           ➡& "</FONT><P>"
45.
46.        If bRowEnd Then
47.            Response.Write "</TD>"
48.            bRowEnd = False
49.        Else
50.            Response. Write "</TD></TR>" & vbCRLF
51.            bRowEnd = True
52.        End If
```

```
53.     End If
54.    Next
55. End If
56. ' check to see if there is an unfilled column
57. If (bRowEnd=False) Then
58. %>
59. <TD VALIGN=TOP ALIGN=LEFT BORDER=1 BGCOLOR="
    ➥#<%=PROP("BGC") %>" WIDTH=290>
60. <FONT SIZE=2 COLOR=#<%=PROP("TBGC")%>>
    ➥Need more on your start page?
61. <A HREF="feedback.htm"><B>Send</B></A> us your ideas.
    ➥</FONT></TD></TR>
62. <%  End If %>
63.
64. <TR>
65. <TD VALIGN=TOP ALIGN=CENTER BORDER=1
    ➥BGCOLOR="#<%=PROP("BGC")%>">
66. <A HREF="summary.asp">
67. <FONT SIZE=3 FACE="Arial, Helv"><B>Change Custom Options
    ➥</B></FONT></A>
68. </TD>
69. <TD VALIGN=TOP ALIGN=CENTER BORDER=1
    ➥BGCOLOR="#<%=PROP("BGC")%>">
70. <A HREF="feedback.htm"><B>Send us feedback</B></A>
71. </TD></TR></TABLE>
72.
73. </CENTER>
74.
75. </BODY>
76. </HTML>
```

The first interesting line is number 5. Using the Defaults property, I have specified values to use for background, text, and both viewed and unviewed link color when the user hasn't selected these. For properties that are mandatory for viewing the page correctly, you have to account for the possibility that the user didn't yet personalize the site. The values of these properties—either personalized or defaults—are then used on lines 13 and 14 to set the colors for this page.

Starting with line 18, the personalized greeting is created for the current user. If this choice was deselected, a simple greeting message with the current (server) date is created (line 21).

The web picks table is created between lines 32 and 62. The code for inserting this table is very similar to the one in the summary file (Listing 17.6), but now the link and description also are inserted. If there was an odd number of picks inserted into the table, the remaining cell is used to display a request for feedback from the user. The page to which the link is pointing isn't implemented.

Adding Personalization Code to the Search Wizard

During personalization, the user could choose which Internet search engines are to be displayed in the search wizard's user interface. To illustrate how few changes need to be applied to the file, Listing 17.7 presents the original source code from Chapter 15's search.asp.

On the CD

LISTING 17.7 - PART OF THE ORIGINAL CODE OF THE SEARCH WIZARD (SEARCH.ASP – CHAPTER 15)

```
84.  <TR>
85.  <TD WIDTH="225" COLSPAN="1">
86.  <FONT FACE="MS Sans Serif, Arial, Helv" SIZE="1">
87.  <BR>
88.       
89.  <INPUT NAME="SearchType" TYPE="RADIO" VALUE="altavista">
     ➥Internet using Alta Vista<BR>
90.       
91.  <INPUT NAME="SearchType" TYPE="RADIO" VALUE="excite">
     ➥Internet using Excite<BR>
92.       
93.  <INPUT NAME="SearchType" TYPE="RADIO" VALUE="infoseek">
     ➥Internet using Infoseek<BR>
94.  </FONT>
95.  </TD>
96.
97.  <TD WIDTH="225" COLSPAN="1">
98.  <FONT FACE="MS Sans Serif, Arial, Helv" SIZE="1">
99.  <BR>
100. <INPUT NAME="SearchType" TYPE="RADIO" VALUE="lycos">
     ➥Internet using Lycos<BR>
101. <INPUT NAME="SearchType" TYPE="RADIO" VALUE="hotbot">
     ➥Internet using HotBot<BR>
102. <INPUT NAME="SearchType" TYPE="RADIO" VALUE="yahoo">
     ➥Internet using Yahoo<BR>
103. </FONT>
```

```
104. </TD>
105. </TR>
```

Only 22 lines need to be replaced with script code to present only the search engines that were selected by the current user during the personalization process. You have to create an instance of the UPD component before you can retrieve the user choices. Listing 17.8 contains the newly added pieces for the search wizard. The entire code can be found on the accompanying CD.

LISTING 17.8 - THE NEWLY ADDED PIECES TO THE SEARCH WIZARD INTERFACE (SEARCH.ASP)

On the CD

```
01. <!--#include file="weblinks.asp"-->
02. <%
03.   Set PROP = Server.CreateObject("MPS.PropertyDatabase")
04.   Response.Expires = 0
05. %>
…
…
89. <%
90. If (PROP("SearchServers").Count > 0) Then
91.    nCount = PROP("SearchServers").Count
92.    nCountHalf = nCount \ 2 + 1
93. %>
94.
95. <TR>
96. <TD WIDTH=225 COLSPAN=1 VALIGN=TOP>
97. <FONT FACE="MS Sans Serif, Arial, Helv" SIZE="1">
98. <BR>
99. <% For j = 1 To nCountHalf
100.    If ("none" <> PROP("SearchServers")(j)) Then
101.    strServer = SearchServers(Clng(
      ➡PROP("SearchServers")(j)))
102.    Response.Write "        "
103.    Response.Write "<INPUT NAME=""SearchType"" TYPE=RADIO
      ➡VALUE=""" & strServer & """>Internet using " & strServer
      ➡& "<BR>"
104.    End If
105. Next%>
106.
107. <TD WIDTH=225 COLSPAN=1 VALIGN=TOP>
108. <FONT FACE="MS Sans Serif, Arial, Helv" SIZE="1">
```

continues

```
109. <BR>
110. <%  For j = nCountHalf+1 To nCount
111.   If ("none" <> PROP("SearchServers")(j)) Then
112.     strServer = SearchServers(Clng(
         ➡PROP("SearchServers")(j)))
113.     Response.Write "<INPUT NAME=""SearchType"" TYPE=RADIO
         ➡VALUE=""" & strServer & """>Internet using " & strServer
         ➡& "<BR>"
114.   End If
115. Next%>
116. </FONT>
117. </TD>
118. </TR>
119. <%  End If %>
...
```

The first five lines are new: the file with the array of search servers is included and a UPD object is created. The replacement code for Listing 17.7 begins on line 89 with the retrieval of the number of search servers selected by the user. After the calculation of the half of this number (line 92), the first nCountHalf search servers are inserted into the first column of the wizard. When done with the first half, the second half is inserted as well, starting with line 107. Notice that the value of the input field for the search server is the same as the name of the server.

With these changes applied, every user then receives a personalized version of the search wizard. Notice that I didn't add the color personalization for this page. This is intended as a pinky exercise for you <g>.

Summary

The sample personalization site presented in this chapter is intended to be a starting point for adding personalization to your own site. The code for gathering personalization information is fully featured, but the pages that demonstrate the use of the personalization information are intended as a reference only, due to the special requirements of every personalization implementation.

You can extend the sample site by sending confirmation e-mail from the summary page and by adding more interesting selections to the personalization pages. For example, you could add restaurant or event categories, or anything that might be of use for the users who are visiting your site.

APPENDIX A

Installing Visual InterDev

The Visual InterDev installation falls into two parts—server installation and client installation. In some cases—for example, an all-in-one development machine—both installation parts are performed on the same machine.

However, most likely there is a separate server machine dedicated to the web server and one or more client computers that access this server with, for example, Microsoft FrontPage or Visual InterDev. Figure A.1 shows the different parts that are installed for the web server and client computers.

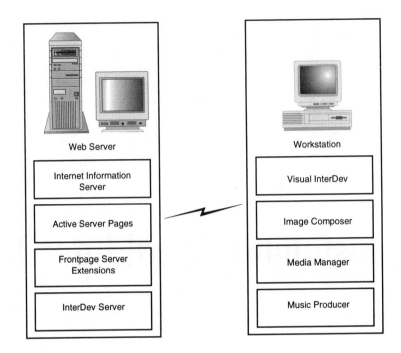

Figure 1.1

Server and client components needed for Visual InterDev installations.

The first two server components, IIS and ASP, are mandatory for the web server to be able to serve active content. The latter two, FrontPage Server Extensions and Visual InterDev Server, are used by client software such as FrontPage or Visual InterDev to connect to the server, retrieve files, and update them on the server.

Note   You don't need to install FrontPage Server Extensions and InterDev Server on the web server in order to run Visual InterDev. Without these, you can still create great web pages. However, without them you can't automatically update and manage the files in a project fashion with your test server. I strongly recommend that you use FrontPage Server Extensions and InterDev Server.

Visual InterDev is the client software that you will use to develop scripts and other active content. The three additional software packages mentioned in this diagram for client software—Image Composer, Media Manager, and Music Producer—come with Visual InterDev. You can use these to manage your media content, such as music and graphics.

Server Components

The server components that need to be installed in order for Visual InterDev to be able to communicate with the web server are as follows:

- Internet Information Server or Personal Webserver

- Active Server Pages

- FrontPage 97 Server Extensions

- Visual InterDev Server

Again, the first two components are needed for any web server that serves ASP pages. The other ones are needed so that Microsoft FrontPage and Visual InterDev can connect to the server and exchange files. The next sections deal with installing these server components.

Internet Information Server

Depending upon the platform you are running on, you need to install different versions of Internet Information Server. Table A.1 is a list of products available from Microsoft for the different platforms.

TABLE A.1
Web Server Software for Different Platforms

Platform	Web server software
Windows NT 4.0 Server	Internet Information Server
Windows NT 4.0 Workstation	Personal Web Server
Windows NT 95	Personal Web Server

Please be aware that Personal Web Server (PWS) for Windows 95 and Windows NT Workstation 4.0 are different products (however, PWS for Windows NT Workstation 4.0 is essentially the same as the Windows NT Server 4.0 version, except minor performance differences). Both Windows NT web servers ship with the operating system. PWS for Windows 95 is included on the Visual InterDev CD-ROM.

When you're installing any of these web server products, you can go with the installation defaults. After all, there's only one portion of these products you must install: the web service. The other parts, such as FTP or Gopher, aren't necessary when you're setting up a server that will be used with Visual InterDev. The following steps guide you through the process of setting up IIS for Windows NT Server 4.0:

1. Start the IIS Setup. Windows NT Setup has added a shortcut to the IIS Setup on the desktop for you. When you still haven't deleted it, you can launch Setup by double-clicking on it. If you have already removed it, you can start setup from the Windows NT CD-ROM. The Setup program's path is %platform%\inetsrv\ inetstp.exe, for example, on Intel platforms the full path is \i386\inetsrv\ inetstp.exe.

2. In the Setup dialog box you can remove the Gopher and FTP services from the options to install when the computer will be used as a web server only. Figure A.2 shows the completed options dialog box.

Figure A.2

Options selected for IIS setup with only web services to be installed.

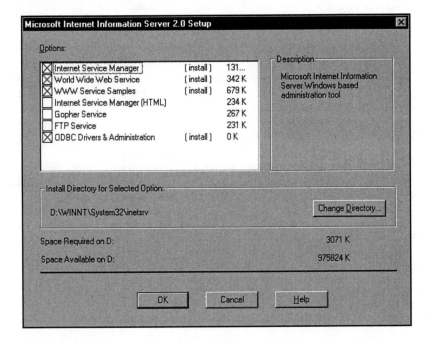

3. After clicking OK, you are asked to enter the directory for your web server's root. Select a directory or leave the default (can be changed later with IIS Service Manager).

4. When you are nearly finished with Setup, you are asked which ODBC drivers to install with IIS. Only SQL Server can be chosen, so select it and go on with the setup.

5. Now Setup finishes and asks to start the services. Select OK.

The web server is now fully functional and can be accessed already. Only the default web pages and the IIS web administrator are installed at this time. To install Active Server Pages, read the next section.

Active Server Pages

Another mandatory part of the web server you need to install is Active Server Pages. There is one distribution of Active Server Pages for all three web server products mentioned in Table A.1. The installation is very straightforward. One caution, however: don't uncheck the option for ODBC 3.0. You need this for the connection pooling feature. The following steps provide a step-by-step installation reference for ASP:

1. Depending on where you received the ASP installation from, starting Setup on your computer might differ. If you obtained ASP from Microsoft's web server (http://www.microsoft.com/iis), then the original setup file is asp.exe. Double-click it to start Setup. When installing with Visual InterDev, a link to the ASP setup is contained on its master setup screen.

2. In the Select Options dialog box presented during Setup leave all options selected. Figure A.3 shows how this dialog box looks.

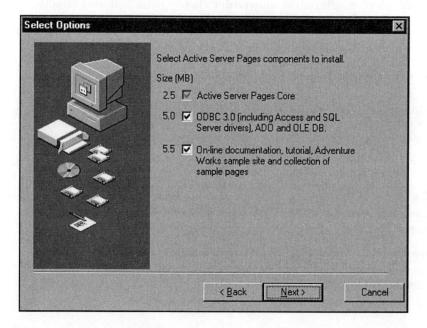

Figure A.3

The Select Options dialog box presented during ASP Setup.

3. Setup asks to stop the WWW service before installing. Allow it to do so.

4. After Setup has finished, the WWW service is restarted.

Now you can serve active content from your web server. With the installation in the preceding outline, a sample site, AdventureWorks, is installed along with ASP. You can check it out to get a first overview of what you can do with ASP (point your browser to `http://localhost/AdvWorks/default.asp`).

FrontPage Server Extensions

Until now, the steps presented for installing IIS and ASP are exactly the same as those needed to install a simple ASP-enabled web server or a development server that can be accessed with Microsoft FrontPage or Visual InterDev. Now you need to add the components that enable these clients to administer the content of a development server. The first software you need to install is FrontPage Server Extensions. Both FrontPage and Visual InterDev can access this server when this software is installed.

The installation of FrontPage Server Extensions can be invoked from Visual InterDev master setup, from FrontPage setup, or from a separate FrontPage Server Extensions setup. Because you will install it along with Visual InterDev, you only have to select this setup part on the Visual InterDev master setup screen. When installing FrontPage Server Extensions, you are presented with very few choices. There are, depending upon your installation, usually only two interesting choices to make during installation:

- Selection of virtual servers to install FrontPage extensions to

- Administrator Setup

If your computer has more than one IP address assigned to its network interface card(s), FrontPage Server Extensions Setup asks you to select the virtual server you want to install the extensions to. Select the servers you need to access with either tool and then go on with installation.

 The setup of FrontPage Server Extensions does not like computer names (the server's name set in the network options) that aren't valid in the sense of Internet computer names (for example: underscores included in the name).

The result is that you aren't able to install the extensions on this computer for no apparent reason. Check before you begin installation to see that your computer's name doesn't include any invalid characters.

Of course, not everybody should be allowed to manage the content of your web server. The setup for the FrontPage Server Extensions asks you to select a username to signify the person who is allowed to manage the content. By default, it proposes the username of the person currently installing the extensions (see Figure A.4).

Select or create a user account that will be used by all team members to manage the site. When you're done with the setup of the FrontPage Server Extension, you need to go on to installing InterDev Server to enable Visual InterDev to talk to the server.

Figure A.4

Username selection for the management of the web server.

Visual InterDev Server

This component adds some extra functionality for Visual InterDev that FrontPage Extensions do not offer. Actually, this is all there is to say about this component. As with FrontPage Server Extensions setup, the setup for Visual InterDev Server can be invoked from the Visual InterDev master setup screen. The installation has no options, so you need simply to install this component to the server computer without any intervention on your side.

Client Components

Now that you have enabled your server computer for management by clients, you still have to install Visual InterDev itself. The following components for the client side are found on the Visual InterDev distribution:

- Visual InterDev
- Image Composer
- Media Manager
- Music Producer

The first component is of the highest interest for the programmers. The other tools can be used to create and manage media content.

Visual InterDev

A lot of preparation work has to be done prior to installing Visual InterDev itself. When you have reached this point, the remaining part is as simple as a normal application setup. You're presented choices about the supporting files to install on the machine (custom setup). As a rule of thumb with development systems, install everything (no one will ever know…).

After setup has finished, you are ready to test your installation. You can do this by creating a new web on the server you have just installed.

See Chapter 4, "Working with Visual InterDev," to learn how to create a new web on the server computer.

Cross Reference

Other Client Components

The remaining three software packages have their own installation routines. I only mention the features of Image Composer, Media Manager, and Music Producer because they're not necessary for running Visual InterDev. However, good graphics and sounds add additional value to your pages.

If you want to create images for your pages, Image Composer, a sprite-based image editing tool, can help you. Just in case you want to add some cool (and royalty-free) sound to your site, Music Producer is your best bet—let Music Producer create your sounds based on your input about style and band composition. And finally, the Media Manager provides extensive information about various media file formats by extending the Windows Explorer with, for example, a new type of folder that closely resembles an artist's portfolio.

Summary

Installing Visual InterDev is a two-step process: preparing the server and then installing Visual InterDev itself. The Visual InterDev package not only includes a development environment, it also includes software for creating and managing images and sounds. Visual InterDev is the programming-focused counterpart to the more design-oriented Microsoft FrontPage 97.

Server-Side Directives

T his appendix is intended to be your single point of reference for the following server-side directives. Each of these directives can be used with Active Server Pages:

◆ Selecting the scripting language in your pages

◆ Including files

◆ Instantiating objects with the <OBJECT> tag

Selecting the Scripting Language

The selection of Scripting languages was presented in Chapter 3, "Foundations for Creating Active Server Pages." You can set the scripting language to all-pages, single-page, or function-level. The next sections show you how.

Registry-Level Scripting Language Changes

By default, the standard scripting language is set to VBScript. If you plan to do most of your project using another scripting language, you will want to change the default.

To change the default to, for example, JScript, follow these steps:

1. Open the Registry editor.

2. Open the key HKEY_LOCAL_MACHINE\SYSTEM\CurrentControlSet\Services \W3SVC\ASP\Parameters

3. Change the entry `DefaultScriptLanguage` from VBScript to Jscript.

4. Stop and restart IIS so changes take effect.

When you're done with this, all your scripts will by default use the JScript engine.

File-Level Scripting Language Changes

If you have set a default scripting language in the Registry, you still may want to program some pages using another scripting language other than the default one. An example for this would be to use VBScript as the default for the entire site, but to use `PerlScript` for doing operating system level programming, a task for which `PerlScript` is exceptionally well-suited.

 Tip Another more convincing argument to set the scripting language on file level is this: you will be distributing your files to a server where it isn't guaranteed that the scripting language you have used is the default.

The syntax for setting the scripting language on file-level looks like the following:

```
<% @ Language=ScriptingLanguage %>
```

`ScriptingLanguage` is what you will be using as default on this page. This statement has to be placed at the beginning of the file before any scripting code.

For example,

```
<% @ Language=JScript %>
```

sets the default scripting language for this page to JScript.

Function-Level Scripting Language Changes

You can even set the scripting language on a per function basis, overriding default and file-level scripting languages. The syntax for controlling scripting languages on a function level is as follows:

```
<SCRIPT LANGUAGE=ScriptingLanguage RUNAT=SERVER>
....
</SCRIPT>
```

You may know the SCRIPT tags from client-side scripting. To distinguish server-side from client-side code, the server-side <SCRIPT> statement has the additional directive RUNAT=SERVER included. Replace ScriptingLanguage with the language of your choice.

Now you have seen three possibilities for setting the scripting language at different levels for your pages. Though setting the scripting language in the registry is a convenient way for defining a standard for all pages, the file-level method is essential if you're planning to deploy your pages to servers where the default language might not be the one you have used on your pages. To mix code written in different languages you can use the last method, which is to set the scripting language at function level. This last method is extremely useful when building code libraries, which you can "link" to your pages with the include statement presented in the next section.

Including Files

If you're creating a site, some elements need to be identical in many pages, like headers, footers, or even some scripting code. You could either duplicate the code (HTML or scripting) needed for these elements in every page you need them (which turns out to be time-consuming when you have to update an element—you need to change it on every page where you incorporated it) or simply create one file which you then include in your pages. File includes are useful—as I have already mentioned—for adding standard elements to each page (for example, footers or navigation bars) or including code libraries (for example, financial calculation) in your pages. The advantage of using included files is that once you change the included file, all changes are automatically incorporated into the pages that have this file included.

The general statement to include files is

```
<!--#INCLUDE FILE¦VIRTUAL="filename"-->
```

The next two sections describe the different behaviors that occur when you use the FILE or VIRTUAL tag.

Virtual Includes

If you use the VIRTUAL keyword, the file is included from a virtual directory of your web server. An example for including a file in your script would be

```
<!--#INCLUDE VIRTUAL="/common/inc/baseline.inc"-->
```

Microsoft recommends that you use the .inc extension for files to be included. This extension isn't vitally necessary for correct operation.

 If you include a file with server-side script code with an .inc extension, it could be downloaded in non-executed form, thus revealing all your code. You can prevent this by sticking to the extension .asp, which can be used with the include statement too, but will execute on download.

File Includes

The FILE keyword includes files relative to the directory where the including file resides. You don't need to provide a fully qualified path relative to the root of your server. It is sufficient to provide a path relative to the path of the current page that includes the file.

```
<!--#INCLUDE FILE="orders/item44.asp"-->
```

This statement includes the item44.asp file from the directory orders into your file.

 If you want to use the syntax ../ for accessing directories below your current directory, you have to set the Registry entry EnableParentPaths to 1.

File includes are an easy way to manage standard elements (headers, footers, and more) and code libraries in central files which, by simply using the include statement, can be incorporated into your pages. All changes to the include files are automatically incorporated into the pages that include these. The next section deals with one of the most important part of Active Server Pages–creating objects to leverage their functionality in your pages.

Creating Objects

You are presented with two choices when creating objects: you can either create them via calls to `Server.CreateObject` or by using the `<OBJECT>` tag. The `Server.CreateObject` method was already discussed at length in Chapter 5, "Programming Active Server Pages." References to the `<OBJECT>` tag were incorporated in many different chapters, however, a single reference section for this was still missing.

The `<OBJECT>` tag poses some restrictions on its use. It can be inserted only in global.asa and objects created with this tag can only have Application or Session scope. One significant advantage to using the `<OBJECT>` tag is that the creation of objects is delayed until they are first used in any page. Furthermore, they are treated like global variables, which are available to all files.

The syntax for the `<OBJECT>` tag is as follows:

```
<OBJECT RUNAT=SERVER SCOPE=scope Id=name [ProgId¦ClassId]=>

➡</OBJECT>
```

You need to replace the *scope* for either `Application` or `Session`. The *Id* takes the name for the instance of the object. In contrast to `CreateObject`, you can use either a `ProgId` or the `ClassId` to create the object.

`ProgId` is the human-readable counterpart for the `ClassId` (this nice 128 Bit globally unique identifier) of any OLE/ActiveX component. It is built the following way (items in square brackets are optional):

```
[Vendor.]Component[.Version]
```

Only this `ProgId` is documented in Active Server Pages Roadmap, therefore I have provided Table B.1 (general components) and B.2 (ADO components) with a mapping of `ProgId` to `ClassId` for ActiveX Server components.

Table B.1
ClassId and *ProgId* for ActiveX Components

Component	Description
Browser Capabilities	ProgId: "MSWC.BrowserType" ClassId: "0ACE4881-8305-11CF-9427-444553540000"

continues

Table B.1, Continued
ClassId and *ProgId* for ActiveX Components

Component	Description
File Access Component	ProgId: "Scripting.FileSystemObject" ClassId: "0D43FE01-F093-11CF-8940-00A0C9054228"
Ad Rotator	ProgId: "MSWC.AdRotator" ClassId: "1621F7C0-60AC-11CF-9427-444553540000"
Content Linking	ProgId: "MSWC.Nextlink" ClassId: "4D9E4505-6DE1-11CF-87A7-444553540000"

Table B.2
ClassId and *ProgId* for ADO objects

Component	Description
Command	ProgId: "ADODB.Command" ClassId: "0000022C-0000-0010-8000-00AA006D2EA4"
Connection	ProgId: "ADODB.Connection" ClassId: "00000293-0000-0010-8000- 00AA006D2EA4"
Recordset	ProgId: "ADODB.Recordset" ClassId: "00000281-0000-0010-8000- 00AA006D2EA4"

Notice that the Parameter object used for parameterized statements is created with the Command.CreateParameter method and not with calls to Server.CreateObject, and is therefore omitted from this table.

The sample code in Listing B.1 instantiates the BrowserCapabilties component using both ProgId and ClassId:

LISTING B.1 - CREATING AN OBJECT WITH THE *<OBJECT>* TAG

```
01. <OBJECT RUNAT=SERVER SCOPE=SESSION ID=testProgId
➥PROGID="MSWC.BrowserType">
02. </OBJECT>
03.
04. <OBJECT RUNAT=SERVER SCOPE=SESSION ID=testClassId
➥CLASSID="Clsid:0ACE4881-8305-11CF-9427-444553540000">
05. </OBJECT>
```

This section was a wrap up of the topic of creating objects in Active Server Pages using the <OBJECT> tag. The tables included here contain all the necessary information to create all additional components delivered with ASP.

Summary

This appendix summarized the different server-side directives that you can use to select a scripting language, including a discussion of files and creating objects with the <OBJECT> tag.

Configuration Tips for Active Servers

T his appendix describes tips and tricks for configuring Internet Information Server with Active Server Pages installed. All sections deal with changes to the registry. My advice is to try these tips on a development server before applying them to a production server.

The tips covered here don't just refer to registry entries of Active Server Pages. The next section, for example, describes a registry key that can be very useful for Active Server Pages applications. However, it's part of the configuration for the WWW service of Internet Information Server.

Setting the Default Logon Domain

In earlier chapters I mentioned that when you install a server with IIS, it creates a local user account for logging in anonymous users. When you create a password-secured area on your server, the accounts and passwords are, by default, looked up in the local computer's user database.

If you're running the web server in a network with a domain server (with the web server and the domain server being different physical computers), you also can use the domain database to validate users, but the logon isn't very efficient:

```
domainname\username
```

Every time a user logs on to the server with the domain account, the username must be preceded by the domain name and a backslash.

 Note If the computer the user is working on is part of the domain, Internet Explorer automatically tries to use the account for this user (including the domain name) to satisfy the logon request. Only if this fails is the user prompted for logon.

To save the user from typing the domain name every time at logon, there is a registry entry for Internet Information that enables you to specify the domain to be used for logon. The name of this registry entry is DefaultLogonDomain and it is located in the registry under the subkey HEKY_LOCAL_MACHINE\SYSTEM\CurrentControlSet\Services\W3SVC\Parameters.

Follow these steps to add the domain name **unlocking** as the default logon domain to your server:

1. Open the registry editor. To do this, select Run from the Start menu and enter **regedit**. Choose OK to launch the registry editor.

2. After the registry editor has opened, navigate to the subkey presented in the preceding text.

3. If the entry DefaultLogonDomain doesn't exist, create a new one with this name by selecting New/String value.

4. Double-click the entry DefaultLogonDomain and enter **unlocking** for the domain (or whatever domain name you want to use).

5. Restart the service to have the changes take effect.

Now all users that belong to this domain no longer need to type
unlocking\username—simply entering **username** is sufficient. Figure C.1 shows a
logon, however, this is not for unlocking (it's merely my own domain).

The user is now automatically logged on to the domain of your choice every time
logon is required. The next section shows how to administer registry settings for the
Session objects created for the users.

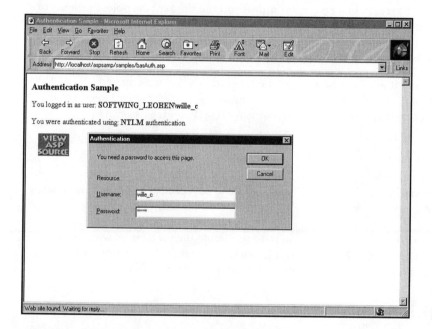

Figure C.1

*An
Authentication
dialog box
requires a domain
name.*

Session Management

Now you are back at the Active Server Pages setup. There are two very important
registry settings for sessions that have a great impact on your server's performance:

◆ Allowing the generation of Session objects

◆ Time period after which unused Session objects are discarded

The second one, of course, can only have an impact on the server's performance
when Session objects are created.

Creation of `Session` Objects

By default, a `Session` object is created for every user visiting the site. This session management involves the creation of a cookie and its transfer between the client and the server for every request and response. Furthermore, each `Session` object needs additional memory for its storage.

The benefits of `Session` objects pay off only if you use the `Session` object's events or store information on a per user basis. If you don't do anything like this, you can do without `Session` objects. Depending upon the traffic to your site, the performance gain may be worth the trouble of playing around in the registry.

The registry key that's used to manage the creation of sessions is named `AllowSessionState` and is located under the subkey for Active Server Pages parameters, `HKEY_LOCAL_MACHINE\SYSTEM\CurrentControlSet\Services\W3SVC\ASP\Parameters`.

 All Active Server Pages parameters that I am describing in this appendix are located under this subkey. Therefore, I won't be repeating it in its entirety again in the sections to follow.

You can set two values; 0 and 1. If you want to disable the creation of sessions, set the value of the entry to 0, otherwise, use 1 if you want to allow the creation of sessions. For the changes to take effect, you need to restart the IIS web service.

Session Timeout

If you have decided to allow session state, there is a second interesting registry entry; `SessionTimeout`. With this entry, you can specify the amount of time ASP maintains the `Session` object for the user when it's not used. After this time period has expired, the resources for this session are freed.

The `timeout` is measured in minutes and you can set it to any value depending upon your needs. If you're creating a site that provides, for example, literature search capabilities, and that directs the user to the appropriate site containing the information, you can expect the user not to spend a lot of time on your server and then to return for another query. On the other hand, if you're providing unique information, your users will stay focused when they leave your site, and you can expect that they won't come back because they have finished investigating your site for this time.

You can adjust the session `timeouts` for each scenario by editing the `SessionTimeout` entry in the registry under the ASP parameters subkey. If you're choosing a high value for `SessionTimeout` and have a heavy-load site, this may create a large number of `Session` objects on your server.

This registry entry has an impact on all sessions created on this web server. If you want to set the timeout on a per-user basis, use the Session.Timeout property to set an individual session timeout for the current user. The following line of code sets the timeout to two hours (120 minutes):

```
Session.Timeout = 120
```

Controlling session timeouts is important for the speed of your web server. Depending on your site's content, you have to decide how long a user might be inactive until he or she requests further content from your server. Because many inactive sessions still need memory, deciding this timeout can be an important decision for a high-volume site. Another speed bottleneck can be the database server—inactive connections to it are intolerable when you have hundreds of users connected to your site at the same time. The next sections show how to avoid inactive connections to the database server.

Connection Pooling

I think connection pooling was one of my favorite topics in this book. It is important enough to be repeated again. The advantage to using connection pooling instead of storing Connection objects for every user is that it is less resource-intensive (creates less idle database connections). Connection pooling is a feature that's part of ODBC 3.0 (installed with ASP) and it is disabled by default. If you want to enable it, you have to set the registry entry StartConnectionPool to 1. To make this change take effect, you have to stop and restart the web server.

 Warning If you're using the connection pooling feature with Microsoft Access, you must have installed the NT 4.0 Service Pack 2 or later, or your system may crash when the IIS service is shut down.

To learn how to implement connection pooling in your ASP pages, please refer to "Database Access with ActiveX Data Objects," (Chapter 7).

 Cross Reference

Scripting

Because Active Server Pages is mainly a scripting environment, there are, of course, interesting registry entries that allow you some control over general scripting features. One of these entries was already presented in Chapter 3—the DefaultScriptLanguage entry. With this, you can determine the default scripting language for your pages. The default value is VBScript, but you can set the option to any language you like best.

More interesting entries are presented in the next two sections covering performance control and error handling.

Performance Control

A major concern of every programming solution is speed. Active Server Pages manages the scripting engines, and therefore has control of loading and unloading engines, caching pre-processed files, and controlling how long a script may take to execute before its execution is terminated by ASP.

The following list contains four registry entries that enable you to modify the behavior of the outlined tasks of ASP.

◆ **ScriptEngineCacheMax:** Defines the number of ActiveX Scripting languages ASP keeps in memory without unloading. The default is to keep thirty engines cached in memory.

◆ **ScriptFileCacheSize:** Specifies the amount of memory in bytes to use for caching of pre-compiled script files. Allowing it to cache pre-compiled scripts greatly improves performance. If you want to cache all scripts, enter **–1**. To cache no scripts, use **0**. By default, -1 is used and all scripts are cached.

 The more RAM your server has, the better the caching performance is.

◆ **ScriptFileCacheTTL:** Specifies the amount of time a script is cached until it is removed from the cache if it hasn't been referenced. The default is to cache for 300 seconds, however, you can set caching to indefinite by using 0xFFFFFFFF.

◆ **ScriptTimeout:** Specifies the amount of time a script may run before it times out. The default is 20 minutes. This value is used as a default for all scripts. If you want to set the `timeout` using scripting code, use the `Server.ScriptTimeout` property (measured in seconds) to specify the `timeout` value a script may run before it is terminated.

If you make changes to any of these registry entries, the web service must be stopped and started in order for the changes to take effect.

Error Handling

Two registryentries give you control of how errors are handled and reported to users. These entries are targeted at production servers where the user doesn't need to see the full error information (description, file, line number), which is of course useful on a development server. The two entries are as follows:

◆ **ScriptErrorsSentToBrowser:** Enables (1) or disables (0) sending of error information to the browser. I recommend that you disable this option when you're using it on a production server (you still have the information in the server log files).

◆ **ScriptErrorMessage:** This is the message sent to the browser when script errors aren't sent to the browser. You can insert informational text for users here.

When changing any of these entries, you do not need to restart the web service. The changes take effect immediately. The installation default is to enable the errors.

 It is strongly recommended that you disable error reporting about production servers because the error messages generated by ASP and its scripting engines are of no use for users browsing your site and unhandled errors give the impression of a badly programmed site.

The most important registry entries to tweak are, in my opinion, those for error handling, because the performance keys are already tuned for optimum performance. If you need very fine control over caching of pre-compiled scripts, then these are of very high value for you.

Summary

This appendix contains a quick tour on the most important registry settings for Active Servers by topic. It showed how to simplify user logon, work with session state, enable connection pooling, and finally, how to optimize the scripting settings of ASP. A complete reference of all entries can be found in the Active Server Pages Roadmap (point your browser to `http://localhost/IASDocs/ASPDocs/roadmap.asp`).

I N D E X

X-Z

NEED TO HOST YOUR ASP SITE?

BitShop, Inc.
The Leader in Microsoft IIS Web Hosting since February 1996!
Your Best Choice for Active Server Pages Web Hosting

Compare Our Features and Prices
Full Details Available on Our Web Site:
http://www.bitshop.com

Features

◆ Dual DS-3 / T-3 Connections for Redundancy

◆ FREE Online Tutorials for ASP Developers

◆ Windows NT 4.0 Servers w/ latest IIS

◆ Active Server Pages Support

◆ Popular ASP Components Pre-Installed FREE

◆ SSL—Secure Servers Available

◆ FrontPage97/Visual Interdev Support

◆ Index Server—NetShow Server

◆ Real Audio/Real Video Servers

◆ 24/7 Monitoring

◆ Databases: SQL Server 6.5, Access, FoxPro

◆ E-Mail: POP3, Exchange Server 5.0

◆ Automated Server Diagnostics and Repair! NO other ISP can offer automated troubleshooting of potential problems BEFORE you notice them!

◆ CoLocate your server on our high speed backbone—starting at $200 per month!

Prices

Basic Virtual Server w/FrontPage
$25.00 per Month*
(Does not include ASP or Database Support)

Level 1 Corporate Site
FrontPage Support
Unlimited E-Mail Forwarders
$35.00 Per Month*
(Does not include ASP or Database Support)

Level 2 Corporate Site
FrontPage Support
Visual Interdev Support
Unlimited E-Mail Forwarders
Active Server Pages Support
Access or FoxPro Database Support
$65.00 Per Month*

All Prices Subject To Change.
Above Accounts Include 25 Megs of Disk Space.
Mention this ad on your sign up form and receive one month FREE hosting!

BitShop ALWAYS supports the latest Microsoft technology. By the time you see this ad we will support newer technologies than are displayed here. Please contact us if you are looking for a site that supports something that is not listed.

US Sales: 1-888-HOST-IIS
Phone: (301)345-6789
Fax: (301)345-6745
http://www.bitshop.com
mailto: sales@bitshop.com

BitShop, Inc.
(888) HOST-IIS

MACMILLAN COMPUTER PUBLISHING USA

A VIACOM COMPANY

Technical Support:

If you need assistance with the information in this book or with a CD/Disk
accompanying the book, please access the Knowledge Base on our Web
site at **http://www.superlibrary.com/general/support**. Our most
Frequently Asked Questions are answered there. If you do not find the
answer to your questions on our Web site, you may contact Macmillan
Technical Support **(317) 581-3833** or e-mail us at **support@mcp.com**.